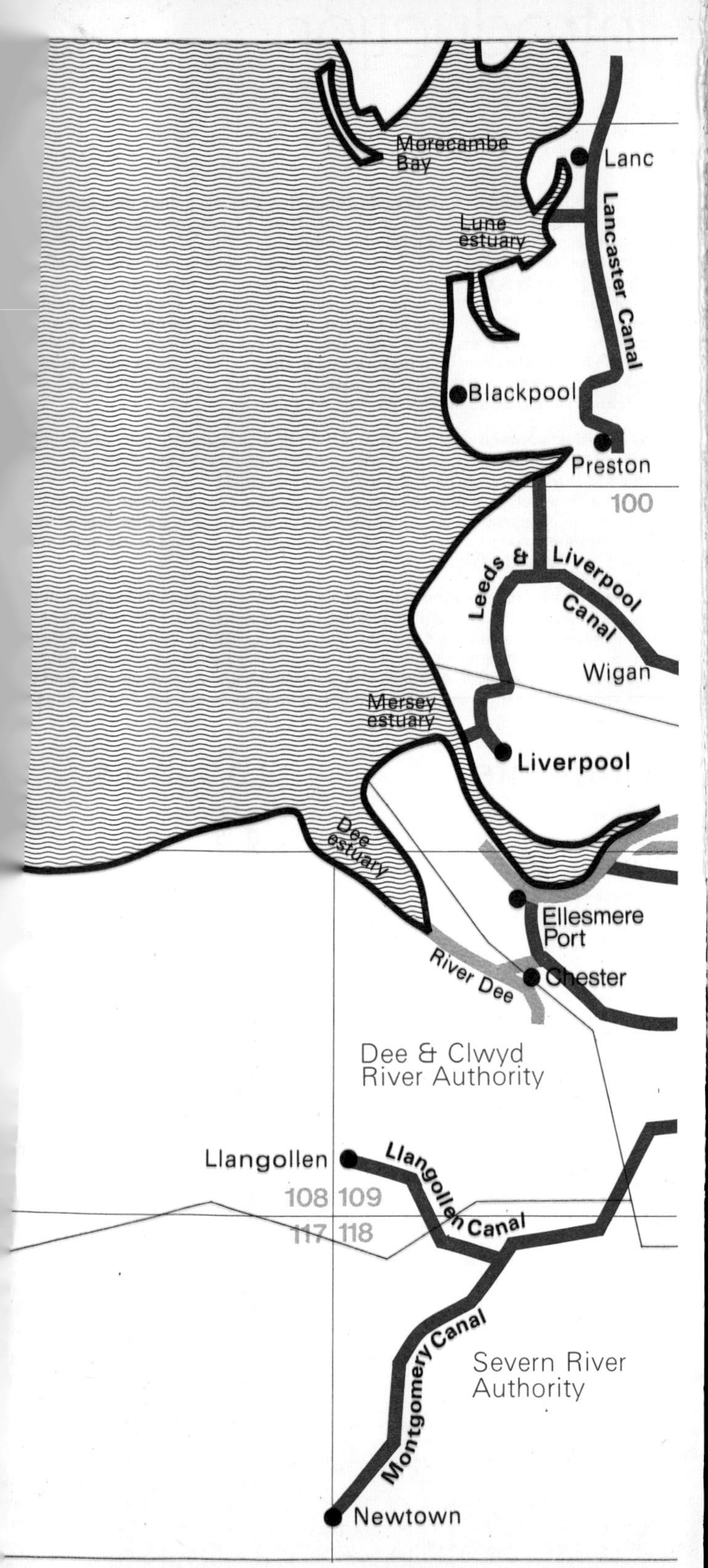

Nicholson's guides to the WATERWAYS

North west

ROBERT NICHOLSON PUBLICATIONS
COMMUNICA-EUROPA

Robert Nicholson Publications
24 Highbury Crescent,
London N5.

Editors: Paul Atterbury and Andrew Darwin

Printed and bound in Great Britain by
Morrison & Gibb Ltd. London and Edinburgh

Robert Nicholson Publications would like to thank all those
who made expert contributions towards the preparation of this
book, especially the staff of BWB.

Further copies of this publication, and others in the series, can be obtained
from your local bookshop or direct from the British Waterways Board,
Willow Grange, Church rd, Watford WD1 3QA.

ISBN 90056820 8

R–12/75–10

Front cover. Tixall Wide on the Staffordshire and Worcestershire canal.

Introduction

Canals today are enjoying a boom in popularity unrivalled s
1790's when 'canal mania' was at its peak. Then, canals we
country as efficient and profitable new transport routes; but
narrow canals is almost finished, the waterways of Britain h
life. Large numbers of people are beginning to realise what
long time: that in a bustling, noisy, dangerous world, the car
to so much that annoys, bores and disturbs us. A 2,000 mile
country, the canals are a part of the English landscape and a
dignified, the rural canal with its charming bridges, archaic l
has achieved a unity with, and enhancement of, the country
since the 18thC has quite equalled.

The contrast between rural and urban canals is dramatic, for
truly enters a world of its own. Slipping unnoticed through th
rare and rewarding glimpse of the Industrial Revolution; and
boatmen but walkers, industrial archaeologists and even fishe
for their quiet enjoyment unspoilt by the bustle and noise of t
see that more and more local councils are making a real effort
canal as a valuable amenity.

There is interest for everyone in the canals: the engineering fe
and flights of locks (all of which amazed a world which had s
Roman times); the brightly decorated narrowboats which use
the wealth of birds, animals and plants on the canal banks; the
architecture of canalside buildings like pubs, stables, lock cott
the sheer beauty and quiet isolation that is a feature of so man

Contents

The Country Code

Guard against fire risks.
Fasten all gates.
Keep dogs under proper control.
Keep to paths across farm land.
Avoid damaging fences, hedges and walls.
Leave no litter.
Safeguard water supplies.
Protect wildlife, wild plants and trees.
Go carefully on country roads.
Respect the life of the countryside.

Symb

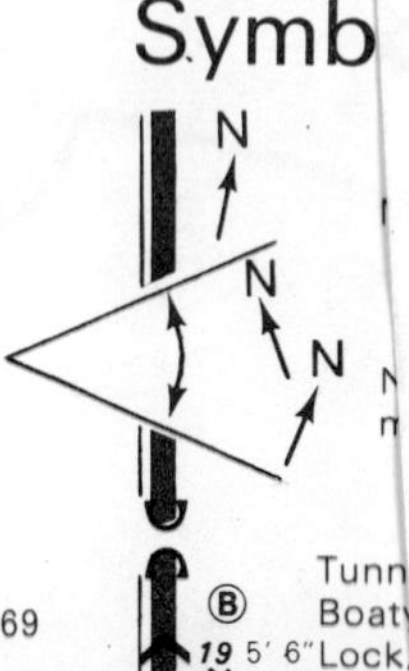

Next to each map
description of the
places of interest a
regarding pubs, res
boatyards etc.

This distance given
of the section is the
mileage on that par

The maps are 2 inch

North west

ROBERT NICHOLSON PUBLICATIONS
COMMUNICA-EUROPA

Robert Nicholson Publications
24 Highbury Crescent,
London N5.

Editors: Paul Atterbury and Andrew Darwin

Printed and bound in Great Britain by
Morrison & Gibb Ltd, London and Edinburgh

Robert Nicholson Publications would like to thank all those
who made expert contributions towards the preparation of this
book, especially the staff of BWB.

Further copies of this publication, and others in the series, can be obtained
from your local bookshop or direct from the British Waterways Board,
Willow Grange, Church rd, Watford WD1 3QA.

ISBN 90056820 8

R–12/75–10

Front cover: Tixall Wide on the Staffordshire and Worcestershire canal.

Introduction

Canals today are enjoying a boom in popularity unrivalled since the halcyon days of the 1790's when 'canal mania' was at its peak. Then, canals were being built all over the country as efficient and profitable new transport routes; but nowadays, when trading on narrow canals is almost finished, the waterways of Britain have obtained a new lease of life. Large numbers of people are beginning to realise what a minority has known for a long time: that in a bustling, noisy, dangerous world, the canals provide a unique antidote to so much that annoys, bores and disturbs us. A 2,000 mile network woven across the country, the canals are a part of the English landscape and a part of our history. Quiet and dignified, the rural canal with its charming bridges, archaic locks and colourful boats has achieved a unity with, and enhancement of, the countryside in a way that nothing since the 18thC has quite equalled.

The contrast between rural and urban canals is dramatic, for it is in a town that the canal truly enters a world of its own. Slipping unnoticed through the town, the canal affords a rare and rewarding glimpse of the Industrial Revolution; and it is here that not only boatmen but walkers, industrial archaeologists and even fishermen find plenty of scope for their quiet enjoyment unspoilt by the bustle and noise of traffic. It is encouraging to see that more and more local councils are making a real effort to use and improve their canal as a valuable amenity.

There is interest for everyone in the canals: the engineering feats like aqueducts, tunnels and flights of locks (all of which amazed a world which had seen nothing like it since Roman times); the brightly decorated narrowboats which used to throng the waterways; the wealth of birds, animals and plants on the canal banks; the mellow, unpretentious architecture of canalside buildings like pubs, stables, lock cottages and warehouses; and the sheer beauty and quiet isolation that is a feature of so many English canals.

Contents

The Country Code

Guard against fire risks.
Fasten all gates.
Keep dogs under proper control.
Keep to paths across farm land.
Avoid damaging fences, hedges and walls.
Leave no litter.
Safeguard water supplies.
Protect wildlife, wild plants and trees.
Go carefully on country roads.
Respect the life of the countryside.

Symbols

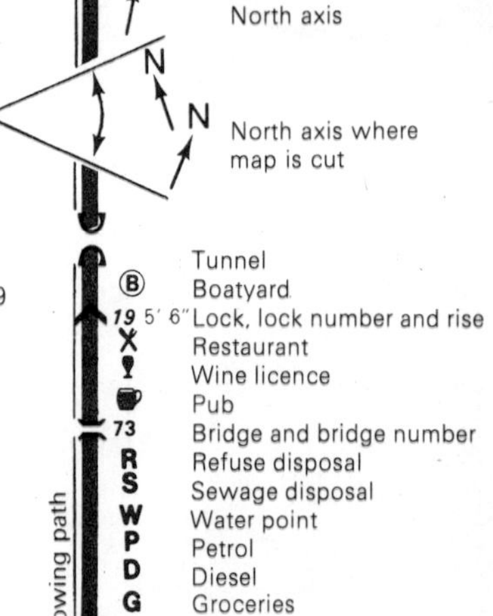

Next to each map will be found a description of the countryside, plus places of interest and details regarding pubs, restaurants, boatyards etc.

This distance given under the name of the section is the approximate mileage on that particular page.

The maps are 2 inches to 1 mile scale.

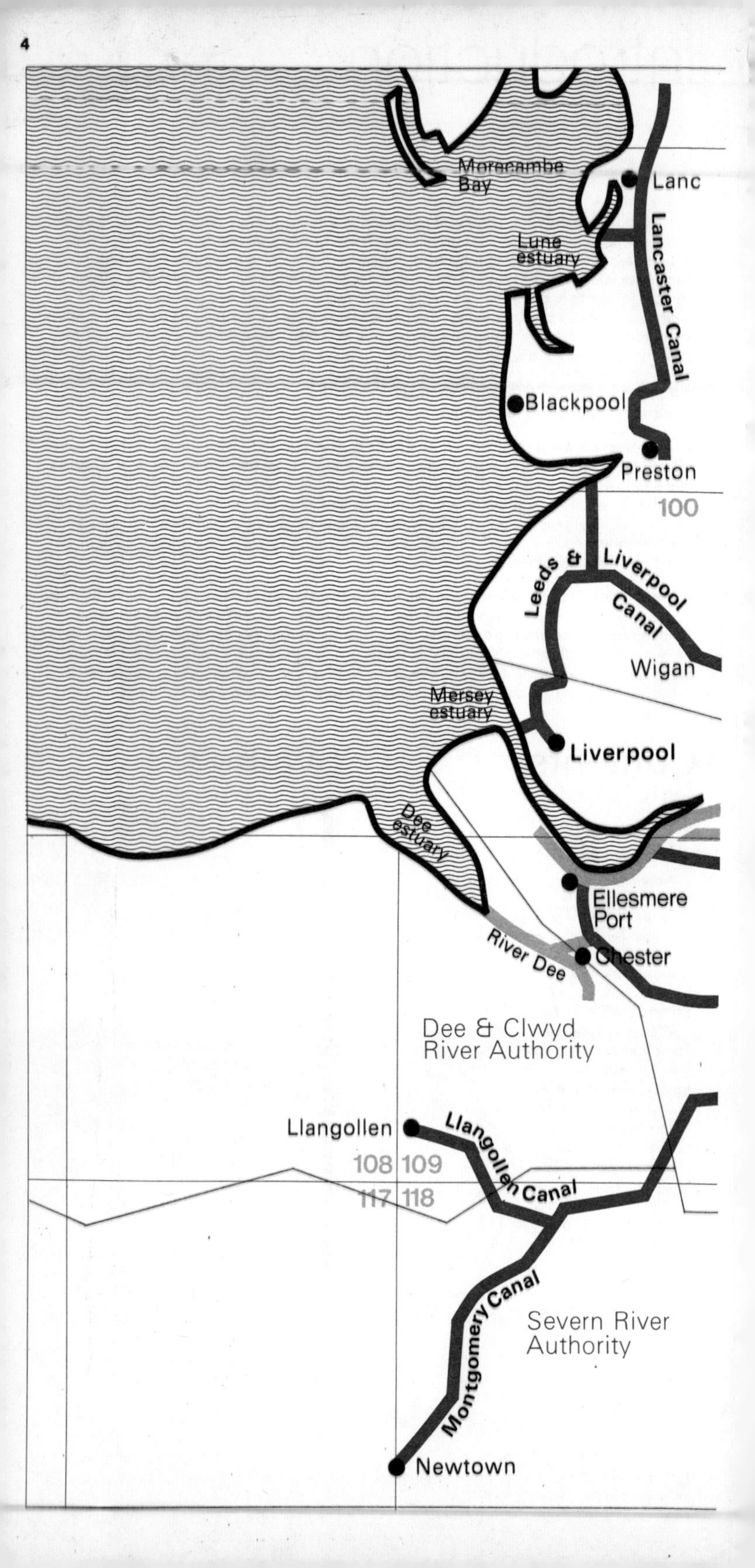
Morecambe Bay
Lanc
Lune estuary
Lancaster Canal
Blackpool
Preston
100
Leeds & Liverpool Canal
Wigan
Mersey estuary
Liverpool
Dee estuary
Ellesmere Port
Chester
River Dee
Dee & Clwyd River Authority
Llangollen
Llangollen Canal
108
109
117
118
Montgomery Canal
Severn River Authority
Newtown

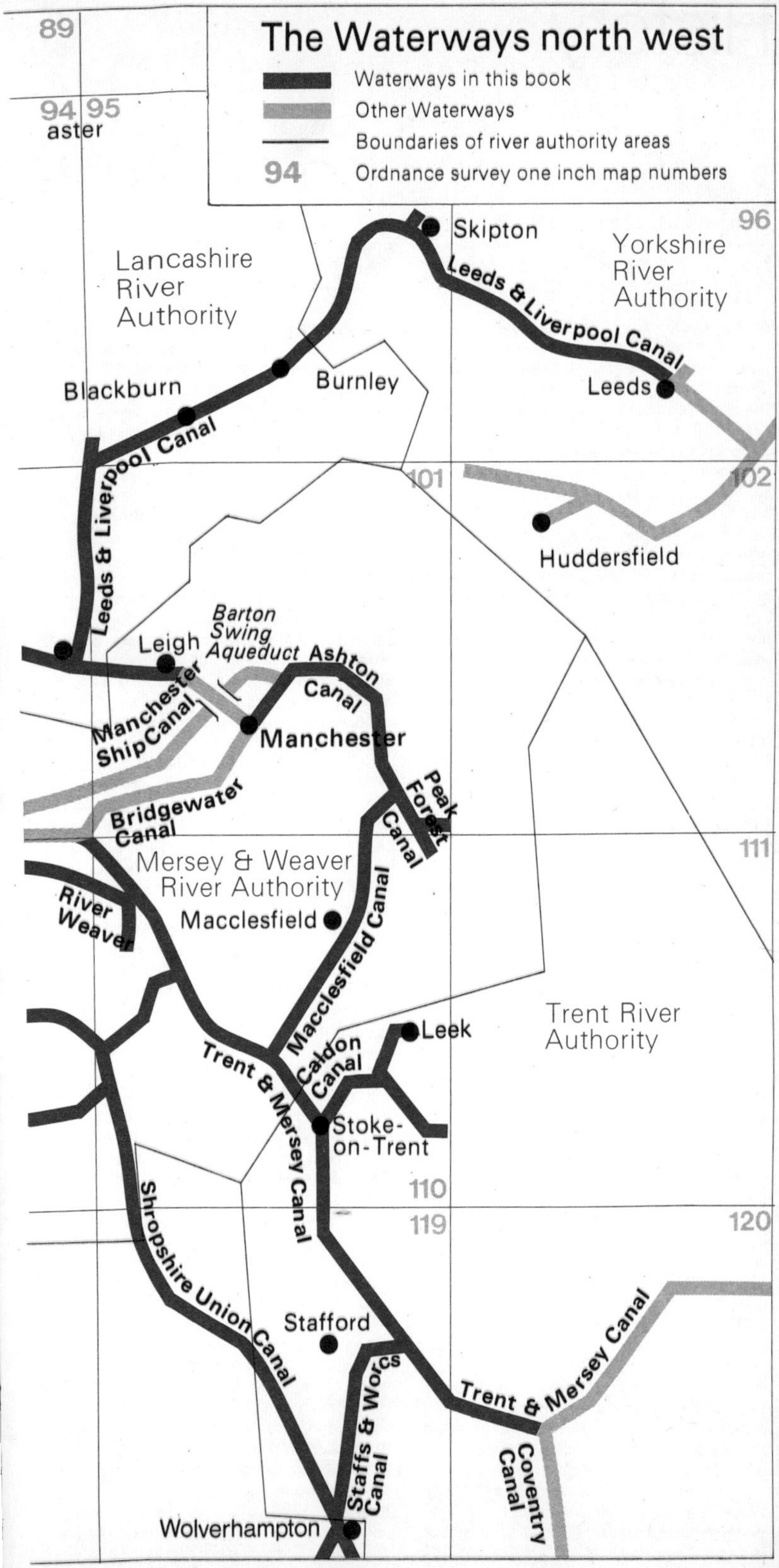

The Waterways north west

Waterways in this book
Other Waterways
Boundaries of river authority areas
94 Ordnance survey one inch map numbers

89
94 95
aster
96
Skipton
Yorkshire River Authority
Lancashire River Authority
Leeds & Liverpool Canal
Leeds
Burnley
Blackburn
Leeds & Liverpool Canal
101
102
Huddersfield
Barton Swing Aqueduct
Leigh
Ashton Canal
Manchester Ship Canal
Manchester
Peak Forest Canal
Bridgewater Canal
Mersey & Weaver River Authority
111
River Weaver
Macclesfield
Macclesfield Canal
Trent River Authority
Leek
Caldon Canal
Trent & Mersey Canal
Stoke-on-Trent
110
119
120
Shropshire Union Canal
Stafford
Staffs & Worcs Canal
Trent & Mersey Canal
Coventry Canal
Wolverhampton

History

River navigations, that is rivers widened and deepened to take large boats, had existed in England since the middle ages; some can even be traced back to Roman times. In 1600 there were 700 miles of navigable river in England, and by 1760, the dawn of the canal age, this number had been increased to 1300. This extensive network had prompted many developments later used by the canal engineers, for example the lock system. But there were severe limitations; generally the routes were determined by the rivers and the features of the landscape and so were rarely direct. Also there were no east-west, or north-south connections.

Thus the demand for a direct inland waterway system increased steadily through the first half of the 18thC with the expansion of internal trade. Road improvements could not cope with this expansion, and so engineers and merchants turned to canals, used extensively on the continent.

One of the earliest pure canals, cut independently of existing rivers, was opened in 1745, at Newry in Northern Ireland, although some authorities consider the Fossdyke, cut by the Romans to link the rivers Trent and Witham, to be the first. However, the Newry is more important because it established the cardinal rule of all canals, the maintenance of an adequate water supply, a feature too often ignored by later engineers. The Newry canal established the principle of a long summit level, fed by a reservoir to keep the locks at either end well supplied. Ten years later, in England, the Duke of Bridgewater decided to build a canal to provide an adequate transport outlet for his coal mines at Worsley. He employed the self-taught James Brindley as his engineer, and John Gilbert as surveyor, and launched the canal age in England. The Bridgewater canal was opened in 1761. Its route, all on one level, was independent of all rivers; its scale of operations reflected the new power of engineering, and the foresight of its creators. Although there were no locks, the engineering problems were huge; an aqueduct was built at Barton over the river Irwell, preceded by an embankment 900 yards long; 15 miles of canal were built underground, so that boats could approach the coal face for loading—eventually there were 42 miles underground, including an inclined plane—the puddled clay method was used by Brindley to make the canal bed watertight. Perhaps most important of all, the canal was a success financially. Bridgewater invested the equivalent of £3 million of his own money in the project, and still made a profit.

Having shown that canals were both practical and financially sound, the Bridgewater aroused great interest throughout Britain. Plans were drawn up for a trunk canal, to link the four major rivers of England: the Thames, Severn, Mersey and Trent. This plan was eventually brought to fruition, but many years later than its sponsors imagined. Brindley was employed as engineer for the scheme, his reputation ensuring that he would always have more work than he could ever handle. The Trent and Mersey, and the Staffordshire and Worcestershire canals received the Royal Assent in 1766, and the canal age began in earnest.

Canals, like the railways later, were built entirely by hand. Gangs of itinerant workmen were gathered together, drawn by the comparatively high pay. Once formed, these armies of 'navigators'—hence 'navvies'—moved through the countryside as the canal was built, in many cases living off the land. All engineering problems had to be solved by manpower alone, aided by the horse and the occasional steam pump. Embankments, tunnels, aqueducts, all were built by these labouring armies kept under control only by the power of the section engineers and contractors.

The Staffordshire and Worcestershire canal opened in 1770. In its design Brindley determined the size of the standard Midlands canal, which of course had direct influence on the rest of the English system as it was built. He chose a narrow canal, with locks 72ft 7in by 7ft 6in, partly for reasons of economy, and partly because he realised that the problems of an adequate water supply were far greater than most canal sponsors realised. This standard, which was also adopted for the Trent and Mersey, prompted the development of a special vessel, the narrow boat with its 30-ton payload. Ironically this decision by Brindley in 1766 ensured the failure of the canals as a commercial venture 200 years later, for by the middle of this century a 30-ton payload could no longer be worked economically.

The Trent and Mersey was opened in 1777. 93 miles long, the canal included 5 tunnels, the one at Harecastle taking 11 years to build. In 1790 Oxford was finally reached and the junction with the Thames brought the four great rivers together. From the very start English canal companies were characterised by their intense rivalries; water supplies were jealously guarded, and constant wars were waged over toll prices. Many canals receiving the Royal Assent were never built, while others staggered towards conclusion, hampered by doubtful engineering, inaccurate estimates, and loans that they could never hope to pay off. Yet for a period canal mania gripped British speculators, as railway mania was to grip them 50 years later. The peak of British canal development came between 1791 and 1794, a period that gave rise to the opening

An early photograph of the Foxton 'staircase'.

'Navvies' (navigators) at work, removing the stop lock at Braunston in the early 1930's.

of the major routes, the rise of the great canal engineers, Telford, Rennie and Jessop, and the greatest prosperity of those companies already operating. At this time the canal system had an effective monopoly over inland transport; the old trunk roads could not compete, coastal traffic was uncertain and hazardous, and the railways were still a future dream. This period also saw the greatest feats of engineering.

The turn of the century saw the opening of the last major cross country routes; the Pennines were crossed by the Leeds and Liverpool canal between 1770 and 1816 while the Kennet and Avon, opened in 1810, linked London and Bristol via the Thames. These two canals were built as broad navigations: already the realisation was dawning on canal operators that the limits imposed by the Brindley standard were too restricting, a suspicion that was to be brutally confirmed by the coming of the railways. The Kennet and Avon, along with its rival the Thames and Severn, also marks the introduction of fine architecture to canals. Up till now canal architecture had been functional, often impressive, but clearly conceived by engineers. As a result the Kennet and Avon has an architectural unity lacking in earlier canals – incidentally another reason to justify its preservation. The appearance of architectural quality was matched by another significant change; canals became straighter, their engineers choosing as direct a route as possible, arguing that greater construction costs would be outweighed by smoother, quicker operation, whereas the early canals had followed the landscape. The Oxford is the prime example of a contour canal, meandering across the midlands as though there were all the time in the world. It looks beautiful, its close marriage with the landscape makes it ideal as a pleasure waterway, but it was commercial folly.

The shortcomings of the early canals were exploited all too easily by the new railways. At first there was sharp competition by canals. Tolls were lowered, money was poured into route improvements; 14 miles of the Oxford's windings were cut out between 1829 and 1834; schemes were prepared to widen the narrow canals; the Harecastle tunnel was doubled in 1827, the new tunnel taking 3 years to build (as opposed to the 11 years of the old). But the race was lost from the start. The 19thC marks the rise of the railways and the decline of the canals. With the exception of the Manchester Ship Canal, the last major canal was the Birmingham and Liverpool Junction, opened in 1835. The system survived until this century, but the 1914–18 war brought the first closures, and through

The rudimentary tools of the early 'navvies'. *Hugh McKnight.*

Worcester and Birmingham Canal.
LOWESMERE WHARF, WORCESTER.

Canal Company's Machine. 181 6
Cheque, No.
Carriage, No.
Gross Weight . .
Tare . . .
Neat Coals, Cwt.
Weighing
Clerk.

Mr.
Bought of
At per Ton
Carriage
Clerk.

Printed by R. Jabet and Co. Herald Office, High-street, Birmingham.

Worcester and Birmingham Canal Company toll ticket, dated 1816. *Hugh McKnight.*

the 1930's the canal map adopted the shape it has today. Effective commercial carrying on narrow canals ceased in the early 1960's although a few companies managed to survive until recently. However, with the end of commercial operation, a new role was seen for the waterways, as a pleasure amenity, a 'linear national park 2000 miles long'.

Water supply has always been the cardinal element in both the running and the survival of any canal system. Locks need a constant supply of water—every boat passing through a wide lock on the Grand Union uses 96,000 gallons of water. Generally two methods of supply were used: direct feed by rivers and streams, and feed by reservoirs sited along the summit level. The first suffered greatly from silting, and meant that the canal was dependent on the level of water in the river; the regular floods from the river Soar that overtake the Grand Union's Leicester line show the dangers of this. The second was more reliable, but many engineers were short-sighted in their provision of an adequate summit level. The otherwise well planned Kennet and Avon always suffered from water shortage. Where shortages occurred, steam pumping engines were used to pump water taken down locks back up to the summit level. The Kennet and Avon was dependent upon pumped supplies, while the Birmingham Canal Navigations were fed by 6 reservoirs and 17 pumping engines. Some companies adopted side ponds alongside locks to save water, but this put the onus on the boatman and so had limited success. Likewise the stop locks still to be seen at junctions are a good example of 18thC company rivalry; an established canal would ensure that any proposed canal wishing to join it would have to lock *down* into the older canal, which thus gained a lock of water each time a boat passed through.

Where long flights or staircase locks existed there was always great wastage of water, and so throughout canal history alternative mechanical means of raising boats have been tried out. The inclined plane or the vertical lift were the favoured form. Both worked on the counterbalance principle, the weight of the descending boat helping to raise the ascending. The first inclined plane was built at Ketley in 1788, and they were a feature of the west country Bude and Chard canals. The most famous plane was built at Foxton, and operated from 1900-1910. Mechanical failure and excessive running costs ended the application of the inclined plane in England, although modern examples work very efficiently on the continent, notably in Belgium. The vertical lift was more unusual, although there were 8 on the Grand Western canal. The most famous, built at Anderton in 1875, is still in operation, and stands as a monument to the ingenuity shown in the attempts to overcome the problems of water shortage.

Engineering features are the greatest legacy of the canal age, and of these, tunnels are the most impressive. The longest tunnel is at Standedge, on the now derelict Huddersfield narrow canal. The tunnel runs for 5456 yards through the Pennines, at times 600ft below the surface. It is also on the highest summit level, 656ft above sea level. The longest tunnel still in use, 3056 yards, is at Blisworth on the Grand Union. Others of interest include the twin Harecastle tunnels on the Trent and Mersey, the first 2897 yards and now disused, the second 2926 yards, Sapperton which carried the Thames and Severn canal through the Cotswolds, and Netherton on the Birmingham Canal Navigation. This, built 1855-58, was the last in England, and was lit throughout by gas lights, and later by electricity.

The Netherton tunnel was built wide enough to allow for a towing path on both sides. Most tunnels have no towing path at all, and so boats had to be 'legged', or

Islington tunnel during construction. *Hugh McKnight.*

walked through.

The slowness and relative danger of legging in tunnels led to various attempts at mechanical propulsion. An endless rope pulled by a stationary steam engine at the tunnel mouth was tried out at Blisworth and Braunston between 1869 and 1871. Steam tugs were employed, an early application of mechanical power to canal boats, but their performance was greatly limited by lack of ventilation, not to mention the danger of suffocating the crew.

An electric tug was used at Harecastle from 1914 to 1954. The diesel engine made tunnel tug services much more practical, but diesel powered narrow boats soon put the tugs out of business; by the 1930's most tunnels had to be navigated by whatever means the boatman chose to use. Legging continued at Crick, Husbands Bosworth and Saddington until 1939.

Until the coming of the diesel boats, the horse reigned supreme as a source of canal power. The first canals had used gangs of men to bow-haul the boats, a left over from the river navigations where 50-80 men, or 12 horses, would pull a 200-ton barge. By 1800 the horse had taken over, and was used throughout the heyday of the canal system. In fact horse towage survived as long as large scale commercial operation. Generally one horse or one mule was used per boat, a system unmatched for cheapness and simplicity. The towing path was carried from one side of the canal to the other by turnover bridges, a common feature that reveals the total dominance of the horse. Attempts to introduce self-propelled canal boats date from 1793, although most early experiments concerned tugs towing dumb barges. Development was limited by the damage caused by wash, a problem that still applies today, and the first fleets of self propelled steam narrow boats were not in service until the last quarter of the 19thC. Fellows, Morton and Clayton, and the Leeds and Liverpool Carrying Co. ran large fleets of steam boats between 1880 and 1931, by which time most had been converted to diesel operation. With the coming of mechanical power the butty boat principle was developed; a powered narrow boat would tow a dumb 'butty' boat, thereby doubling the load without doubling the running costs. This system became standard until the virtual ending by the late 1960's of carrying on the narrow canals. Before the coming of railways, passenger services were run on the canals; packet boats, specially built narrow boats with passenger accommodation, ran express services, commanding the best horses and the unquestioned right of way over all other traffic. Although the railways killed this traffic, the last scheduled passenger service survived on the Gloucester and Berkeley canal until 1935.

The traditional narrow boat with its colourful decoration and meticulous interior has become a symbol of English canals. However this was in fact a late development. The shape of the narrow boat was determined by Brindley's original narrow canal specification, but until the late 19thC boats were unpainted, and carried all male crews. Wages were sufficient for the crews to maintain their families at home. The increase in railway competition brought a reduction in wages, and so bit by bit the crews were forced to take their families with them, becoming a kind of water gipsy. The confines of a narrow boat cabin presented the same problems as a gipsy caravan, and so the families found a similar answer. Their eternally wandering home achieved individuality by extravagant and colourful decoration, and the traditional narrow boat painting was born. The extensive symbolic vocabulary available to the painters produced a sign language that only these families could understand, and the canal world became far more enclosed, although outwardly it was more decorative. As the canals have turned from commerce to pleasure, so the traditions of the families have died out, and the families themselves have faded away. But their language survives, although its meaning has mostly vanished with them. This survival gives the canals their characteristic decorative qualities which make them so attractive to the pleasure boatman and to the casual visitor.

The Cross Keys at Filance bridge on the Staffs & Worcester.

Practical information cruising

Licences

Pleasure craft using the Board's canals must be licensed and those using the Board's rivers must be registered under the British Waterways Act 1971. Charges are based on the length of the boat and a canal craft licence covers all the navigable waterways under the Board's control. Permits for permanent mooring on the canals are also issued by the Board. Apply in each case to:

Craft Licensing Office,
British Waterways Board,
Willow Grange,
Church Road,
Watford WD1 3QA.
(Watford 26422).

The licensing officer will supply you with a list of BWB navigations. The canals in the Manchester area that are not under BWB jurisdiction are dealt with on page 171.

Getting Afloat

There is no better way of finding out the joys of canals than by getting afloat. The best thing is to hire a boat for a week or a fortnight from one of the boatyards on the canals. (Each boatyard has an entry in the text, and most of them offer hire cruisers; brochures may be easily obtained from such boatyards). A list showing the address of all boatyard on the canal system is available from the BWB at Watford.

General Cruising

Most canals are saucer shaped in section and so are deepest in the middle. However very few have more than 3-4ft of water and many have much less. Try to keep to the middle of the channel except on bends, where the deepest water is on the *outside* of the bend. When you meet another boat, the rule of the road is to keep to the right; slow down, and aim to miss the approaching boat by a couple of yards; do not steer right over to the bank unless the channel is particularly narrow or badly overgrown, or you will most likely run aground. The deeper the draught of the boat, the more important it is to keep in the middle of the deep water, and so this must be considered when passing other boats. If you meet a loaded working boat, keep right out of the way. Working boats should always be given precedence, for their time is money. If you meet a boat being towed from the bank, pass it on the outside rather than intercept the towing line. When overtaking, keep the other boat on your starboard, or right, side.

Speed

There is a general speed limit of 4mph on most British Waterways Board canals. This is not just an arbitrary limit; there is no need to go any faster, and in many cases it is impossible to cruise even at this speed. Canals were not built for motor boats, and so the banks are easily damaged by excessive wash and turbulence. Erosion of the banks makes the canal more shallow, which in turn makes running aground a more frequent occurrence. So keep to the limits and try not to aggravate the situation. It is easy to see when a boat is creating excessive turbulence by looking at the wash. If in doubt, slow down.

Slow down also when passing moored craft, engineering works and anglers.

Slow down when there is a lot of floating rubbish on the water; old planks and plastic bags may mean underwater obstacles that can damage a boat or its propeller if hit hard.

Slow down when approaching blind corners, narrow bridges and junctions.

Running aground

The effective end of commercial traffic on the narrow canals has meant a general reduction in standards of dredging. Canals are now shallower than ever, and contain more rubbish than ever. Running aground is a common event, but is rarely serious, as the canal bed is usually soft. If you run aground, try first of all to pull the boat off by reversing the engine. If this fails, use the boat hook as a lever against the bank or some solid object, in combination with a tow rope being pulled from the bank. Do not keep revving the engine in reverse if it is obviously having no effect; this will merely damage both your propeller and the canal bed by drawing water away from the boat. Another way is to get your crew to rock the boat from side to side while using the boat hook or tow rope. If all else fails, lighten your load; make all the crew leave the boat except the helmsman, and then it will often float off quite easily.

Remember that if you run aground once, it is likely to happen again as it indicates a particularly shallow stretch—or you are out of the channel.

In a town it is common to run aground on sunken rubbish, for example old oil drums, bicycle frames, bedsteads etc; this is most likely to occur near bridges and housing estates. Use the same methods, but be very careful as these hard objects can easily damage your boat or propeller.

Remember that winding holes are often silted up; do not go further in than you have to.

Mooring

All boats carry metal stakes and a mallet

How a lock works

Plan: lock filling

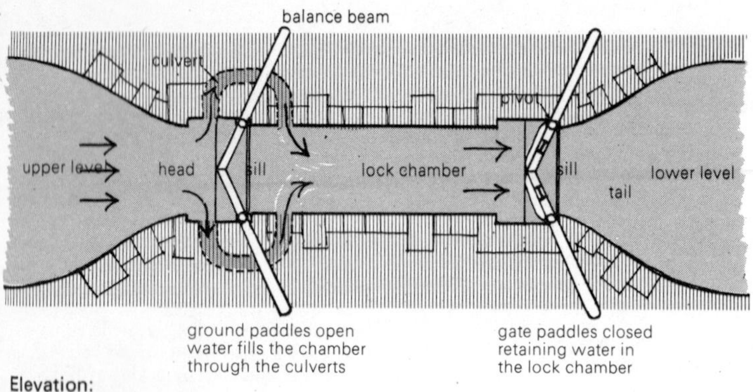
balance beam
culvert
pivot
upper level
head
sill
lock chamber
sill
lower level
tail
ground paddles open
water fills the chamber
through the culverts
gate paddles closed
retaining water in
the lock chamber

Elevation: lock emptying

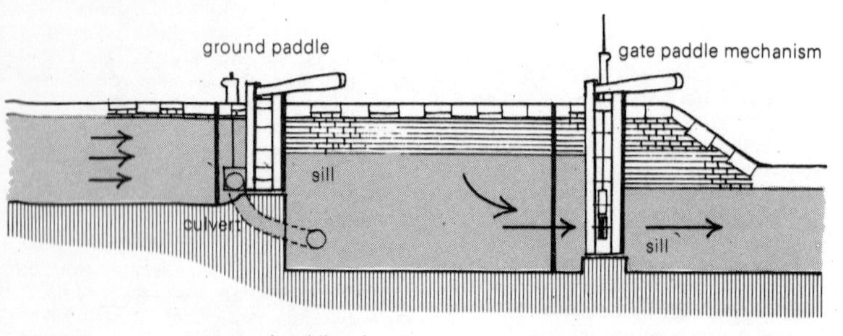
ground paddle
gate paddle mechanism
sill
culvert
sill
ground paddles closed
preventing water from
the upper level filling
the chamber
gate paddles open
water flows from the
chamber to the
lower level

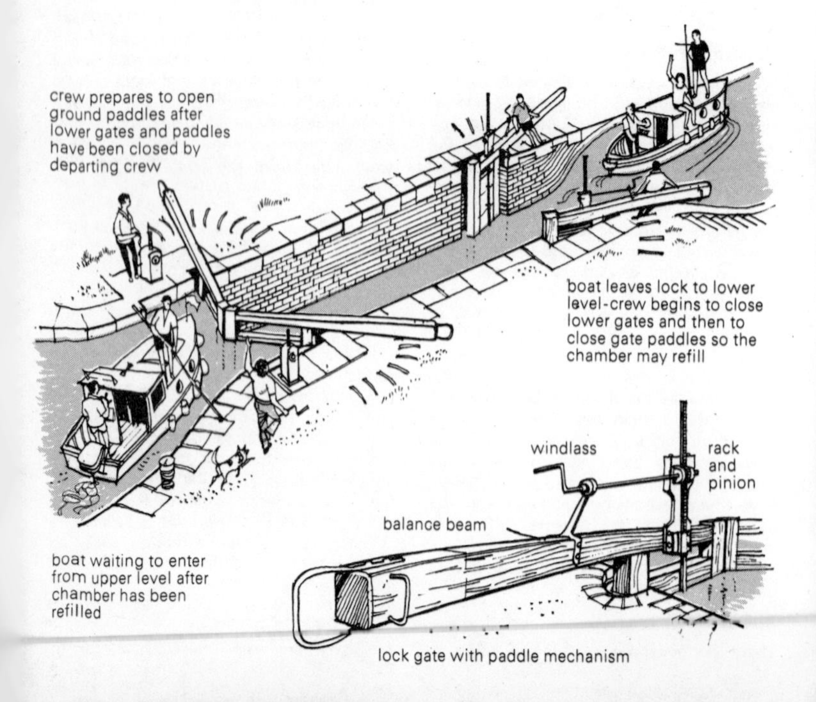
crew prepares to open
ground paddles after
lower gates and paddles
have been closed by
departing crew
boat leaves lock to lower
level-crew begins to close
lower gates and then to
close gate paddles so the
chamber may refill
windlass
rack
and
pinion
balance beam
boat waiting to enter
from upper level after
chamber has been
refilled
lock gate with paddle mechanism

These are used for mooring when there are no rings or bollards in sight, which is usually the case. Generally speaking you may moor anywhere to BWB property but there are certain basic rules. Avoid mooring anywhere that could cause an obstruction to other boats; do not moor on a bend or a narrow stretch, do not moor abreast boats already moored. Never moor in a lock, and do not be tempted to tie up in a tunnel or under a bridge if it is raining. Pick a stretch where there is a reasonable depth of water at the bank, otherwise the boat may bump and scrape the canal bed—an unpleasant sensation if you are trying to sleep. For reasons of peace and quiet and privacy it is best to avoid main roads and railway lines.

Never stretch your mooring lines across the towpath; you may trip someone up and face a claim for damages. This means that you should never tie up to trees or fences.

There is no need to show a riding light at night, except on major rivers and busy commercial canals.

So long as you are sensible and keep to the rules, mooring can be a pleasant gesture of individuality.

Locks

A lock is a simple device, relying for its operation on gravity, water pressure and manpower.

On the opposite page, the plan (top) shows how the gates point uphill, the water pressure forcing them together. Water is flooding into the lock through the underground culverts that are operated by the ground paddles; when the lock is full, the 'top' gates (on the left in the drawing) can be opened. One may imagine a boat entering, the crew closing the gates and paddles after it.

In the elevation, the bottom paddles have been raised—opened—so the lock empties. A boat would of course float down with the water. When the lock is 'empty', the bottom gates can be opened and the descending boat can leave the lock.

Remember that:

1. For reasons of safety and water conservation, all gates and paddles must always be left closed when you leave a lock.

2. When going *up* a lock, a boat should be tied up to prevent it being thrown about by the rush of incoming water; but when going *down* a lock, a boat should never be tied up, or it will be left high and dry.

3. Windlasses should *not* be left slotted on the paddle spindle. If the ratchet slips (and they are often worn) the spindle will spin round and the windlass will fly off, probably into the lock or into someone's face.

4. Be very careful when operating locks in wet weather: the lockside is often slippery and the wooden planks across the gates can be downright treacherous.

Knots

You do not need to know much about knots as there is one that is generally useful, the clove hitch. This is simple, strong, and can be slipped on and off easily. Make two loops in a rope, and pass the right hand one over the left; then drop the whole thing over a bollard, post or stake and pull it tight. See diagram below.

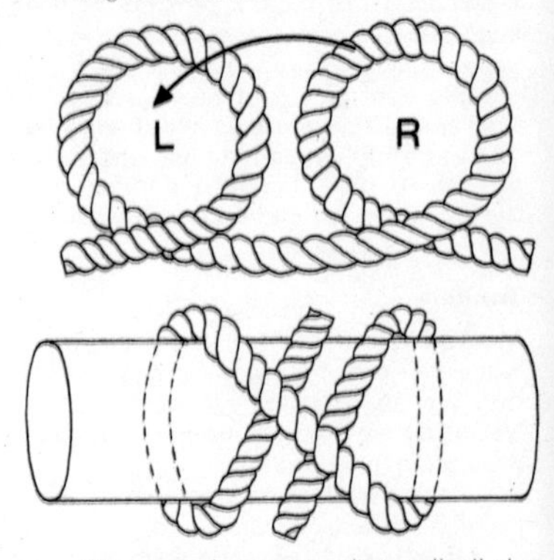

When leaving a mooring coil all the ropes up again. They will then be out of the way, but ready if needed in a hurry. Many a sailor has fallen overboard after tripping on an uncoiled rope.

Fixed bridges

At most bridges the canal becomes very narrow, a means of saving building costs developed by the engineers. As a result careful navigation is called for if you are to avoid hitting either the bridge sides with the hull or the arch with the cabin top. As when entering a lock, the best way to tackle 'bridgeholes' is to slow down well in advance and aim to go straight through, keeping a steady course. Adjustments should be kept to a minimum for it is easy to start the boat zig-zagging, which will inevitably end in a collision. One technique is to gauge the width of the approaching bridgehole relative to the width of the boat, and then watch one side only, aiming to miss that side by a small margin—say 6in; the smaller you can make the margin, the less chance you have of hitting the other side of the bridge. If you do hit the bridge sides when going slowly it is not likely to do much damage; it will merely strengthen your resolve to do better next time.

Moveable bridges

Moveable bridges are an attractive feature of some canals; they cannot be ignored as they often rest only 2 or 3ft above the water. Generally they are moved either by being swung horizontally, or raised vertically. Operation is usually manual, although some have gearing to ease the movement. There are one or two mechanized moveable bridges; these are very rare, and they have clear instructions at control points. Before operating any moveable bridge make sure that any road traffic approaching is aware of your intention to open the bridge. Use protective barriers if there are any and remember to close the bridge again after you.

Swivel bridges, which are moved horizontally, are usually simple to operate. They do however demand considerable strength, and many are difficult for one person.

Lift bridges, which are moved vertically, are raised by pulling down a balance beam. The heaviest member of the crew should swing on the chain that hangs from the beam. Once the bridge is up the beam should be sat on or otherwise held as in some cases it fails to counterbalance the bridge. Serious damage could be caused to the boat and to the helmsman if the bridge were allowed to fall while the boat was passing through. A draw bridge is another, more traditional type of lift bridge; the method of operation is the same.

Tunnels

Many people consider a canal incomplete without one or two tunnels, and certainly they are an exciting feature of any trip. Nearly all are easy to navigate, although there are a few basic rules:

Make sure your boat has a good headlight in working order.

If you can see another boat in the tunnel coming towards you, it is best to wait until it is out before entering yourself. It is in fact possible for craft of 7ft beam to pass in many tunnels, but it can be unnerving to meet another boat. If you do, keep to the right as usual.

In most tunnels the roof drips constantly, especially under ventilation shafts. Put on a raincoat and some form of hat before going in.

A notice on the tunnel portal will give its length, in yards, and will say whether unpowered craft are permitted to use it.

Care of the engine

Canal boats are powered by one of three types of engine; diesel, petrol and petrol/oil or two-stroke. However basic rules apply to all three. Every day before starting off, you should:

Check the oil level in the engine.
Check the fuel level in the tank.

If your engine is water-cooled, check that the filter near the intake is clean and weedfree. Otherwise the engine will overheat which could cause serious damage.

Check the level of distilled water in the battery, and ensure that it is charging correctly.

Lubricate any parts of the engine, gearbox or steering that need daily attention.

Check that the propeller is free of weeds, wire, plastic bags and any other rubbish. Although this is an unpleasant task, it is a constant necessity and will remain so as long as canals continue to be used as public rubbish dumps. The propeller and the water filter should be checked whenever there is any suspicion of obstruction or overheating—which may mean several times a day.

When navigating in shallow water, keep in mind the exposed position of the propeller. If you hit any underwater obstruction put the engine into neutral immediately. When running over any large floating object put the engine into neutral and wait for the object to appear astern before re-engaging the drive.

Respect should be shown to the engine. Remember that this simple maintenance could make the difference between trouble-free cruising and tiresome breakdowns.

Fuel

Petrol engines and petrol/oil motors are catered for by some boatyards and all roadside fuel stations. Fuel stations on roads near the canal are shown in the guide, and these should be considered when planning your day's cruise. Running out is inconvenient; remember you may have to walk several miles carrying a heavy can.

Diesel powered boats pose more of a problem in obtaining fuel, although their range is generally greater than that of petrol powered craft. Most boatyards sell marine diesel, which is tax-free and therefore very much cheaper (the heavy tax on fuels is aimed only at road vehicles). The tax-free diesel, which contains a tell-tale pink dye to prevent it being used in road vehicles, can only be sold by boatyards, which are still few and far between on the canals. BWB yards may let you have enough to reach the next boatyard. Some, but by no means all roadside fuel stations sell diesel, but at the higher price. A further complication is that diesel engines must not be allowed to run out of fuel, as their fuel system will need professional attention before they can run again. The simple rule about fuel is—think ahead.

Water

Fresh water taps occur irregularly along the canals, usually at boatyards, BWB depots, or by lock cottages. These are marked on the maps in the guide. Ensure that there is a long water hose on the boat (BWB taps have a ½-inch slip on hose connection).

Lavatories

Canal boats are generally fitted with chemical lavatories which have to be emptied from time to time. Never empty them over the side or just tip them into the bushes. Either empty them at the sewage disposal points marked on the maps, or dig deep holes with the spade provided. Some BWB depots and boat yards have lavatories for boat crews.

Litter

Some canals are in a poor state today because they have long been misused as unofficial dumps for rubbish, especially in towns. Out of sight is only out of mind until some object is tangled round your propeller. So keep all rubbish until you can dispose of it at a refuse disposal point.

BWB Byelaws

Although no one needs a 'driving licence' to navigate a boat on the waterways, boat users should remember that they incur certain responsibilities and duties to the BWB and to other waterway users, e.g. a knowledge of correct sound signals. These liabilities are contained in the BWB Byelaws, which should be obtained by all prospective navigators by sending 12½p to the Secretary, British Waterways Board, Melbury House, Melbury Terrace, London NW1 6JX.

Practical information walking

There are public rights of way over many of the canal towing paths in the north west. Some of them are indicated by 'public footpath' signs. (Maps showing rights of way can be inspected at Local Authority offices.) The Board are willing to arrange with Local Authorities for the public to be given access to all the towing paths and for their condition to be improved.

Prospective towpath walkers are warned that over the years constant erosion of the canal banks by the wash of motor boats has meant that in places the towpath has become narrow and difficult to negotiate, especially as at the same time the towpath hedge often manages to outstrip efforts to keep it trimmed and tidy. For these reasons a pair of waterproof boots is a useful item for a canalside walk.

Since most canal bridges are still the splendid old hump-backed variety, persons visiting a canal by motor car should remember to park well away from the bridge to avoid causing an obstruction to other traffic.

Finally, all readers are reminded that at the moment the canals are unspoilt, friendly, peaceful and greatly appreciated by all who use them. It is to be hoped that they remain so.

'Fishing' by Regents Park.

Practical information fishing

This section has been written by Bill Howes, well known angling correspondent and author of many books on the subject.

Most of these cross-country waterways have natural reed-fringed and grassy banks, and in addition to the delightful surroundings the fishing is generally good. In most areas there has been a steady improvement in the canal fishing in recent years and in many places new stocks of fish have been introduced. Good stocks of quality bream and roach have gone into several canals in the past couple of years, and this has improved the sport considerably.

The popular quarry are roach, perch and bream, but the canals also hold dace, tench, chub and carp in places, in addition to pike and other species in particular areas.

Canals afford good hunting grounds for those seeking specimen fish, that is fish above average size, and these are liable to be encountered on almost any water, yet some areas are more noted for big fish than others. The canals also make good venues for competition fishing, and in most places nowadays matches are held regularly at week-ends throughout the season.

The Statutory Close Season for coarse fish is March 15 to June 15 inclusive, but in some areas, notably the Yorkshire River Authority, the Close Season is from February 28 to May 31. The Close Season for pike in some areas is March 15 to September 30.

Permits and fishing rights

Most parts of the canal system are available to anglers. The big angling associations e.g. the Airedale AA, Cheshire AA, County Palatine AA, Leeds & District ASA, Liverpool & District AA, Northern AA, Northwich AA, Shropshire Union Canal AA and Warrington AA, rent fishing rights from the BWB over extensive areas on the canal system. In most cases day-tickets are available.

On arrival at the canal-side it is always advisable to make enquiries as to who holds the fishing rights, and to obtain a permit if one is required *before* starting to fish.

Remember, also, that a River Authority rod licence is required in addition to a fishing permit. It is essential to obtain this licence from the relevant River Authority *before* starting to fish. Some fishing permits and licences are issued by bailiffs along the bank, but local enquiry will help to determine this.

A canalside pub or a local fishing tackle shop are good places to enquire if permission or day tickets are required for the local stretch of water. Canal lock-keepers are usually knowledgeable about the fishing rights in the immediate locality, and often a lock-keeper may be found who issues day tickets on behalf of an angling association, or owner.

A lock-keeper is always worth talking to, for apart from knowing who holds the fishing rights, he often knows some of the better fishing areas, as well as local methods and baits which may be considered most successful.

The fishing rights on most canals are owned by the British Waterways Board and many miles of good fishing are leased to clubs and angling associations. They also issue day tickets on certain lengths, so it is worth enquiring at the local British Waterways office when planning a trip. Special arrangements are made for fishing from boats. Consult BWB at Nantwich (65122).

Once permission has been obtained it would be advisable to find out if there are any restrictions imposed, since some clubs and associations ban certain baits, or have restrictions on live-baiting for pike; and on some fisheries pike fishing is not allowed before a specified date.

Other restrictions may concern size-limits of fish, and this certainly applies to the London AA canal fisheries. Some River Authority by-laws prohibit the retention of under-sized fish in keep nets. A local club holding the fishing rights may have imposed their own size-limits in order to protect certain species. Such restrictions are generally printed on permits and licences.

Tackle

In the slow moving, sluggish waters the float tackle needs to be light and lines fine in order to catch fish.

When fishing for roach and dace lines of 1½lb to 2lb breaking strain are the maximum strength normally needed in order to get the fish to take a bait—particularly when the water is clear, or on the popular reaches which are 'hard-fished'.

Fine tackle also means small hooks, and hook sizes 16 and 18—or even as small as 22 at times. Such light gear is also effective when fishing for the smaller species, such as gudgeon and bleak. This tackle will require a well-balanced float to show the slightest indication of a bite.

Bait

Baits should be small, and maggots, casters (maggot chrysalis), hempseed, wheat, tiny cubes of bread crust, or a small pinch of flake (the white crumb of a new loaf) may take fish.

Barbel

Common Bream

Chub

Freshwater Eel

River Lamprey

Minnow

Pike

Ruffe

Stickleback

Bleak

Bullhead

Common Carp

Dace

Gudgeon

Perch

Roach

Rudd

Tench

Brown Trout

But it pays to experiment with baits; bait which is effective on one occasion will not necessarily prove to be as effective the next. With slight variations, similar fishing methods can be used effectively on the majority of waterways.

Northern anglers who regularly compete in contests on canals use bloodworms as bait. They have become extremely skilful in using this tiny bait and often take fish on bloodworms when all other baits fail. Bloodworms are the larvae of a midge, and are a perfectly natural bait. The anglers gather the bloodworms from the mud and, apart from a wash in clean water, the baits are ready for use.

A popular groundbait which has had great success is known as 'black magic'! This is a mixture of garden peat and bread crumbs mixed dry and carried to the water. When dampened and mixed it can be thrown in in the usual way.

The basis of most groundbaits is bread, and many other materials may be added. But always avoid stodgy mixtures for canal fishing. Canals are not waters which respond to heavy groundbaiting tactics.

It is far better to use a cloud-bait, and this can be purchased ready for use. Some successful midland anglers wet their cloud-bait with milk instead of water to increase the cloud effect.

Methods

Once the swim – that is the area of water to be fished – has been decided upon, and the tackle set up, use the plummet to find the depth and adjust the float.

It usually pays to plumb the depth of the swim before fishing, but be cautious when doing so in clear waters. At times it may be best to find the depth by trial and error.

Often most fish will be caught from around mid-water level, but always be prepared to move the float further up the line in order to present the bait closer to the bottom, where the bigger fish are usually to be found.

At frequent intervals toss a few samples of the hook-bait into the top of the swim to keep the fish interested.

Fish vary in different swims, and on different waters, in the way they take a bait and this creates a different bite registration. It may be found that the fish take the hook-bait quickly, causing the float to dip sharply or dive under the surface. The strike should be made instantly, on the downward movement. On some canals the fish are even quicker – and perhaps gentler – not taking the float under at all, and in this case the strike should be made at the slightest unusual movement of the float.

Roach and dace abound in many lengths and although working the float tackle down with a flow of water takes most fish, better quality fish – also bream – are usually to be taken by fishing a laying-on style, with the bait lying on the bottom. This method can often be best when fishing areas where there is no flow at all.

This can be done with float tackle, adjusted to make the distance from float to hook greater than the depth of water, so that when the float is at the surface the bait and lower length of line are lying on the bottom.

The alternative method of fishing the bottom is by legering, the main difference in the methods being in the bite indication. Without the float a bite is registered at the rod-tip where, if need be, a quiver-tip or swing-tip may be fitted. These bite detectors are used extensively on Midland and Northern waters.

Legering is a method often used in the south, where in some southern canals barbel and chub are quite prolific. These species grow to good sizes in canal waters – chub up to 7lb and barbel up to 14lb have been taken – but these are exceptional and the average run of fish would be well below those weights. Nevertheless, both species are big fish and big baits and hooks may be used when fishing for them.

Many bigger than average fish – of all species – have been taken by fishing the bait on the bottom. Whatever the style of leger fishing, always choose the lightest possible lead weight, and position it some 12 to 18 inches up from the hook. There are no hard and fast rules governing the distance between lead and hook, so it pays to experiment to find the best to suit the conditions.

Anglers who regularly fish the northern, and midland canals invariably use tiny size 20 and 22 hooks, tied to a mere ¾lb b.s. line, and when float-fishing use a tiny quill float – porcupine or crow quill. A piece of peacock quill is useful because it can be cut with scissors to make it suit prevailing conditions.

Such small floats only need a couple of dust-shot to balance them correctly, and usually the midland anglers position this shot on the line just under the float so that the bait is presented naturally. Once the tackle has been cast out the bait falls slowly through the water along with hook-bait samples, which are thrown in at the same time. This is called 'fishing on the drop'. A fine cloud-bait is also used with this style.

Canals which have luxuriant weed growth harbour many small fish, which are preyed upon by perch. These move in shoals and invariably the perch in a shoal are much the same size. Usually the really big perch are solitary, so it pays to rove the canal and search for them.

Perch are to be caught from almost any canal and although they may be caught by most angling methods, the most effective is usually float-fishing. The fishing depth can vary according to conditions, time of year, and actual depth of the canal, so it pays to try the bait at varying depths. The usual baits for perch are worms, small live-baits (minnows etc) and maggots. Close by the wooden lock gates are very often good haunts for perch.

In certain places canals and rivers come together and take on the characteristics of the river (i.e. with an increased flow) and different methods are needed. These places are often noted for splendid chub (and sometimes barbel) in addition to roach and other species. Trotting the stream is a popular and effective fishing style.

Weather

Weather conditions also have to be taken into consideration. Canals usually run through open country and catch the slightest breeze. Even a moderate wind will pull and bob the float, which in turn will agitate the baited hook. If bites are not forthcoming under such conditions then it may be best to remove the float and try a straightforward leger arrangement.

When legering, the effects of the wind can be avoided by keeping the rod top down to within an inch or two of the water level—or even by sinking the rod-tip below the surface. Anglers in the north and midlands have devised a wind-shield for legering which protects the rod-tip from the wind and improves bite detection.

Nevertheless, in some circumstances a slight wind can be helpful because if a moderate breeze is blowing it will put a ripple on the water, and this can be of assistance in fishing in clear waters.

Where to fish

Most canals are narrow and this makes it possible to cast the tackle towards the far bank where fish have moved because they had been disturbed from the near bank. Disturbance will send the fish up or downstream and often well away from the fishing area. So always approach the water quietly, and remember to move cautiously at all times. When making up the tackle to start fishing it is advisable to do so as far back from the water as possible to avoid scaring the fish. It pays to move slowly, to keep as far from the bank as possible, and to avoid clumping around in heavy rubber boots.

If there is cover along the bank—shrubs, bushes, tall reeds and clumps of yellow flag iris—the wise angler will make full use of it.

There are some canals which are not navigable, and these are generally weedy. At certain times in the season the surface of the water disappears under a green mantle of floating duckweed, which affords cover and security for the fish. It is possible to have the best sport by fishing in the pockets of clear water which are to be found.

Some canals have prolific growths of water lilies in places, and are particularly attractive for angling. They always look ideal haunts for tench, but they can also be rather difficult places from which to land good fish.

Tench are more or less evenly distributed throughout the canals and the best are found where weed growth is profuse. It may be best to fish small areas of clear water between the weeds. Groundbait can encourage tench to move out from the weed beds, and to feed once they are out. Sometimes it is an advantage to clear a swim by dragging out weeds or raking the bottom. This form of natural groundbaiting stirs the silt which clouds the water, and disturbs aquatic creatures on which the fish feed. Sometimes a tench is hooked within minutes of raking.

Bream seem to do well in canals and some fairly good fish up to 5lb may be taken. Some canals are noted for shoals of big bream, where it is possible to catch over 50lb of them at a session. Any deep pools or winding holes (shown as ∩ on map) are good places to try, particularly when fishing a canal for the first time.

Other places worth fishing are cattle drinks' regularly used by farm animals. These make useful places to fish for bream, roach and dace. The frequent use of these drinking holes colours the water, as the animals stir up the mud, and disturb various water creatures. The coloured water draws fish into the area—on the downstream side of the cattle drink when there is the slightest flow.

Pike are to be found in every canal in the country, and these grow big. They are predators, feeding on small fish (which gives a sure indication of the most effective baits.) Any small live fish presented on float tackle will take pike. The best places to fish are near weed beds and boats which have been moored in one place a long time.

As a general rule, never fish in locks on navigable canals, or anywhere that could obstruct the free passage of boats. Remember that you will inconvenience yourself as well as the boatman if you have to move in a hurry, or risk a broken line.

British Waterways Board
The BWB Fisheries Officer at Watford welcomes specific enquiries about fishing on BWB canals from individuals, associations and clubs. He will also supply the name and address of the current Secretary of each Angling Association shown on page 18.

River Authorities
Refer to the map on pages 4 and 5 showing the areas covered.

Dee & Clwyd River Authority
2 Vicars lane,
Chester. (45004).
(Rod licence required).

Lancashire River Authority
48 West Cliff,
Preston,
Lancs. (54921).
(No rod licence required).

Mersey & Weaver River Authority
PO Box 12,
Liverpool road,
Great Sankey,
near Warrington. (Penketh 5531).
(No rod licence required).

Severn River Authority
Portland House,
Church street,
Great Malvern,
Worcs. (Malvern 61511).
(Rod licence required).

Trent River Authority
206 Derby road,
Nottingham. (42300)
(Rod licence required).

Yorkshire River Authority
21 Park Square South,
Leeds. (29404).
(Rod licence required).

Natural history

Stretches of water always add to the natural history interest of an area. The water itself provides a habitat for some wildlife and the verges too have their special plants and animals. The canals of north west England are no exception and a walk along the tow-ing path can be full of interest. These canals support a large variety of native fish and in some areas, where warm water is discharged from industrial cooling plants, tropical fish thrive. Some aquarists have a bad habit of throwing unwanted exotic water weeds into the nearest canal or stream and, in warm water areas, these may grow excessively, sometimes blocking the watercourse. Fish-spawn on these weeds will hatch, given the right conditions. The result has been that guppies, black mollies, catfish and cichlids have survived for long periods and some species have bred.

The number of species of fish is controlled by the purity of the water, and fish such as the gudgeon and roach, which can tolerate pollution, are found even when the Leeds and Liverpool Canal in the industrial area of Merseyside was heavily polluted as—happily—it is not today. Where the water is cleaner, other species such as perch and eels can live. Young eels, known as elvers, migrate in shoals up the Shropshire Union Canal. They began life in the Caribbean Sea and have travelled many hundreds of miles back to the canals which their parents left on their long journey to the salt water breeding grounds. Near Burscough carp, bream and tench are found and sometimes pike also. Near Blackburn trout have been introduced and one of over three pounds has been caught. Where the Leeds and Liverpool Canal climbs up to the limestone hills, large chub and a few crayfish live. Crayfish are shrimp-like crustaceans, about 3" long, beloved by chub. They live in holes and dead specimens are often found in mud dredged from canals. (Observant towpath walkers will notice them where the canal has been recently dredged). The presence of crayfish in a canal indicates good clean water.

The bitterling was recently discovered in the Llangollen Canal. It has a most interesting life history, being hatched inside a fresh-water mussel shell, where it lives safe from enemies until it is ready to lead an independent existence.

A slug-pearl has been reported in a fresh-water mussel shell from the Shropshire Union Canal. Frogs, toads and newts may be found in backwaters, ponds or lakes near the canals, although they have been so heavily collected that they are now hard to find.

Water spiders are interesting creatures which, although breathing air, live entirely in the water. They store air in a web which assumes a bell shape as it becomes distended with air. Each bubble is brought down from the surface trapped between the legs and abdomen of the spider. Water skaters, which skim over the surface, and water boatmen, which swim upside down just below the surface film, are two bugs sure to be found where the water is quiet. A number of flying insects pass the first stage of their lives below the surface. Among these are may-flies (chief fly taken by fish), caddis flies (with larvae living in tubes made of tiny stones, sticks and leaves which they cement together), and dragonflies, whose larvae are voracious feeders. There are several beetles which live entirely in the water and the largest of these is the great diving beetle, about 1¼ inches long. It is carnivorous and ferocious, attacking creatures, including fish, much larger than itself.

Near the Llangollen Canal red squirrels and adders are occasionally found. These beautiful snakes should not be killed. Although poisonous, they are timid, and will seldom attack if left alone. There are few British aquatic mammals but two of them, water voles and water shrews, are found in the quieter parts of the area. Foxes, rabbits and hares live in suitable country near the canals, and cause the canal maintenance staff a lot of trouble when their burrowing takes place in the canal banks.

Many of our most beautiful wild flowers grow in or near the water. Visitors to the canals should look in spring for the great pond sedge which grows in clumps up to four feet high and has dark brown flower spikes. Soon after this, in May, the yellow flag opens its large yellow flowers and in wet patches may be seen marsh marigolds and lesser celandine with shiny yellow petals. Along the banks grows the hoary willow herb or codlins and cream, a tall plant with rose-madder or occasionally white flowers. Purple loosestrife has shaggy spikes of purple flowers, and comfrey hanging bells of white, pink, purple and occasionally blue. Other plants of the bankside are the blue greater skullcap, mauve marsh woundwort, white gypsywort, yellow bur marigold, blue water forget-me-not, greenish-white angelica and mauve water mint. A plant with leaves like those of the yellow flag, but with inconspicuous green flower-spikes, is the sweet flag. The leaves have a very sweet smell when crushed and were used in mediaeval times to strew on floors.

Growing out of the water in some places will be found the reedmace, often wrongly called bulrush, with long, dense brown flower spikes and wide grass-like leaves. The true bulrush also grows in the canals and has no obvious leaves, bearing its sprays of brown flowers near the tip of thick round stems. Both plants may grow to six feet or more in height.

Three large grasses grow in shallow water at the edges of canals. They spread rapidly and may choke the waterway if not controlled. The true reed, used for thatching, has purplish brown heads, the great reed grass spreading heads of greenish brown and reed canary grass has soft pinkish sprays. Another plant, looking like a grass or rush when not in flower, is the flowering rush, with pink three-petalled flowers in a large umbel. Among other plants which grow in the water is the common yellow waterlily, called brandy bottle from the shape of the seed capsules. An uncommon plant which looks similar, though it is in fact a member of the gentian family, is the fringed waterlily, whose smaller yellow flowers have deeply fringed petals. Water violet has whorled spikes of delicate lilac blossoms and arrowhead large three-petalled white flowers. The name describes the shape of the leaves.

Some plants grow entirely under water, like the hornwort which has finely divided leaves and very tiny flowers. Water milfoil is similar but the tiny spike of flowers does emerge from the water. Duckweeds, free-floating plants consisting of just one or two leaves and very tiny flowers, cover still water with a green carpet. All four British species are found in these canals. Water persicaria, with dense spikes of pink flowers, may grow in the water, when its oval leaves float on the surface, or on land. The aquatic and terrestrial forms are quite different in appearance.

Wild damsons and crab-apples are frequently found along canals, especially the Shropshire Union, and all towing-path hedges are a well-known source of blackberries. These grow also in many cuttings on the offside—where they are accessible only by boat.

These are but a fraction of the many hundreds of interesting plants which grow in or near the canals. Butterflies, moths and many other creatures have not even been mentioned, but local Natural History Societies and Naturalists' Trusts are always willing to help those in search of knowledge.

Enquiries should be addressed in the case of Natural History Societies to the Council for Nature, c/o The Royal Zoological Society of London, Regents Park, London NW1, or for the Trusts to the Society for the Promotion of Nature Reserves, The Manor House, Alford, Lincolnshire.

Birds

The slow, noisy flap of a grey-and-black heron rising from the water's edge; a chirrup of alarm as the white tail of a moorhen disappears into the reeds; the circle of ripples where a dabchick has just dived—these are just a few of the signs of the abundant birdlife which may be encountered along our waterways. From a quietly progressing boat much more can be seen and, with a little practice, the names and distinguishing features of the commonest birds can be learned. A great many birds are associated with water without being 'water birds' proper, but here we will look only at this main group, the birds whose whole life is intimately connected with water in that they either swim in it or wholly depend on it for food.

Swimming birds fall into three main groups. Grebes are long-necked diving birds; five species breed in Britain, but much the most likely one to be seen on inland waterways is the tiny, brown-and-russet dabchick, a round-bodied bird which seems to spend more time beneath the water than on the surface and which can be most elusive and difficult to watch. Ducks, geese and swans are a large and diverse group, and here we need only mention the two most abundant species, the familiar mute swan (which is actually quite a vocal bird at times) and the mallard or wild duck. The latter is well enough known too, the drake being a handsome bird with a bottle-green head, a narrow white collar and a largely greyish body, and the duck wearing quieter, mottled brown plumage. Moorhens and coots may be confusing to the beginner, but are in fact easy to tell apart. The slightly larger coot is entirely black but for a white bill, while the moorhen is browner on the back, shows a white line along its side and a white 'horseshoe' under its upright tail. It also has a red-and-yellow bill.

Two birds, both unmistakeable, live almost completely on fish which they obtain without swimming. The heron is a large, long-necked, long-legged bird, blue-grey above with white below, who wades silently in the shallows or stands motionless near the bank, suddenly spearing fish with a lightning thrust of its dagger-like bill. Its long neck is withdrawn in flight, when it appears as a very large, broad-winged bird with blackish flight feathers.

The kingfisher is a very small bird, not much larger than a sparrow, with a large head and, again, a substantial dagger-shaped bill. It is a wary bird, most often seen as a flash of incredible blue flying off low over the water, but at close range it is among the most handsome of all British birds, brilliant blue and blue-green above and brick-red below, with a flash of white behind the eye and vivid red feet.

Several types of gulls may be met with feeding on or over water, of which the two most likely are the common gull and the black-headed gull. Both are rather small gulls, white below and pale grey above. The common gull shows black-and-white wing-tips, green legs and a yellowish bill, while the black-headed sports a chocolate-brown hood in spring and summer (and a small dark patch behind the eye at other times of the year) and has red legs and a dark red bill. The white leading edges to the latter's wings are a safe guide to its identity at any season.

Swallows and martins regularly feed over water and, although a little confusing at first, the three species are readily identifiable. Sand martins are brown above and whitish below; house martins are blue-black above with a conspicuous white rump and gleaming white underparts—and swallows are a deep, metallic blue above, with long tail-streamers, dark chestnut and blue on the face and upper breast and more creamy underparts. The superficially similar but unrelated swift is larger with long, sickle-shaped wings and is sooty-black all over.

Of the numerous small birds which live alongside water, only a few can be mentioned here. Wagtails are slender, long-tailed birds which, as their name implies, wag their tails up and down almost constantly. Pied wagtails are the commonest, and are attractive in black, white and grey plumage; grey wagtails are more colourful than their name suggests, having slate-grey upper parts and yellow underparts, the latter being brightest under the very long tail; male yellow wagtails are vivid yellow birds with greenish upperparts, while the females are somewhat duller and browner. Reed and sedge warblers are small, brownish birds with pale underparts which live in thick, waterside vegetation. Both have long, complicated songs of great richness and variety. Given a good view, they can be told apart by the fact that the reed warbler is uniformly coloured above, while the sedge warbler is streaked darker and has a distinct, creamy-white stripe over the eye. The reed-bunting is a rather sparrow-like bird in general appearance, pale below, streaked brown above, and showing white outer tail-feathers. The male is very distinctive with his black head and bib and contrasting white collar. These are just a few of the commonest birds you might see: there are many more. Bird-watching is a fascinating hobby anywhere—if you would like to know more about it your local library will be able to produce dozens of books telling you how to learn. The Royal Society for the Protection of Birds at The Lodge, Sandy, Bedfordshire (Sandy 80551) will be delighted to welcome new members.

Shropshire Union

Maximum dimensions

Autherley to Nantwich, and Middlewich branch
Length: 72'
Beam: 7'
Headroom: 8'
Nantwich to Ellesmere Port
Length: 72'
Beam: 13' 3"
Headroom: 8'
Hurleston to Llangollen
Length: 72'
Beam: 6' 10"
Headroom: 7'

Mileage

Shropshire Union main line
Autherley Junction (Staffs & Worcs Canal) to Norbury: 15½ miles 2 locks
Market Drayton: 27 miles, 7 locks
Hurleston Junction (Llangollen Canal): 40¾ miles, 29 locks
Barbridge Junction (Middlewich Branch): 42 miles, 29 locks
Chester Junction with Dee Branch: 58 miles, 43 locks
Ellesmere Port junction with Manchester Ship Canal: 66½ miles, 47 locks

Middlewich Branch
Middlewich (Trent & Mersey Canal) to Barbridge Junction: 10 miles, 4 locks

Llangollen Branch
Hurleston Junction (S.U. main line) to Frankton Junction (Montgomery Branch): 29 miles, 19 locks
Pontcysyllte Aqueduct: 40 miles, 21 locks
Llangollen: 44½ miles, 21 locks
Llantisilio canal terminus: 46 miles, 21 locks

Montgomery Branch
Frankton Junction (Llangollen Branch) to Newton canal terminus: 35 miles, 25 locks

The Chester Canal

In 1772 an enabling Act was passed for a canal from the river Dee in Chester to join the Trent & Mersey Canal at Middlewich, with a spur to Nantwich. The building of the Trent & Mersey was the cause of this new venture, for it was seen as a threat to the future of the river Dee navigation and the port of Chester. The new canal was designed to bolster Chester as an alternative port to Liverpool, and so was planned as a barge canal, with locks 80ft by 14ft 9in. Work started in Chester in the middle of 1772 and progressed very slowly. There were engineering and financial problems, and the main line of the new canal was altered to terminate at a basin and warehouses just outside Nantwich: the proposed line to Middlewich was now to be a branch. The Nantwich–Chester link was completed in 1779, but the spur to Middlewich was not built until 54 years later. When the Nantwich–Chester canal was finished, arguments with the Dee River Company delayed the building of the river lock. By this time competition with the Trent & Mersey was out of the question. Although regular freight and fast passenger services were run, the canal was wholly uneconomic and in 1787 the company collapsed. In 1790 it was revived and the canal repaired, for the directors saw the publication of the plans of the Ellesmere Canal as their last chance to complete the line to Middlewich.

The Ellesmere Canal

In 1791 a plan was published for a canal from the Mersey to the Severn, to pass through Chester, the iron and coal fields around Ruabon, Ellesmere and Shrewsbury. There were to be branches to the limestone quarries at Llanymynech, and to the Chester Canal via Whitchurch. The new terminus on the Mersey was to be at the little fishing village of Netherpool, known after 1796 as Ellesmere Port. After extensive arguments about routes, the company received its Act in 1793. William Jessop was appointed engineer, and work began. By 1796 the Wirral line from Chester to Ellesmere Port was open, and was immediately successful, carrying goods and passengers (in express 'fly-boats') to Liverpool. The same year, the Llanymynech branch was completed. The company continued to expand and build inwards, but failed to make the vital connections with the Dee and the Severn; the line south to Shrewsbury never got further than Weston, and the line northwards to Chester stopped at Pontcysyllte. By 1806 the Ellesmere company had opened 68 miles of canal, which included lines from Hurleston on the Chester Canal to Plas Kynaston via Frankton, and from Chester to Ellesmere Port; there were branches to Llanymynech, Whitchurch, Prees and Ellesmere, and a navigable feeder to Llangollen; the two great aqueducts at Chirk and Pontcysyllte were complete. However it was a totally self-contained system, its only outlet being via the old Chester Canal at Hurleston. Despite this, the Ellesmere Canal was profitable; it serviced a widespread local network, and gave an outlet to Liverpool (via the river Mersey) for the ironworks and coalfields that were grouped at the centre of the system. This profitability was dependent upon good relations with the Chester Company. An attempted take-over in 1804 failed, but in 1813 the inevitable merger took place, and the Ellesemere & Chester Canal Company was formed.

The Montgomery Canal

When the Ellesmere plans were published, they inspired a separate company to plan a canal from Newtown northwards to join the Llanymynech branch of the Ellesmere Canal at Carreghofa. The canal was authorised in 1793, and by 1797 the line was open from Carreghofa to Garthmyl. The Montgomery Canal was mainly agricultural; apart from the limestone, it existed to serve the farms and villages through which it passed, and so was never really able to make a profit. The lack of capital and income greatly delayed the completion of the western extension to Newtown, which was not finally opened until 1821, having been financed by a separate company. So the 35-mile length that later became known as the Montgomery Canal was in fact built by three separate companies over a period of thirty years.

The Birmingham & Liverpool Junction Canal

The future prosperity of the Ellesmere & Chester was limited by the lack of an outlet to the south, without which its trade could never be more than local. So the company was much cheered by the plans for the Birmingham & Liverpool Junction Canal which received its Act in 1825. The line from Nantwich to Autherley, on the Staffordshire & Worcestershire Canal, would give a direct link between Liverpool and the Midlands, and thus with the canal network as a whole. After serious engineering difficulties the canal was opened in 1835, shortly after the opening of the long planned branch from the Chester Canal to the Trent & Mersey at Middlewich, providing access to Manchester and the Potteries. Railway competition was close at hand by this date, and so the Birmingham & Liverpool Junction and Ellesmere & Chester companies worked closely together to preserve their profits. Ellesmere Port was greatly enlarged, and by 1840 steam haulage was in use on the Wirral line and on the Mersey itself. In 1845 the two companies merged, and then shortly after were re-formed as the Shropshire Union Railways and Canal Company.

The Shropshire Union

The Shropshire Union Railways & Canal Company was formed under the shadow of railway expansion. Its initial plans were to build railways instead of canals, on the principle that it would halve the construction costs to lay a railway along the bed of an existing canal. By 1849 this plan had been abandoned, for the slow development of railways in Wales had shown the company that canals could still be profitable. Throughout the mid-19th century the Shropshire Union network remained profitable, and did not experience the steady decline of other major canal systems. The London and North Western Railway Company was a major shareholder in the Shropshire Union, and they were very happy to let the canals remain as they provided the company with a significant tentacle into Great Western Railway territory. As a result the Shropshire Union was allowed to expand steadily; in 1870 the company owned 213 narrow boats, and in 1889 there were 395. By 1902 this fleet had increased to 450 boats. A few branches were threatened with closure on the grounds of unprofitability, but no such closures were in fact carried out. The flourishing trade continued until the 1914-18 war, which started a pattern of regular heavy losses from which the company was never able to recover. In 1921 the company gave up canal carrying, and sold most of its fleet of boats to private operators. Locks were closed at weekends, and standards of maintenance began to slip. In 1922 the Shropshire Union Company was bought out by the London and North Western Railway, which then was swallowed in turn by the newly-formed London Midland and Scottish Railway. Despite these changes the network remained open, although trade declined rapidly. Many traders were driven away by the lack of maintenance, which meant that most boats could only operate half empty. In 1936 a breach occurred on the Montgomery Canal one mile south of Frankton Junction; the company set out to repair the damage and then changed their minds. (The Weston Line had been similarly abandoned after a breach in 1917.) With trade at a standstill there were no complaints, and in 1944 an Act was passed making closure official. This Act also officially abandoned 175 miles of the old Shropshire Union network. Out of this mass closure only the main line and the Middlewich branch remained, although the Llangollen branch luckily also escaped closure, being retained as a water supply channel. Nowadays it is the most popular cruising canal in the country.

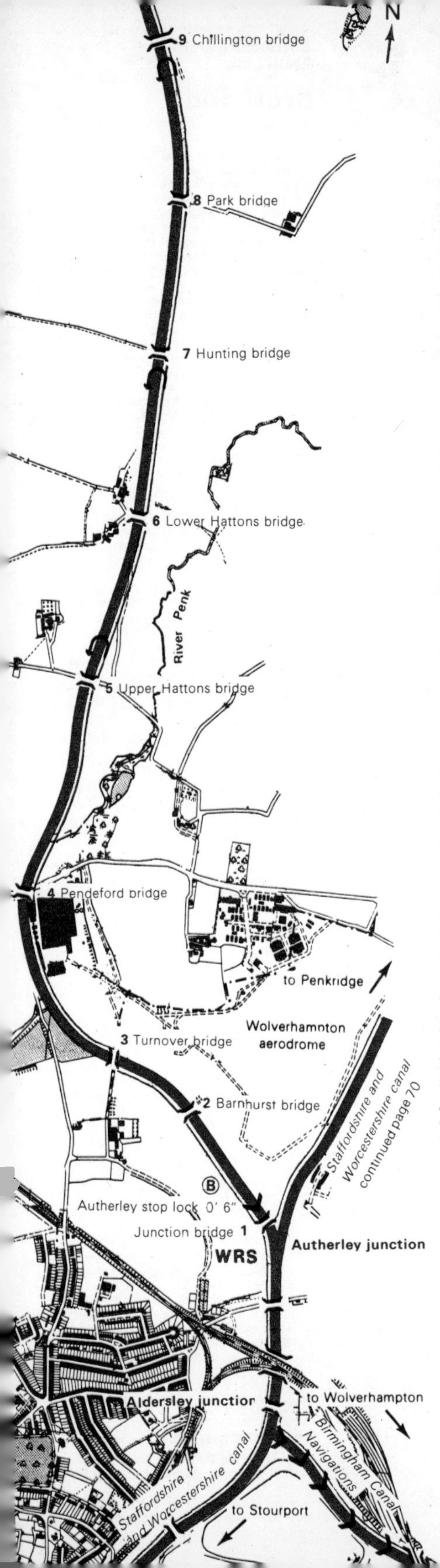

9 Chillington bridge
8 Park bridge
7 Hunting bridge
6 Lower Hattons bridge
River Penk
5 Upper Hattons bridge
4 Pendeford bridge
to Penkridge
Wolverhampton aerodrome
3 Turnover bridge
2 Barnhurst bridge
Staffordshire and Worcestershire canal continued page 70
Autherley stop lock 0' 6"
Junction bridge 1
WRS
Autherley junction
Aldersley junction
to Wolverhampton
Birmingham Canal Navigations
Staffordshire and Worcestershire canal
to Stourport

Autherley Junction

5 miles

The Shropshire Union Canal leaves the Staffordshire & Worcestershire canal at Autherley Junction, and runs straight along the side of Wolverhampton Aerodrome at Pendeford. Passing the Wolverhampton Boat Club, the canal soon enters a short cutting, which is through rock, and narrow in places. Emerging briefly into the green and quiet countryside that is found along the whole length of this navigation, the canal plunges into a deep, long cutting that is typical of this particular stretch.

Autherley Junction
An important and busy canal junction, where in 1830 Thomas Telford brought his Birmingham & Liverpool Junction Canal (now part of the Shropshire Union system) to join the much older Staffordshire & Worcestershire canal (built by James Brindley and opened in 1772). There is a former canal toll office here, also a boatyard and a boatclub. The stop lock has a fall of only about 6ins: it was insisted upon by the Staffs & Worcs company to prevent the newer canal 'stealing' water from them. Autherley Junction is sometimes confused with Aldersley Junction, ½ mile to the south, where the Birmingham Canal Navigations join the Staffs & Worcs canal from the east after falling through the Wolverhampton flight of 21 locks.

BOATYARDS & BWB

Water Travel Autherley Junction, Tettenhall, Wolverhampton, Staffs. (Wolverhampton 782371). Hire cruisers. Sewage & refuse disposal, water, diesel, petrol, gas, chandlery. Slipway up to 45 foot, moorings, winter storage. Boat & motor sales & repairs. Steel boats built & fitted out. Bar, groceries. Lavatory. *Open daily throuthout year.*
Boat trips 'Compton Queen' runs trips from Autherley for parties of up to 40. Enquiries to Mr Gregory, 83 Aldersley rd, Tettenhall, Wolverhampton. (Wolverhampton 753851). Hire cruisers and Autherley moorings (on the Staffs & Worcs canal) also available from this address.

FISHING THE SHROPSHIRE UNION

There are roach, dace, eels, bream, perch, pike and gudgeon to be caught throughout the 150 miles of the Shropshire Union system which is available to anglers. A few clubs and associations lease fishing rights, and visiting anglers can obtain permits from local bailiffs or tackle shops.
The tench and carp are particularly wary. However they can be caught by float-fishing a laying-on style with a bunch of 4 or 5 maggots on a size 12 hook. These tactics have accounted for tench to 3½lb and carp to 14lb.
There is good fishing for most species at *Autherley, Brewood, Norbury, Market Drayton, Audlem, Nantwich, Calveley, Beeston Castle* and *Chester.*

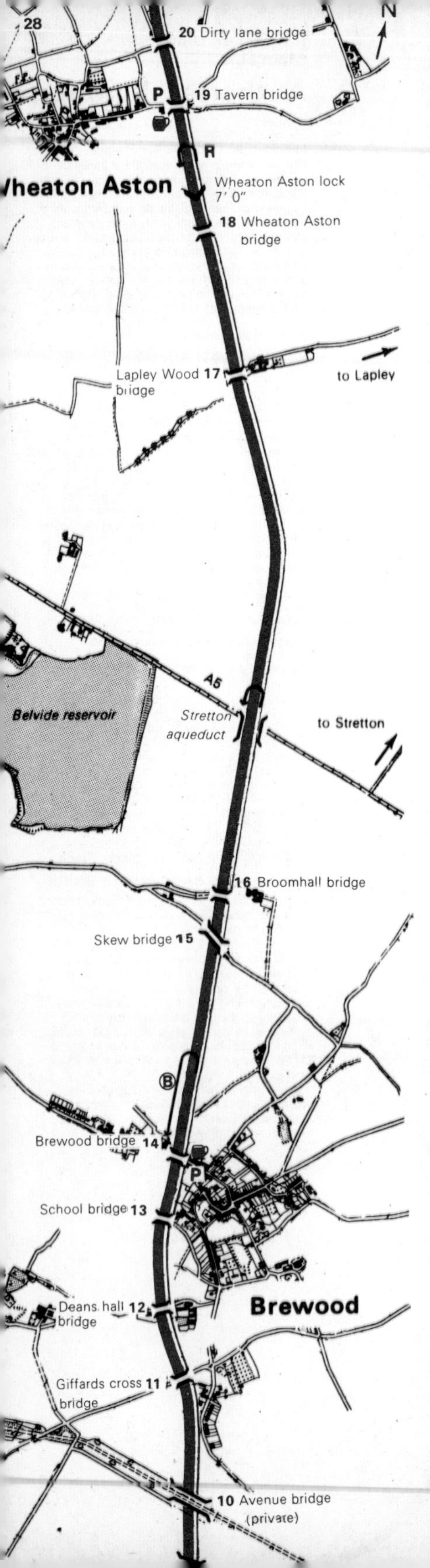

Shropshire Union Main Line

Brewood

4½ miles

Leaving the balustraded Avenue bridge (10), which leads westward to Chillington Hall, the canal curves in a bold cutting past the village of Brewood and its attractive wharf–recently turned into a boatyard–and moves north west along a very straight embankment. The head bank of the big Belvide reservoir can be seen on the west side; its feeder stream enters the canal just south of Stretton Aqueduct. This solid but elegant cast iron structure carries Telford's canal over Telford's road (the Holyhead road–A5). Crossing the aqueduct by boat tends to give the canal traveller an air of great superiority over the teeming motorists below. After another long wooded cutting the canal reaches Wheaton Aston Lock. This lock marks the end of the long 'pound' from Autherley and the beginning of the 17-mile level that lasts almost to Market Drayton.

Wheaton Aston
Staffs. PO, tel, stores, garage. Overrun by new housing. The village green around the church (rebuilt in 1857) is a memento of a more pleasant past. The garage beside the canal repairs boats' engines and sells chandlery; while at the lock cottage local hand-painted canal ware may be bought.

Lapley
Staffs. ¾ mile NE of bridge 17. The central tower of the church dominates the village. It is an interesting building with fine Norman windows, an old Dutch font and traces of mediaeval paintings on the nave wall. The church as we see it now was completed in the 15thC.

Stretton
1 mile NE of Stretton Aqueduct off the A5. The church was rebuilt in 19thC but retains its original chancel and fragments of mediaeval glass in the east window.
Stretton Hall Built in 1620 to designs by Inigo Jones. Most interesting features are the vast fireplace with steps up to it for chimneysweep boys, and the remarkable staircase suspended by chains from the roof. The house is private.

Belvide Reservoir
A large nature reserve open to naturalists. The Royal Society for the Protection of Birds is developing the reserve to include displays and hides, enabling enthusiasts to have a greater opportunity to observe the many species of birds. There is only private club fishing and no sailing on the reservoir, so as to preserve the bird sanctuary.

Brewood
Staffs. Pop 7,100. EC Wed. PO, tel, stores, bank, garage. The name (pronounced 'Brood') derives from Celtic 'Bre' meaning 'hill', thus giving 'wood on the hill'. It originally consisted of a Roman fort on Beacon Hill to defend Watling st. but is now a beautiful, quiet village with some extremely attractive Georgian houses in groups. The village church is a tall, elegant building which has been greatly restored but still contains a 16thC font and several 16thC effigies and 17thC monuments commemorating the Giffard family of Chillington Hall.

Chillington Hall
1½ miles west of canal, south west of Brewood, this has been the home of the Giffard family since the 12thC. The existing hall was built in the 18thC, and the wooded park in which it stands was designed by 'Capability Brown'. The hall is approached by an avenue of trees, at the eastern end of which is Giffard's Cross. This is said to mark the spot where Sir John Giffard in 1513 shot a wild panther with his cross bow, thus saving the lives of a woman and her child. The panther, a gift from a friendly Oriental, had escaped from its cage. *Open May-Aug Thur 14.30-17.30.* (Brewood 850260).

BOATYARDS & BWB

Countrywide Cruisers The Wharf, Brewood, Staffs. (850166). Just north of bridge 14. Hire cruisers. Refuse & sewage disposal, water, diesel, gas, chandlery, slipway up to 70 foot, moorings,

winter storage. Boat & motor sales & repairs, agents for Yamaha. Groceries. Lavatory. *Open daily throughout year.*
Boat trips 12 berth camping boat & 50-seater narrow boat 'David', both with crew, available for charter: operate from Brewood. Enquiries to Canal Transport Services, Norton Canes Dock, Lime lane, Pelsall, Staffs. (Brownhills 4370).

PUBS

Hartley Arms Canalside, at Tavern Bridge, Wheaton Aston.
Coach & Horses Wheaton Aston.
Swan Brewood (850330).
Lion Brewood (850235).
Admiral Rodney near Brewood Church.
Boat Canalside, at Brewood Bridge.

CARAVANS & CAMPING

Sunny Bank Caravan Park Lapley. (Wheaton Aston 283). ¼ mile from canal. Overnight caravan stops. No tents permitted.

Cruising on the Shropshire Union.

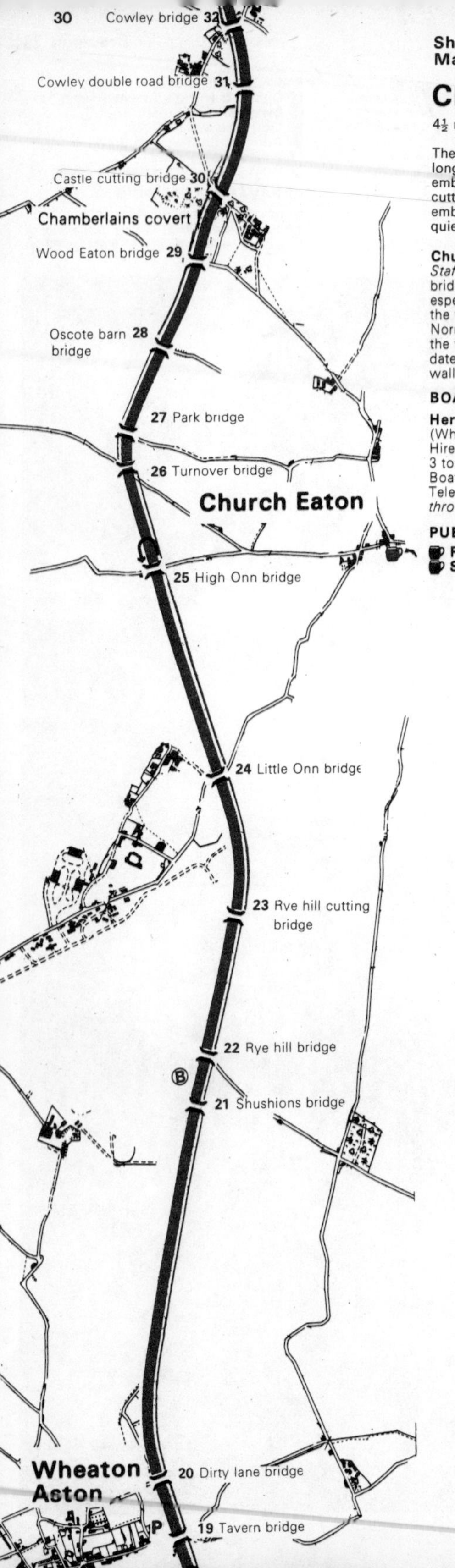

Shropshire Union Main Line

Church Eaton

4½ miles

The canal now proceeds along the very long pound, alternately in cuttings and on embankments. Both offer interest; the cuttings for their rich vegetation, and the embankments for the excellent views over quiet, unspoilt grazing land.

Church Eaton
Staffs. EC Wed. PO, tel, stores. 1 mile NE of bridge 25. Parts of the old village remain, especially at the end of the village street in the vicinity of the fine church. St Editha's, a Norman structure with the spire added to the tower in the 15thC. The east window dates from about 1400 and almost fills the wall.

BOATYARDS & BWB

Heron Cruisers Little Onn, Stafford, (Wheaton Aston 840040). At bridge 21. Hire cruisers, day boats. Dustbins, gas, 3 ton crane, moorings, winter storage. Boat & motor sales & repairs. Groceries. Telephone. Lavatories. *Open daily throughout year.*

PUBS

Royal Oak Church Eaton
Swan Church Eaton.

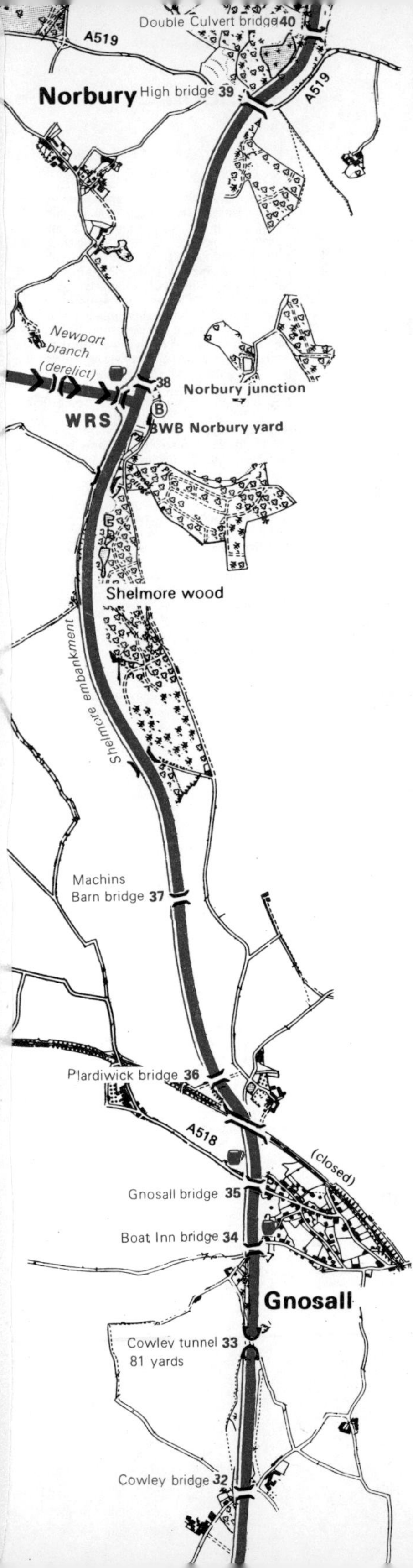

Norbury Junction

$4\frac{3}{4}$ miles

The canal now enters the very deep and almost vertical cutting that terminates in Cowley tunnel. North of the tunnel is Gnosall; shortly after this, the canal moves round the side of Shelmore Wood and crosses the mighty Shelmore Embankment before reaching Norbury Junction, where the Newport branch used to lock down from the main line. North of here is the long Grub Street cutting which features the well known High Bridge with a masonry strut, carrying a short telegraph pole, built across its tall arch.

Norbury Junction
This was once the outlet for the Shrewsbury, Newport and Trench branches on to the rest of the Shropshire Union Canal system. There is a long flight of locks from the junction down to Newport, but these are now closed and the Shropshire canals are disused and forgotten. Norbury Junction is still full of interest, however: there is a boatyard, a canal maintenance yard and a popular canalside pub. A converted horse-drawn narrowboat runs regular trips up and down the canal from the junction.

Shelmore Embankment
The construction of this great embankment 1 mile long, just south of Norbury Junction, was the source of endless grief and expense to the Birmingham & Liverpool Junction Canal Company in general and to Thomas Telford, their engineer, in particular. It was an enormous task anyway to shift the millions of cubic feet of earth to build the bank; but while the contractors struggled to complete it, the bank slipped and collapsed time and again. By early 1834, Shelmore Embankment was the only unfinished section of the whole canal. It was not until 1835, after $5\frac{1}{2}$ years solid work on it and well after Telford's death, that the embankment was completed by William Cubitt and the B&LJ Canal was opened as a through route.

Gnosall
Staffs. PO, tel, garage, stores. The main feature of interest in the village is the Church of St Laurence, a mile east of the canal. It is a 15thC building with original Norman tower arches. The east window has fine decorated tracery, framing modern stained glass.

Cowley Tunnel
This short tunnel was originally intended to be much longer–700 yards–but most of it was opened out at an early stage in construction (during the early 1830s) because of dangerous faults in the rock, and now only 81 yards remain. The tunnel is unlined, and to the south of it a very steep narrow cutting through solid rock stretches a considerable distance–an awe-inspiring sight to a boatman.

BOATYARDS & BWB

BWB Norbury Yard Woodseaves 253. At Norbury Junction. Water, lavatory, refuse & sewage disposal.
Shropshire Union Cruises The Wharf, Norbury Junction, Norbury, Stafford. (Woodseaves 292). Hire cruisers. Sewage & refuse disposal, water, diesel, petrol, gas, chandlery, drydock, slipway up to 55 foot, moorings, winter storage. Boat & motor sales & repairs, agents for Mercury, Marina, Callumcraft, Island Plastics, Nautacraft. Steel & fibreglass boats built and fitted out. Milk. Lavatories. *Open daily throughout year.*
Boat trips 'Iona' is a horse-drawn narrowboat operating from Norbury Junction. (Available by charter to parties up to 48 strong. Enquiries to Shropshire Union Cruises: see above).

PUBS

Junction Inn Canalside, at Norbury Junction.
Navigation Canalside, at bridge 35.
Royal Oak Gnosall.
Boat Canalside, at Boat Inn bridge.

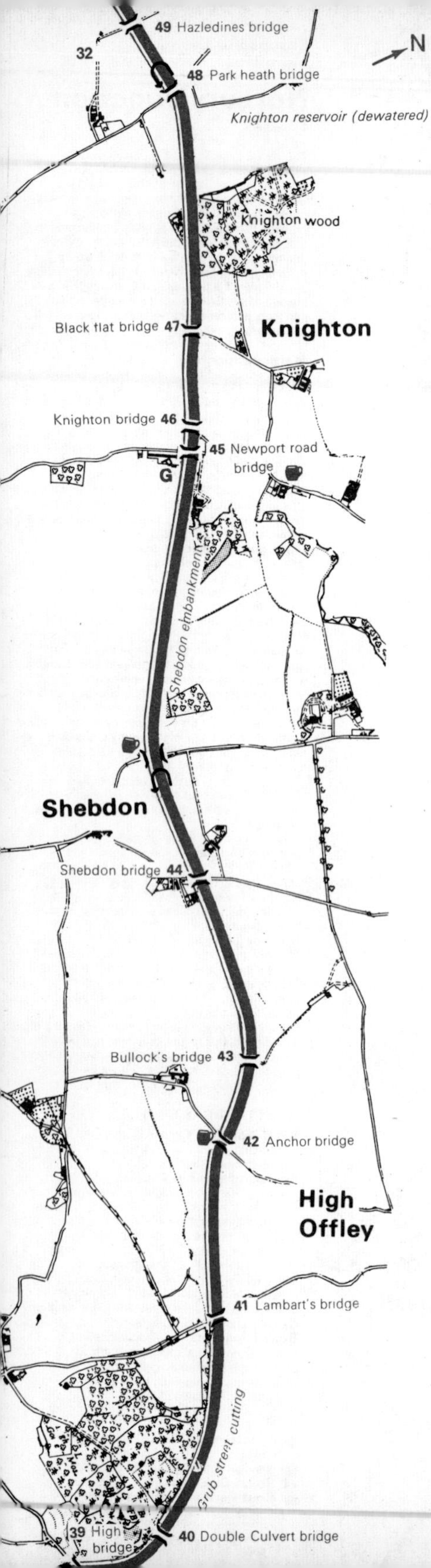

N

Shropshire Union Main Line

Shebdon

5 miles

The canal moves out of Grub Street cutting and, passing the village of High Offley on a hill to the north, continues in a north westerly direction through the quiet open farmland that always accompanies this canal. Along this stretch are two canalside pubs—both amaze the traveller by their very survival, situated as they are on quiet roads and an even quieter canal. The great Shebdon embankment is heralded by an aqueduct; at the far end is a large ex-chocolate factory (now producing only dried milk), whose goods used to be carried to and from Bournville (on the Worcester & Birmingham Canal) by canal boat. Knighton post office, stores and telephone are by bridge 45; Knighton Reservoir—now empty—lies to the north.

High Offley
Staffs. Tel. Hilltop farming village, scattered round a large 15thC church. Good views in all directions.

PUBS

Haberdashers Arms Knighton, ½ mile NE of bridge 45.

Wharf Inn Canalside, below Shebdon aqueduct.

Anchor Inn Canalside, at Offley Bridge (42).

Royal Oak High Offley.

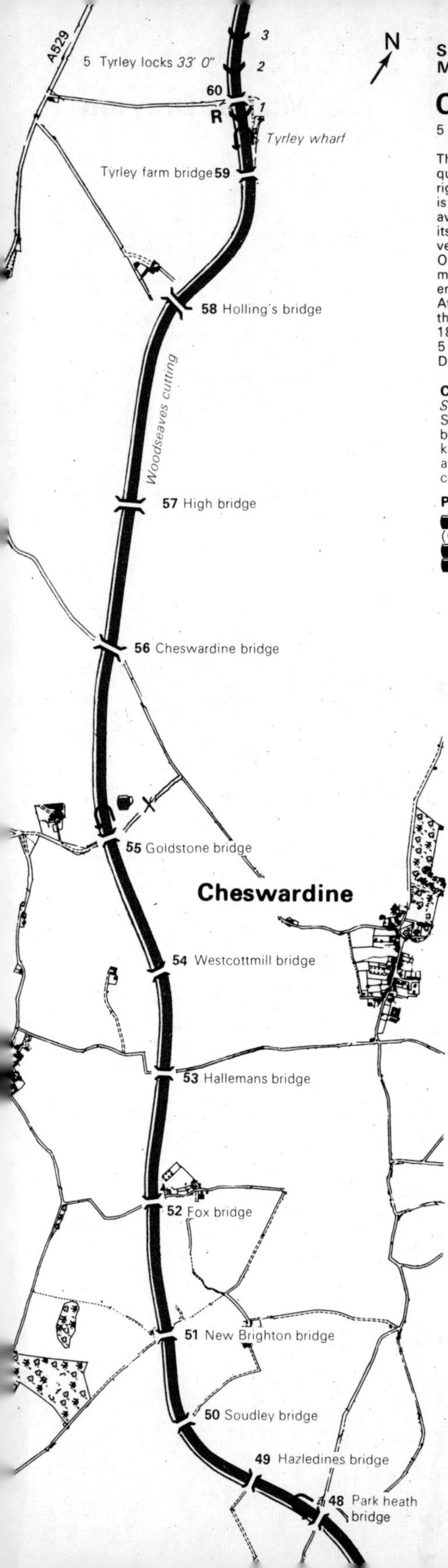

Cheswardine

5 miles

The canal continues north west through the quiet, empty landscape. Hills rise to the right, while the massive bulk of the Wrekin is clearly visible to the south west, 15 miles away. After passing Goldstone Wharf, with its thriving pub, the canal plunges into the very deep rock cutting near Woodseaves. One can hardly fail to be impressed by the magnitude of a work like this, cut as it was entirely by men without powered machines. At the north end of this wooded cutting is the delightful group of buildings (dated 1840) comprising Tyrley Wharf; here the 5 Tyrley locks begin the fall towards Market Drayton.

Cheswardine
Salop. PO, tel, stores, garage, EC varies. Situated 1 mile up a long hill east of bridge 55, the village has a traditional, well-knit feeling about it. The church is sited on a rise overlooking the village street. It contains some good 19thC glass.

PUBS

Wharf Tavern Canalside, at bridge 55. (Cheswardine 226). Dinners, light lunch.
Fox & Hounds Cheswardine.
Red Lion Cheswardine.

A529
5 Tyrley locks *33' 0"*
3
2
1
60
R
Tyrley wharf
Tyrley farm bridge **59**
58 Holling's bridge
Woodseaves cutting
57 High bridge
56 Cheswardine bridge
55 Goldstone bridge
Cheswardine
54 Westcottmill bridge
53 Hallemans bridge
52 Fox bridge
51 New Brighton bridge
50 Soudley bridge
49 Hazledines bridge
48 Park heath bridge
N

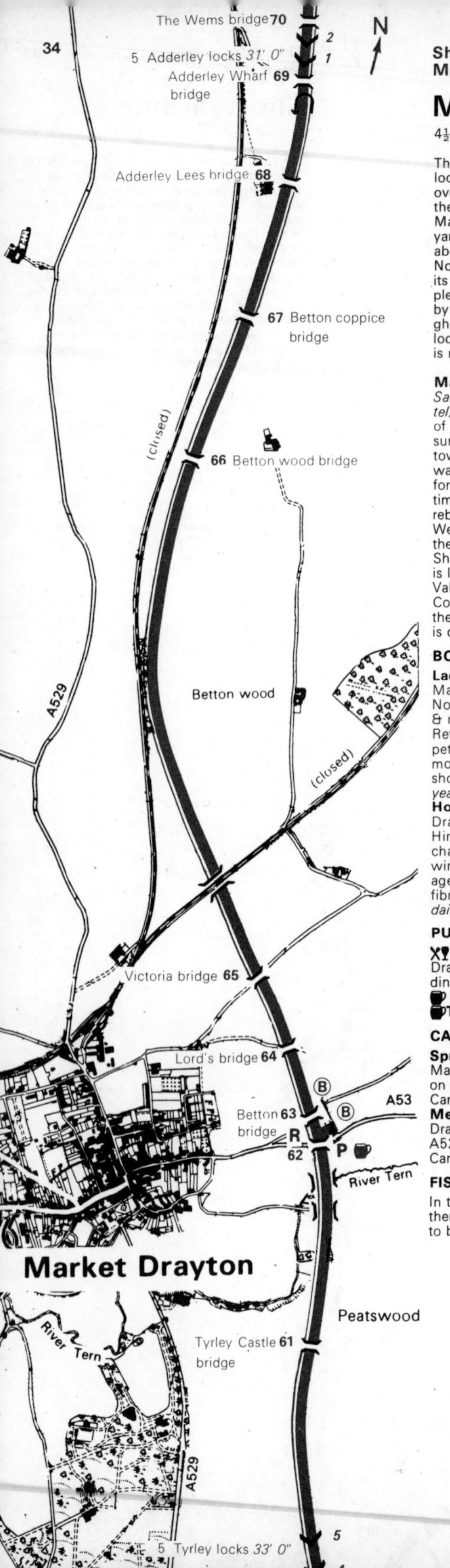

Shropshire Union Main Line

Market Drayton

4½ miles

The canal continues to fall through Tyrley locks, which in places are almost roofed over by trees, then crosses a minor road and the river Tern via aqueducts, and arrives at Market Drayton. There are two large boatyards here, so there are always many boats about and great care is needed in navigation. North of Market Drayton the canal regains its peaceful isolation, passing through a pleasant wooded cutting (which is alleged by the superstitious to shelter a vociferous ghost) before arriving at the five Adderley locks. The railway running beside the canal is now closed.

Market Drayton
Salop. Pop 6,200. EC Thur. MD Wed. PO, tel, stores, garage, bank. On the west bank of the canal, it is the market centre for the surrounding district, and is a very attractive town with some splendid old buildings. It was destroyed by fire in 1651, but fortunately picturesque black and white timberframing was again used for the rebuilding, the best of which is the National Westminster Bank in the market square and the adjacent Sandbrook Vaults (1653) in Shropshire st. The parish Church of St Mary is large and well-sited overlooking the Tern Valley and dates from the 12thC. The Corbet Arms Hotel is a fine centre-piece to the main square but heavy through-traffic is damaging these buildings.

BOATYARDS & BWB

Ladyline (Drayton Marina), Bretton rd, Market Drayton, Salop. (2267/3101/3102). North of bridge 63. Boat & motor sales & repairs, agents for most major firms. Refuse & sewage disposal, water, diesel, petrol, gas, chandlery. Slipway up to 50 foot, moorings, winter storage. Lavatory, showers, telephone. *Open daily throughout year.*

Holidays Afloat The Boatyard, Market Drayton, Salop. (2641). At bridge 62. Hire cruisers, dustbins, water, petrol, gas, chandlery, slipway up to 38 foot, moorings, winter storage. Motor sales & repairs, agents for Evinrude. Steel, wood & fibreglass boats built & fitted out. *Open daily throughout year.*

PUBS

Corbet Arms hotel High st, Market Drayton. (2961). Restaurant: lunches & dinners.

Sandbrook Vaults Market Drayton.

Talbot Canalside, at bridge 62.

CARAVANS & CAMPING

Springfields Caravan Site Little Drayton, Market Drayton. (2873). 1 mile from canal, on A53. Overnight caravan & tent stops. Caravans for hire.

Meiklejohn Farm Pell Wall, Market Drayton. (2973). ½ mile from canal on A529. Overnight caravan & tent stops. Caravans for hire.

FISHING

In the *Market Drayton* to *Nantwich* lengths there are good bream, of 2lb to 3lb average, to be caught from the wider pools.

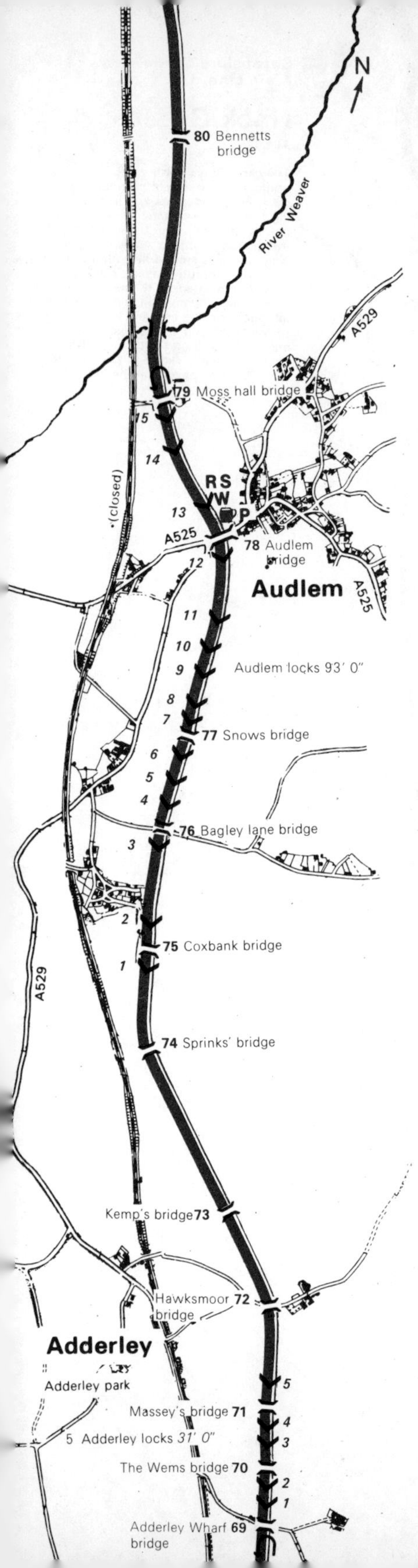

Audlem

4½ miles

Adderley locks, the middle of the 3 main groups of locks between Autherley & Nantwich, are shortly followed by the 15 locks in the Audlem flight, lowering the canal by over 90ft to the dairylands of southern Cheshire. The locks are close together and provide over 2 hours energetic navigating; there is an attractive cottage at the top lock, and a canalside pub in Audlem. The bottom of the locks is marked by a well restored canal stable and just to the north a minor aqueduct over the tiny river Weaver.

Audlem
Ches. Pop 1,300. PO, tel, stores, garage, bank. Some pleasant houses are grouped around the church in this expanding and well-kept canalside village. The massive shape of the 15thC church seems to spill down from its hillock in battlemented layers. The colonnaded structure at its foot was once a butter market. There are some mellow old buildings on the canal wharf that ask to be renovated. Elsewhere, there is a 17thC grammar school.

Adderley
Salop. PO, tel, garage. A rather under-populated village, bisected by the now closed railway and flanked by the large Shavington and Adderley Parks. The unusual church, set by itself, was rebuilt of red sandstone in 1801 in neo-classical style. In 1958 a large portion of the church was closed to reduce maintenance costs, including the tower dated 1712, the transepts and the chancel. As a result the much smaller interior is better suited to contemporary needs and feels more like a large formal drawing room than a cold decaying church.

Shavington Hall Adderley. An impressive red brick house dating from 1685 with 19thC additions and alterations. A fine park surrounds the house, which is not open to the public.

PUBS

Bridge Canalside, at Audlem Bridge.
Crown Audlem.
Lamb hotel Audlem (238). Food. (Baths available for dirty customers.)
Lord Combermere Audlem.

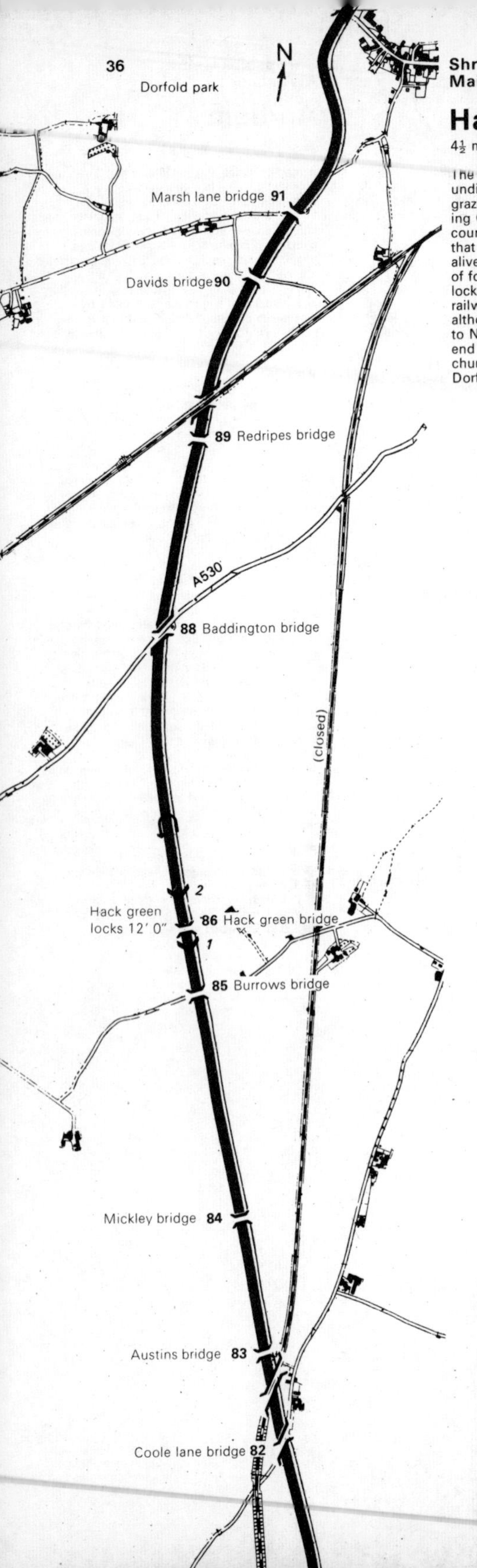

Shropshire Union Main Line

Hack Green

4½ miles

The canal flows northwards through an undisturbed stretch of pastoral land. Cows graze either side, clearly intent on maintaining Cheshire's reputation as a prime dairy county. It is a chilling thought to reflect that in 1968 hardly a single beast was left alive for miles around here after the ravages of foot and mouth disease. Hack Green locks briefly interrupt the navigation. The railway accompanying the canal is closed, although the line crossing from Shrewsbury to Nantwich and Crewe is still open. At the end of this section the tower of Nantwich church is clearly visible to the east, while Dorfold Park appears on the left.

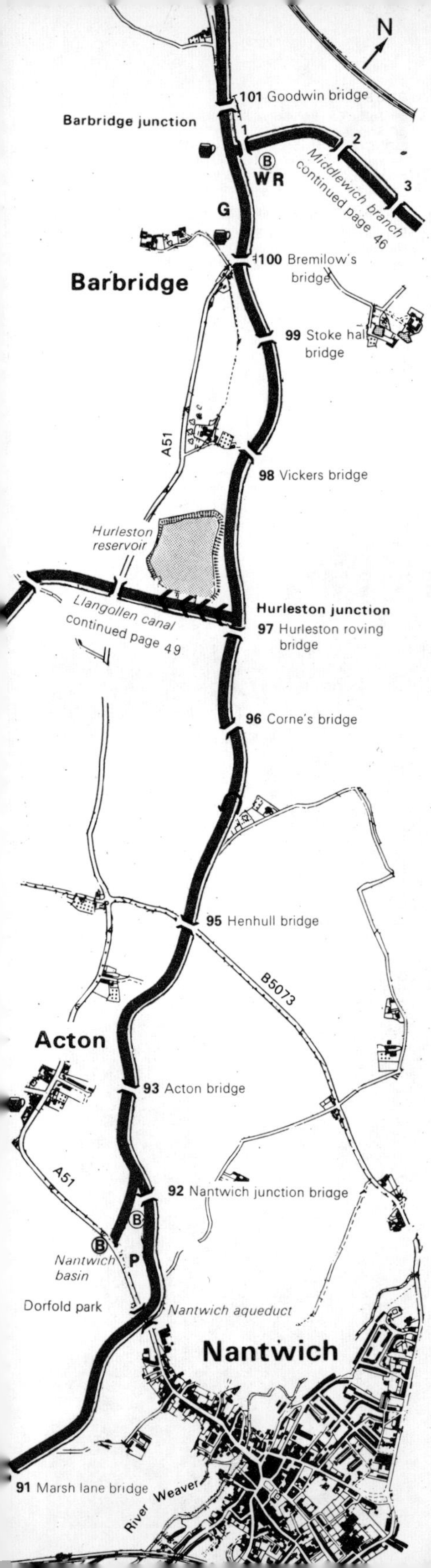

Nantwich

4½ miles

Swinging round Dorfold Park on a long embankment, the canal crosses the Nantwich-Chester road on a fine cast iron aqueduct and soon reaches an oblique canal junction at Nantwich basin: this is where Telford's narrow Birmingham & Liverpool Junction Canal joins the older Chester Canal. The stop-gates to be seen at each end of the embankment are a precaution against flooding in the event of a breach or damage to the aqueduct. The wide bridgehole at the next and all subsequent bridges reveals the difference in gauge of the 2 canals. The Chester Canal's wideness is complemented by its sweeping course, as it curves gracefully round the hillside to Hurleston Junction. Here the Llangollen canal branches off up 4 narrow locks on its way to North Wales (see page 49). Meanwhile the main line of the Shropshire Union soon reaches Barbridge (*PO, tel, stores, garage*) where there is a junction with the Middlewich branch. This branch (see page 46) connects the Shropshire Union system to the Trent & Mersey Canal.

Acton
Ches. PO, tel, stores. A small village with a large church of red stone and an old pub with a mounting block outside.

Dorfold Hall
¼ mile SW of Nantwich Basin. Built by Ralph Wilbraham in 1616, this beautiful Jacobean house is approached along an avenue of trees. The panelled rooms contain fine furnishings and family portraits. (Nantwich 65245). *Open May-Sep Mon 14.00-17.00.*

Nantwich Basin
A busy canal basin, once the terminus of the isolated Chester canal from Nantwich to Ellesmere Port. When the B & LJ Canal was first authorised in 1826, Telford intended to bring it from Hack Green across Dorfold Park and straight into Nantwich Basin; but the owner of the Park refused to allow it and forced the company to build the long embankment right round the Park and the iron aqueduct over the main road. This proved a difficult and costly diversion since, as at Shelmore, the embankment repeatedly collapsed. Today the old canalside cheese warehouses have been skilfully restored by the BWB and there are two boatyards and a boat club based here.

Nantwich
Cheshire. Pop 11,000. EC Wed. MD Thur, Sat. All services. A very fine old town, prosperous since Roman times because of its salt springs, which made it the country's main salt mining centre until the 19thC. The town was devastated by fire in 1583 but rebuilt in fine Tudor style. Many of the half-timbered houses still remain. Two especially interesting buildings on the road into town from the basin are the Cheshire Cat Inn and a tiny cottage built in 1502 and restored in 1971. In London road are the Tollemache Almshouses built in 1638 by Sir Edmund Wright, who became Lord Mayor of London in 1641.

Church of St Mary Church lane. Focal point of the town centre, it is a large and magnificent red sandstone church which stands behind its former graveyard, now an open green. It dates from the 14thC though it was greatly restored in 1885. It has an unusual octagonal tower and the vaulted chancel contains 20 ornate 14thC choir stalls with canopies.

Churche's Mansion Hospital street, Nantwich (65933). In the centre of the town is this fine example of an Elizabethan merchant's half-timbered house built in 1577, with oak-panelling interior. A 'Son Sans Lumiere', a 25 minute history in sound, is staged on the first floor (during daylight hours). The mansion houses a restaurant. Cuisine is mainly English: the many specialities include jugged hare and smoked trout. L 12.00-14.00, D 19.00-20.30 (closed Dec 24-28). Must book D. Good Food Guide since 1957.

BOATYARDS & BWB

Ladyline (Barbridge Marina), nr Nantwich Ches. (Wettenhall 682/683). Situated just on the Middlewich branch.
Hire cruisers. Sewage & refuse disposal, water, diesel, gas, chandlery. Slipway up to 50 foot, moorings, winter storage. Boat & motor sales & repairs, agents for most major firms. Lavatory. Groceries. *Open daily throughout year.*
S.C. Cummins Martin st, Crewe, Ches. (57411). Adjoining the Nantwich Basin. Hire cruisers, steel boats built & fitted out.
British Waterways Hire Cruiser Base Basin End, Chester rd, Nantwich, Ches. (65122). At Nantwich Basin. Hire cruisers, sewage & refuse disposal, water, petrol, moorings. *Closed winter weekends and summer Suns.*

PUBS

Jolly Tar Barbridge Junction.
Star Acton.
Crown Hotel Nantwich (55283). Restaurant: lunches and dinners daily. An interesting old coaching house, built in the late 16thC.

CARAVANS & CAMPING

Brookfield Caravan Site Brookfield Park, Nantwich. (Nantwich 64951). 1 mile from canal, off A530. Overnight caravan stops. No tents permitted.

Tyrley top lock.

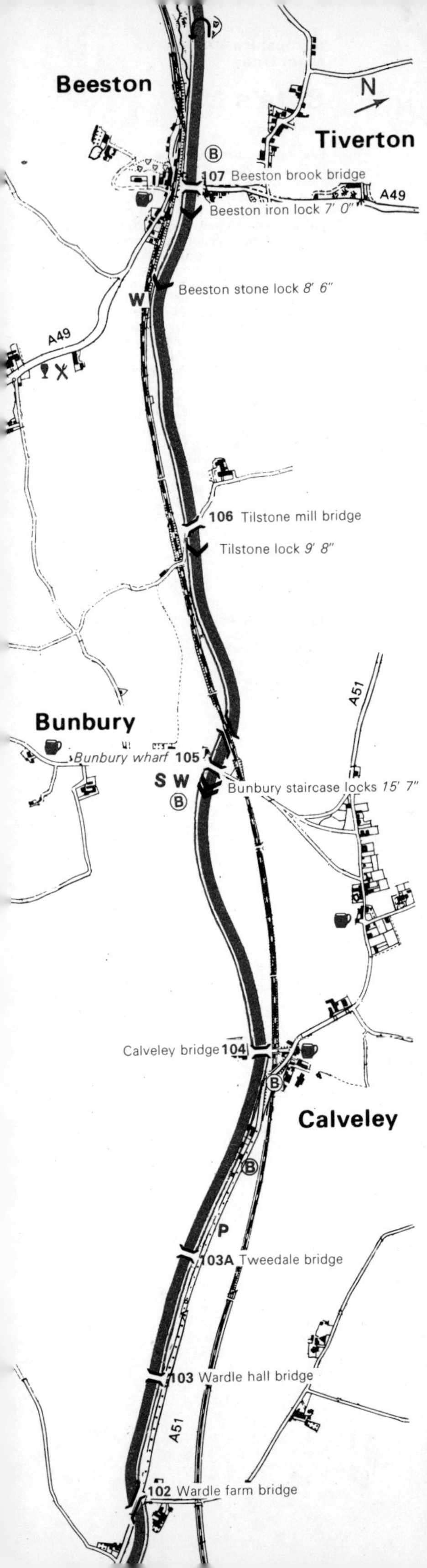

Bunbury

4½ miles

The canal moves almost westwards now along a busy main road, passing an enormous radar scanner. At Calveley, large modern cheese warehouses remind the traveller that Cheshire cheese is not merely local produce but a major export. Here the towpath changes sides and the Crewe–Holyhead railway joins the canal. At Bunbury Wharf two 'staircase' locks require thought before action: they are also 14ft wide, like all subsequent locks between here and Chester. There is a fine range of stables beside Bunbury locks, and a former warehouse beside the bridge which still displays the Shropshire Union Railways & Canal Company's name on its gable wall. Beyond the wharf, wooded hills crowd in on the canal, which flows like a river through a narrow valley. There are occasional views to the west of the ruined Beeston Castle on its isolated hill. An old water mill beside Tilstone lock is now used as an outdoor activities base by the local Scout group. At Beeston two contrasting lock-chambers are encountered: one is made of stone, the other of cast iron flanged plates to overcome running sand below it. The water point at the stone lock is in the lockside lobby. There were once similar lobbies at all locks on the S.U. main line: only 3 now survive. Up the hill to the north of the 2 locks is Tiverton (*PO, tel, stores, garage*).

Bunbury
Ches. EC Wed, Sat. PO, tel, stores, garage, bank. A mile SW of Bunbury locks, the village is bigger than it looks at first, being virtually split into 3 sections. The attractive part is nearest, around the church. This is an outstanding building: supremely light, airy and spacious, it stands as a fine monument to workmanship of the 14th and 15thC, and represents a powerful contrast to the unimaginative architecture that characterises so many modern buildings.

Calveley
Ches. Tel, stores, garage. This rather insignificant village has been practically overwhelmed by the canal, road & railway that carve their respective ways through it. Old wharf buildings now house a boatyard.

BOATYARDS & BWB

Beeston Pleasure Craft Beeston Wharf, nr Tarporley, Ches. (Tarporley 595). Just west of bridge 107 (Beeston brook bridge). Hire cruisers. Sewage & refuse disposal, water, diesel, petrol, gas. Slipway up to 50 foot, moorings, winter storage, boat & motor sales & repairs.

Dartline Cruisers The Canal Wharf, Bunbury, nr Tarporley, Ches. (Bunbury 638). At Bunbury locks. Hire cruisers, sewage & refuse disposal, dustbins, water, diesel, gas, chandlery. Slipway up to 25 foot, moorings, winter storage. Boat & motor sales & repairs, agents for Lister. Steel boats built & fitted out. Lavatories.

Primo Continental Engineering Calveley Wharf, nr Tarporley, Ches. (Bunbury 564/5). Agents for DTN diesel engines. Slipway facilities at Venetia Pleasure Boat Centre (see page 47).

Middlewich Marina Calveley Filling Station, Calvely, nr Tarporley, Ches. (Bunbury 544). ½ mile east of bridge 104 (Calveley bridge). Hire cruisers. Water, diesel, petrol, gas, chandlery, slipway up to 70 foot, moorings, winter storage.

PUBS

Wild Boar Motor Lodge Inn Beeston. (Bunbury 309/550). This is an enormous mock Tudor building. The restaurant is French, the menu ambitious. There is also a grill room offering a quicker service and simpler food. L 12.30-14.30, D 19.00- 22.30 (closed Sun D). Must book D, no dogs. Good Food Guide since 1967.

Beeston Castle hotel, Beeston.

Nags Head Bunbury

Dysart Arms Bunbury, by the church.

Tollemache Arms ½ mile NE of Bunbury Wharf. Food.

Davenport Arms Calveley, nr the wharf.

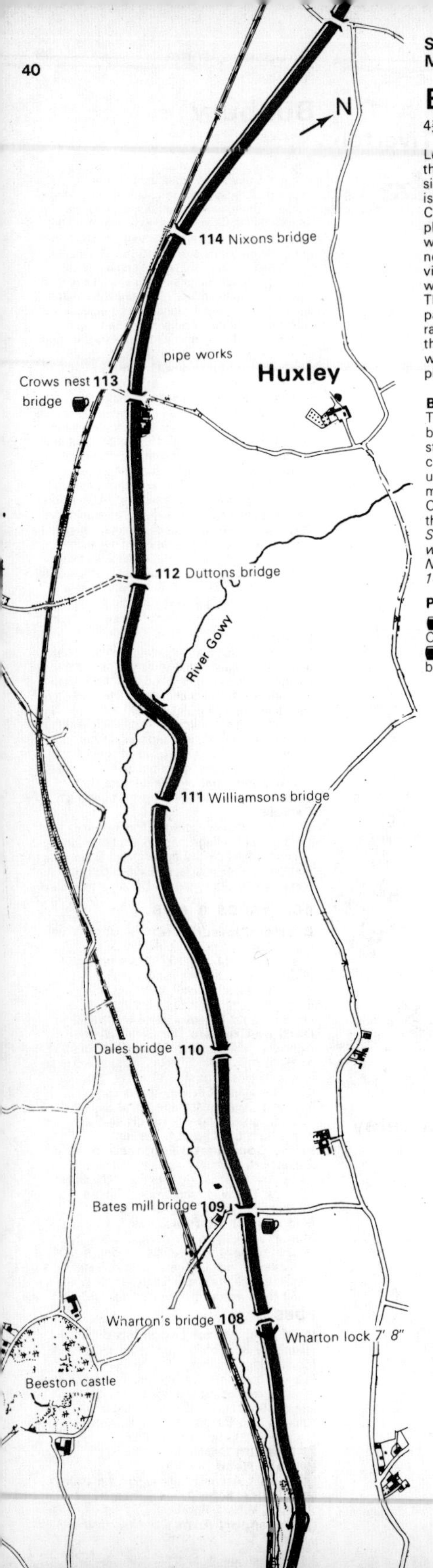

Shropshire Union Main Line

Bate's Mill

4¾ miles

Leaving Beeston, the canal moves out of the narrow valley into more open countryside. From Wharton lock an excellent view is obtained of the massive bulk of Beeston Castle, a landmark which can be seen from places up to 30 miles away. As one moves westward, the romantic-looking turrets of neighbouring Peckforton Castle come into view, revealing the long ridge of hills of which Beeston Castle forms the eastern end. The countryside here is flat and quiet, and packed with cows and buttercups. The railway accompanies the canal for some of the way: so does the tiny river Gowy, which fed the old Bate's Mill. There is a pipe works near Crow's Nest Bridge.

Beeston Castle
The impressive ruins of a 13thC castle built by the Earl of Chester. Situated on top of a steep hill dominating the surrounding countryside, it was in an ideal, almost unassailable position. From the castle, one may have a remarkable view of the Cheshire Plain, and one can see the well in the courtyard. It is 360ft deep. *Open: May-Sep daily 9.30-19.00. Mar, Apr, Oct weekdays 9.30-17.30. Sun 14.00-17.30. Nov-Feb weekdays 10.00-16.30, Sun 14.00-16.30.*

PUBS

Aldersey Arms hotel 200yds SW of Crow's Nest bridge.

Royal Oak Canalside, at Bate's Mill bridge.

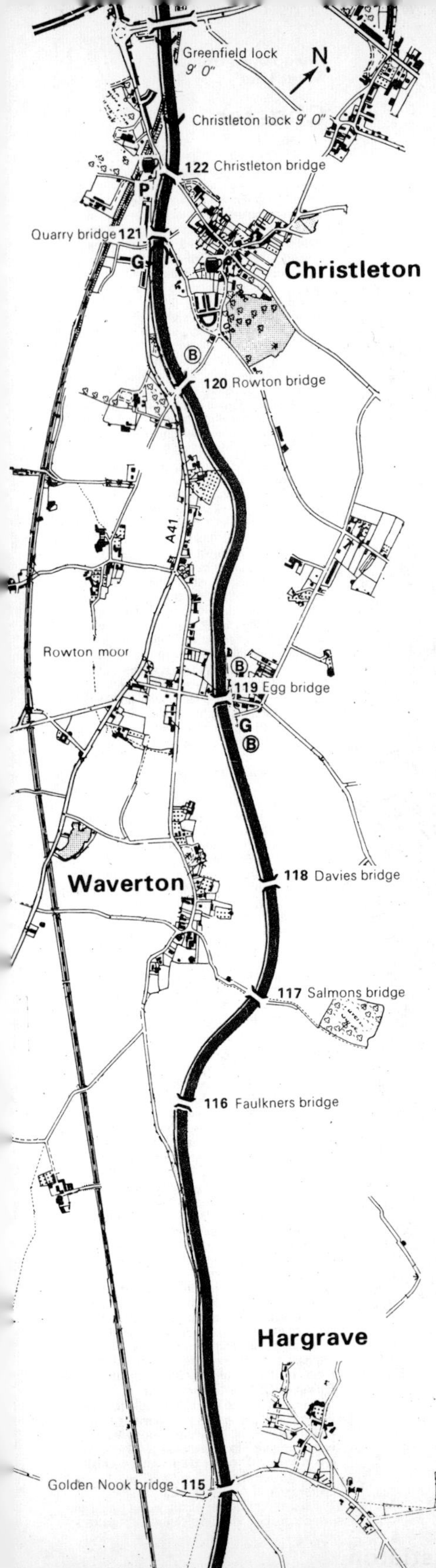

Christleton

4½ miles

The canal continues through the flat but very green landscape of the Cheshire Plain past Waverton with its conspicuous church tower and, past a fine brick mill by Egg Bridge, along through the unprepossessing Rowton Moor to the delightful village of Christleton. Here the towers and chimneys of Chester come into view and the railway dives under the canal in a short tunnel. Nearly all motorists sound their horn before crossing Christleton bridge, so this is a bad place for an overnight mooring.

Christleton
Ches. PO, tel, stores. A very pleasant village near the canal, well worth visiting. The village green is still very much the centre of the village: church and pub are beside it, as are several well-kept elegant houses. It is refreshing to find a village so near to a big town that has so defiantly retained its identity.

Battle of Rowton Moor It was here, three miles from Chester, that the last major battle of the Civil War took place in 1645. The Parliamentarians completely routed the Royalists who, still under fierce attack, retreated to Chester. It is said that King Charles I watched the defeat from the walls of Chester, but it is more probable that he only saw the final stages under the walls of the city. Charles fled, leaving 800 prisoners and 600 dead and wounded.

Waverton
Ches. PO, tel, stores. The sturdy church tower carries a pleasing, modest spire. Inside the church, which was greatly restored by the Victorians, the low aisle arches lend a certain cosiness to the building.

BOATYARDS & BWB

Deans Marina Rowton bridge, Christleton, nr Chester. (Chester 35523). Dustbins, water, diesel, petrol, gas, chandlery. Slipway up to 25 foot, moorings. Boat & motor sales & repars, agents for most leading firms. Lavatories. *Open daily throughout year.*

S. Weaver 1a Fox lane, Eggbridge, Waverton, Chester. (Chester 36604). Just north of bridge 119 (Egg bridge). Hire cruisers, slipway up to 40 foot, moorings, winter storage, telephone. *Open daily throughout year.*

Holiday Makers (Cheshire) Waverton Mill, Eggbridge lane, Waverton, Chester. (Chester 36456). Just south of bridge 119 (Egg bridge). Narrowboat hire.

PUBS

Ring O' Bells Christleton.
Ye Old Trooper Canalside, at Christleton Bridge.

CARAVANS & CAMPING

Netherwood House Whitchurch rd, Rowton. (Chester 35583). Canalside. Overnight caravan stops. No tents permitted.

FISHING

Good sport is to be had at *Egg Bridge, Waverton* with bream and roach. A single caster, or chrysalis, float-fished at the far bank generally works well on this canal, and a single maggot on size 18 hook is a good early season float-bait.

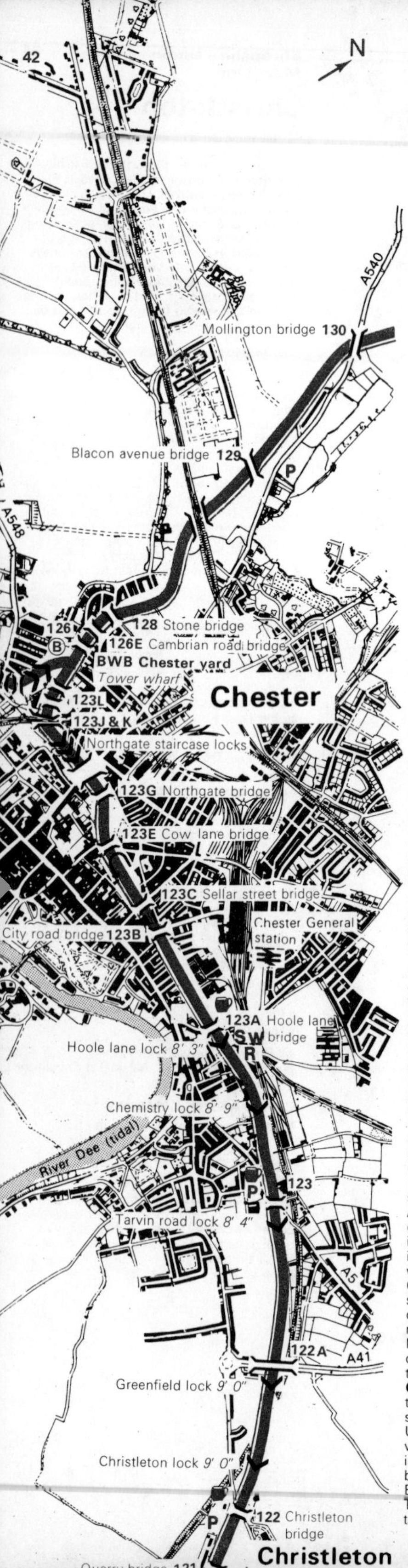

Shropshire Union Main Line

Chester

4¼ miles

This is a most interesting and unusual stretch of canal. Leaving Christleton, the canal drops down into the ancient city of Chester through 5 locks: none of these have top gate paddles, and they all take rather long to fill. The canal goes straight through the middle of the town and is very much open to view. Passing a large lead works—with its tall chimney and 'shot tower'—and a great variety of bridges, the navigation approaches the old city and suddenly curves round into a very steep rock cutting: the city wall is high up on one side. King Charles' Tower stands on the wall. Soon the Northgate locks (a 'staircase') are reached: at the bottom is a sharp right turn to Tower Wharf, a good place to tie up for the night. There is a boatyard at the head of the arm leading down into the river Dee.

Chester
Ches. Pop 60,000. EC Wed, MD Tue, Thur. All services. There is a wealth of things to see in this Roman city, which is the sort of place that is enjoyable to walk round even in the rain. It is in fact an excellent town to see on foot, partly because a costly new inner ring road has obviously generated more traffic congestion than it has alleviated, but more especially because of the amazing survival of almost all the old city wall. This provides Chester with its best and rarest feature—one can walk right round the city on this superb footpath, over the old city gates and past the defensive turrets, including King Charles' Tower above the canal, which contains an exhibition depicting the Civil War. Chester is in fact the only city in England with its walls still complete in their two mile circuit. Portions of the original Roman work still remain, but in the Middle Ages several gates and towers were added, one of which—the Eastgate—has, since 1897 carried an elaborate clock to commemorate Queen Victoria's Diamond Jubilee. Other splendid features are the race course—the Roodee—(just outside the city wall and therefore well inside the modern town) where Chester Races are held each year in May, July and September—it can easily be overlooked for free from the road that runs above and beside it; the superb old cathedral; the bold new theatre; the 'Rows'—unique double-tier mediaeval shopping streets; and the immense number of old and fascinating buildings throughout the town, such as Leche House, God's Providence House and Bishop Lloyd's Palace in Watergate street.

Chester Cathedral Northgate st. A magnificent building of dark red stone on the site of a 10thC minster. In 1092 the Earl of Chester and St Anselm founded a Benedictine abbey, which was dissolved in 1540, but in the following year it was made a cathedral and the seat of a bishop. The monastery buildings still remain; in the cathedral the 14thC choir stalls with their intricate carvings depict the Tree of Jesse showing the genealogy of Christ.

Abbey Square Outside the cathedral, opposite the Victorian town hall, the square is entered through a massive gateway built in 1377, where the Chester Mystery Plays were performed.

Church of St John the Baptist St John's st. Impressive 12thC church that was built on the site of an earlier Saxon church. The nave contains fine examples of austere Norman pillars and arcades. The ruins of the choir at the east end still remain, as well as those of the tower which collapsed in 1573.

Chester Castle Grosvenor rd. The original timber structure c1069 was replaced by stone walls and towers by Henry III. Unfortunately in 1789 the defensive walls were removed to make way for the incongruous Thomas Harrison group of buildings, which include the Grand Entrance and Assize Courts.
The main part of the castle is occupied by troops of the Cheshire Regiment, but the

13thC Agricola Tower is open to the public. The County Archives, which include numerous documents relating to the canal, are kept here.

Museum of the Cheshire Regiment Situated inside the tower of the Castle, it contains relics of many wars, including maps, plans, photographs and standards. *Open Apr-Oct 10.30-18.00; Nov-Mar 10.30-16.00.*

Grosvenor Museum Grosvenor st. Exhibits the archaeology and natural history of Chester. Fine collection of Anglo-Saxon coins. *Open May-Sep: Mon-Fri 10.00-18.30, Sat 10.00-19.00, Sun 14.30-18.30.*

Stanley Palace Watergate st. Beautifully timbered house built in 1591 as the town house of the Stanleys, Earls of Derby. It was restored in 1935 and is now used as the headquarters of the English-Speaking Union. *Open Mon-Fri 10.00-16.00.*

Northgate Locks
Hewn out of solid rock, these three staircase locks lower the canal by 33 feet, an impressive feat of engineering and a suitable complement to the deep rock cutting nearby. The locks are now sandwiched between a large new flyover and a low railway bridge.

The Dee Branch
This branch into the tidal River Dee runs through 3 wide locks from Taylor's boatyard near Tower Wharf. There used to be a large basin below the second lock, but this has now been filled in. The bottom lock and bridge are new, having been built to replace an old single-tracked swing bridge on a main road. There is a very sharp bend into the branch from Tower Wharf. Anyone wishing to take a boat into the River Dee *must* give at least 24 hours notice to the BWB section inspector (Chester 25732) during working hours. (The bottom lock has to be kept padlocked to prevent silting up at high water.) It is practicable to enter or leave the river Dee at this point only for 1 hour either side of high water, since there is insufficient water at the entrance for the rest of the time.

BOATYARDS & BWB

J.H. Taylor & Sons Cambrian View, Chester (26041). At junction with Dee branch. Shipwrights, wooden boats built. Repair and fit out all types of boats. Engine repairs. Drydock, 7 slipways up to 36 foot long. Chandlery. *Open daily*

BWB Chester Yard Tower Wharf. (Chester 25732). Drydock, 30ft slipway.

PUBS

Pied Bull Northgate.
Ye Olde Custom House Watergate.
Lock Vaults by Hoole Lane Lock
Bridge near Tarvin road lock.
The Courtyard 13 St Werburgh street, Chester (21447). Housed in what was once a sweet factory, two restaurants here provide alternative services. In the evening one may choose between the bistro and music or the main restaurant. Consistent specialities have been the roast rib of beef and various pâtés; and the proprietors describe the lunchtime salads as exciting. L 12.00-14.30, D bistro 18.00-23.00 Tue-Sat, Restaurant 19.00-23.00. Must book D (closed public hols, Sun). Main restaurant in Good Food Guide since 1969.

Youth Hostels
Hough Green House, 40 Hough Green, Chester. (22231).

FISHING

In the vicinity of *Chester* there is particularly good fishing.

i TOURIST INFORMATION CENTRE

Chester Town Hall. (40144).

Preparing to descend Northgate Locks, in Chester.

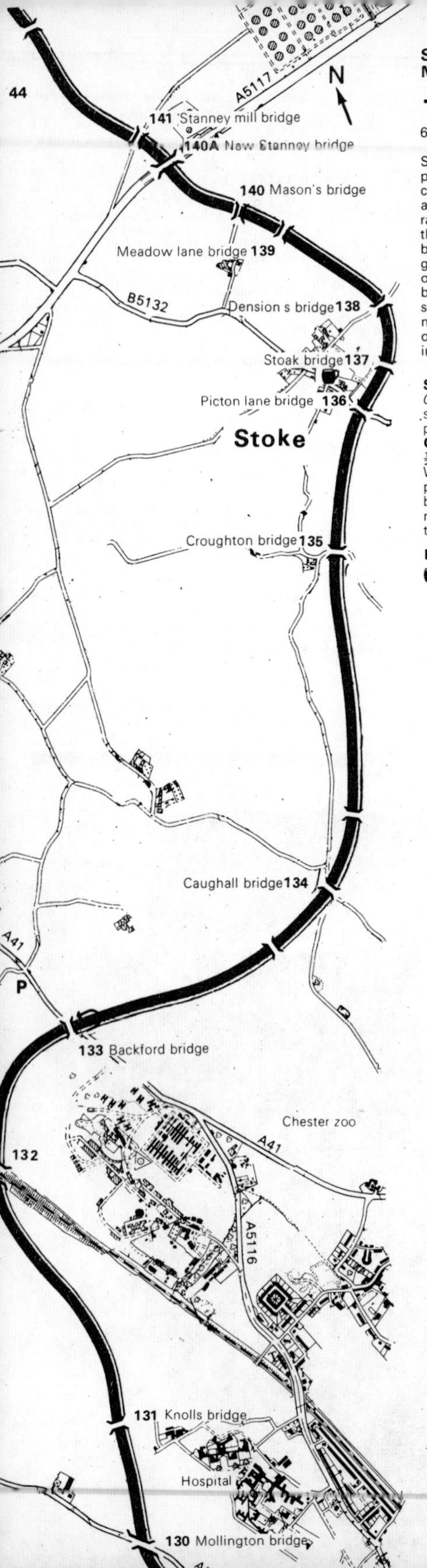

Shropshire Union Main Line

The Wirral

6 miles

Sweeping northwards along the lockfree pound from Chester to the Mersey, the canal enters for the last time open country as it crosses the Wirral. The handsome stone railway viaduct over the navigation carries the Chester-Birkenhead line; here one turns briefly eastwards, passing along a shallow green and peaceful valley. Chester Zoo is only ½ mile south of the cast iron Caughall bridge. Stoak (or Stoke–alternative spellings) church is conspicuous from the navigation; north of the village, the distant oil refineries and chimneys herald the industrial activity along Merseyside.

Stoak

Ches. Tel. There is little of interest in this scattered village except a pleasant country pub and a small, pretty church.

Chester Zoo

½ mile south of Caughall Bridge (134). Wide variety of animals shown as much as possible without bars and fences, enhanced by attractive flower gardens and its own miniature canal. Largest elephant house in the world. *Open daily 9.00-dusk.*

PUBS

Bunbury Arms Stoak.

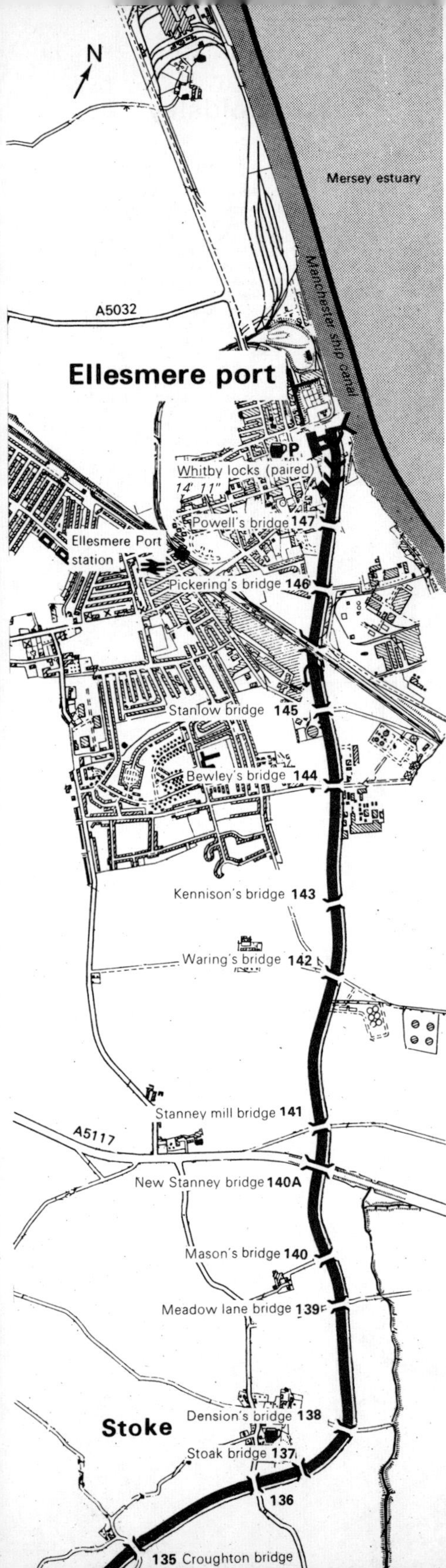

Ellesmere Port

3¾ miles

The canal now rapidly enters an area of large scale industries. Oil refineries and chemical works seem to predominate in a gaunt, manmade landscape in which the canal is completely forgotten and shunned by industry which it fostered long ago. The docks and basins of the port itself, where the Shropshire Union Canal meets the Manchester Ship Canal, are—or were—very extensive. They are leased to the Ship Canal Co. by the BWB. Acres of docks, locks, wharves and vast warehouses are all laid out to handle the great tonnages of goods that used to be transhipped here; but now the whole network is disused, except for the wharf area at the entrance to the Ship Canal. Telford's famous warehouses in which the narrowboats and barges were loaded and discharged under cover were recently set alight by local hooligans and had to be demolished in the interests of safety; locks and basins are suffering from indiscriminate dumping of rubbish and old barges; and the whole area, while still absolutely fascinating for anyone interested in industrial archaeology, is somewhat depressing. One bright spot here is that at least there is still access for boats from the Shropshire Union through several wide locks down into the Manchester Ship Canal. But no pleasure boat may enter the Ship Canal without previously seeking permission from the Manchester Ship Canal Company (see page 171). Boat owners should remember that amongst other conditions the company insists on before considering granting entry to pleasure boats is that every boat should carry conventional navigation lights; an anchor and cable, at least 50 fathoms of rope, and third party insurance cover worth at least £50,000.

Ellesmere Port
Ches. Pop 58,000. EC Wed. MD Fri. All services. The proposed Wirral motorway may be built through this town.

Stanlow Abbey
Beside the Mersey, 1½ miles east of the canal on Stanlow Point. Remains of the Cistercian abbey founded in 1178 by John, Baron of Halton. Now isolated by the Ship Canal.

PUBS

- **Bulls Head** Ellesmere Port.
- **Horse and Jockey** Ellesmere Port.

FISHING

At *Ellesmere Port* the canal is particularly noted for big bream, plus a variety of other species. It is a matter of finding a bream shoal if sport is to be assured.

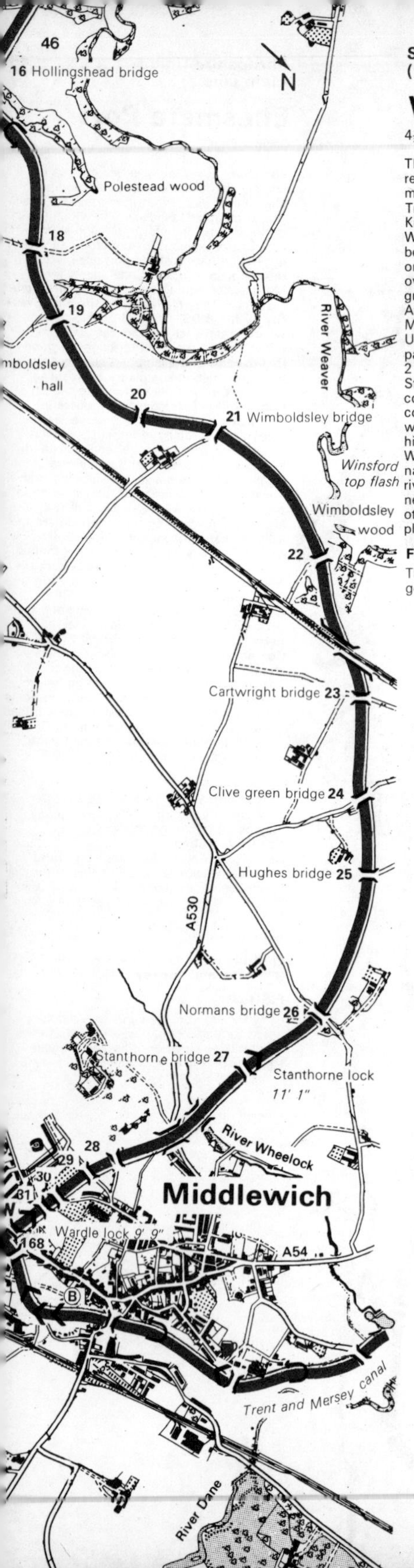

Shropshire Union (Middlewich Branch)

Wimboldsley

4½ miles

The Middlewich branch is a very quiet, remote canal, passing only one village and much unspoilt countryside. It leaves the Trent and Mersey (see page 88) just below Kings lock and immediately climbs up Wardle lock. This section used in fact to belong to the Trent & Mersey—a branch only about 20 yards long—and the bridge over the entrance to the branch is grandiosely inscribed 'Wardle Canal 1829'. At the head of the lock begins the actual Middlewich branch of the former Shropshire Union Railways & Canal Company. It passes a rapid succession of bridges and 2 minor aqueducts, then up the deep Stanthorne lock and out into open countryside interspersed with woods. The course of the canal is generally south-westerly, following the side of a shallow hill. This yields views to the west over Winsford Top Flash (which is the limit of navigation to adventurous boatmen on the river Weaver). The busy electric railway nearby generates a certain amount of noise; otherwise this is a peaceful and very pleasant stretch.

FISHING

The *Middlewich* branch throughout is a good fishing area for most species.

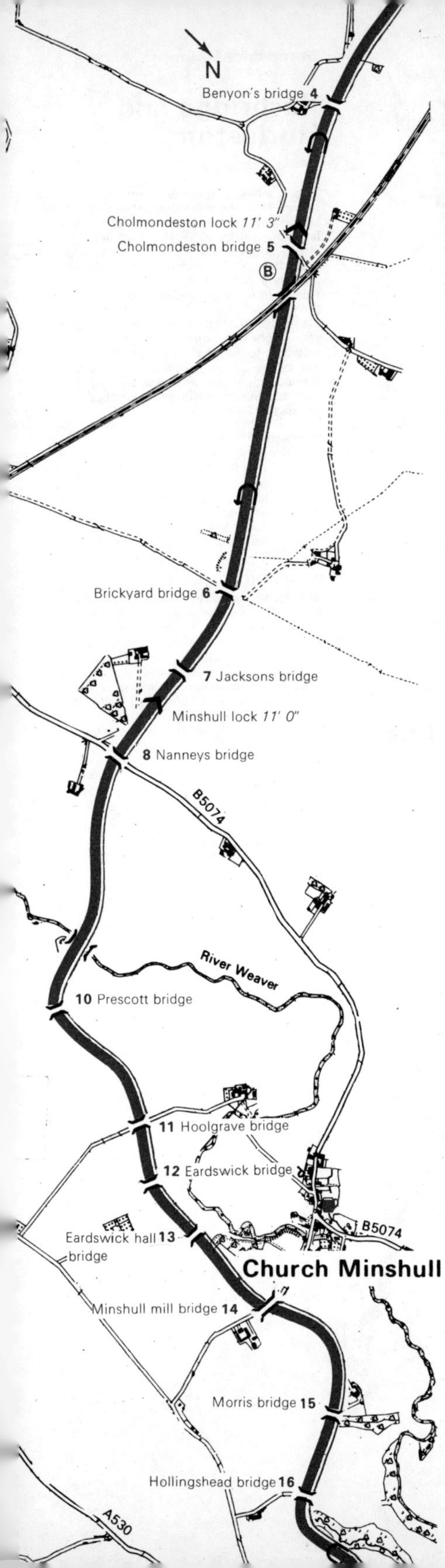

Church Minshull

$5\frac{1}{4}$ miles

This is another very quiet, remote stretch of canal. Church Minshull is passed, then the Weaver is crossed on a high embankment. Here the canal leaves the side of a ridge of low hills and runs through flatter country for a straight mile to Cholmondeston lock, where there is a boatyard. The Crewe to Chester railway line crosses here. Above the lock the pleasant and quite untouched pasture lands continue right through to the main line of the Shropshire Union Canal at Barbridge Junction.

Church Minshull
Ches. PO, tel, stores, garage. An old and mellow village beside the river Weaver. The notable 18thC church in the centre of the village is the subject of a Preservation Order. It is certainly the core of this most attractive place—and next to it is an old country pub.

BOATYARDS & BWB

Venetia Pleasure Boat Centre
Cholmondeston, nr Nantwich, Ches. (Wettenhall 251). At bridge 5 (Cholmondeston bridge). Sewage & refuse disposal, water, diesel, petrol, gas, chandlery. Slipway up to 30 foot, moorings. Boat sales & repairs, agents for Buckingham & Dawn Craft. Motor sales & repairs, agents for Crescent and Chrysler. Boats fitted out. Groceries. Lavatories. *Open daily throughout year.*

PUBS

Badgers Arms Church Minshull.

N
Benyon's bridge 4
Cholmondeston lock 11' 3"
Cholmondeston bridge 5
B
Brickyard bridge 6
7 Jacksons bridge
Minshull lock 11' 0"
8 Nanneys bridge
B5074
River Weaver
10 Prescott bridge
11 Hoolgrave bridge
12 Eardswick bridge
Eardswick hall 13 bridge
B5074
Church Minshull
Minshull mill bridge 14
Morris bridge 15
Hollingshead bridge 16
A530

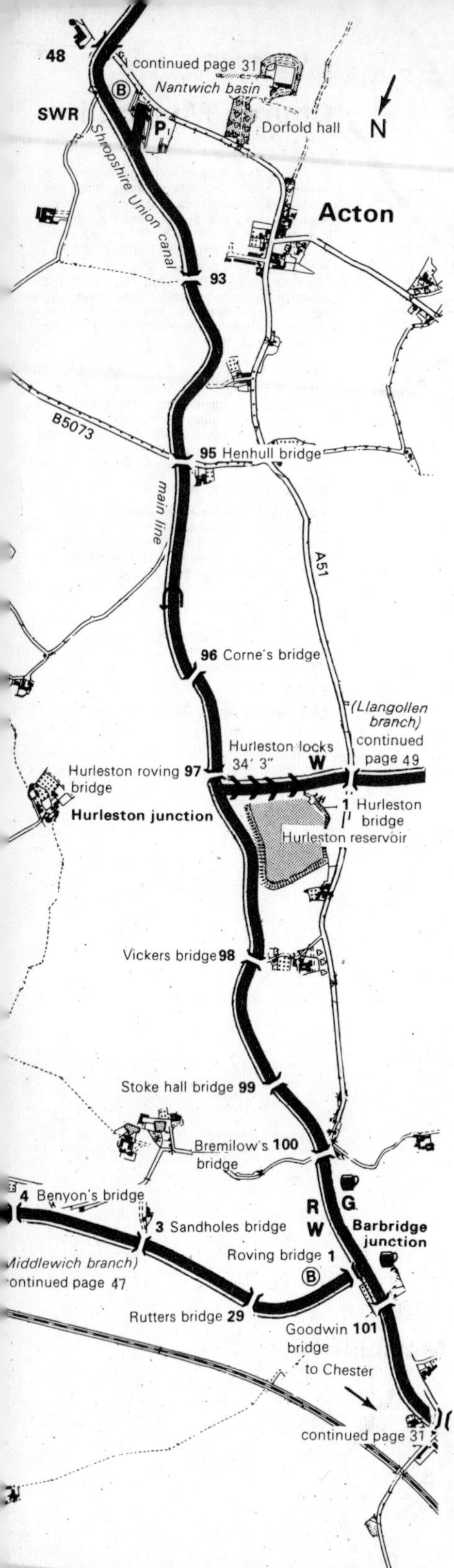

Barbridge and Hurleston

4 miles

This is a busy section where the Middlewich branch joins the main line of the Shropshire Union at Barbridge junction. There is a large boatyard and usually much activity at the junction. The main line to the south leads through Barbridge and out into open country. After 1½ miles the head bank of Hurleston reservoir appears; at its far end is the equally busy Hurleston junction. The Llangollen canal descends here through a steep flight of 4 narrow locks, beside the reservoir, to join the main line. (For the Shropshire Union main line north from Barbridge junction, see page 37. For the main line south of Hurleston junction, see page 27.)

Hurleston Reservoir
This stores most of the millions of gallons of water that flow daily down the Llangollen canal from the river Dee at the head of the canal at Llantisilio. The water is treated by the Mid Cheshire Water Board for public supply. This is a good example of a cruising waterway being used for another profitable purpose.

BOATYARDS & BWB

British Waterways Hire Cruiser Base Basin End, Chester rd, Nantwich, Ches. (65122). At Nantwich Basin. Hire cruisers, sewage & refuse disposal, water, petrol, moorings. *Closed winter weekends and summer Suns.*

Lady line (Barbridge Marina) nr Nantwich, Ches. (Wettenhall 682/683). Situated on Middlewich branch. Hire cruisers, sewage & refuse disposal, water, diesel, gas chandlery, slipway up to 50 foot, moorings, winter storage. Boat & motor sales & repairs, agents for most major firms. Lavatories. Groceries. *Open daily throughout year.*

PUBS

Kings Arms Barbridge. Canalside, at Bremilow's bridge.

Jolly Tar Barbridge junction.

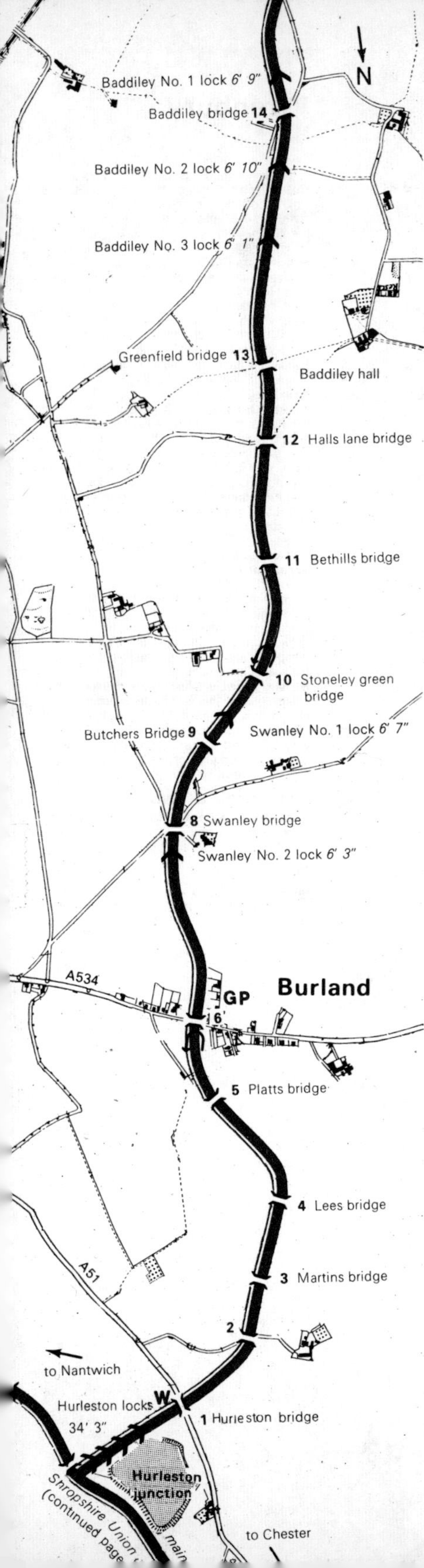

Burland

4½ miles

The Llangollen rapidly establishes its character as a quiet and pretty canal. Considering the spectacular scenery further west, it is hardly surprising that this is the most popular cruising waterway in the country—so much so, in fact, that in the height of the summer up to 400 boats a week use the canal. Leaving Hurleston, the canal runs through a very shallow valley past the hamlet of Burland to Swanley locks. There is an old canalside house at Swanley bridge (8) with a beautiful garden and weeping willows overhanging the water. The next three locks encountered are Baddiley locks; the tall Georgian house surrounded by trees to the west of the bottom lock is Baddiley Hall.

Burland
Ches. Tel, stores, garage. A straggling settlement by the canal, useful as a supply centre; the general store here is open every day. And the petrol station is almost beside the canal.

FISHING THE LLANGOLLEN CANAL

The Llangollen branch of the Shropshire Union canal is a coarse fish water holding some big fish, mainly roach, perch, pike and bream plus gudgeon. But this is more of a specimen hunter's water, and few if any contests are held here.
Bread flake is a good bait for specimen fish, but a useful and often successful standby is the redworm.

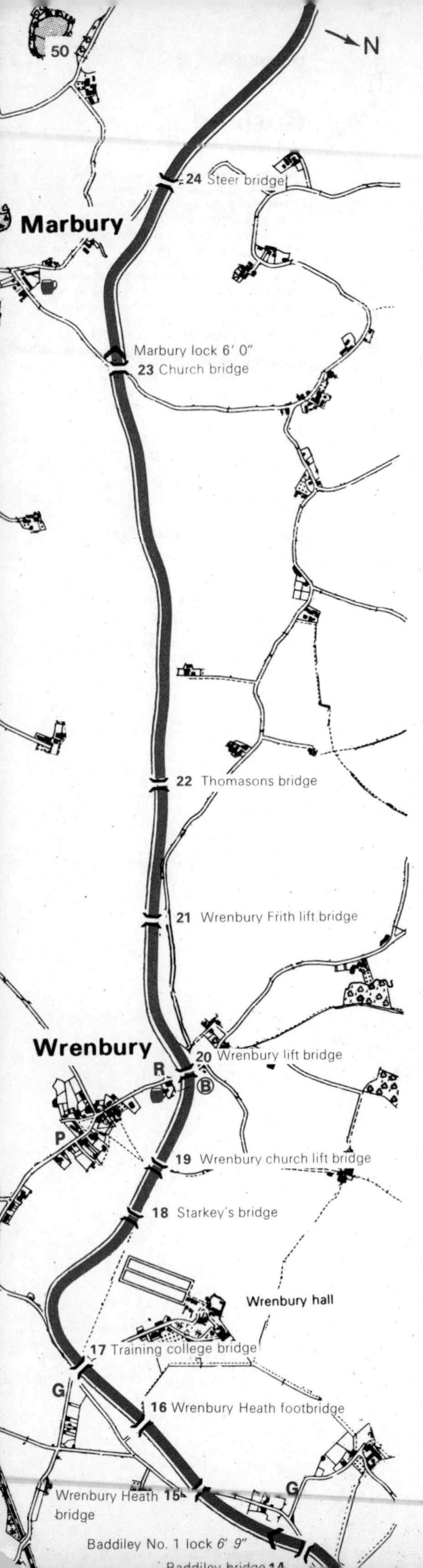

Wrenbury

$5\frac{1}{4}$ miles

The canal moves past Wrenbury Hall, formerly the home of Sir John Stapleton Cotton (one of Wellington's generals) and now a college, towards Wrenbury. The old farmhouse west of bridges 14 and 15 sells local honey, cheese, eggs, milk, etc. Wrenbury Wharf is a delightful spot. The bridge is an old-fashioned wooden lift bridge, of a type often seen in Holland and Van Gogh's paintings. There are some fine warehouses and a former mill here, and a nearby pub. Beyond the wharf, the soft green Cheshire countryside leads to Marbury lock. The tall obelisk visible to the south is at distant Combermere Park.

Marbury
Ches. PO, tel, stores. An enchanting village $\frac{1}{2}$ mile south of Marbury lock. Centred on an old farm, the village boasts several other old and timbered buildings. The church is a gem, and its setting is unrivalled: it stands on top of a little hill that overlooks a beautiful mere. The church grounds contain not just a graveyard but a garden, and the interior is correspondingly attractive and interesting. The sympathetically restored rectory stands next door.

Wrenbury
Ches. PO, tel, stores, garage, station. A quiet village $\frac{1}{4}$ mile from the wharf. There are some thatched cottages and a large church. It is indeed refreshing to find a railway station still operating today in a village as small as this. The line goes from Crewe to Shrewsbury.

St Margaret's Church Overlooking the village green, this is a large, battlemented church with an early 16thC west tower and 18thC chancel and pulpit. The interior is very light and airy and contains a number of fine monuments of the last century, as well as several brasses.

BOATYARDS & BWB

Just Boats Sumners Hill, Wrenbury, nr Nantwich, Ches. (Aston 236). In the old Wrenbury Mill. Hire cruisers.

PUBS

- **Swan** Marbury.
- **Cotton Arms** near Wrenbury bridge.

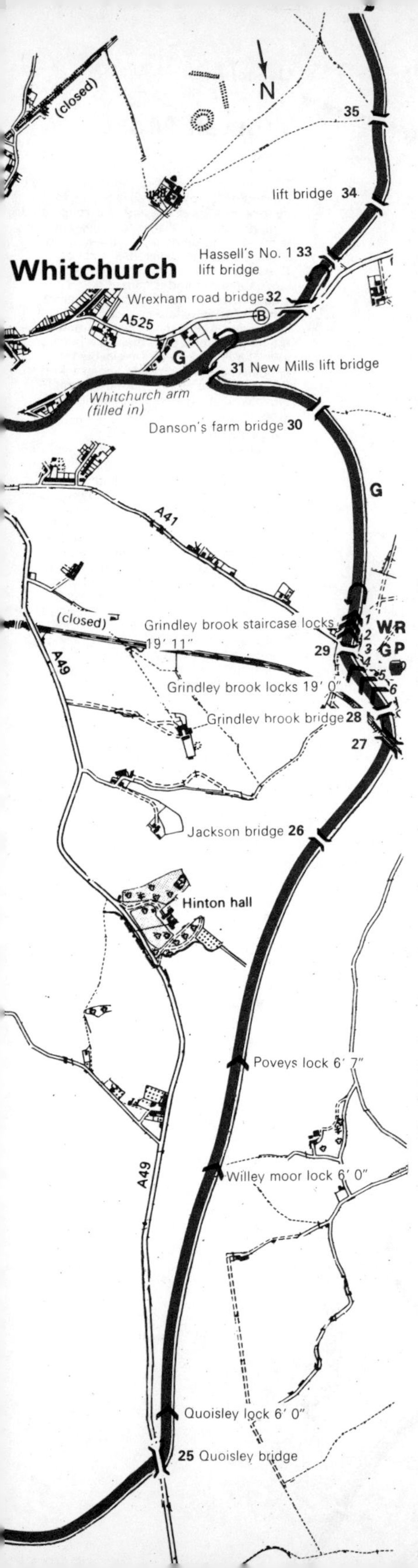

Grindley Brook

$5\frac{1}{4}$ miles

The canal continues to rise through a series of isolated locks as the sides of the valley begin to encroach on either side. Hinton Hall, a large Victorian building, is shrouded in trees on the side of a hill. At the end of a straight stretch a massive railway embankment precedes a sharp bend to the bottom of the 6 locks at Grindley Brook; care should be exercised on the approach to the locks, and any boats stopping to visit the garage or pub nearby should remain below the railway embankment. The first 3 locks are followed at the A41 bridge by 3 'staircase' locks. Anyone requiring assistance or advice should look for the lock-keeper, whose curious angled house is at the top lock. There is a convenient post office/ stores beside the staircase locks, and $\frac{1}{4}$ mile south of the locks is a canalside cottage where provisions can be bought: roast chickens and excellent home made cakes are the speciality. The canal now swerves round the side of a hill near Whitchurch: the first of a spattering of lift bridges marks the entrance to the long-abandoned Whitchurch Arm. A farm 100 yards up the arm sells home dairy produce.

Whitchurch

Salop. EC Wed, MD Fri. PO, tel, stores, garage, bank, station. Pop 7,100. A very fine town with some beautiful old houses of all periods in the centre. The streets are narrow and there is much to discover by wandering around. The striking church of St Alkmund on the hill was built in 1713, after the old church, called the Norman White Church—hence the name of the town—'fell ye 31 of July 1711'. Oxford Canal connoisseurs will recognise its similarity to the magnificent church of the same vintage at Banbury. It has very big windows: indeed the whole church is on a grand scale. There are plenty of splendid pubs in the town, but unfortunately none near the canal.

BOATYARDS & BWB

Bridge Canal Cruisers Wrexham rd, Whitchurch, Salop (2012). Near bridge 32 (Wrexham road bridge). Hire cruisers, also day boat. Dustbins, water, diesel, petrol, gas, chandlery, slipway up to 30 foot. Moorings, winter storage. Boat & motor sales & repairs. Boats fitted out. Lavatories. *Open daily throughout the year.*

PUBS

Black Bear Whitchurch (2648). Booked meals in pub; pies etc.
Red Cow Whitchurch (2852). Sandwiches and pies.
White Bear Whitchurch (2638). Food. B & B.
Horse and Jockey Grindley Brook, nr bottom lock.

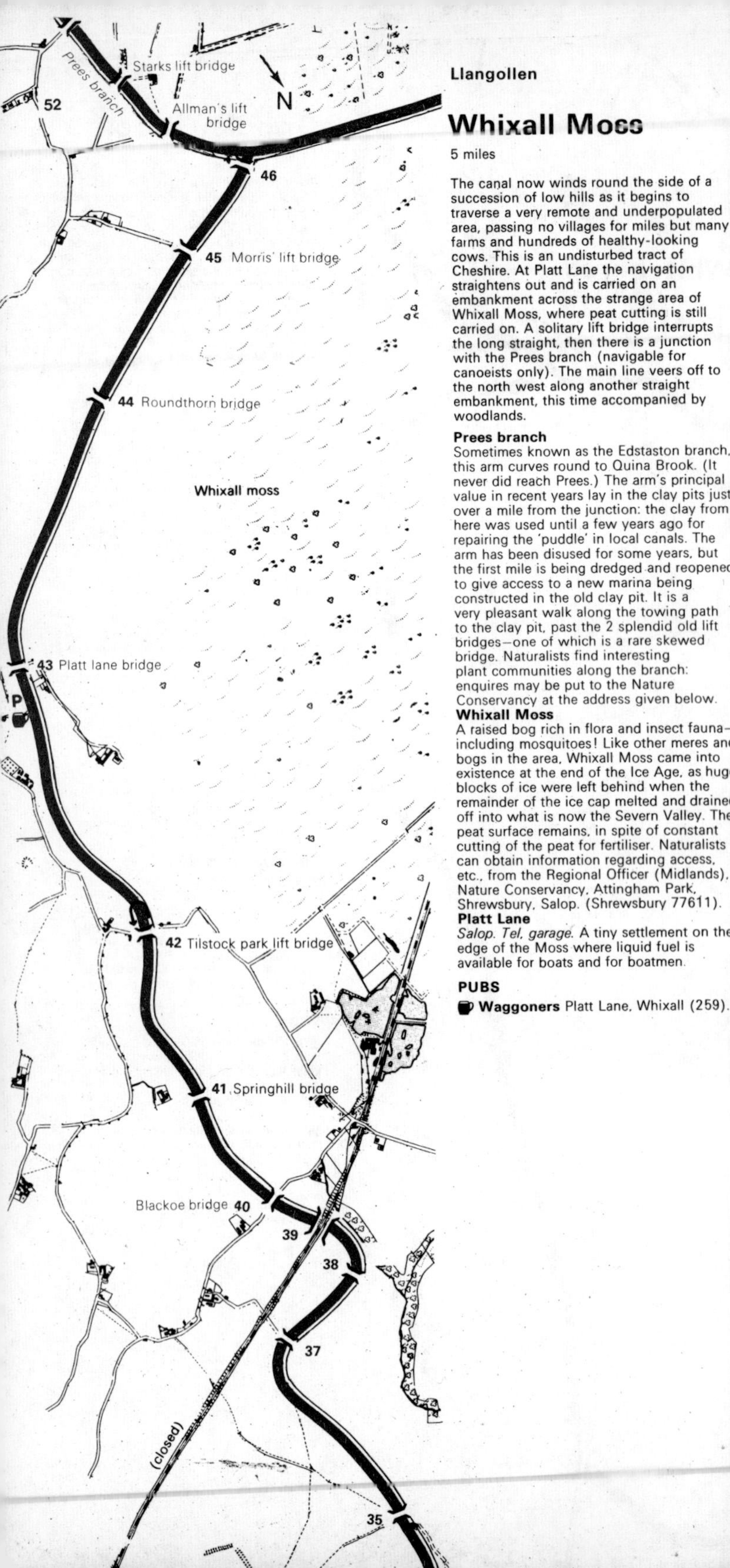

Whixall Moss

5 miles

The canal now winds round the side of a succession of low hills as it begins to traverse a very remote and underpopulated area, passing no villages for miles but many farms and hundreds of healthy-looking cows. This is an undisturbed tract of Cheshire. At Platt Lane the navigation straightens out and is carried on an embankment across the strange area of Whixall Moss, where peat cutting is still carried on. A solitary lift bridge interrupts the long straight, then there is a junction with the Prees branch (navigable for canoeists only). The main line veers off to the north west along another straight embankment, this time accompanied by woodlands.

Prees branch
Sometimes known as the Edstaston branch, this arm curves round to Quina Brook. (It never did reach Prees.) The arm's principal value in recent years lay in the clay pits just over a mile from the junction: the clay from here was used until a few years ago for repairing the 'puddle' in local canals. The arm has been disused for some years, but the first mile is being dredged and reopened to give access to a new marina being constructed in the old clay pit. It is a very pleasant walk along the towing path to the clay pit, past the 2 splendid old lift bridges—one of which is a rare skewed bridge. Naturalists find interesting plant communities along the branch: enquires may be put to the Nature Conservancy at the address given below.

Whixall Moss
A raised bog rich in flora and insect fauna—including mosquitoes! Like other meres and bogs in the area, Whixall Moss came into existence at the end of the Ice Age, as huge blocks of ice were left behind when the remainder of the ice cap melted and drained off into what is now the Severn Valley. The peat surface remains, in spite of constant cutting of the peat for fertiliser. Naturalists can obtain information regarding access, etc., from the Regional Officer (Midlands), Nature Conservancy, Attingham Park, Shrewsbury, Salop. (Shrewsbury 77611).

Platt Lane
Salop. Tel, garage. A tiny settlement on the edge of the Moss where liquid fuel is available for boats and for boatmen.

PUBS

Waggoners Platt Lane, Whixall (259).

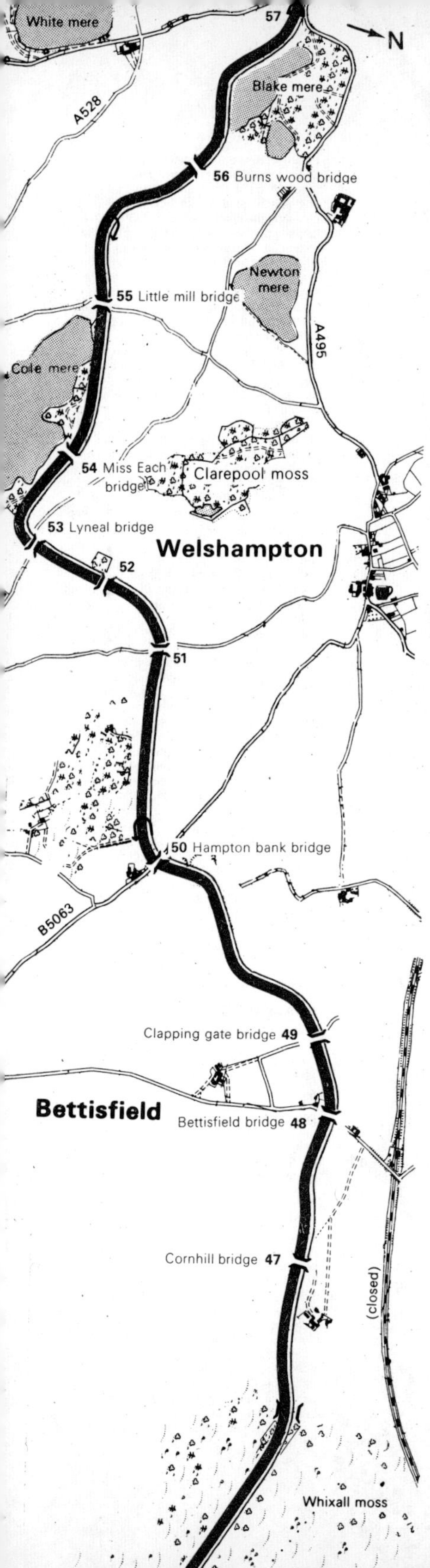

Bettisfield

5½ miles

Leaving Whixall Moss, the canal passes Bettisfield and begins to wind this way and that, passing into Wales and out again. Soon the open countryside gives way to the hilly wooded landscape that precedes Ellesmere and contains several beautiful meres. The canal skirts first Cole Mere, which is below and mostly hidden from it by tall trees; there is a delightful timbered cottage at the west end. Then the navigation runs right beside Blake Mere: this is a charming little lake, surrounded by steep and thickly wooded hills. It is inhabited by many fish, and also ducks and other wild birds. One plunges immediately afterwards into the 87-yard Ellesmere Tunnel and out into the open parkland beyond.

Welshampton
PO, tel, stores, garage. 1 mile west of bridge 50, the village contains the only pub since Platt Lane.

Bettisfield
Flintshire. PO, tel, stores (off-licence). There is little life in Bettisfield now: the pub and railway have closed and the station has become a private house. The church occupies a good position on the hill—it is a pretty Victorian building.

PUBS

Sun Welshampton.

CARAVANS & CAMPING

Fernwood Caravan Park Lyneal, nr Ellesmere. (Bettisfield 221). Canalside. Overnight caravan stops. No tents permitted.

FISHING

Blake Mere, Cole Mere and White Mere are Ellesmere Angling Club waters, but all three are open for coarse fishing to members of the public who have obtained day tickets from: W. Clay & Sons, Scotland st, Ellesmere; or Colesmere Post Office, Colesmere; or Mr E. Done, Whitemere. Day tickets permit bank fishing only in Blake Mere, but both bank and boat fishing in Cole Mere and White Mere. No canal fishing (even from boats) is permitted between Colemere Bridge 53 and Ellesmere Bridge 58

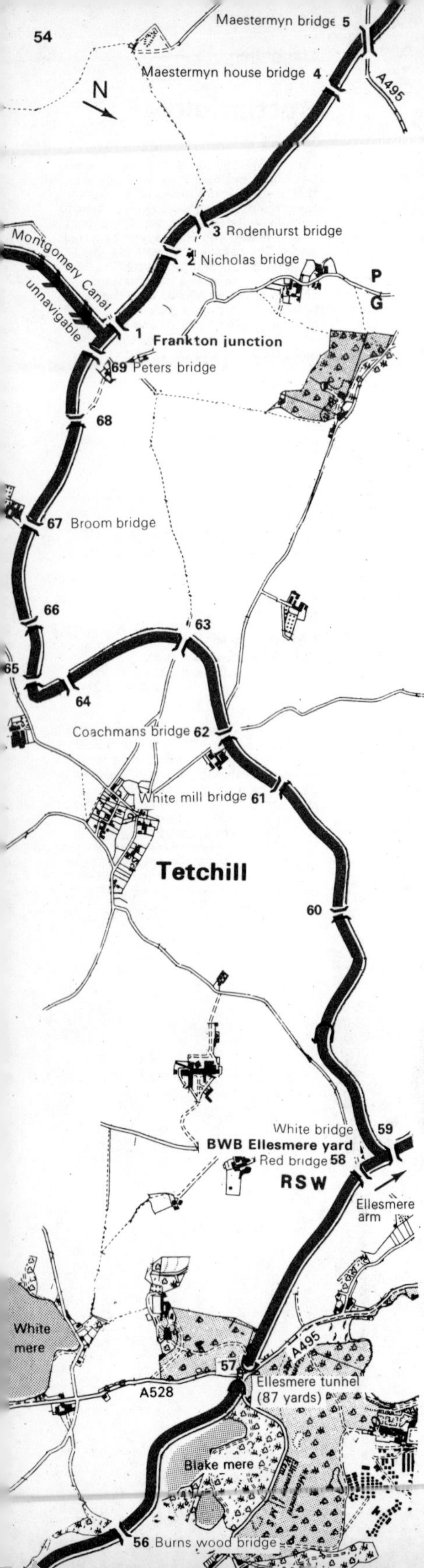

Ellesmere

$6\frac{1}{4}$ miles

Leaving Blake Mere and the tunnel, one soon arrives at Ellesmere. The town itself is reached via a short arm: at the end of the arm is a large dairy and good moorings close to the centre of town. Old warehouses and a small canalside crane testify to the canal trading that used to be carried on from here. The main line of the canal to Llangollen bears round sharply to the south west at the junction: the fine old buildings here house the BWB maintenance yard with all sorts of facilities for pleasure boats. Within the yard is 'Beech House', once the canal company's office. Beyond the yard, the country once again becomes quiet and entirely rural, while the canal's course becomes very winding. Frankton Junction is where boats used to branch off down the old Montgomery Canal south to Newtown (see page 60): the canal is derelict now, and the staircase locks by the junction have been disused since 1936. West of this junction, the bridge numbering on the Llangollen Canal starts at no. 1 again, because originally the Llangollen was only a branch of the Montgomery line.

Tetchill
Salop. PO, tel, stores, garage. A small farming village, quiet and unpretentious. There is no sign of a church.

Ellesmere
Salop. Pop 2,300. EC Thur. PO, tel, stores, garage, bank. This handsome 18thC market town with its narrow winding streets is an attractive place to visit. There are many tall red brick houses and several terraces of old cottages. It takes its name from the large and beautiful Mere beside it. The castle that once defended the people of Shropshire from their barbarous Celtic neighbours was destroyed long ago, and its ancient site is now used as a bowling green with a fine view of the surrounding countryside. It is hard today to associate this town with Ellesmere Port (see page 45). Yet the latter, then just a small village called Netherpool on the river Mersey, was chosen by the canal's builders as little Ellesmere's trade outlet to the sea.

St. Mary's Church Standing on a hill overlooking the mere, the general appearance of this large red stone church is Victorian, belying its mediaeval origins. It contains a mediaeval chest hewn out of a solid block of oak, many fine effigies and a beautiful 15thC octagonal font.

BOATYARDS & BWB

BWB Ellesmere Yard at junction with Ellesmere Arm. Water; refuse & sewage disposal. Drydock for hire. (Ellesmere 2549).

PUBS

Bridgewater Arms hotel Ellesmere (2312). Restaurant: lunches and dinners daily.

Swan Ellesmere.

White Hart Ellesmere. A very old timbered building.

FISHING

In the Ellesmere area there are good stocks of all species, including quality tench, bream, and pike. A few noted swims here always seem to produce fairly good catches. All day fishing on the Llangollen Canal is controlled by the Shropshire Union Canal Angling Association—tickets available from their bailiffs at 15p per day. Match fishing permits and permits to fish from pleasure boats are issued by BWB at Nantwich: details on page 174.

In the waters of Ellesmere itself there is boat-fishing only: tickets are available from the warden at the Mere. Rowing boats may be hired.

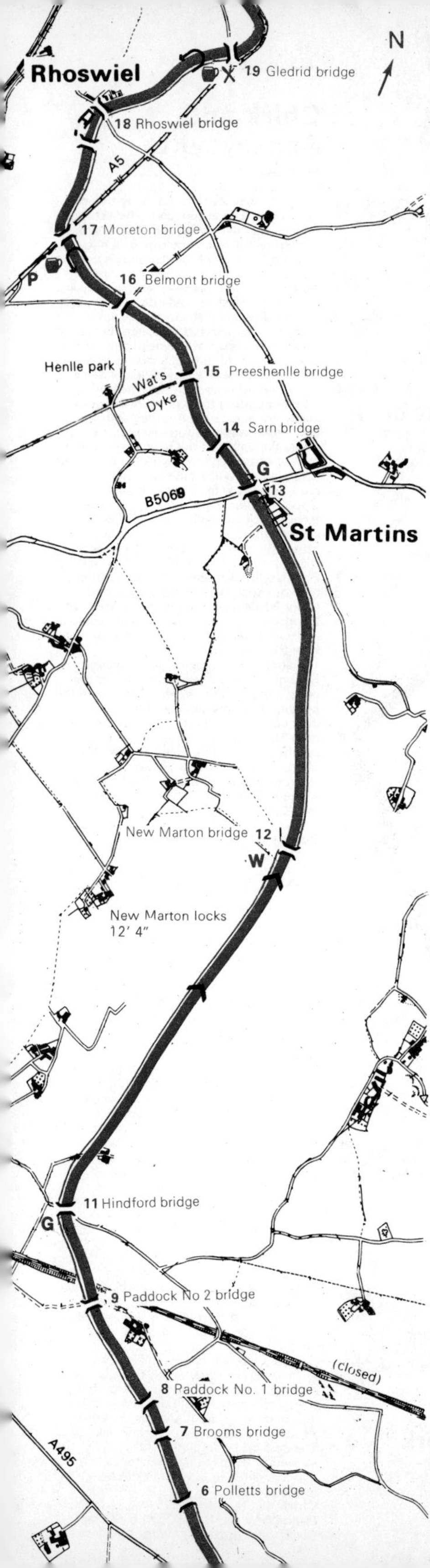

Henlle Park

5½ miles

The navigation continues to run west and north through quiet, green countryside. At Hindford bridge a canalside farm sells all sorts of provisions and serves teas, coffees, etc. (*closed Fridays:* tel Whittington Castle 327). Beyond, the canal climbs through the 2 New Marton locks – the last to be encountered on the way to Llangollen. Gradually the land becomes hillier as one passes Wat's Dyke and Henlle Park. There is a quick taste of industry – mainly worked out coal mines – before the A5 joins the navigation near Chirk Bank.

Rhoswiel

Salop. PO, tel, stores. A tiny mining village on the Welsh border; the canal runs through it in a slight cutting.

PUBS

New Inn Gledrid, Chirk. (3250). Canalside, at bridge 19 and on A5 road. Restaurant: lunches and dinners daily. (B & B).

N
Rhoswiel
19 Gledrid bridge
18 Rhoswiel bridge
A5
17 Moreton bridge
P
16 Belmont bridge
Henlle park
Wat's Dyke
15 Preeshenlle bridge
14 Sarn bridge
G
13
B5069
St Martins
New Marton bridge 12
W
New Marton locks
12' 4"
11 Hindford bridge
G
9 Paddock No 2 bridge
(closed)
8 Paddock No. 1 bridge
7 Brooms bridge
A495
6 Polletts bridge

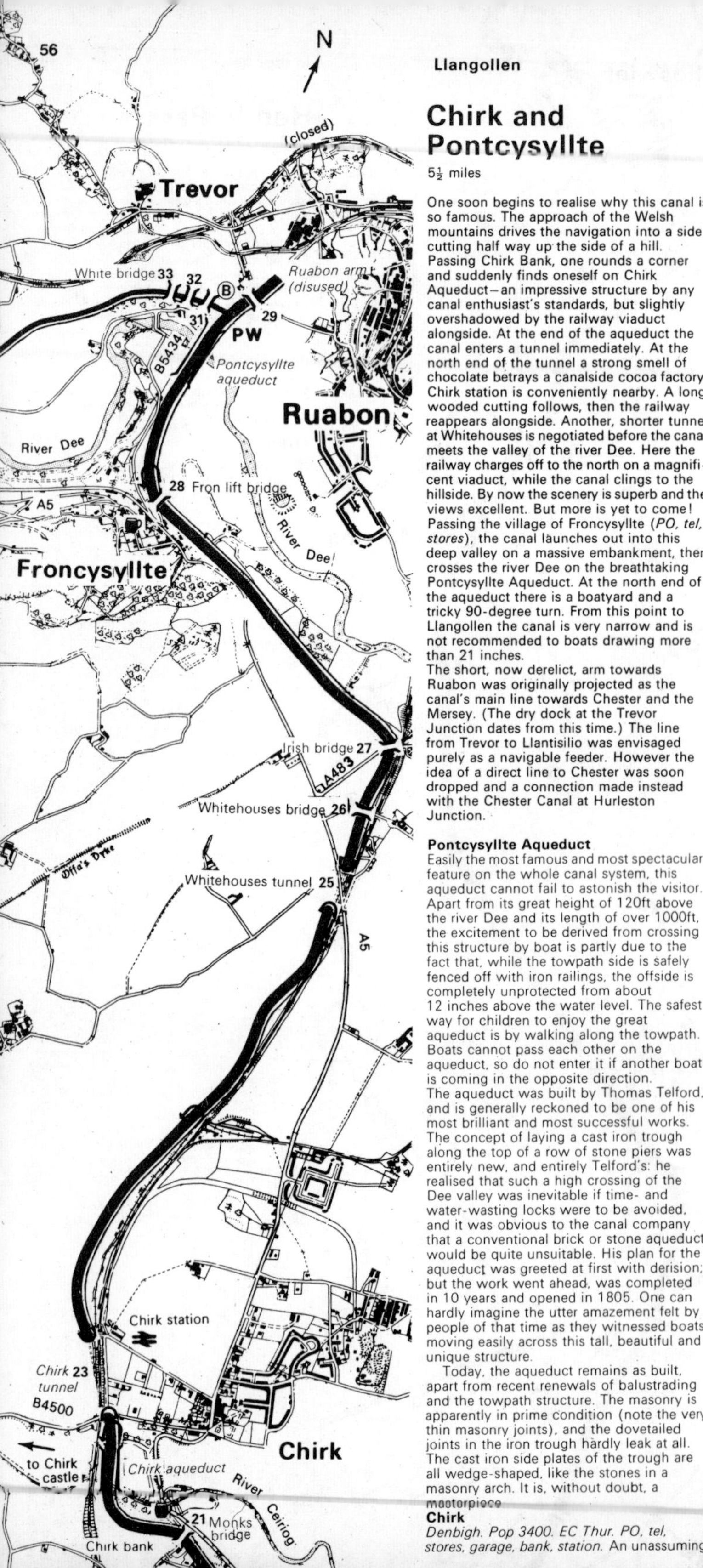

Chirk and Pontcysyllte

5½ miles

One soon begins to realise why this canal is so famous. The approach of the Welsh mountains drives the navigation into a side cutting half way up the side of a hill. Passing Chirk Bank, one rounds a corner and suddenly finds oneself on Chirk Aqueduct—an impressive structure by any canal enthusiast's standards, but slightly overshadowed by the railway viaduct alongside. At the end of the aqueduct the canal enters a tunnel immediately. At the north end of the tunnel a strong smell of chocolate betrays a canalside cocoa factory; Chirk station is conveniently nearby. A long wooded cutting follows, then the railway reappears alongside. Another, shorter tunnel at Whitehouses is negotiated before the canal meets the valley of the river Dee. Here the railway charges off to the north on a magnificent viaduct, while the canal clings to the hillside. By now the scenery is superb and the views excellent. But more is yet to come! Passing the village of Froncysyllte (*PO, tel, stores*), the canal launches out into this deep valley on a massive embankment, then crosses the river Dee on the breathtaking Pontcysyllte Aqueduct. At the north end of the aqueduct there is a boatyard and a tricky 90-degree turn. From this point to Llangollen the canal is very narrow and is not recommended to boats drawing more than 21 inches.

The short, now derelict, arm towards Ruabon was originally projected as the canal's main line towards Chester and the Mersey. (The dry dock at the Trevor Junction dates from this time.) The line from Trevor to Llantisilio was envisaged purely as a navigable feeder. However the idea of a direct line to Chester was soon dropped and a connection made instead with the Chester Canal at Hurleston Junction.

Pontcysyllte Aqueduct

Easily the most famous and most spectacular feature on the whole canal system, this aqueduct cannot fail to astonish the visitor. Apart from its great height of 120ft above the river Dee and its length of over 1000ft, the excitement to be derived from crossing this structure by boat is partly due to the fact that, while the towpath side is safely fenced off with iron railings, the offside is completely unprotected from about 12 inches above the water level. The safest way for children to enjoy the great aqueduct is by walking along the towpath. Boats cannot pass each other on the aqueduct, so do not enter it if another boat is coming in the opposite direction.

The aqueduct was built by Thomas Telford, and is generally reckoned to be one of his most brilliant and most successful works. The concept of laying a cast iron trough along the top of a row of stone piers was entirely new, and entirely Telford's: he realised that such a high crossing of the Dee valley was inevitable if time- and water-wasting locks were to be avoided, and it was obvious to the canal company that a conventional brick or stone aqueduct would be quite unsuitable. His plan for the aqueduct was greeted at first with derision; but the work went ahead, was completed in 10 years and opened in 1805. One can hardly imagine the utter amazement felt by people of that time as they witnessed boats moving easily across this tall, beautiful and unique structure.

Today, the aqueduct remains as built, apart from recent renewals of balustrading and the towpath structure. The masonry is apparently in prime condition (note the very thin masonry joints), and the dovetailed joints in the iron trough hardly leak at all. The cast iron side plates of the trough are all wedge-shaped, like the stones in a masonry arch. It is, without doubt, a masterpiece

Chirk

Denbigh. Pop 3400. EC Thur. PO, tel, stores, garage, bank, station. An unassuming place whose 18thC village centre is full of A5 traffic. Most of Chirk is in Wales but a few houses on the south side are in England, including the Bridge Inn, which, unlike some pubs in Wales, is open on Sundays.

Chirk Castle 1 mile west of Chirk Tunnel. Built in 1310, it has been the home of the Myddelton family since 1595. The interior rooms are richly decorated and the entrance gates are a remarkable example of wrought-iron work, made in 1719. There are traces of Offa's Dyke within the park.

Chirk and Whitehouses tunnels
Neither of these tunnels is wide enough for 2 boats to pass—although each tunnel has a towing path running through it. Chirk tunnel is 459 yards long, Whitehouses tunnel is 191 yards.

Chirk Aqueduct
Opened in 1801, this is a splendidly massive brick and stone aqueduct carrying the canal in a narrow cast iron trough from England into Wales. The river Ceiriog flows 70ft below, and the great railway viaduct is beside and a little higher than the aqueduct.

BOATYARDS & BWB

Anglo-Welsh Narrow Boats Canal Wharf, Trevor, Llangollen, Den. (Ruabon 2337). At the junction with the Ruabon Arm. Hire narrow boats. Sewage & refuse disposal, water, diesel, petrol, gas. Drydock. Sale & repair of diesel engines. Local shops, telephone, lavatories.

PUBS

Aqueduct Froncysyllte.
Britannia Froncysyllte.
Hand hotel Church st, Chirk (2479). Restaurant lunches and dinners (*except Sun evening*).
Bridge Chirk Bank (Chirk 3213). 'Last pub in England', on the A5 downhill from bridge 21. Sandwiches etc.

Pontcysyllte Aqueduct, which carries boats 120 feet above the river Dee.

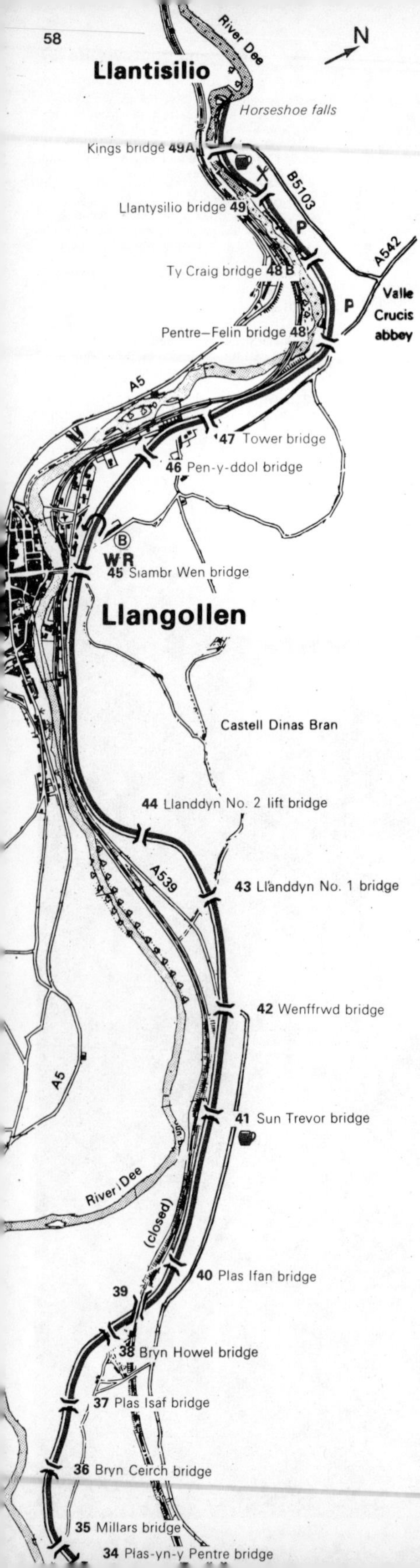

Llantisilio
River Dee
N
Horseshoe falls
Kings bridge 49A
B5103
Llantysilio bridge 49
P
A542
Ty Craig bridge 48B
Valle Crucis abbey
P
Pentre–Felin bridge 48
A5
47 Tower bridge
46 Pen-y-ddol bridge
B
WR
45 Siambr Wen bridge
Llangollen
Castell Dinas Bran
44 Llanddyn No. 2 lift bridge
A539
43 Llanddyn No. 1 bridge
42 Wenffrwd bridge
A5
41 Sun Trevor bridge
River Dee
(closed)
40 Plas Ifan bridge
39
38 Bryn Howel bridge
37 Plas Isaf bridge
36 Bryn Ceirch bridge
35 Millars bridge
34 Plas-yn-y Pentre bridge

Vale of Llangollen

5 miles

This is another stretch of very great beauty. All the way to Llangollen the navigation sidles along the tree-covered mountains, with views down into the Vale of Llangollen. In places the mountainside is very steep, making the canal so narrow that only one boat can negotiate the channel at a time. This incredible canal passes high above Llangollen, but it doesn't stop there: the tiny channel continues as a navigable feeder to weave up the valley to Llantisilio. At this delightful spot the Horseshoe Falls (in fact a large semi-circular weir built by Telford across the river Dee) provide the water which is constantly passed from the river through a sluice and meter into the canal. Then it flows past Llangollen and the aqueducts, right back down to Hurleston reservoir—to the tune of 6 million gallons a day.

Navigational note
There is **no** turning point west of the winding hole at Llangollen, so no boats longer than about 10ft should venture up the feeder. However the towpath is in excellent shape and it makes a very enjoyable walk. There are good temporary moorings and other BWB facilities at Llangollen.

Llantisilio
The village is set on a steep hillside among trees that overlook the Horseshoe Falls. The Victorian church is of interest: parts of the interior are taken from the nearby Valle Crucis Abbey, and the south window still contains 16thC glass.
Valle Crucis Abbey 1½ miles north west of the town. Picturesque ruins of the Cistercian abbey founded in 1201 by Madoc, Lord of Powys. The abbey fell into neglect after the Dissolution of the Monasteries in 1539.
Eliseg's Pillar ¼ mile north of the abbey. Erected in 18thC to commemorate Eliseg, who built the fortress on the top of Dinas Bran.
Llangollen
Denbighs. Pop 3000. EC Thur, MD Tue. PO, tel, stores, garage, bank. Renowned for its International Musical Eisteddfod every July, it is in one of the finest stretches of the Dee valley. The canal runs along the hillside overlooking the town, which is built steeply along the fast flowing river. The centre of the town is on the south side of the 14thC bridge across the Dee, and contains many stone-built Victorian buildings. Great centre for pony trekking and other outdoor pursuits, especially climbing and walking. The parish church of St. Collen in Church street is a fine 13thC building, enlarged in 1865 and containing a superb carved oak ceiling. One place well worth a visit is the Llangollen Pottery in Regent st, where the pottery is all hand-made and hand-decorated—a fascinating sight. For details of visiting times phone Llangollen 2249. The railway is closed—it must have been a beautiful line.
Plas Newydd On southern outskirts of town. An attractive black and white timbered house which, from 1779-1831, was the home of the eccentric Lady Eleanor Butler and Miss Sarah Ponsonby, known as the 'Ladies of Llangollen'. Their visitors, who included Browning, Tennyson, Walter Scott and Wordsworth, presented them with antique curios, which are now on display in the elaborately panelled rooms. Part of the 12-acre grounds is a public park. *Open May-Sep Mon-Sat 10.30-19.30, Sun 11.00-16.00.*
Castell Dinas Bran ½ mile north of canal. The ruins of the castle built for Eliseg, Prince of Powys, are conspicuous from boats approaching the town, and stand on an 1100ft mountain accessible to energetic walkers from various points along the canal. It was once an important fortress, defending Wales from the English

marauders. It has been in ruins since the 16thC but is now being worked on. From the summit there is a glorious view of the district.

BOATYARDS & BWB

Welsh Canal Holiday Craft The Wharf, Llangollen, Den. (Market Drayton 2641 or Chester 35180). Hire narrow boats. Dustbins, petrol, gas. Drydock. 15 cwt crane. *Open as required through season.*
Boat trips Horse-drawn boat trips. Party bookings Easter-end of Sep, daily public trips from end of June onwards.

PUBS

Chain Bridge hotel near Horseshoe Falls. (Llangollen 2215). Meals and residential.
Royal hotel Llangollen (2202). Meals and residential.
Royal Oak Llangollen. Pub in a very old barn.
Sun Trevor hotel near bridge 41. Meals and residential; telephone outside.

CARAVAN & CAMPING

Abbey Farm Caravan Site Horse Shoe Pass rd, Llangollen. (2283). 1 mile from the canal. Overnight caravan and tent stops.
Ddol Hir Pony Trekking Farm & Caravan Park Glyn Ceiriog. (331). 6 miles from canal, on B4500. Overnight caravan & tent stops.

YOUTH HOSTELS

Tyndwr Hall, Llangollen, (2330).

PONY TREKKING

Tyndwr Trekking Centre, Llangollen. (2328).

The river Dee in Llangollen.

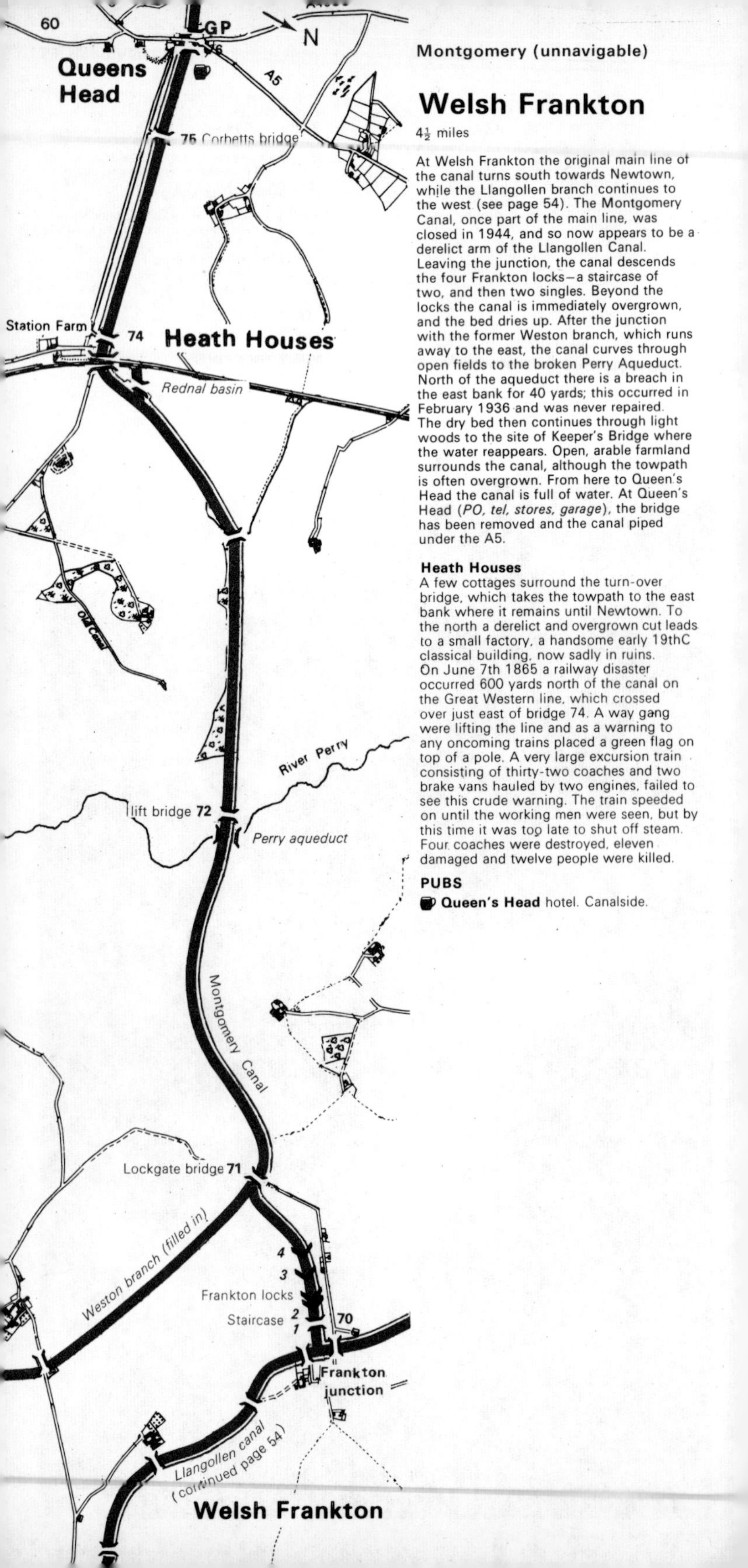

Welsh Frankton

$4\frac{1}{2}$ miles

At Welsh Frankton the original main line of the canal turns south towards Newtown, while the Llangollen branch continues to the west (see page 54). The Montgomery Canal, once part of the main line, was closed in 1944, and so now appears to be a derelict arm of the Llangollen Canal. Leaving the junction, the canal descends the four Frankton locks—a staircase of two, and then two singles. Beyond the locks the canal is immediately overgrown, and the bed dries up. After the junction with the former Weston branch, which runs away to the east, the canal curves through open fields to the broken Perry Aqueduct. North of the aqueduct there is a breach in the east bank for 40 yards; this occurred in February 1936 and was never repaired. The dry bed then continues through light woods to the site of Keeper's Bridge where the water reappears. Open, arable farmland surrounds the canal, although the towpath is often overgrown. From here to Queen's Head the canal is full of water. At Queen's Head (*PO, tel, stores, garage*), the bridge has been removed and the canal piped under the A5.

Heath Houses

A few cottages surround the turn-over bridge, which takes the towpath to the east bank where it remains until Newtown. To the north a derelict and overgrown cut leads to a small factory, a handsome early 19thC classical building, now sadly in ruins. On June 7th 1865 a railway disaster occurred 600 yards north of the canal on the Great Western line, which crossed over just east of bridge 74. A way gang were lifting the line and as a warning to any oncoming trains placed a green flag on top of a pole. A very large excursion train consisting of thirty-two coaches and two brake vans hauled by two engines, failed to see this crude warning. The train speeded on until the working men were seen, but by this time it was too late to shut off steam. Four coaches were destroyed, eleven damaged and twelve people were killed.

PUBS

Queen's Head hotel. Canalside.

Maesbury Marsh

5 miles

The canal continues south through arable land. After the three Aston locks the level remains constant, the canal crossing the rolling fields on low embankments or through shallow cuttings. Much of this section holds water, although stretches are very overgrown. Canoeing and fishing are both possible. After Maesbury Marsh, still a picturesque canalside village, two bridges have been filled and piped, the bed gradually dries up, and the towpath is so overgrown that it becomes impassable. Between Redwith and Crickheath it is necessary to leave the towpath and walk along the marshy canal bed for a while. The many farms along the canal are served by a large number of original brick accommodation bridges.

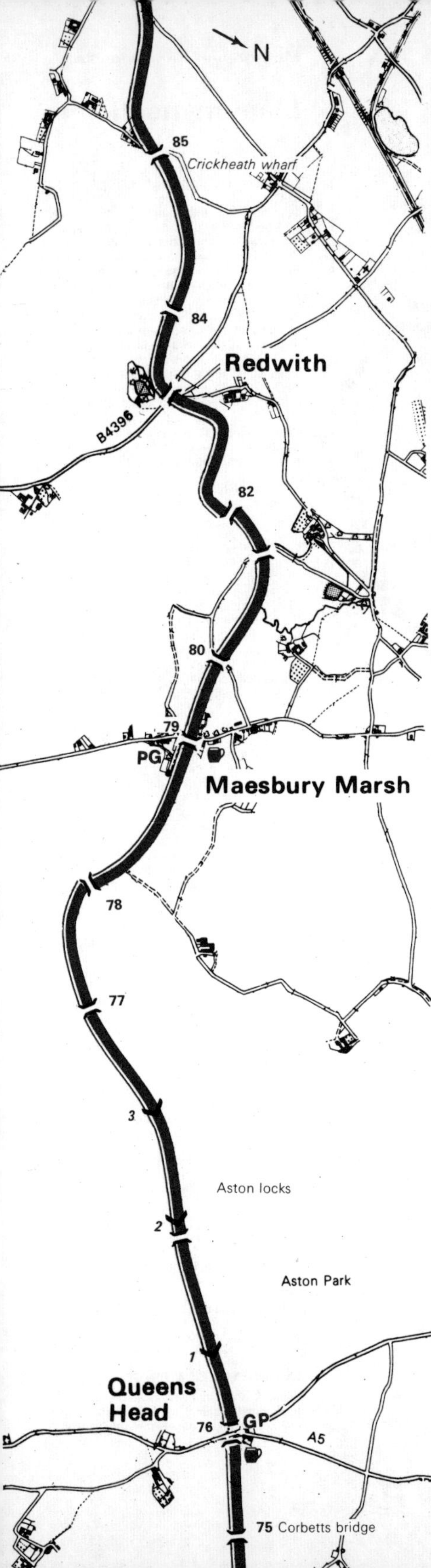

Crickheath
The picturesque wharf at Crickheath is now overgrown, the pretty stone cottage empty and the canal dry. Ten years ago it was possible to swim (illegally, of course) in the basin.

Maesbury Marsh
PO, tel, stores, garage. A pretty village clustered round the disused wharf, Maesbury still feels like a canal village; although it is 35 years since the last boat called at the wharf, the crane still stands beside the canal. The main warehouse was destroyed by fire recently, but there are still canal buildings to be seen—like those at the old coal wharf north of the pub, and the stone stables in the garage yard. After the closure of the canal to navigation Maesbury became a centre for fishing, attracting parties from all over the country.

PUBS

Navigation Maesbury Marsh. Canalside.

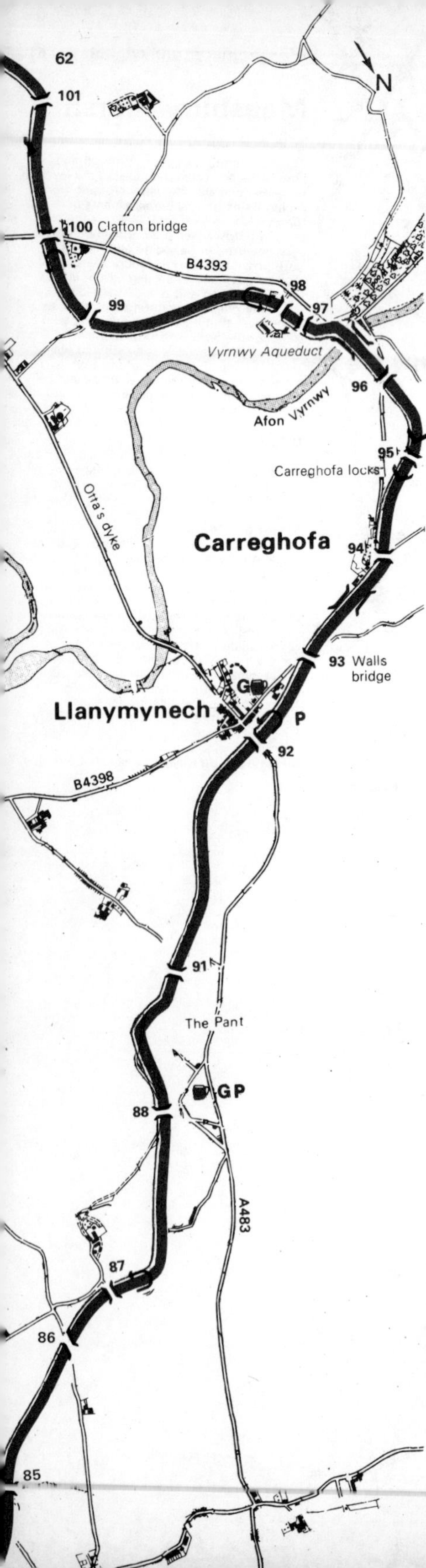

Montgomery (unnavigable)

Llanymynech

5 miles

The dry overgrown bed of the canal continues south through rolling farmland to the Pant, where the steep limestone hills dominate the west bank. The hills continue and become higher, causing the canal to meander. South of the Vyrnwy Aqueduct the canal follows the course of the hills to the west, often running through woods in an embanked sidecutting. Part of the bed has been filled in and the canal piped as it passes the Pant, but water reappears north of Llanymynech and then continues throughout the section, although very shallow and overgrown in places. Two locks at Carreghofa continue the descent, while the unnavigable Tanat feeder joins the canal between the locks. Offa's Dyke follows the canal to the east along here, after crossing at Llanymynech. At Maerdy Bridge, the road bridge has been dropped, and the canal piped under the A483.

Vyrnwy Aqueduct
Opened in 1796, the stone aqueduct across the river Vyrnwy is one of the canal's original features. Its building was fraught with problems; one arch collapsed during construction, and after completion subsidence distorted the whole structure, necessitating the addition of iron braces in 1823. The distortion also caused continual leakage problems; in 1971 repairs were undertaken to try yet again to stop the leak. To the north a long embankment precedes the aqueduct, partly of earth and partly of brick arches, which makes it altogether a much longer structure than appears at first sight.

Offa's Dyke
Offa's Dyke, which runs from Chepstow to Prestatyn, passes near the canal at several points in this area. Though at times only fragmentary, its 168-mile course has been designated as a long-distance public footpath. It was constructed by Offa, King of Mercia between 750 and 800AD to mark the boundary with Wales. The structure consisted of a long mound of earth with a ditch on the west side, though now it is often hardly recognisable as such.

Llanymynech
PO, tel, stores, garage, fish and chips.
A Victorian village built round a crossroads, tall gaunt houses lining the roads. Several railways and the canal made it a communications centre, but all are now gone, and so the village has lost its original reason for existence. Offa's Dyke and the Anglo-Welsh border run through the village, their line actually passing through the bar of the Lion Hotel; it is possible to drink with one foot in each country. The church is very interesting, a 19thC French style Norman building with a lateral bell tower. A replica of an 11thC building, the church is remarkably accurate in detail. Norman revival buildings were rare in the 19thC.

The Pant
PO, tel, stores, garage. A scattered village of bungalows and late Victorian terrace houses, The Pant grew up around the limestone quarries, one of the main reasons for the existence of the canal. The canal wharf is now filled, and almost invisible, but lime-kilns cut into the rock face serve as a reminder of the trade.

PUBS

Four Crosses Inn Four Crosses. (400 yards E of Clafton bridge).
Dolphin Llanymynech.
Lion hotel Llanymynech. (234).

CARAVAN & CAMPING

Tanat Caravan Park Llanymynech. (Llansantffraid 259). ¾ mile from canal, off A483. Overnight caravan & tent stops.

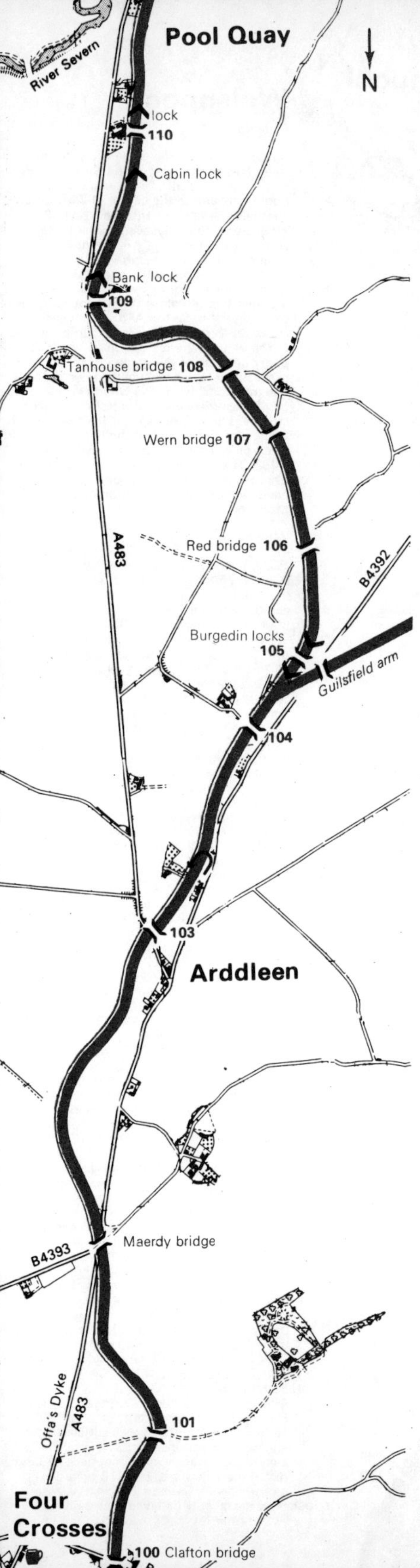

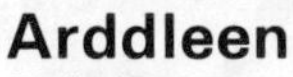

Arddleen

5 miles

The canal continues south through rolling countryside, dominated by hills to the west. The position of the canal on the western side of the Severn valley allows good views across the valley. At Burgedin two locks lower the canal to its bottom level. Immediately north of the locks the Guilsfield arm runs away to the west for two miles, terminating at Tyddyn; like the whole canal this was built to serve agriculture, particularly with lime produced from canal-borne limestone and coal. Legally abandoned in 1944 along with other branches of the Shropshire Union system, the arm is now wholly derelict and overgrown. South of Burgedin the canal crosses the open fields on a long high grassy embankment before returning to the flank of the steep wooded hills by Pool Quay. The long views to the east continue, interrupted at times by the occasional woods which descend to the canal bank. Before Pool Quay three single locks at Cabin start the climb to the summit at Newtown. The A483 flanks the canal to the east and accompanies it to Welshpool, while before Pool Quay the canal swings down to run parallel to the river Severn, following it closely all the way to Newtown.

Four Crosses
PO, tel, stores, garage. Main road village built along Offa's Dyke.

PUBS

Four Crosses Inn Four Crosses.

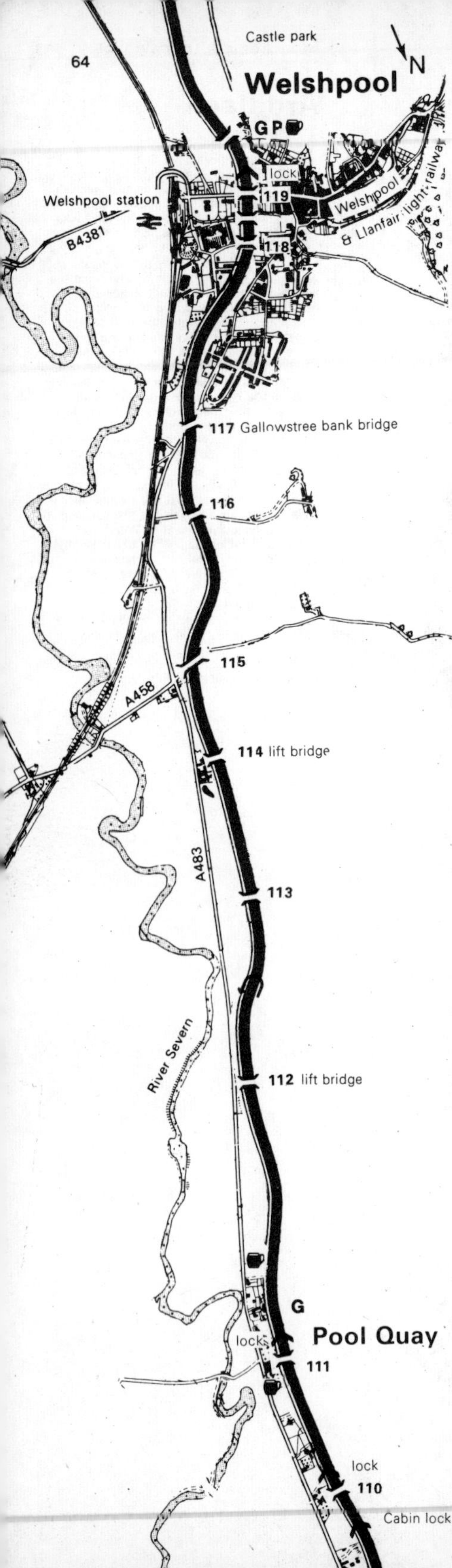

Montgomery (unnavigable)

Welshpool

4½ miles

Continuing south the canal clings to the steep hills to the west of the Severn valley, often in a wooded side cutting. Locks at Pool Quay and in the centre of Welshpool continue the rise towards Newtown. Before Welshpool there are several draw bridges; all are now permanently in the down position. Although overgrown the canal is in good condition, with water throughout most of the section. However there is a dropped bridge before Welshpool, with the canal piped under the A483. The canal is attractive through Welshpool, partly because of the voluntary work begun in 1969, and partly because of the gardens that run down to the water to the north of the town centre. The traditional basin and wharf are now used by Montgomeryshire County Council as a storage depot. After leaving the town the canal runs at the foot of the landscaped grounds of Powis Castle, flanked by the A483. The Earl of Powis is President of the Shropshire Union Canal Society, which campaigns for the restoration of the Montgomery Canal.

Welshpool
Montgom. Pop 6800. EC Thur, MD Mon. PO, tel, stores, garage, bank, station, cinema. Welshpool is a handsome Georgian town, built along a wide main street that climbs up the hill to the west. Although plagued by traffic and parked cars, Welshpool still retains the character of a market town. The canal runs through the east of the town, passing attractive gardens and the traditional wharf and warehouse. Recently the Shropshire Union Canal Society and the Waterways Recovery Group have spent many weekends working on the canal at Welshpool and have greatly improved the stretch through the town, thus adding considerably to the appearance of Welshpool, and strengthening their argument for restoration of the canal as a whole. From Welshpool lock to the site of bridge 117 the canal is now in excellent condition. A converted narrow boat, operated by the Shropshire Union Canal Society, carries passengers along the restored section on Sundays, or by prior arrangement at other times.
Powysland Museum Salop rd. Founded in 1874 to illustrate the archaeology, history, and literature of the local area. *Open 14.00-16.30 except Wed & Sun.*
Powis Castle *NT property.* Access from High st. The seat of the 5th Earl of Powis, this impressive building has been continuously inhabited for over 500 years. It is a restored mediaeval castle with late 16thC plasterwork and panelling, and has on display many fine paintings, tapestries, early Georgian furniture and relics of Clive of India. The castle is in the centre of beautiful 18thC terraced gardens and a park containing the tallest tree in Britain, a Douglas fir. *Open June-Sep 14.00-18.00. Closed Sun & Mon.*
Welshpool & Llanfair Railway
This is a delightful narrow-gauge railway restored and run by enthusiasts. In the summer, little steam-hauled trains run up and down the line, which was originally 9 miles long. So far only part of the line has been reopened, as much work remains to be done on the Welshpool end. However a bus service from Welshpool connects the town with the present terminus of the railway, some 4 miles to the west along the A458. Copies of the timetable may be obtained from Llanfair station, Llanfair Caereinion, Montgom. (Llanfair Caereinion 441).
Buttington
Montgom. ½ mile east of bridge 115. The church is a mediaeval building, restored in 1876. The village has twice suffered from attempted invasions—in 894 by the Danish army which was evicted from here by King Alfred the Great, and in 1916 by a presumptuous German Zeppelin, whose crew mistakenly believed that the Welsh would offer less resistance than the English.

Breidden Hills
East of Buttington are the three peaks of the Breidden Hills which dominate the flat landscape of the Shropshire plain. The Breidden Crag (1324ft), increasingly defaced by quarrying, is best climbed from Criggion. An 18thC pillar on the summit commemorates Admiral Rodney.

Pool Quay
PO, tel, stores. The village is scattered along the A483, little clusters of cottages and farms sheltering from the noise between the road and the canal. The lock, bridge and cottage in the village centre form an attractive group.

PUBS

Plenty in Welshpool of all types.
Powis Arms Pool Quay. (Free House).

FISHING

At Welshpool there is a good head of various coarse fish, and this makes it a popular place for visiting anglers.

Berriew aqueduct over the river Rhiw.

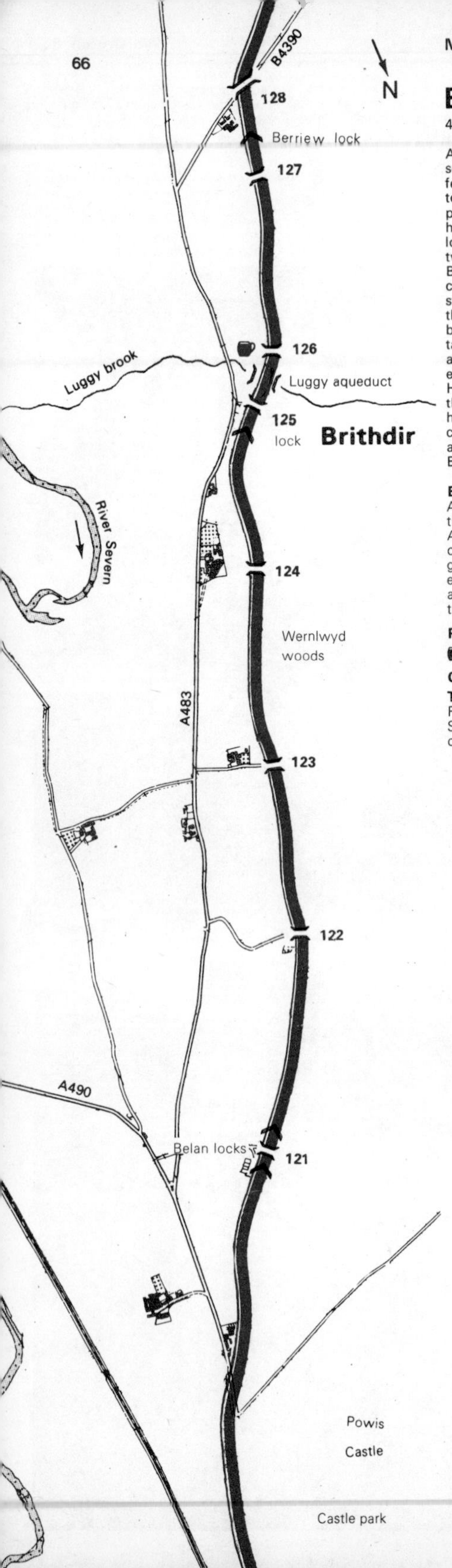

Brithdir

$4\frac{1}{2}$ miles

After Welshpool the canal turns more to the south west, leaving the river Severn for a few miles. The A483 also runs further away to the east, leaving the canal to flow in peace through woods at the foot of the hills which rise steeply to the west. Four locks continue the rise towards Newtown, two at Belan and then two singles north of Berriew. Although heavily overgrown the canal appears to be in good condition, and still in water despite the reed growth. As the canal approaches Newtown the scenery becomes more dramatic and more spectacular; woods give the canal the appearance of a river, only the side-cut embankments revealing its artificiality. Hidden by foliage in the pound between the two Belan locks are the half-sunken hulks of two narrow boats, trapped in the canal after the 1936 breach and later abandoned. The grander of the two is the Berriew, built as a 'fly boat'.

Brithdir
A small main road settlement, built round the pub. To the south is the Luggy Aqueduct, a small iron trough carrying the canal over the fast flowing stream. Overgrown and almost hidden from view, the elegant cast iron balustrades of the aqueduct contrast strangely with the tangled foliage.

PUBS

Horseshoes Brithdir. Camping nearby.

CARAVAN & CAMPING

Tavern Caravan Site Railway Inn, Forden, nr Welshpool. (Forden 237). 3 miles SE of Belan Locks, off B4388. Overnight caravan stops. No tents permitted.

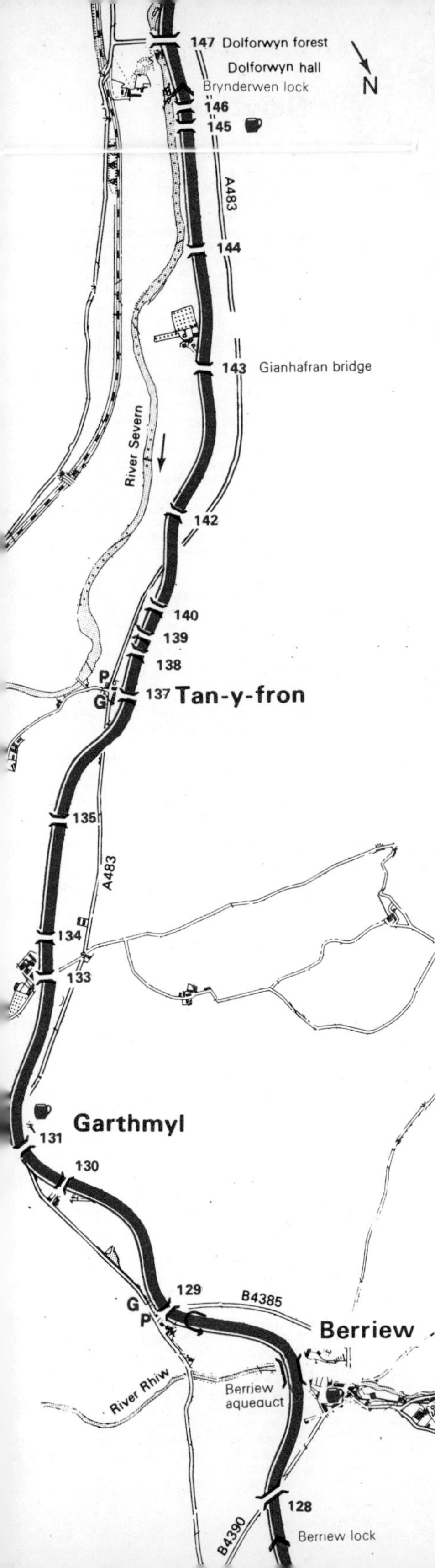

Garthmyl

5 miles

Continuing south west, the canal runs through woods south of Berriew and then swings back towards the river Severn as the valley is narrowed by the hills sweeping in from the east. Steep wooded hills flank the canal to the west. The A483 follows the canal very closely, breaking up the peace and quiet of the scenery. The canal is very weedy and overgrown, although there is some water throughout most of the section. Three road bridges have been replaced by culverts and there are several immovable swing bridges. One lock continues the rise towards Newtown, raising the canal above the level of the steadily rising Severn whose waters flow swiftly beside the canal from Abermule to Newtown.

Tan-y-fron
Tel, stores, garage. Main road settlement.
Garthmyl
Tel. Main road settlement that was once beside the canal. The wharf buildings can still be identified, looking rather incongruous as the wharf has long vanished and the canal is out of sight, piped under the road.
Berriew
Montgom. PO, tel, stores, garage. A two-arched brick aqueduct carries the canal over the beautiful wooded valley of the river Rhiw. Originally built of stone, the aqueduct was reconstructed in 1889 and although it appears quite sound, the canal has had to be piped across it because of leakage. The village of Berriew lies to the west, climbing the steep slopes of the fast-flowing river which cascades over rocks beneath the houses. In the centre of the village is a handsome 18thC single span stone arch across the river; the black and white painted timber framed and stone houses are ranged on either side. The black and white gives the village a great unity, regardless of style or period. The village is undoubtedly picturesque, and has been voted the Best Kept Village in Wales; but this has not spoilt it, for it is still quiet, pretty and self-contained. The church—a Victorian restoration of a mediaeval building—is set attractively among trees to the west. The vicarage is dated 1616.

PUBS

Nags Head hotel Garthmyl. Canalside.
Lion hotel Berriew.
Talbot hotel Berriew. (Free House).

CARAVAN & CAMPING

Argae Hall Select Caravan Park
Garthmyl. (Berriew 216). 400yds from canal. Overnight caravan stops. No tents permitted. Caravans for hire. Awarded 'Best Kept Caravan Site in Wales' trophy in 1971.

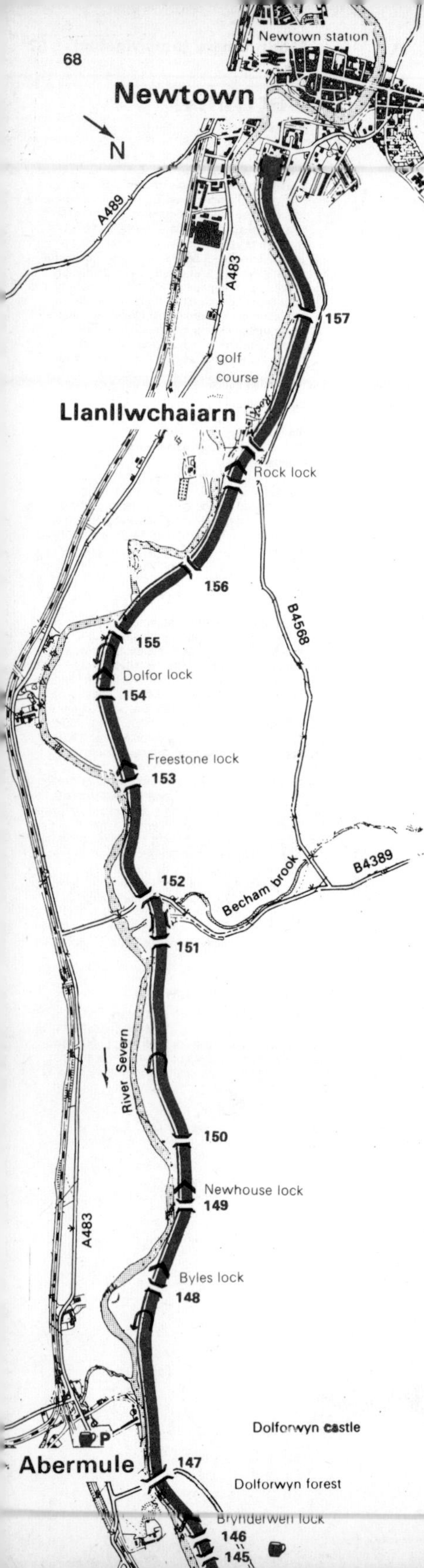

Newtown

4½ miles

The canal continues south west towards Newtown along the wooded west side of the Severn valley. Canal and river flow side by side, the river providing the water for the canal via a feeder at Penarth and at one time by a pumping-station at Newtown. Hills flank the valley, offering excellent views across it. The river flows fast, often leaping over rocks in its narrow course. Five single locks raise the canal to its summit level at Newtown. The canal deteriorates rapidly during this section, ultimately becoming dry until, finally, infilling conceals the canal completely as it enters Newtown. The once-busy basin and the last half mile have vanished under a new road, and the canal now terminates by the old pumping-station, whose tall chimney rises forlornly into the sky. The length from the top lock into the town (including the pumping house) now belongs to Newtown Corporation.
The entry to Newtown is very attractive; the canal runs in a wooded cutting past the lock at Llanllwchaiarn, overlooked by the church, while to the east there are glimpses through the trees of the river Severn down below the level of the canal.

Newtown
Montgom. Pop 5500. PO, tel, stores, garage, bank, station, cinema. Built round the Severn which sweeps round the town in a gentle curve. Prosperous as a woollen manufacturing town from the 18thC; the industry has now ceased. Its growth in the early 19thC prompted the building of the canal, as a means of supplying coal and raw materials. It still looks like a prosperous Victorian town with its large handsome buildings, rich in terracotta decoration, and wide streets. Further development is limited by the narrowness of the Severn valley, and so the town is preserved at its point of maximum development. Its former importance as a wool town is commemorated in the Textile Museum in Commercial st, where old machinery and equipment are exhibited. One may also visit the birthplace—and tomb—of Robert Owen (1771-1858), a great humanitarian and inspiration of the Co-operative movement.

Abermule
Montgom. PO, tel, stores, garage. The trees of Dolforwyn Forest sweep down to the river Severn and the canal from the west. The village of large handsome houses suffers from the the main road. The best feature is the iron bridge carrying the road jointly over the canal and the Severn. After a plain girder bridge across the canal it develops into a beautiful elegant single span arch leaping across the river. Into the curve of the arch are cast the words: 'This second iron-bridge constructed in the county of Montgomery was erected in the year 1852'. By the post office is a pump in working order.

PUBS

Plenty of pubs and hotels in Newtown.
Dolforwyn hotel and restaurant Abermule. 100yds W of bridge 145.
Waterloo Arms hotel Abermule.

CARAVAN & CAMPING

Glandulais Farm Newtown. (381). 3 miles from the canal, on A492. Overnight caravan & tent stops. Caravans for hire.
Hazeldene Pool rd, Newtown. (6865). ¼ mile from canal. Overnight caravan & tent stops.

FISHING

Tickets for match and day fishing from Llanllwchaiarn lock to the old warehouse and lock facing Dolforwyn hotel are obtainable from Abermule lock house. The towpath is good and the fishing excellent in places.

Staffordshire & Worcestershire

Maximum dimensions

Autherley to Great Haywood
Length: 72′
Beam: 7′
Headroom: 7′

Mileage

Autherley Junction (Shropshire Union Canal): to Penkridge lock: 10½ miles, 7 locks
Weeping Cross (for Stafford): 15¾ miles, 11 locks
Great Haywood Junction (Trent & Mersey Canal): 20½ miles, 12 locks

Construction of this navigation was begun immediately after that of the Trent & Mersey, to effect the joining of the rivers Trent, Mersey and Severn. After this, only the line down to the Thames was necessary to complete the skeleton outline of England's narrow canal network.

Engineered by James Brindley, the Staffs & Worcs was opened throughout in 1772, at a cost of rather over £100,000. It stretched 46 miles from Great Haywood on the Trent & Mersey to the river Severn, which it joined at what became the bustling canal town of Stourport. The canal was an immediate success. It was well placed to bring goods from the Potteries down to Gloucester, Bristol and the West Country; while the Birmingham Canal, which joined it halfway along at Aldersley Junction, fed manufactured goods northwards from the Black Country to the Potteries via Great Haywood.

Stourport has always been the focal point of the canal, for the town owed its birth and rapid growth during the late 18th century to the advent of the canal. It was here that the cargoes were transferred from narrowboats into Severn Trows for shipment down the estuary to Bristol and the south west.

The Staffordshire & Worcestershire canal soon found itself facing strong competition. In 1815 the Worcester & Birmingham canal opened, offering a more direct but heavily locked canal link between Birmingham and the Severn. The Staffs & Worcs answered this threat by gradually extending the opening times of the locks, until by 1830 they were open 24 hours a day.

When the Birmingham & Liverpool Junction canal was opened from Autherley to Nantwich in 1835, traffic bound for Merseyside from Birmingham naturally began to use this more direct, modern canal, and the Staffs & Worcs lost a great deal of traffic over its length from Autherley to Great Haywood. Most of the traffic now passed along only the ½-mile stretch of the Staffs & Worcs canal between Autherley and Aldersley Junctions. This was, however, enough for the company, who levied absurdly high tolls for this tiny length. The B & LJ company therefore co-operated with the Birmingham Canal company in 1836 to promote in Parliament a Bill for the 'Tettenhall & Autherley Canal and Aqueduct'. This remarkable project was to be a canal 'fly-over', going from the Birmingham Canal right over the profiteering Staffs & Worcs and locking down into the Birmingham & Liverpool Junction canal. In the face of this serious threat to bypass its canal altogether, the Staffs & Worcs company gave way and reduced its tolls to a level acceptable to the other 2 companies. In later years the device was used twice more to force concessions out of the Staffs & Worcs.

In spite of this setback, the Staffs & Worcs maintained a good profit, and high dividends were paid throughout the rest of the 19th century. When the new railway companies appeared in the west midlands, the Staffs & Worcs Canal Company would have nothing to do with them; but from the 1860s onwards, railway competition began to bite, and the company's profits began to slip. Several modernisation schemes came to nothing, and the canal's trade declined. Like the other narrow canals, the Staffordshire & Worcestershire faded into obscurity as a significant transport route by the middle of this century, although the old canal company proudly retained total independence until it was nationalised in 1947. Now the canal is used almost exclusively by pleasure craft.

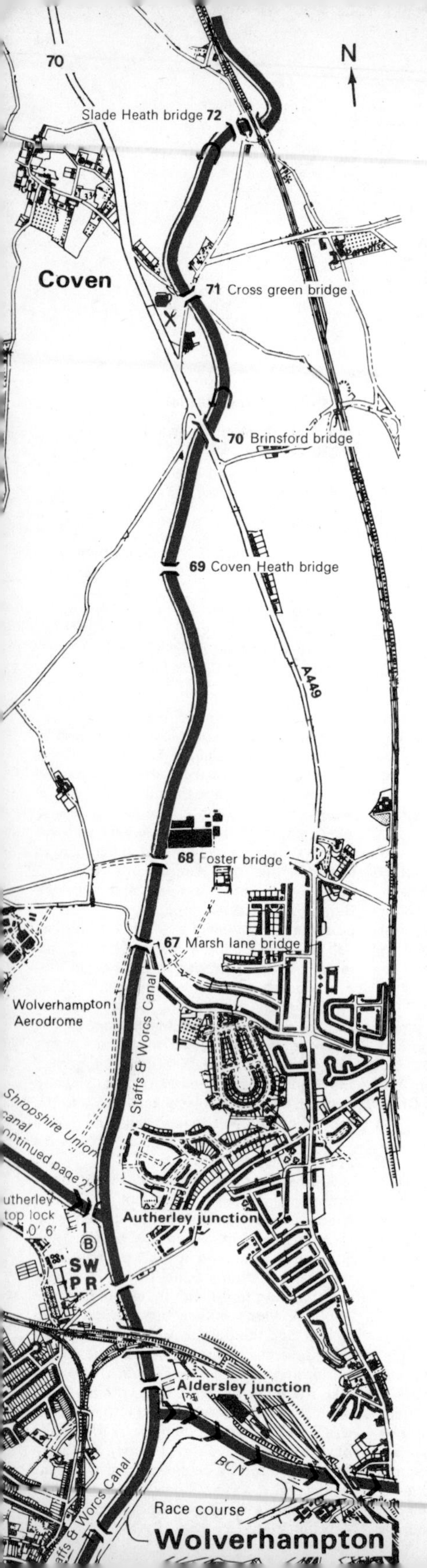

Coven

4¾ miles

Leaving Autherley and the junction with the Shropshire Union Canal (see page 27), the Staffs & Worcs Canal continues its winding course from Stourport and the river Severn towards the Trent & Mersey Canal at Great Haywood. Passing Wolverhampton aerodrome, the canal runs through a very narrow cutting through rock: there is room for only one boat here, so a good lookout should be kept for oncoming craft. Soon the navigation leaves behind the suburbs of Wolverhampton and enters pleasant farmland. The bridges need care: although the bridgeholes are reasonably wide, the actual arches are rather low. The age of this canal shows itself in its extremely twisting course after passing the railway bridge. There are few real centres of population along this stretch, which comprises largely former heathland.

Coven
Staffs. PO, tel, stores, garage. The only true village on this section, Coven lies beyond a dual carriageway northwest of Cross Green Bridge. There is a large number of shops, including a launderette.

Autherley Junction
A busy canal junction with a full range of boating facilities on the Shropshire Union Canal. (See page 27.)

BOATYARDS & BWB

Water Travel Autherley Junction, Tettenhall, Wolverhampton, Staffs. (Wolverhampton 782371). Hire cruisers. Sewage & refuse disposal, water, diesel, petrol, gas chandlery. Slipway up to 45 foot, moorings, winter storage. Boat & motor sales & repairs. Steel boats built & fitted out. Bar, groceries. Lavatory. *Open daily throughout year.*

PUBS

Anchor Canalside, by Cross Green bridge. Steak bar.

FISHING THE STAFFS & WORCS CANAL

The fishing is in pleasant surroundings, and the canal holds chub, bream, tench (laying-on with bread flake early in the season), roach, carp and pike along its various lengths. There are some sheltered swims: if these are approached cautiously, good quality fish can be taken from close in to the bank. Casters and maggots are favourite bait. This canal has produced many specimen fish, including perch over 1lb and carp of 6 to 7lb. However small fish predominate.
In the short section of the Staffs & Worcs canal from Autherley to Great Haywood Junction, there are bream, perch and pike. There has been a roach shortage, but the fishing is beginning to pick up and small roach are being caught again. There are also tench and carp. This canal has been restocked in several places by local clubs.

Gailey Wharf

7 miles

Hatherton Junction marks the entrance of the former Hatherton branch of the Staffs & Worcs Canal into the main line. This branch used to connect with the Birmingham Canal Navigations. The branch is closed now, but water is still fed down the locks into the Staffs & Worcs Canal, which explains the unusual clearness of the water hereabouts. There is a very handy all-purpose shop at the junction, surrounded by delightful rose gardens. Not far away, a big tar distillery is encountered astride the canal in what used until recently to be woodlands. Gailey Wharf is about a mile further north: it is a small canal settlement that includes a post office and a large, round tollkeeper's watchtower. The canal itself disappears under Watling Street and falls rapidly through another 5 locks towards Penkridge. The M6 motorway comes alongside for half a mile, screening the reservoirs which feed the canal. These are very attractive locks: many of them are accompanied by little brick bridges.

Gailey and Calf Heath Reservoirs
½ mile east of Gailey Wharf, either side of the M6. The three are feeder reservoirs for the canal though rarely drawn on. The public has access to them as nature reserves to study the wide variety of natural life, especially the long established heronry which is thriving on an island in Gailey Lower reservoir. In the Gailey Upper, fishing is available to the public from the riparian owner and in Gailey Lower a limited number of angling tickets are available on a season ticket basis each year from BWB, Nantwich Basin, Chester rd, Nantwich, Cheshire. (65122). There is club sailing on two of the reservoirs.

BOATYARDS & BWB

Gailey Canal Cruisers Calf Heath Marina, Kings rd, Calf Heath, nr Wolverhampton, Staffs. (Walsall 27138). At Hatherton junction. Hire cruisers, dustbins, water, diesel, gas, chandlery, drydock, 50 cwt crane, moorings. Boat & motor repairs. Cafe & grocery shop. Telephones & lavatory. *Open throughout year, closed winter Suns.*

PUBS

Cross Keys Canalside, at Filance bridge 84. Once again a proper canal pub. Water available for water-borne drinkers.

FISHING

In the Hatherton section there are mainly small roach, and plenty of gudgeon, with some perch and pike. This section has been restocked on several occasions and local clubs frequently hold contests here.

N
Princefield bridge 85
Filance lock 10' 3" 37
Filance bridge 84
(closed)
Lynehill bridge 83
A449
Otherton bridge 82
Otherton lock 10' 3' 36
81
Rodbaston bridge 80
Rodbaston lock 8' 6" 35
Bogg s lock 8' 6" 34
33 Brick kiln lock 8' 0"
M6 motorway
P 79
Gailey wharf
WR
32 Gailey lock 8 ft. 6 ins.
Watling street
A5
78 Gravelly way bridge
Calf heath Woods
ar
stillery
77 Calf heath bridge
Hatherton branch (disused)
B
Long Moll's 76 bridge
Hatherton junction
G
Deepmore bridge 75
73 Laches bridge
74 Moat House bridge

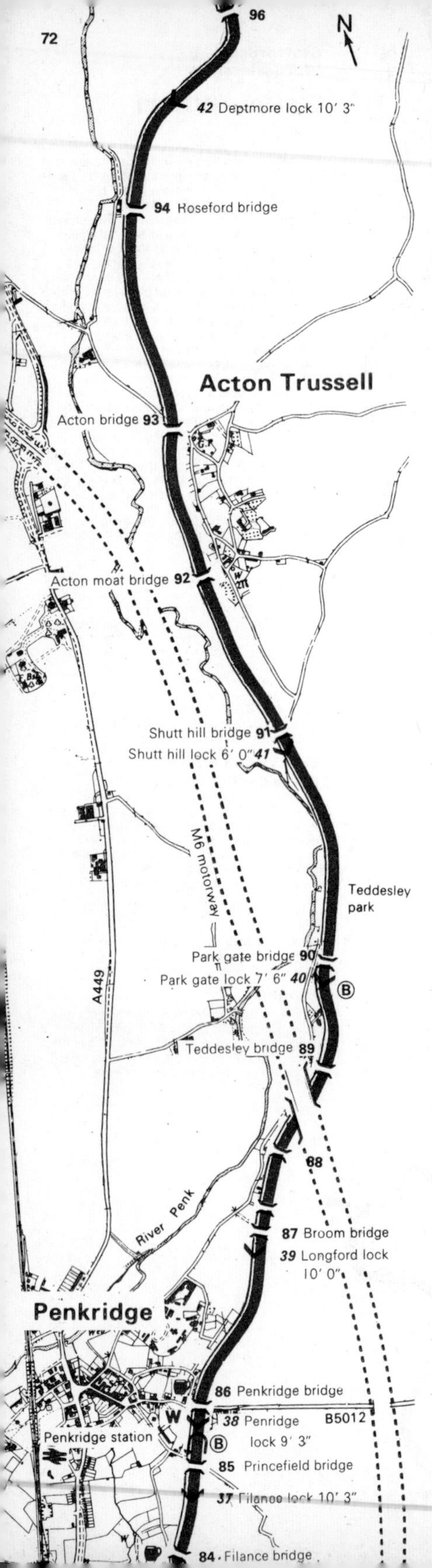

Staffordshire & Worcestershire

Penkridge

4¾ miles

The navigation now passes through Penkridge and is soon approached by the little river Penk: the two water courses share the valley for the next few miles. Apart from the noise of the motorway, this is a quiet and pleasant valley: there are plenty of trees, a handful of locks and the large Teddesley Park alongside the canal. At Acton Trussell the M6 roars off to the north west and the canal moves along to the blissful isolation that surrounds Deptmore lock. There is an inhabited lock cottage here; the residents' easiest means of access to the 'civilised' world is by boat to Radford Bridge.

Acton Trussell
Staffs. PO, tel, stores. A village overwhelmed by modern housing: much the best way to see it is from the canal. The 15thC church stands to the south, overlooking the navigation. There is a very fine old house at Acton Moat bridge.

Teddesley Park
On the east bank of the canal. The Hall, once the family seat of the Littletons, was used during the last war as a prisoner-of-war camp, but has since been demolished. Its extensive wooded estate still remains.

Penkridge
Staffs. EC Wed, MD Mon. Pop 3400. PO, tel, stores, garage, bank, station. Above Penkridge lock is a good place to tie up in this village, which is relatively old. It is bisected by a trunk road, but luckily most of the village lies to the east of this road. The church is tall and sombre, and looks well kept. Early English—mostly 12thC, but restored in the 1880s. There is a fine Dutch 18thC wrought iron screen, and the tower is believed to date from about 1500.

BOATYARDS & BWB

Teddesley Boating Centre Park Gate Lock, Teddesley rd, Penkridge, Staffs. (2437/2477/2467). Hire cruisers & narrow boats. Sewage & refuse disposal, water, diesel, gas, chandlery. Slipway up to 15 foot, moorings, winter storage. Boat & motor sales & repairs. Steel boats built & fitted out. *Open daily throughout year.*

Bijou Line Penkridge Wharf, Cannock rd, Penkridge, Staffs (2732). At Penkridge lock. Hire cruisers & narrow boats. Chandlery, boat repairs, inboard motor sales & repairs. Steel boats built & fitted out. *Open throughout the year, closed winter Sats.*

Wright Marine Wolverhampton Road, Penkridge, Staffs. (3181). Not on the canal. Steel boats built & fitted out to order.

PUBS

Boat Canalside, by Penkridge lock.
Horse & Jockey Penkridge.
Littleton Arms Penkridge. (2287). Food; B & B.

FISHING

The Acton Moat stretch at Penkridge has yielded perch to 3lb since a large stock was introduced from the Blythfield Reservoir (not BWB's) a few years ago. There are a few really big perch in the swims, and a lobworm is a good bait for catching them.

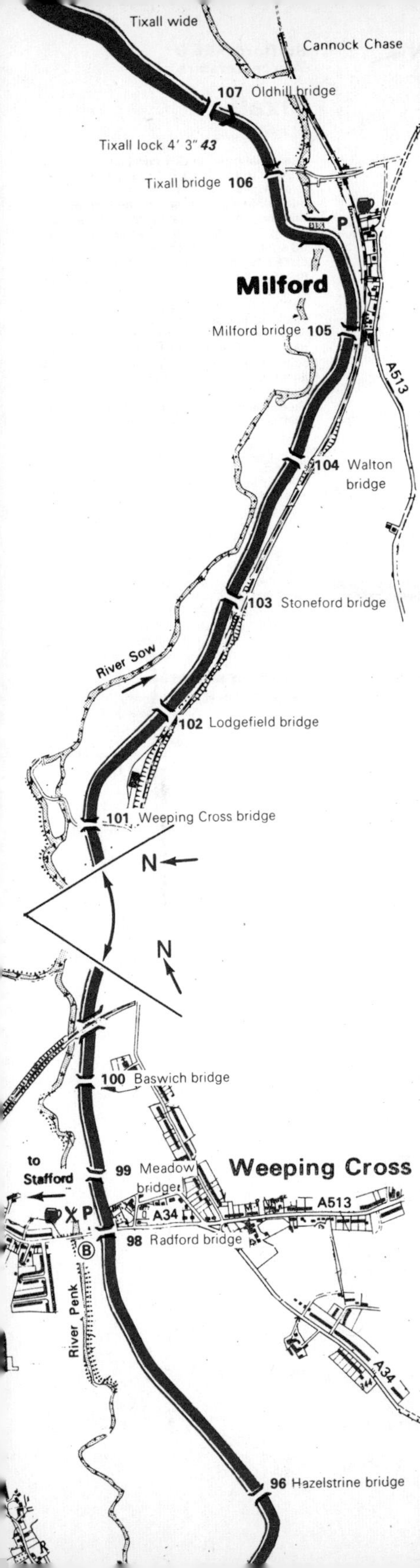

Sow Valley

5¼ miles

Flowing north along the shallow Penk valley, the canal soon reaches Radford Bridge, the nearest point to Stafford (about 1½ miles to the centre of town—there is a frequent bus service). A mile north of here the canal bends around to the south east and follows the river Sow. The Sow is a pretty valley and the canal water is very clean, in spite of the occasional industrial works. At Milford the navigation crosses the Sow via an aqueduct—an early structure by James Brindley, carried heavily on low brick arches. Tixall lock offers some interesting views in all directions: the castellated entrance to Shugborough railway tunnel at the foot of the thick woods of Cannock Chase, and the distant outline of Tixall Gatehouse.

Milford
Staffs. PO, tel, stores, garage. The village straggles parallel and close to the canal but access is obstructed by the busy railway: it is best reached from Tixall bridge (106). Milford is an estate village on the fringes of Cannock Chase; there is a great big green near the pub. Milford Hall is hidden by trees.

The Stafford Branch
Just west of bridge 101 one may see the remains of the lock that used to take a branch off the Staffs & Worcs to Stafford. The branch, 1 mile long, was unusual in that it was not a canal but the canalised course of the river Sow, which joins the river Penk just by the former lock (Baswich lock). The branch has not been used for years, but there is a pleasant walk along the river into Stafford from the pipe-bridge over the canal near bridge 100.

Stafford
Staffs. Pop 54,000. EC Wed, MD Tue, Fri, Sat. All services. This town is well worth visiting, since there is here a remarkable wealth of fine old buildings—including even the main post office. The Market Square survives, its best feature being—yet again!—the National Westminster Bank. There is a handsome City Hall complex of ornamental Italianate buildings, circa 1880. The robust-looking gaol stands nearby; and the church of St Mary's stands in very pleasing and spacious grounds. There are some pretty back alleys: Church Lane contains a splendid-looking eating house, and at the bottom of the lane a fruiterer's shop is in a thatched cottage built in 1610. All this in the middle of a town as large as Stafford is truly rewarding.

Museum & Art Gallery The Green. (Stafford 2151). On first floor of Stafford central library. Small museum with exhibits depicting the art, history and industrial development of the locality. *Open Mon-Fri 10.00-19.00, Sat 10.00-17.00.*

BOATYARDS & BWB

Radford Marine Radford Wharf, Stafford. (3519). At bridge 98 (Radford bridge). Refuse & sewage disposal, water, diesel, gas, chandlery. Slipway up to 25 foot, winter storage. Boat sales & repairs, agents for Microplus. Outboard engine sales & repairs. Groceries. Lavatory. *Open daily throughout year.*

PUBS

Barley Mow Milford. Steak bar.
X **Trumpet** Canalside, at Radford bridge. Grills.
X **Bear Inn** Greengate, Stafford (51070). *Dinner daily.*
Chains Martin st, Stafford.
Nag's Head Mill st, Stafford
X **Vine** hotel Salter st, Stafford (51071). Restaurant: lunches and dinners (*except Sun*). B & B.
X **Ye Old Soup Kitchen** Church Lane. Light meals.

FISHING

In the Stafford area local club contests are regularly held—the winning weights are usually about 5lb and made up of small fish.

Tixall wide
Cannock Chase
107 Oldhill bridge
Tixall lock 4' 3" 43
Tixall bridge 106
Milford
Milford bridge 105
A513
104 Walton bridge
103 Stoneford bridge
River Sow
102 Lodgefield bridge
101 Weeping Cross bridge
N
N
100 Baswich bridge
to Stafford
99 Meadow bridge
Weeping Cross
A513
A34
98 Radford bridge
River Penk
A34
96 Hazelstrine bridge

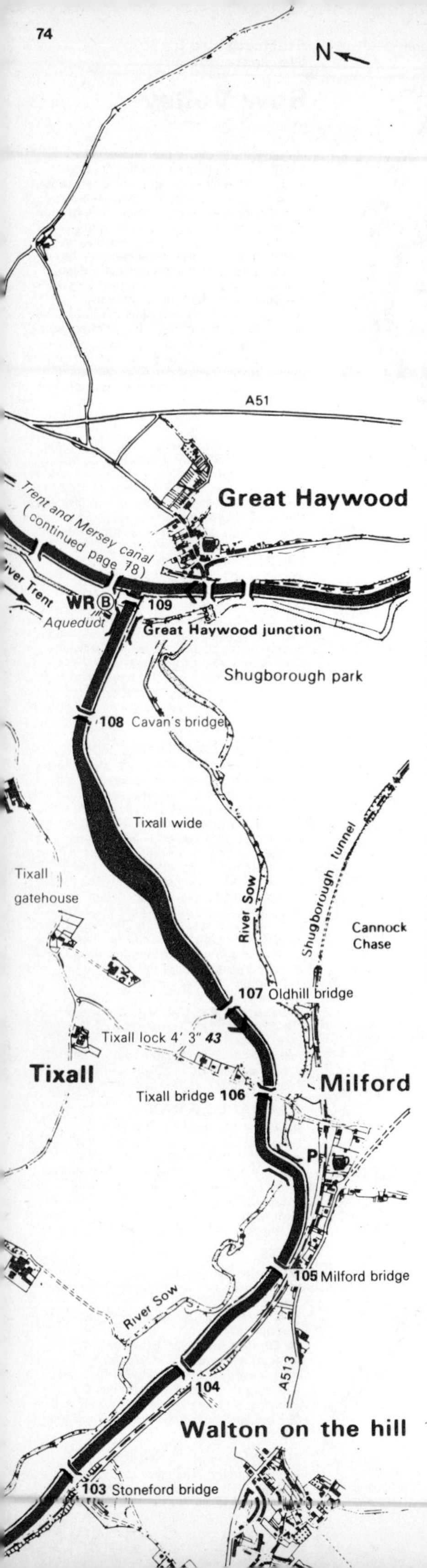

Staffordshire & Worcestershire

Tixall

$3\frac{1}{4}$ miles

The canal now quickly completes its journey to the Trent & Mersey Canal at Great Haywood. It is a length of waterway quite unlike any other. Proceeding along this very charming valley, the navigation enters Tixall Wide—an amazing and delightful stretch of water so broad that one could drive a full length narrowboat round and round in circles. The Wide is noted for its kingfisher population. Up on the hill to the north is the equally remarkable shell of Tixall Gatehouse, while woods across the valley conceal Shugborough Hall (see page 78). The river Trent is met, on its way south from Stoke-on-Trent, and crossed on an aqueduct. There is a mill, wharf and towpath bridge across Haywood Junction. Great Haywood Junction is now in a Conservation Area and is due for a 'facelift' in 1972.

Tixall
Staffs. PO, tel, stores. A quiet and unspoilt hamlet facing the wooded slopes of Cannock Chase. Just to the east are the stables and the Gatehouse of the long-vanished Tixall Hall. This massive square Elizabethan building is fully 4 storeys high and completely derelict, standing alone in a field; one can only wonder at the size of the former hall with a gatehouse as huge as this. It is clearly visible from the canal: indeed Tixall Wide may have been made to resemble a 'broad' purely because it was in full view of the Gatehouse and the Hall.

BOATYARDS & BWB

Anglo Welsh Narrowboats The Canal Wharf, Mill lane, Great Haywood, Staffs. (Little Haywood 711). At Great Haywood Junction. Hire narrow boats. Sewage disposal, water, diesel. Boat & motor repairs. Lavatories. *Open daily throughout year.*

PUBS

Barley Mow Milford. Steak bar.

FISHING

Anglers catch good quality roach around here, particularly in the early morning and late evenings, when roach to 1lb are taken as well as tench of 2lb and over. There are also some perch and pike, where the water is very clear, so the angler must always move cautiously if he is to stand any chance of catching quality fish.

Trent & Mersey

Maximum dimensions
Fradley to Great Haywood
Length: 72′
Beam: 7′
Headroom: 6′ 3″
Great Haywood to Middlewich
Length: 72′
Beam: 7′
Headroom: 5′ 9″
Middlewich to Anderton
Length: 72′
Beam: 14′ 6″
Headroom 7′
Anderton to Preston Brook
Length: 72′
Beam: 7′
Headroom: 7′

Mileage
Fradley Junction to
Great Haywood Junction (Staffs & Worcs Canal): 12¾ miles, 5 locks
Stone: 22 miles, 9 locks
Stoke top lock and (Caldon Canal): 32 miles, 23 locks
Harding's Wood Junction (Macclesfield Canal) 37¾ miles, 23 locks
King's lock, Middlewich (junction with branch): 50 miles, 54 locks
Anderton Lift (for river Weaver): 60¼ miles, 58 locks
Preston Brook north end of tunnel and junction with Bridgewater Canal: 67 miles, 59 locks

This early canal was originally conceived partly as a roundabout link between the ports of Liverpool and Hull, while passing through the busy area of the Potteries and mid-Cheshire, and terminating either in the river Weaver or in the Mersey. One of its prime movers was the famous potter Josiah Wedgwood (1730-1795). Like the Duke of Bridgewater a few years previously, he saw the obvious enormous advantages to his—and others'—industry of cheap, safe and rapid transport which a navigation would offer compared with packhorse carriage (the only alternative then available). Wedgwood was greatly assisted in the promotion of the canal by his friends, notably Thomas Bentley and Erasmus Darwin. Pamphlets were published, influential support was marshalled; and in 1766 the Trent & Mersey Canal Act was passed by Parliament, authorising the building of a navigation from the river Trent to Runcorn Gap, where it would join the proposed extension of the Bridgewater Canal from Manchester.

The ageing James Brindley was—of course—appointed engineer of the new canal. Construction began at once and much public interest was excited in this remarkable project, especially in the great 2900-yard tunnel under Harecastle Hill.

Once opened in 1777 the Trent & Mersey Canal was a great success, attracting much trade in all kinds of commodities. Vast tonnages of china clay and flints for the pottery industry were brought by sea from Devon and Cornwall, then transhipped into canal boats on the Mersey and brought straight to the factories around Burslem, taking finished goods away again. Everyone near the canal benefited: much lower freight costs meant cheaper goods, healthier industries and more jobs. Agriculture gained greatly from the new supply of water, and of stable manure from the cities.

The Trent & Mersey soon earned its other name (suggested by Brindley) as the Grand Trunk Canal—in the 67 miles between Fradley Junction and Preston Brook Junction, the Trent & Mersey gained connection with no less than 8 other canals or significant branches.

By the 1820s the Trent & Mersey was so busy that the narrow and slowly-sinking tunnel at Harecastle had become a serious bottleneck for traffic. Thomas Telford was called in; he recommended building a second tunnel beside Brindley's old one. His recommendation was eventually accepted by the Company, and a tremendous burst of energy saw the whole tunnel completed in under 3 years, in 1827. A much-needed towpath was included in this tunnel.

Although the Trent & Mersey was taken over in 1845 by the new North Staffordshire Railway Company, the canal flourished until the Great War as a most important trading route. Today there is practically no trade at all along the canal except by the Anderton Canal Carrying Company, but it is assured (by statute) of a future as a pleasure cruising waterway.

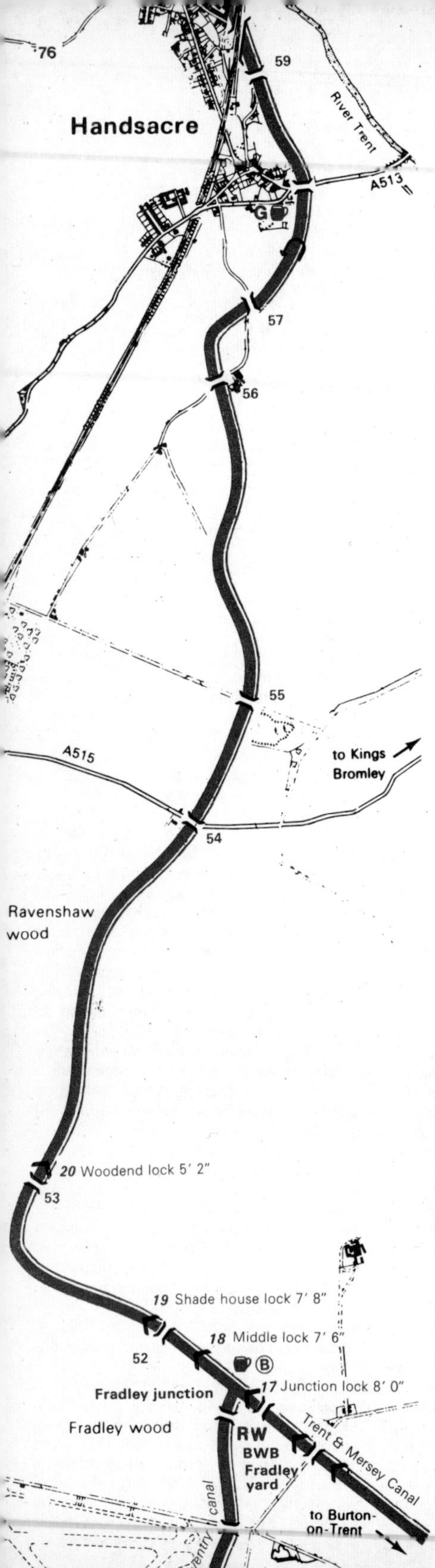

Fradley Junction

5¼ miles

Leaving the Coventry Canal at Fradley Junction, the Trent & Mersey climbs past wooded heathland and abruptly changes course from southwest to northwest, a direction it generally maintains right through to its terminus at Preston Brook, over 67 miles away. The isolated Woodend lock introduces a further stretch of woodland; beyond this the canal winds towards Armitage as the river Trent and the railway converge on either side.

Kings Bromley
Staffs. PO, tel, stores. A village 1½ miles north of bridge 54, along the A515. There are some pleasant houses and an old mill to be seen here, as well as what is reputed to have been Lady Godiva's early home. The Trent flows just beyond the church, which contains some old glass and a 17thC pulpit and font.

Fradley Junction
A canal junction that has everything: boatyard, pub, canal maintenance yard, a flight of locks and an uncaring isolation from modern roads and towns.

BOATYARDS & BWB

BWB Fradley Yard Fradley Junction. (Burton-on-Trent 790236). Sewage & refuse disposal, water, diesel. Drydock, slipway up to 20 foot, moorings. Telephone, lavatories. *Open daily throughout year.*
Swan Line Cruisers Fradley Junction Alrewas, Burton-on-Trent. (790332). Hire narrow boats. Diesel, chandlery, drydock. Boat repairs. Steel boats built & fitted out. Groceries. *Open daily throughout year.*

PUBS

Crown Handsacre. Canalside, at bridge 58. Grocer and fish & chips nearby.
Swan Fradley Junction. A true canal pub, although there are no real old boatmen calling here now.

CARAVANS & CAMPING

Woodside Caravan Park Fradley Junction. (Burton-on-Trent 790407 & Yoxhall 483). 100yds from canal. Overnight caravan stops. No tents permitted.

FISHING THE TRENT & MERSEY CANAL

Along the whole length of the Trent & Mersey Canal from Fradley Junction to Preston Brook there is often good roach fishing—although some of the competitions held along these reaches have produced disappointing weights. Other fish which are known to inhabit this canal are bream, tench, perch, pike, gudgeon and carp. The specimen hunter could find a big tench, or a double figure pike along the Trent & Mersey.
Most of the fishing is held by local clubs and Associations, and most of it is available on permit to visiting anglers who should ask local BWB staff or enquire at local tackle shops. Match and day-ticket fishing between Colwich lock and Wolseley bridge is controlled by BWB. Tickets are obtainable from the bailiff—Mr J. Bates, 12 Wolseley Close, Colwich, nr Stafford. Permits for match and day fishing on the Coventry Canal from Fradley Junction to Huddlesford Junction (4 miles away) can be obtained from the BWB at Nantwich (details on page 174).

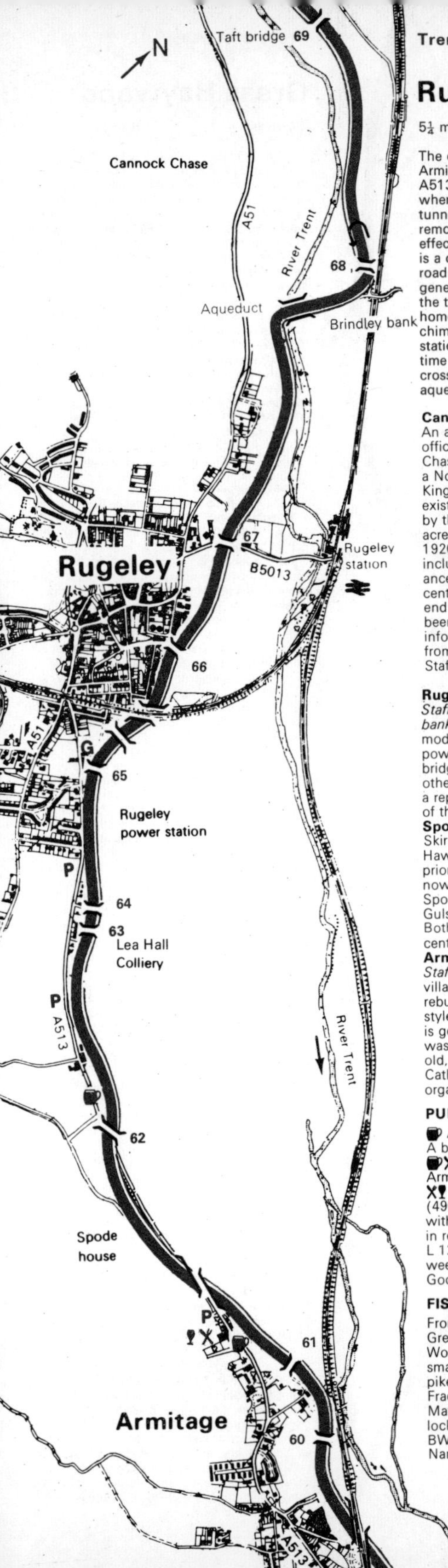

Rugeley

5¼ miles

The canal now skirts Armitage, passing the Armitage pottery and church. Then the A513 crosses the canal on a new bridge where the short (130 yards) Armitage tunnel used to run before its roof was removed in 1971 to combat the subsidence effects of coal being mined nearby. There is a distinguished restaurant just across the road here, very much a rarity on canals in general and this area in particular. West of the tunnel stands Spode House, a former home of the pottery family. The towers and chimneys of the colliery and huge power station come into view; they take a long time to recede. North of the town, the canal crosses the river Trent via a substantial aqueduct.

Cannock Chase
An area of outstanding natural beauty and officially designated as such in 1949. The Chase is all that remains of what was once a Norman hunting ground known as the King's Forest of Cannock. Much of the existing forest has been planted and tended by the Forestry Commission, about 7000 acres of land having been acquired since 1920. Flora and fauna are abundant and include a herd of fallow deer whose ancestors have grazed in this area for centuries. Shugborough Park is at the north end of the Chase. Three nature trails have been laid out in Cannock Chase: information about these may be obtained from the Head Warden, 3A Tixall road, Stafford (61967).

Rugeley
Staffs. Pop 18,000. PO, tel, stores, garage, banks, station. An unexciting place with a modern town centre and a dominating power station. There are two churches by bridge 67: one is a heap of 14thC ruins, the other is the parish church built in 1822 as a replacement. Cannock Chase rises west of the town.

Spode House
Skirted by the canal. Spode House and Hawkesyard Priory stand side by side. The priory, which is only a small community now, was founded in 1897 by Josiah Spode's grandson and his niece Helen Gulson when they lived at Spode House. Both are now used as a conference centre.

Armitage
Staffs. PO, tel, stores, garage. A main road village, whose church is interesting: it was rebuilt in the 19thC in a Saxon/Norman style, which makes it rather dark. The font is genuine Saxon, however, and the tower was built in 1690. The organ is 200 years old, and enormous: it came from Lichfield Cathedral and practically deafens the organist at Armitage.

PUBS

Ash Tree Canalside, at bridge 62. A boat club is based here. Water point.

Plum Pudding Canalside, west of Armitage. Food.

Old Farmhouse Restaurant Armitage (490353). A very popular English restaurant with many specialities ranging from pigeon in red wine to fresh lemon meringue pie. L 12.00-14.00, D 19.00-21.00 (closed at weekends). Essential to book D, no dogs. Good Food Guide since 1965.

FISHING

From Fradley Junction through Rugeley to Great Haywood Junction and the Staffs & Worcs Canal, there are plenty of generally small fish—mainly roach, bream, perch and pike. The favourite reaches are between Fradley Junction and Armitage.
Match and day fishing between Alrewas lock and Woodend lock are controlled by BWB. Permits obtainable from their Nantwich office (see page 174).

Great Haywood

5½ miles

One now enters an immensely attractive area that is full of interest. Accompanied by the river Trent, the canal moves up a narrowing valley bordered by green slopes on either side, Cannock Chase being clearly visible to the south. Wolseley Hall has gone, but Bishton Hall (now a school) still stands: its very elegant front faces the canal near Wolseley Bridge. Passing Colwich, an important railway junction, the canal reaches the perimeter of Shugborough Park: the impressive façade of the Hall can be seen across the parkland. At Great Haywood Junction the Staffs & Worcs Canal (see page 74) joins the Trent & Mersey from the west under a graceful towing path bridge. Here the Trent valley becomes much broader and more open. Hoo Mill lock is a busy spot: a boatyard stretches either side of it. North of the lock a busy road joins the hitherto quiet canal for a while. To the west is Ingestre Hall.

Great Haywood

Staffs. PO, tel, stores. Centre of the Great Haywood and Shugborough Conservation Area, the village is not particularly beautiful but is closely connected in many ways to Shugborough Park, to which it is physically linked by the very old Shugborough Bridge, where the crystal clear waters of the river Sow join the heavily polluted Trent on its way down from Stoke. Haywood lock is beautifully situated between this packhorse bridge (which is an Ancient Monument) and the unusually decorative railway bridge that leads into Trent Lane. The lane consists of completely symmetrical and very handsome terraced cottages: they were built by the Ansons to house the people evicted from the former Shugborough village.

There is an interesting-looking Roman Catholic church in Great Haywood: the other curious feature concerns the Anglican church. About 100yds south of Haywood lock is an iron bridge over the canal. This bridge, which now leads nowhere, used to carry a private road from Shugborough Hall which crossed both the river and the canal on its way to the church just east of the railway. This was important to the Ansons, since the packhorse bridge just upstream is not wide enough for a horse and carriage, and so until the iron bridge was built the family had to *walk* the 300yds to church on Sunday mornings!

Shugborough Hall

NT property. This splendid mansion is very close to the canal and should certainly be visited. The present house dates from 1693, but was substantially altered by James Stuart around 1760 and by Samuel Wyatt around the turn of the 18thC. It was at this time that the old village of Shugborough was bought up and demolished by the Anson family so that they should enjoy more privacy and space in their park. Family fortunes fluctuated greatly for the Ansons, the Earl of Lichfield's family; eventually crippling death duties in the 1960s brought about the transfer of the estate to the National Trust. The Trust have leased the property to Staffordshire County Council, who now manage the whole estate.

The house has been recently restored at great expense. There are some magnificent rooms and many treasures inside.

Museum of Staffordshire Life

This excellent establishment, which is effectively Staffordshire's county museum, is housed in the old stables adjacent to Shugborough Hall. Open since 1966, it is superbly laid out and contains all sorts of exhibits concerned with old country life in Staffordshire. Amongst other things it contains an old fashioned laundry, the old gun-room and the old estate brew-house, all completely equipped. Part of the stables contains harness, carts, coaches and motor cars. There is an industrial annexe up the road, containing a collection of preserved

steam locomotives and some industrial machinery.
House, grounds and museum open March-October, Tue-Sat 11.00-17.30, Sun 14.00-17.30. Closed Mon. (Industrial annexe open weekends only.) All enquiries to Little Haywood 388.
Access to Hall, Park and Museum: just walk across the long footbridge that straddles the Trent. Motorists have to leave their machine by the canal in Great Haywood, or must drive right round to the south side of the park.

Shugborough Park
There are some remarkable sights in the large park that encircles the Hall. Thomas Anson, who inherited the estate in 1720, enlisted in 1744 the help of his famous brother, Admiral George Anson, to beautify and improve the house and the park. And in 1762 he commissioned James Stuart, a neo-Grecian architect, to embellish the park. 'Athenian' Stuart set to with a will, and the spectacular results of his work can be seen scattered round the park. The stone monuments that he built have deservedly extravagant names like the Tower of the Winds, the Lanthorn of Demosthenes, etc.

BOATYARDS & BWB

Kingfisher Line Hoo Mill Lock, Great Haywood, Staffs. (Little Haywood 384). Hire cruisers. Petrol, gas, slipway up to 35 foot, moorings, winter storage. Boat & inboard motor repairs. Boats fitted out. *Open daily throughout year.*

Anglo Welsh Narrowboats The Canal Wharf, Mill lane, Great Haywood, Staffs. (Little Haywood 711). At Great Haywood Junction. Hire narrow boats. Sewage disposal, water, diesel. Boat & motor repairs. Lavatories. *Open daily throughout year.*

PUBS

Coach & Horses near bridge 77. Lunches and dinners. (Weston 324).
Clifford Arms Great Haywood. Bed & breakfast.
Fox & Hounds Great Haywood.
Lamb & Flag Little Haywood.
Red Lion Little Haywood.
Wolseley Arms near bridge 70.

Tixall Gatehouse, on the Staffordshire & Worcestershire canal near Great Haywood Junction.

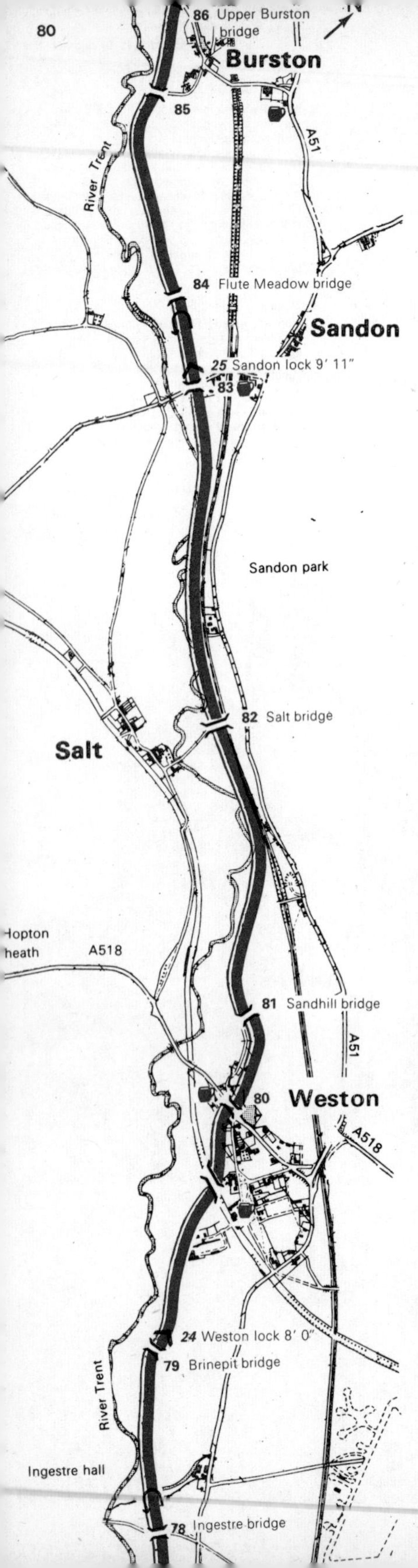

Sandon Park

4½ miles

Continuing up the Trent valley past Ingestre Hall and Park, the canal enjoys a length in which locks are few and far between. Weston (*PO, tel, stores*) is left behind and railway and main road converge as the valley narrows. The wooded Sandon Park rises steeply on the north bank; the canal passes now through quiet meadows to the little village of Burston.

Burston
Staffs. Tel. A hamlet apparently untouched by modern times, in spite of the proximity of 3 transport routes. Most of the village is set around the village pond. A very quiet place.

Sandon
Staffs. Tel. A small estate village clustered near the main gates to Sandon Park. The main road bisecting the place is enough to send any canal boatman scurrying back to the safety of the pretty Sandon lock. There is a pub, however, opposite the park gates. All Saints Church, up the hill, is 13thC to 15thC with a Norman font and a 17thC wall painting.

Sandon Park
The Jacobean house, seat of the Earl of Harrowby, is closed to the public, but the beautiful gardens covering 50 acres are open to visitors in the summer. There are several tall monumental columns in the park. Access from Sandon village. *Open Sun 14.00-19.00. Apr-Aug.*

Battle of Hopton Heath
This was fought 1½ miles west of Weston. An inconclusive Civil War battle on the 19th March 1643, it reflected the strategic importance to both sides of Stafford, only 4 miles south west of the battlefield. In the engagement, 1800 Parliamentarians met 1200 Royalists (mostly cavalry). Supported by 'Roaring Meg'—a 29-pound cannon—the Royalists took the initiative, making several bold and effective cavalry charges against the enemy. However the Roundheads' musketry fought back strongly, and after the Royalist leader (the Earl of Northampton) was killed, the Cavaliers weakened and fell back. Eventually both sides were exhausted and nightfall brought an end to the battle. Casualties—at under 200—were surprisingly light, and neither side could claim a victory. The Cavaliers returned to Stafford, but 2 months later they lost the town for good to the Roundheads.

Chartley Moss
3 miles north east of canal at Weston, off the A518. A nature reserve, rich in spiders, that is a quaking bog. The vegetation grows on a floating surface of peat that is only 10ft thick in places. Visitors' permits obtainable from The Regional Officer (Midlands), Nature Conservancy, Attingham Park, Shrewsbury, Salop. (Shrewsbury 77611/4).

Ingestre Hall
½ mile south west of bridge 78. Originally a Tudor building, the Hall was rebuilt in neo-Gothic style following a disastrous fire in 1820. The house is surrounded by large attractive gardens. Now a residential arts centre, open to visitors only on the *first Sat in July*. (Weston 225).

PUBS

Greyhound Burston.
Dog & Doublet Sandon.
Holly Bush Salt.
Access from a stile near bridge 82; then walk up the lane.
Saracen's Head Weston, by bridge 80.
Woolpack Weston.

FISHING

From Great Haywood junction to Stone there are many species, mainly roach, bream, gudgeon, pike and some tench.

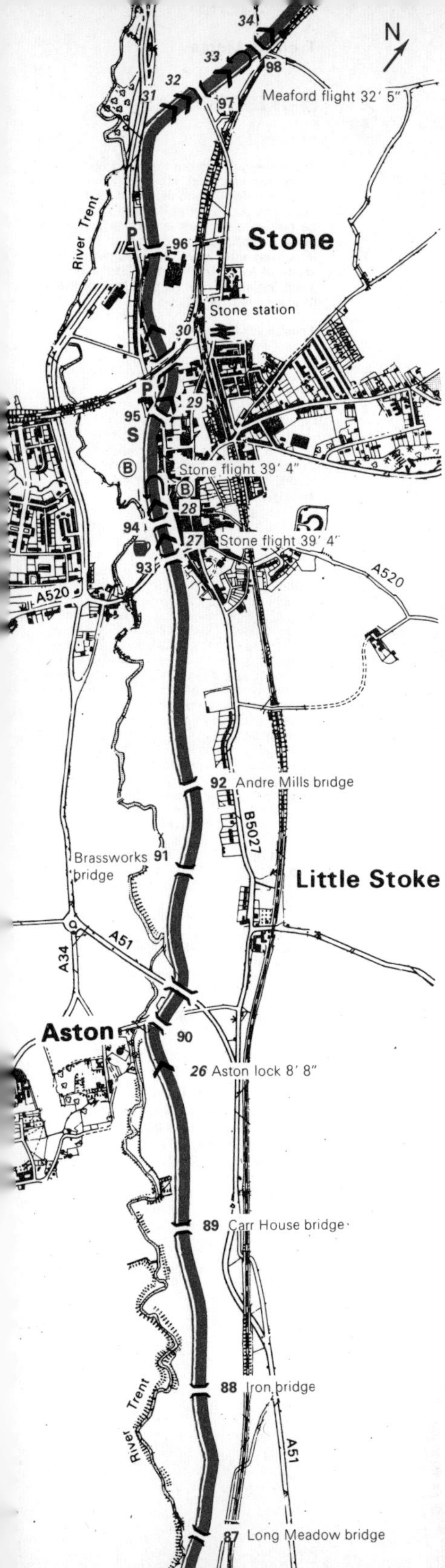

Stone

4¾ miles

The 100-year old tower of Aston church is prominent as the canal continues up through the quiet water meadows of the Trent valley. Soon Stone is entered; below the bottom lock is a good place to tie up for the night—a lockside pub and all shops are very close by. These locks are deeper than most on a narrow canal—their average rise is about 10 ft. Just above the second lock is a boatyard and 3 drydocks: there is another boatyard a few yards further on. Lock 29 is accompanied by a little tunnel under the road for boat horses. The Stone locks are followed by another flight of 4, climbing up the valley to Meaford. Here the electric railway line draws alongside.

Stone
Staffs. Pop 10,000. EC Wed, MD Tue, Thur, PO, tel, stores, garage, bank, station, cinema. A busy and pleasant town with excellent boating and shopping facilities. The old priory church began to fall down in 1749, so in 1753 an Act of Parliament was obtained to enable the parishioners to rebuild it. The new church (St Michael's in Lichfield rd) was consecrated in 1758, having cost £5000: it is a handsome building in open ground (no graves) on a slope at the east end of the town.

BOATYARDS & BWB

Stone Boatbuilding Company (Midland Luxury Cruisers) Newcastle rd, Stone, Staffs. (2688). Midway between bridges 94 and 95. Hire cruisers and narrow boats. Sewage & refuse disposal, water, diesel, petrol, gas, chandlery. Slipway up to 40 foot, moorings. Boat sales & repairs, agents for Ailsa Craig, Chrysler, Johnson, Seagull. Motor sales & repairs, agents for Dejon, Mayland, Shetland, Yamaha. Fibreglass & steel boats built & fitted out. Lavatories. *Open daily throughout year.*
Canal Cruising Stone, Staffs. (3982). Above lock 28. Hire cruisers. Diesel, gas. Drydock, winter storage. Boat & motor sales & repairs. Steel hull conversions, boats fitted out. Telephone, lavatories. *Open daily throughout year.*
J. Malkin Malkin Narrow Boats, 4 4 Monument lane, Tittensor, Stoke-on-Trent, Staffs. (Barlaston 2574). Hire cruiser (embark at Canal Cruising Company's Wharf).

PUBS

Crown & Anchor Stone.
Crown hotel High st, Stone (3535). Lunches and dinners in this establishment designed by Henry Holland in 1779.
Star Canalside, at Stone bottom lock. Apparently no 2 rooms are on the same level in this 13-room pub.

FISHING

In the Stone area carp have been stocked in several places along the canal and there are also bream, roach, pike and gudgeon—and of course eels.

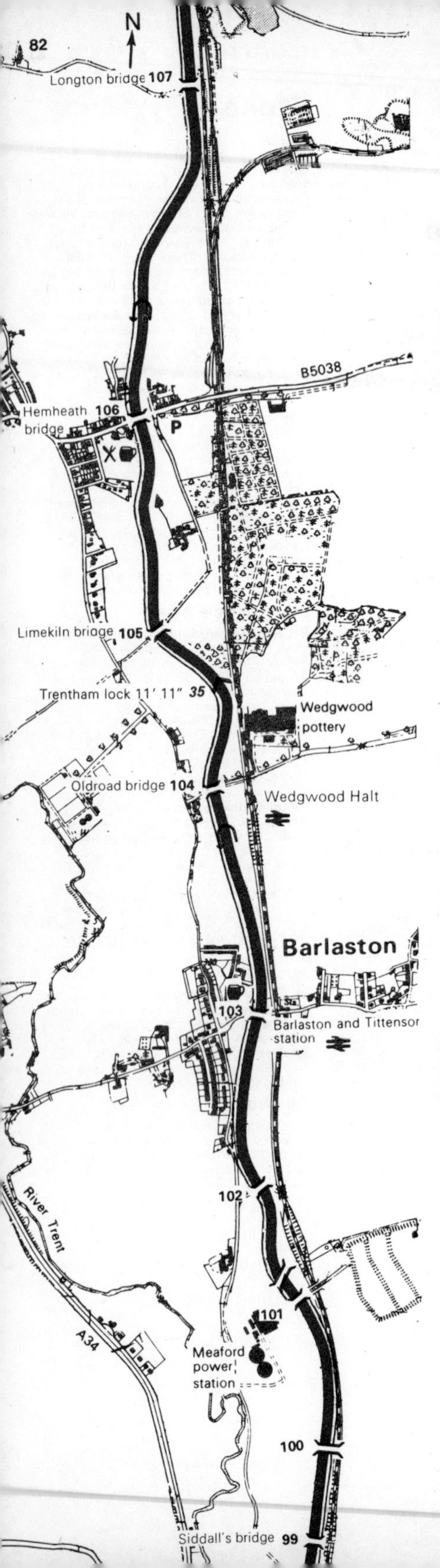

Barlaston

$4\frac{3}{4}$ miles

The valley widens out now and becomes flatter and less rural. Meaford power station and the railway flank the canal as it approaches straggling Barlaston. Just before Trentham lock is the Wedgwood pottery, set back from the canal. The factory is conveniently served by Wedgwood Halt. North of Hem Heath bridge, Stoke-on-Trent looms up with its periphery of bleak industrial wastelands.

Trentham Gardens
1 mile west of bridge 106. The Hall, which was built by Barrie and which formerly belonged to the Duke of Sutherland, was demolished in 1909 except for the ball-room and orangery. Now used as a leisure centre, the place possesses formal Italian gardens and, among other facilities, a lake for fishing and boating, an open air swimming pool, and a miniature railway. Concerts are held in the ballroom.

Wedgwood Factory
The Wedgwood Group is the largest china and earthenware manufacturer in the world. It was started in 1759 in Burslem by the famous Josiah Wedgwood, the 'Father of English Potters', who came from a small pottery family. By 1766 he was sufficiently prosperous to build a large new house and factory which he called Etruria—a name suggested by his close friend Dr Erasmus Darwin—to use the canal, of which he was a promoter, for transport. It was here that he produced his famous Jasper unglazed stoneware with white classical portraits on the surface. He revolutionised pottery making with his many innovations and after his death in 1795 the company continued to expand. In the 1930s the Wedgwoods decided to build a new factory because mining subsidence had made Etruria unsuitable. The Etruria factory has unfortunately since been demolished but the large new factory began production in 1940 in Barlaston and is still the centre of the industry, with six electric tunnel ovens which produce none of the industrial smoke that is commonly associated with the Potteries. The Wedgwood museum at Barlaston has a vast range of exhibits of Wedgwood pottery. The works is only a few yards from the canal, accessible from bridge 104.
Open: Tours of the factory, museum and shop can be arranged by contacting the Personnel Manager (Barlaston 2141). Tours Mon-Fri 10.10, 11.35, 13.45, 15.10. The tour at 15.10 is not held on Fri. Children under 12yrs are not allowed round the factory.

PUBS

Roebuck hotel (Hunting lodge restaurant) near Hem Heath bridge.

Plume of Feathers Barlaston. Canalside.

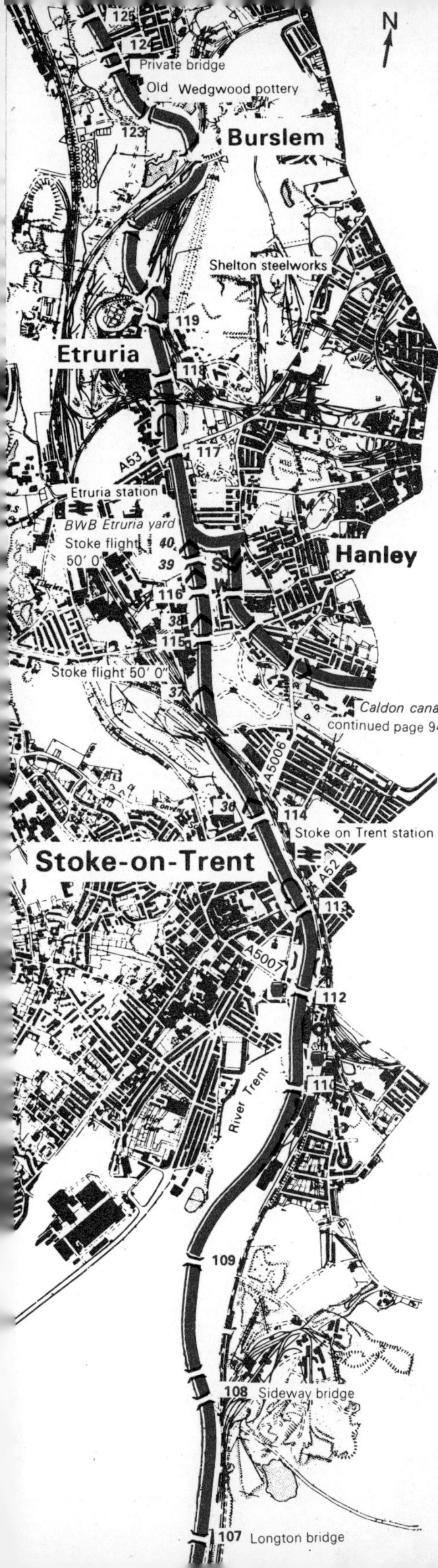

Stoke-on-Trent

5 miles

This is an intensely industrial length of canal, passing right through Stoke-on-Trent with all its factories and warehouses. The signs of the pottery industry are everywhere, like rows and rows of lavatories and washbasins ranged along the windows of Doulton's Sanitary Pottery. But the most remarkable manifestation of the industry is the 'bottle kilns'—the brick furnaces shaped like gigantic bottles about 30 feet high that still stand, cold and disused now (but, happily, to be preserved), at the side of the canal. Near Stoke-on-Trent station can be seen the remains of the canal arm to Newcastle under Lyme; what is left of the arm is now used as a boat club mooring. Unfortunately Josiah Wedgwood's original factory in Etruria no longer exists. This entire area tends to bemuse some canal travellers by its overpowering industries and total disregard for the canal that was once its lifeblood; but industrial archaeologists are not alone in enjoying seeing what is made in this proud and prosperous town and the incongruity of scenes like pleasure boats creeping through the roaring Shelton steelworks (an interesting scene at night). Note: the canal bridges in Stoke are mostly very low, with a minimum of 6ft 8ins headroom.

Stoke-on-Trent
Staffs. Pop 272,000. EC Thur, MD Wed, Fri, Sat. All services. The city was formed in 1910 from a federation of 6 towns (Burslem, Fenton, Hanley, Longton, Stoke and Tunstall) but became known as The Five Towns in the novels of Arnold Bennett. The thriving pottery and coal industries are the source of the city's great prosperity, but they also brought in their wake their inevitable dirt and ugliness. Many of the pottery factories have in recent years been dealing with the problem and are open to the public for visits by prior arrangement *(for details contact the Citizens' Advice Bureau, 46 Marsh st, Hanley: Stoke-on-Trent 29427)*. One to visit is the famous Spode China works which is right in the centre of the town in Church st. The Town Hall in Glebe st is an imposing and formal 19thC building. Opposite the Town Hall is the parish church of St Peter, a 19thC structure in Perpendicular style which contains a commemorative plaque to Josiah Wedgwood, who is also remembered in the bronze statue that welcomes visitors at the station.

City Museum and Art Gallery Broad st, Hanley (Stoke-on-Trent 22714). As one might expect, it contains one of the world's most outstanding collections of ceramics including work from Egypt, Persia, China, Greece and Rome. The historical development of pottery manufacture in Stoke-on-Trent is also traced from Roman times to the present day. *Open weekdays 10.00-18.00. Sun 14.30-17.00.*

BOATYARDS & BWB

BWB Etruria Yard at junction with Caldon Canal. (Stoke-on-Trent 25597). Water, sewage disposal, lavatory.

PUBS

Obviously there are plenty near the canal. But 3 where reasonable moorings are nearby are:

Bridge Etruria, by Wedgwood factory site.

Red Lion near bridge 112 (moor south of bridge). Extravagantly decorated externally.

Dolphin Canalside, by bridge 110.

FISHING

In and around Stoke-on-Trent the canal has been stocked heavily with thousands of good quality fish by the local angling clubs. The re-stocking programmes have included bream and roach, and some carp have also been released.

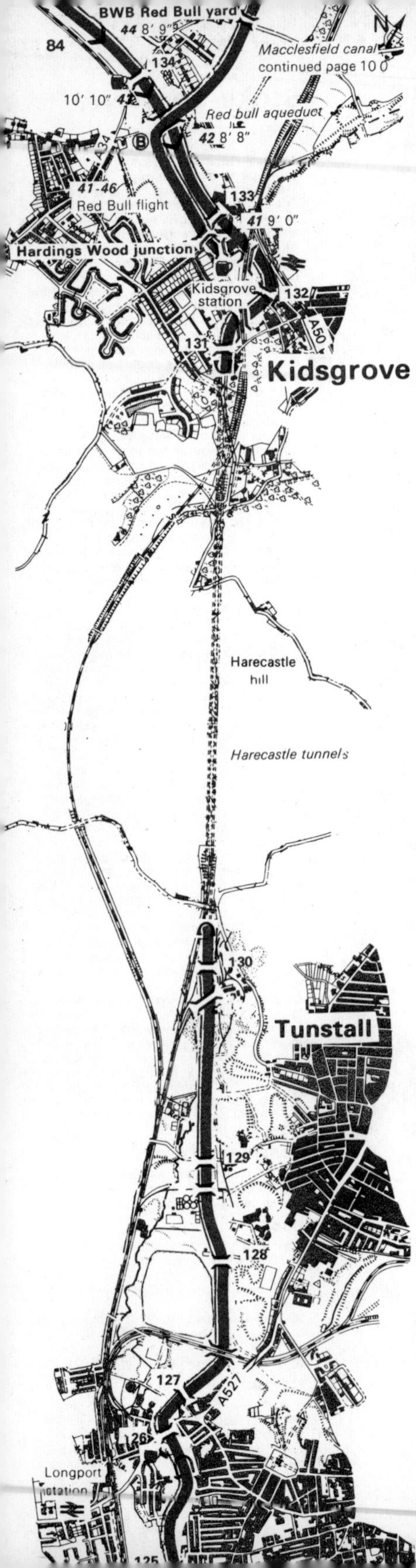

Harecastle Hill

5 miles

The canal continues for a while through a heavily industrial area mostly connected with the pottery business and its needs. Before long the navigation abandons its very twisting course and makes a beeline for Harecastle Hill and the tunnels through it. (The odd colour of the water here is caused by local ironstone strata.) Only one of the tunnels is navigable now. The tunnel is too long to see through, so no boat may proceed through it in either direction until the boat crew has reported to the tunnel keeper and perused the instructions at the entrance. (See navigational note below.) At the north end of the tunnel, the navigation passes Kidsgrove station: just beyond it is Harding's Wood Junction with the Macclesfield Canal where there are 2 pubs and a grocer. The Trent & Mersey proceeds to descend from the summit level through a flight of paired narrow locks. Just below the second lock, the Macclesfield Canal crosses to T & M on Red Bull Aqueduct. By now the industrial built-up area of the Potteries is being rapidly replaced by pleasant countryside.

Kidsgrove
Staffs. Pop 22,000. All services. Originally a big iron and coal producing town, Kidsgrove was much helped in its growing size and prosperity by the completion of the Trent & Mersey Canal, which gave the town an outlet for these goods. James Brindley is buried in the town in a churchyard at Newchapel.
St Saviour's church Butt Lane. This building is unusual in looking quite unlike a church. Built in 1878, it was designed in black and white Tudor style.
The three Harecastle tunnels
There are altogether 3 parallel tunnels through Harecastle Hill. The first, built by James Brindley, was completed in 1777, after 11 years work. To build a 9ft wide tunnel 1¾ miles long represented engineering on a scale quite unknown to the world at that time, and the world was duly impressed.
Since there was no towpath in the tunnel the boats—which were of course all towed from the bank by horses in those days—had to be 'legged' through by men lying on the boat's cabin roof and propelling the boat by 'walking' along the tunnel roof. (The towing horse would have to be walked in the meantime over the top of the hill.) This very slow means of propulsion, combined with the great length of the narrow tunnel and the large amount of traffic on the navigation, made Harecastle a major bottleneck for canal boats. So in 1822 the Trent & Mersey Canal Company called in Thomas Telford, who recommended that a second tunnel be constructed alongside the first one. This was done: the new tunnel was completed in 1827, with a towpath, after only 3 years work. Each tunnel then became one-way until in the 20thC Mr Brindley's bore had sunk so much from mining subsidence that it had to be abandoned. An electric tug was introduced in 1914 to speed up traffic through Telford's tunnel; this service was continued until 1954.
The 3rd tunnel through Harecastle Hill was built years after the other two, and carried the Stoke–Kidsgrove railway line. It runs 40ft above the canal tunnels and is slightly shorter. This tunnel was closed in the 1960s: the railway line now goes round the hill and through a much shorter tunnel. Thus 2 out of the 3 Harecastle tunnels are disused.
Navigational note
A tunnel keeper is on duty at each end of the tunnel from April to October, 5 days a week, from 8.00 to 17.00. Boat crews wishing to go through during these hours should call at the tunnel keeper's lobby: he will telephone through to the other end to see if the way is clear.
At weekends in summer, when the tunnel

keepers are off duty, northbound boats should enter the tunnel between dawn and 11.00; southbound boats should enter between 13.00 and dusk.
Boats should not go through at night: if they meet anyone else doing the same thing, they may have to reverse for up to a mile in pitch darkness. Any boats wishing to go through outside the summer season may find no tunnel keepers in attendance, so they should telephone the Section Inspector at Etruria top lock (Stoke-on-Trent 25597) in advance.
Boats should take care when in the tunnel itself. Subsidence has lowered considerable lengths of it and restricted the headroom drastically. A loading gauge at each end will show whether any particular boat will get through. The other slight obstacle is that Mr Telford's splendid towpath has sunk—along with everything else—and this can present a hazard. However the towpath is now gradually being taken out by BWB engineering staff to allow boats to pass centrally beneath the tunnel roof where there is the maximum headroom. Not surprisingly, unpowered boats are not allowed to enter Harecastle tunnel.

BOATYARDS & BWB

BWB Red Bull Yard north of bridge 134. Water, sewage disposal, toilets.
David Piper Red Bull Basin, Church Lawton, Stoke-on-Trent, Staffs. (Kidsgrove 4754). On Macclesfield canal. Diesel, slipway up to 60 foot, moorings, winter storage. Boat & motor sales & repairs. Steel boats built & fitted out. Lavatory.

PUBS

Red Bull Canalside, in the Red Bull flight of locks.
Blue Bell at junction with Macclesfield Canal.
Canal Tavern opposite the Blue Bell.
Bridgewater Arms near bridge 126.

The northern entrance to Telford's Harecastle New Tunnel. (Brindley's earlier tunnel, now abandoned, is to the right).

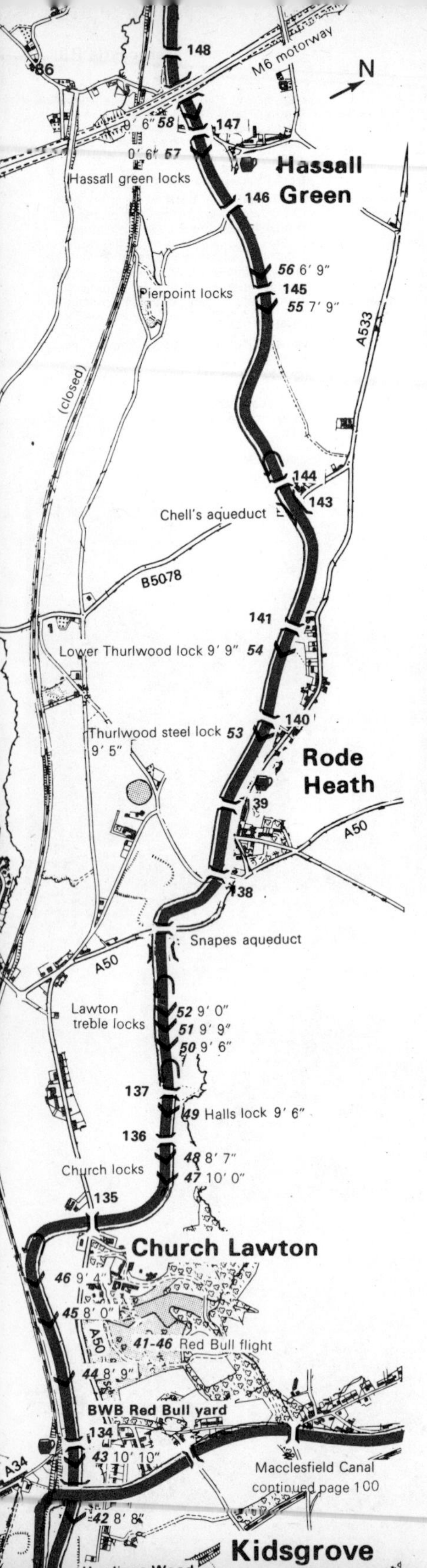

Rode Heath

5¼ miles

Leaving behind the spire of Church Lawton, the canal continues to fall through a heavily locked stretch. The countryside is entirely rural and pleasant, slightly hilly and wooded. Two minor aqueducts are encountered, but the locks are more interesting: they are all pairs of narrow locks, side by side. The interconnecting paddle between the locks was installed so that one lock could act as a 'side-pond' to the other—an ingenious water-saving device which also speeded trade. Some of the duplicate locks are unusable or even filled in, but many of them are in good condition, so that a boatman can choose whichever lock is set for him. One of the strangest locks on the whole canal system is Thurlwood Steel lock, a gigantic affair with a massive steel superstructure, constructed in 1957 to combat local brine-pumping subsidence. There is a conventional lock adjoining, which is considerably easier to use. At Hassall Green a canalside *PO, tel and stores* can be found just by the new concrete bridge. The M6 motorway crosses nearby.

Rode Heath
PO, tel, stores. A useful shopping area approachable from bridge 139.

BOATYARDS & BWB

BWB Red Bull Yard north of bridge 134. Water, sewage disposal, lavatory.

PUBS

Romping Donkey Hassall Green. A pretty country pub.

Broughton Arms Rode Heath. Canalside.

FISHING

From Harding's Wood junction to Middlewich there is good general coarse fishing, with fair roach, some bream and tench, and the occasional carp. Roach to 2lb have been caught, and bream to around 3lb.

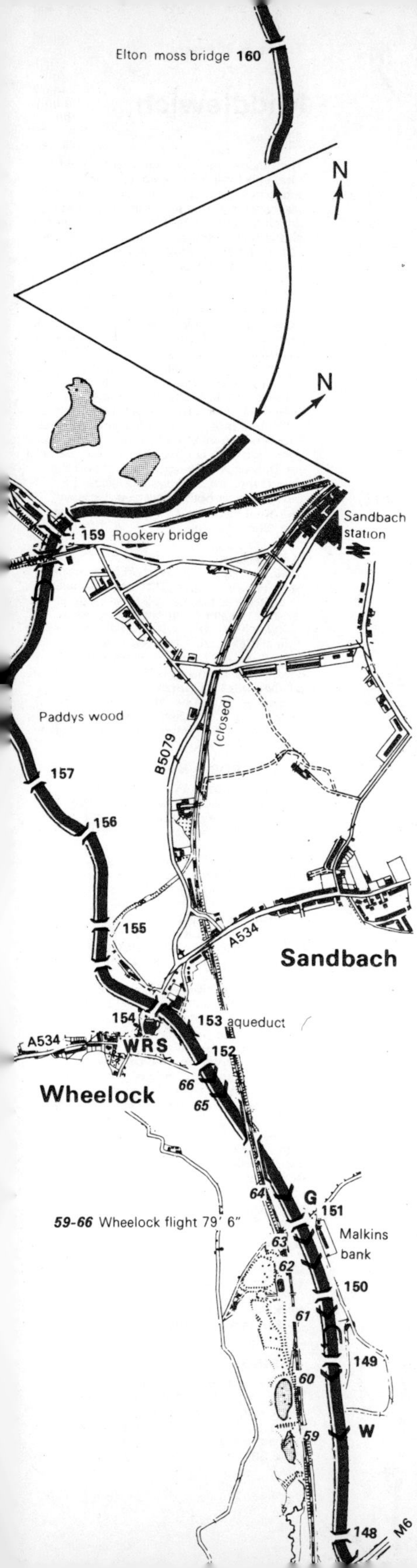

Wheelock

$4\frac{1}{2}$ miles

The canal now descends the Wheelock flight of 8 locks, which are the last paired locks one sees when travelling northwards. The countryside continues to be quiet and unspoilt but unspectacular. The pair of locks halfway down the flight has a curious situation in the little settlement of Malkin's Bank: overlooked on each side by terraced houses, the boatman can get the distinct feeling that his lock operating routine is a very public performance. At the bottom of the flight is the village of Wheelock: west of here the navigation curls round the side of a hill before entering the very long-established salt-producing area that is based on Middlewich. The 'wild' brine pumping and rock-salt mining that has gone on hereabouts has resulted in severe local subsidence: the effect on the canal has been to necessitate the constant raising of the banks as lengths of the canal bed sink. This of course means that the affected lengths tend to be much deeper than ordinary canals. Non-swimmers beware of falling overboard.

Sandbach
Ches. Pop 11,700. EC Tue, MD Thur. PO, tel, stores, garage, bank, station. $1\frac{1}{2}$ miles N of Wheelock. An old market town that has maintained its charm despite the steady growth of its salt and chemical industries.
Ancient Crosses In the cobbled market place on a massive base stand two superb Saxon crosses, believed to commemorate the conversion of the area to Christianity in the 7thC. They suffered severely in the 17thC when the Puritans, who were totally unamused by religious trappings, broke them up and scattered the fragments for miles. After years of searching for the parts, George Ormerod succeeded in re-erecting the crosses in 1816, with new stone replacing the missing fragments.
St Mary's Church High st. A large, 16thC church with a handsome battlemented tower. The most interesting features of the interior are the 17thC carved roof and the fine chancel screen.
The Old Hall Hotel An outstanding example of Elizabethan half-timbered architecture, which was formerly the home of the lord of the manor, but is now used as an hotel. (Sandbach 3757).

Wheelock
Ches. EC Tue. PO, tel, stores, garage. Busy little main road village on the canal.

PUBS

- **Cheshire Cat** Wheelock. Canalside.
- **Nag's Head** Wheelock.

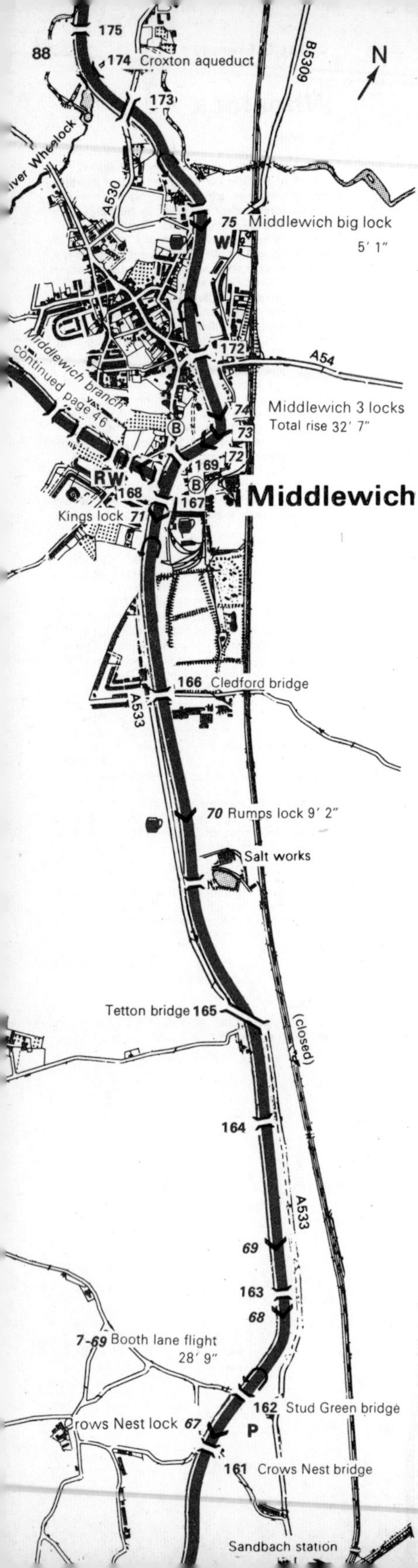

Middlewich

4¾ miles

The navigation now begins to lose the rural character it has enjoyed since Kidsgrove. Falling through yet more locks, the canal is joined by a busy main road which accompanies it into increasingly flat and industrialised landscape, past several salt works and into Middlewich, where a branch of the Shropshire Union leads off westwards towards that canal at Barbridge. (See page 46.) The Trent & Mersey skirts the centre of the town, passing through 3 consecutive narrow locks and arriving at a wide (14ft) lock (which has suffered from subsidence) with a pub beside it. This used to represent the beginning of a wide, almost lock-free navigation right through to Preston Brook, Manchester and Wigan (very convenient for the salt industry when it shipped most of its goods by boat), but Croxton Aqueduct had to be replaced many years ago, and is now a steel structure only 8ft 2ins wide. The aqueduct crosses the river Dane, which flows alongside the navigation as both water courses leave industrial Middlewich and move out into fine open country.

Middlewich
Ches. Pop 8000. EC Wed. PO, tel, stores, bank, garage. A town that since Roman times has been dedicated to salt extraction. Most of the salt produced here goes to various chemical industries. Subsidence from salt extraction has prevented redevelopment for many years, but a big new renewal scheme is now in progress.
St. Michael's Church A handsome mediaeval church which was a place of refuge for the Royalists during the Civil War. It has a fine interior with richly carved woodwork.

BOATYARDS & BWB

Andersen Boats Wych House lane, Middlewich, Ches. At Middlewich 3 locks. Refuse disposal, water, diesel, gas, chandlery, slipway up to 40 foot. Boat sales & repairs, motor sales & repairs, agents for Evinrude & Selva. Steel boats built & fitted out. Grocery and gift shop. Lavatories. *Open daily throughout year.*
Olympus Narrowboats Wych House lane, Middlewich, Ches. (061 225 2561) At Middlewich 3 locks. Hire cruisers & narrow boats. Same firm as Andersen Boats.
Willow Wren Kearns Canal Terrace, Lewin st, Middlewich, Ches. (2460). At bridge 169. Narrow boats and a 12 berth camping boat for hire. Sewage & refuse disposal, water, diesel, petrol, gas, chandlery. Drydock, moorings, boat repairs. Lavatories. *Open daily throughout summer, closed winter Suns.*
Kings Lock Boatyard Booth lane, Middlewich, Ches. (Middlewich 3234 or Crewe 55914 in the evening). At junction with Middlewich branch. Dustbins, diesel, gas chandlery. Moorings & winter storage. Boat & motor repairs. Steel boats built & fitted out. Telephone, lavatories. *Open daily throughout summer, closed some winter Suns.*

PUBS

Big Lock Middlewich. Canalside.
Cheshire Cheese Lewin st. Middlewich. Food.
Kings Lock Middlewich. Canalside.
Kinderton Arms Close to canal 1 mile S of Middlewich.

FISHING

For fishing in the Shropshire Union Canal and local rivers contact Mr C. Clare, Kings Lock, Middlewich. For general information on match fishing and fishing from boats contact BWB at Nantwich: details on page 38.

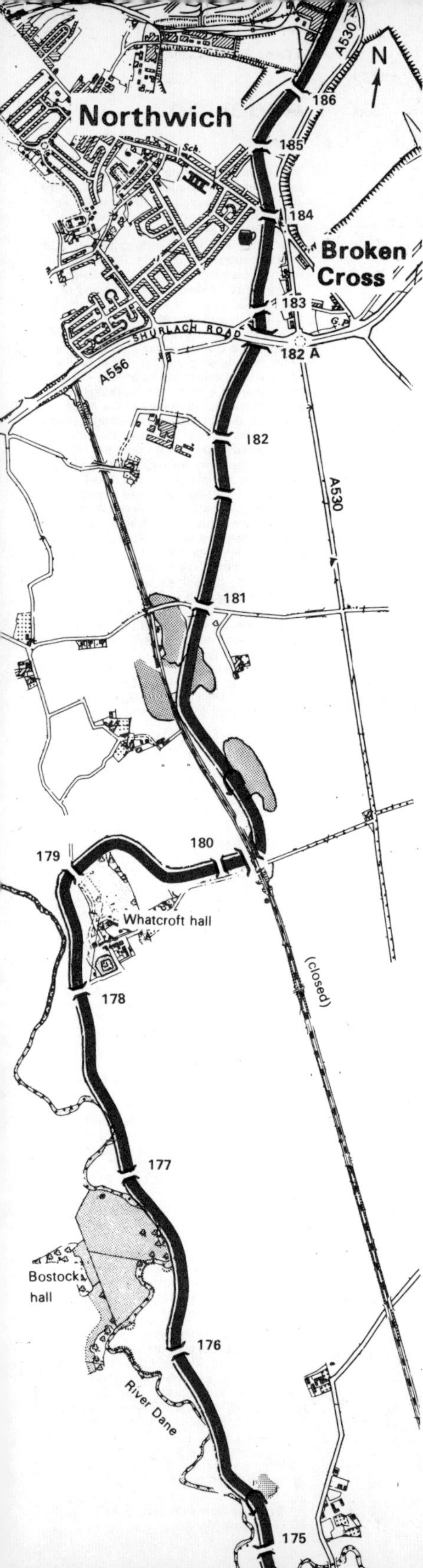

Dane Valley

$5\frac{1}{2}$ miles

Initially, this is a stretch of canal as beautiful as any in the country. Often overhung by trees, the navigation winds along the side of a hill as it follows the delightful valley of the river Dane. The parkland on the other side of the valley encompasses Bostock Hall, a school for subnormal children.

At Whatcroft Hall (privately owned), the canal circles around to the east, passing under a derelict railway before heading for Northwich and shedding its beauty and solitude once again as it re-enters a semi-industrial area. The outlying canal settlement of Broken Cross acts as a buffer between these two very different lengths of canal.

Note: There are several privately-owned wide 'lagoons' caused by subsidence along this section of the Trent & Mersey, in some of which repose the hulks of abandoned barges and narrowboats. Navigators should be wary of straying off the main line, since the offside canal bank is often submerged and invisible just below the water level.

For notes on Northwich see page 118.

PUBS

Old Broken Cross Canalside, at bridge 184. An attractive old canal pub.

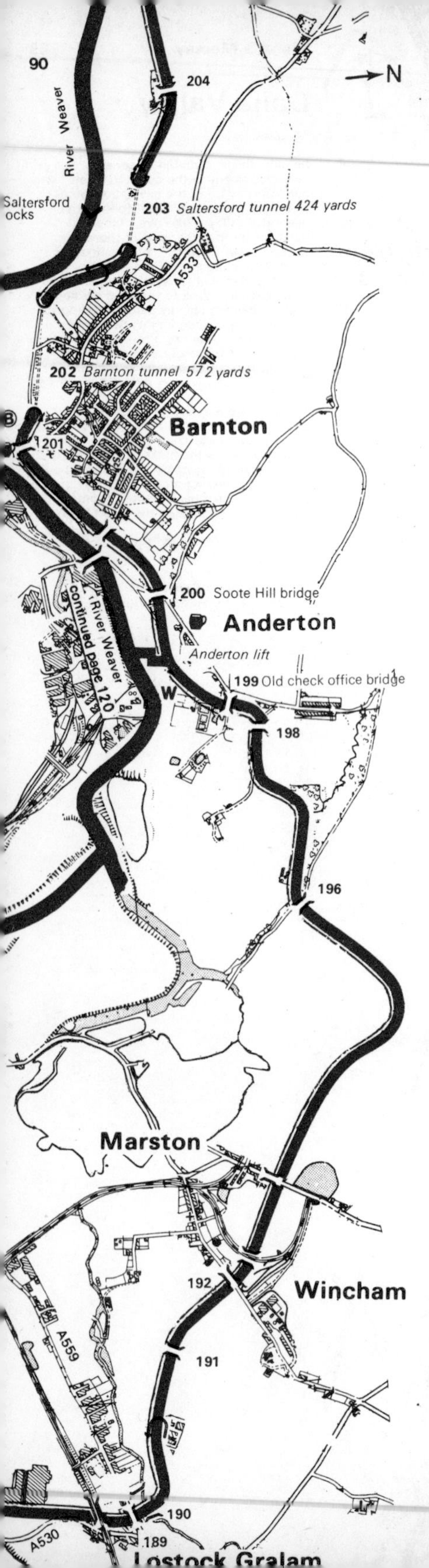

River Weaver continued page 120

Anderton

5½ miles

This is another length in which salt mining has determined the nature of the scenery. Part of it is heavily industrial, with enormous I.C.I. works dominating the scene; much of it is devastated but rural (just), some of it is nondescript, and some of it is superb countryside. Donkey engines can still be seen in surrounding fields pumping brine. Leaving the vicinity of Lostock Gralam and the outskirts of Northwich, one passes Marston and Wincham (*PO, tel, stores*). Just west of the village, one travels along a ½ mile stretch of canal that was only cut in 1958, as the old route was about to collapse into—needless to say—underground salt workings. Beyond a short wooded embankment is Anderton (*PO, tel, stores*)—the short entrance canal to the famous boat lift down into the Weaver Navigation is on the left. The main line continues westward, winding along what is now a steep hill and into Barnton Tunnel. At the west end one emerges onto a hillside overlooking the river Weaver, with a marvellous view straight down the huge Saltersford Locks. Now Saltersford Tunnel is entered: beyond it, one finds oneself in completely open country again. Henceforth, the salt extraction industry can be safely forgotten.

Anderton may soon benefit from the construction here of an exciting new Museum of Inland Navigation. This will house (floating) canal boats of many types, as well as all kinds of exhibits concerned with canals, their construction, operation and traditions.

Anderton Lift
An amazing and enormous piece of machinery built in 1875 by Leader Williams (later Engineer of the Manchester Ship Canal) to connect the Trent & Mersey to the flourishing Weaver Navigation, 50ft below. As built, the lift consisted of 2 water-filled tanks counterbalancing each other in a vertical slide, resting on massive hydraulic rams. It worked on the very straightforward principle that making the ascending tank slightly lighter—by pumping a little water out—would assist the hydraulic rams (which were operated by a steam engine and pump) in moving both tanks, with boats in them, up or down their respective slide.
In 1908 the lift had to have major repairs, so it was modernised at the same time. The troublesome hydraulic rams were done away with; from then on each tank—which contained 250 tons of water—had its own counterweights and was independent of the other tank. Electricity replaced steam as the motive power.
The lift is still fully operational. One of the most fascinating individual features of the canal system, it draws thousands of sightseers every year. *It is open for boats Mon-Fri 8.00-16.30, Sat 8.00-10.30. (Charge £2 per single trip, £3 return.) Maximum beam 15ft. Also open on Sundays by prior arrangement.* Telephone Northwich 75252.

Marston
Ches. Tel. A salt-producing village, suffering badly from its own industry. The numerous gaps in this village are presumably caused by the demolition or collapse of houses affected by subsidence. Waste ground abounds.

BOATYARDS & BWB
Olympus Leisure Cruising Tunnel Wharf, Barnton, Tunnel End, Northwich, Ches. Hire cruisers, camping boats and day hire. Water, refuse, petrol, gas. Boats operate from yard near Barnton Tunnel. Enquiries to 39 George St, Manchester. (061-228 2561).

PUBS
Red Lion Barnton, just east of bridge 201.
Stanley Arms Anderton, near the lift.
New Inn Marston.

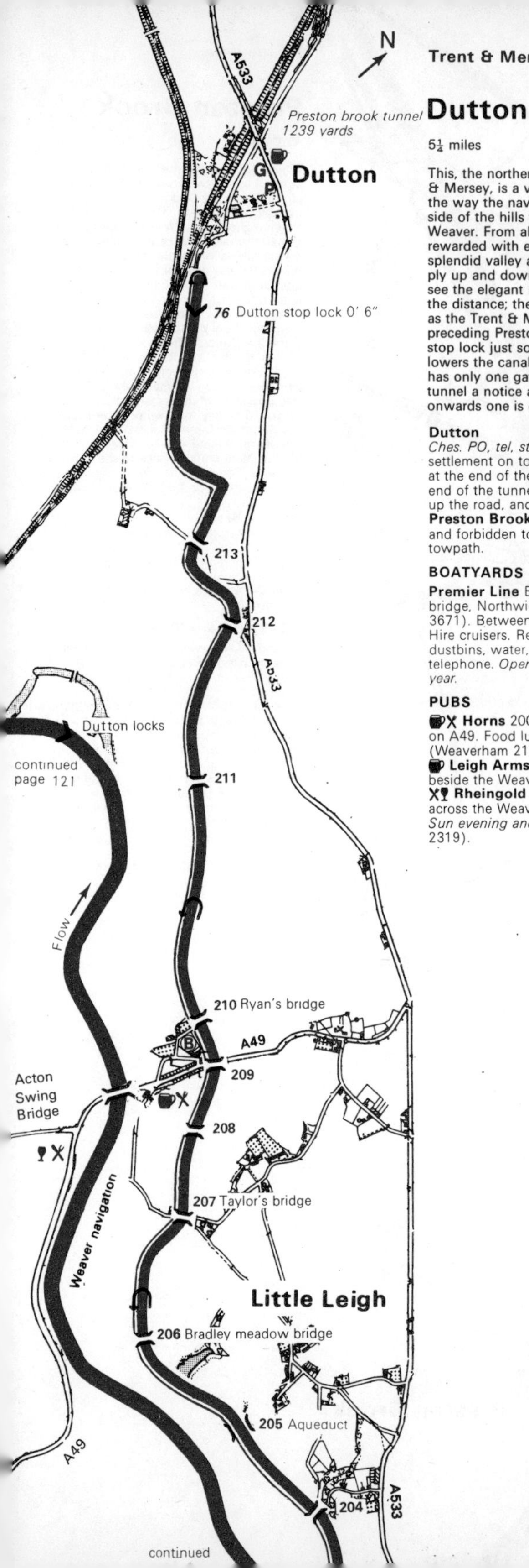

Dutton

5¼ miles

This, the northernmost stretch of the Trent & Mersey, is a very pleasant one. Most of the way the navigation follows the south side of the hills that overlook the river Weaver. From about 60ft up, one is often rewarded with excellent views of this splendid valley and the large vessels that ply up and down it. At one point one can see the elegant Dutton railway viaduct in the distance; then the 2 waterways diverge as the Trent & Mersey enters the woods preceding Preston Brook Tunnel. There is a stop lock just south of the tunnel, which lowers the canal level by a mere 6ins: it has only one gate. At the north end of the tunnel a notice announces that from here onwards one is on the Bridgewater Canal.

Dutton
Ches. PO, tel, stores, garage. Small settlement on top of Preston Brook tunnel, at the end of the lane uphill from the south end of the tunnel. There is a large hospital up the road, and a pub.
Preston Brook tunnel 1239 yards long and forbidden to unpowered craft. No towpath.

BOATYARDS & BWB

Premier Line Bartington Wharf, Acton bridge, Northwich, Ches. (Weaverham 3671). Between bridges 210 and 209. Hire cruisers. Refuse & sewage disposal, dustbins, water, diesel. Groceries, telephone. *Open daily throughout the year.*

PUBS

Horns 200 yards south of bridge 209, on A49. Food lunchtime and evenings. (Weaverham 2192).
Leigh Arms ¼ mile south of bridge 209, beside the Weaver. Sandwiches.
Rheingold Restaurant Acton bridge, across the Weaver. Meals served *except Sun evening and all Mon.* (Weaverham 2319).

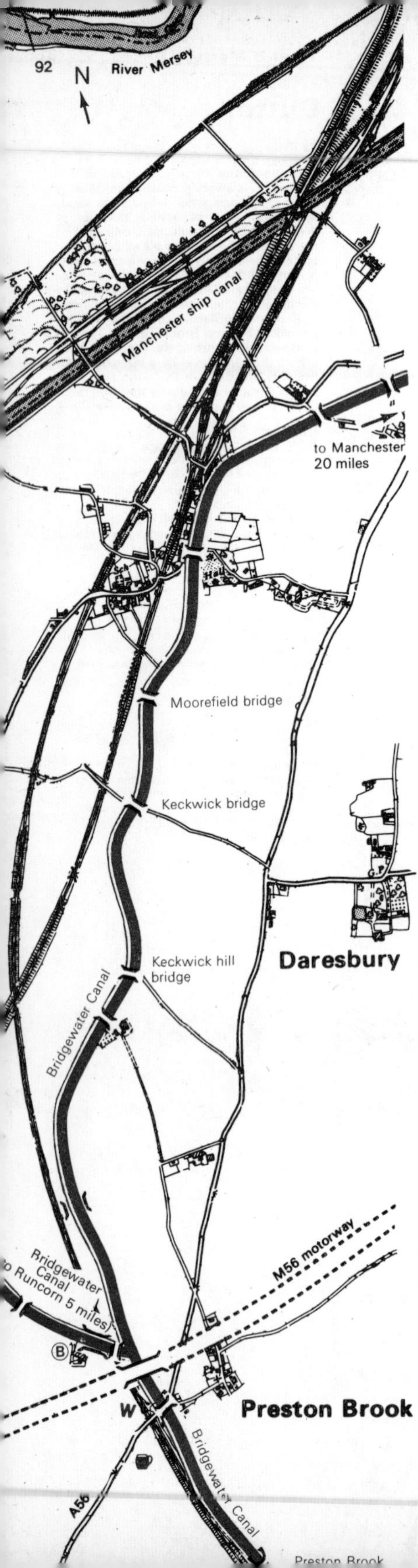

Preston Brook

4¼ miles

Emerging from the north end of Preston Brook Tunnel, the Trent & Mersey flows straight into the Bridgewater Canal, with no obvious junction. This is in fact the Preston Brook branch of the Bridgewater Canal: the main line of the canal is met ¾ mile further on, at the new motorway bridge. To the west of the junction is an aqueduct over the railway; beyond it is a large boatyard. 5 miles further is the terminus of the Bridgewater Canal at Runcorn, now unfortunately a dead end since the Runcorn & Weston Canal was closed in 1966 and its flight of locks filled in. The other way—northwards along the Bridgewater Canal—leads in a long lock-free pound to Manchester, Leigh and Wigan. One day this will provide access up the Rochdale Canal to a restored Ashton Canal and thence—via the Peak Forest and Macclesfield canals—back to the Trent & Mersey. (See page 171 for a map showing canal connections from Preston Brook.)

Preston Brook
Ches. Tel, stores. A settlement that is apparently left breathless by the various lines of transport that plough through it. The railway, now being electrified, is the main West Coast line from London to Glasgow.

BOATYARDS & BWB

Inland Waterway Holiday Cruises
Preston Brook, Runcorn, Ches. (Aston 376). On Bridgewater Canal. Dustbins, water, diesel, petrol, gas, chandlery, drydock, slipway up to 25 foot, moorings, winter storage, boat & motor repairs. Boats fitted out. Telephone. Pairs of full-sized 'hotel boats' run by this firm cruise the canals in summer, picking-up passengers all over the system. 12 berth camping barge and 48 passenger excursion narrowboat also available for hire. *Open daily throughout year.*

PUBS

Red Lion Preston Brook. 100yds W of the bridge.

N
River Mersey
Manchester ship canal
to Manchester 20 miles
Moorefield bridge
Keckwick bridge
Keckwick hill bridge
Daresbury
Bridgewater Canal
Bridgewater Canal to Runcorn 5 miles
M56 motorway
Preston Brook
A56
Bridgewater Canal

Caldon

Maximum dimensions

Length: 72′
Beam: 7′
Headroom: 6′ 6″

Mileage

Caldon Canal
Etruria Top Lock (Trent & Mersey Canal) to
Hanley: 2 miles, 3 locks
Foxley: 4½ miles, 3 locks
Stockton Brook Summit: 7 miles, 9 locks
Hazelhurst Junction (Leek Branch):
9½ miles, 9 locks
Leek terminus: 12¼ miles, 9 locks
Cheddleton flint mills: 11½ miles, 12 locks
Froghall terminus: 17½ miles, 17 locks

The Caldon Canal—or, more correctly, the Caldon Branch of the Trent & Mersey Canal—was designed as an outlet for the Caldon limestone quarries near Froghall on to the canal system. It was opened as a single branch to Froghall in 1779, tramways being constructed to bring the vast quantities of limestone down from Caldon Low quarries a couple of miles to the east. Froghall became a very busy terminus. 18 years later the Caldon's owners, the Trent & Mersey Canal Company, decided to build a secondary branch from the Caldon Canal to Leek, the main purpose of the extension being to use the line as a feeder from their new reservoir at Rudyard. The fact that the feeders from Rudyard had to enter the summit level of the canal, and the later advent of the railway, brought about significant changes in the layout of the canal between Endon and Hazelhurst, resulting in the curious 'cross-over' junction that exists at Denford today.

In 1811 yet another branch was completed from Froghall down the Churnet Valley for 13 miles to Uttoxeter. This branch was shortlived, however. In 1845 a railway line was built, much of the track using the canal bed. One can still trace the remaining sections of the Uttoxeter branch near the railway.

The limestone from Froghall remained the chief commodity carried on the Caldon Canal for years. With its 17 locks and roundabout route the Caldon must have been an obvious target for railway competitors. However, the canal, with the rest of the Trent & Mersey, was owned by a railway company (the North Staffordshire Railway) from the 1840s onward, so presumably the NSR saw no point in competing against itself.

But at the beginning of the 20thC a new railway line was eventually opened and inevitably canal traffic slumped badly. After that time the canal gradually deteriorated until it became more or less unnavigable in the early 1960s.

Since then, the Caldon Canal Society has been formed to lead the struggle to reopen the canal; public interest has grown and local authorities have recognised the great recreational potential of this beautiful canal for the thousands of people living in the nearby Potteries. Much has already been achieved in the way of essential works by BWB and volunteer efforts: the canal can now be navigated by shallow-draught boats from Etruria to Leek. The main line from Hazelhurst Locks down to Froghall Basin is still closed, but happily its future as a fully navigable waterway for pleasure boats is now more or less secure; for early in 1972 agreement was reached between Stoke City Council, Staffordshire County Council and the British Waterways Board to restore this 8-mile section of the canal. This will represent a splendid addition to the cruising network, and a much-needed 'linear park' for the Potteries.

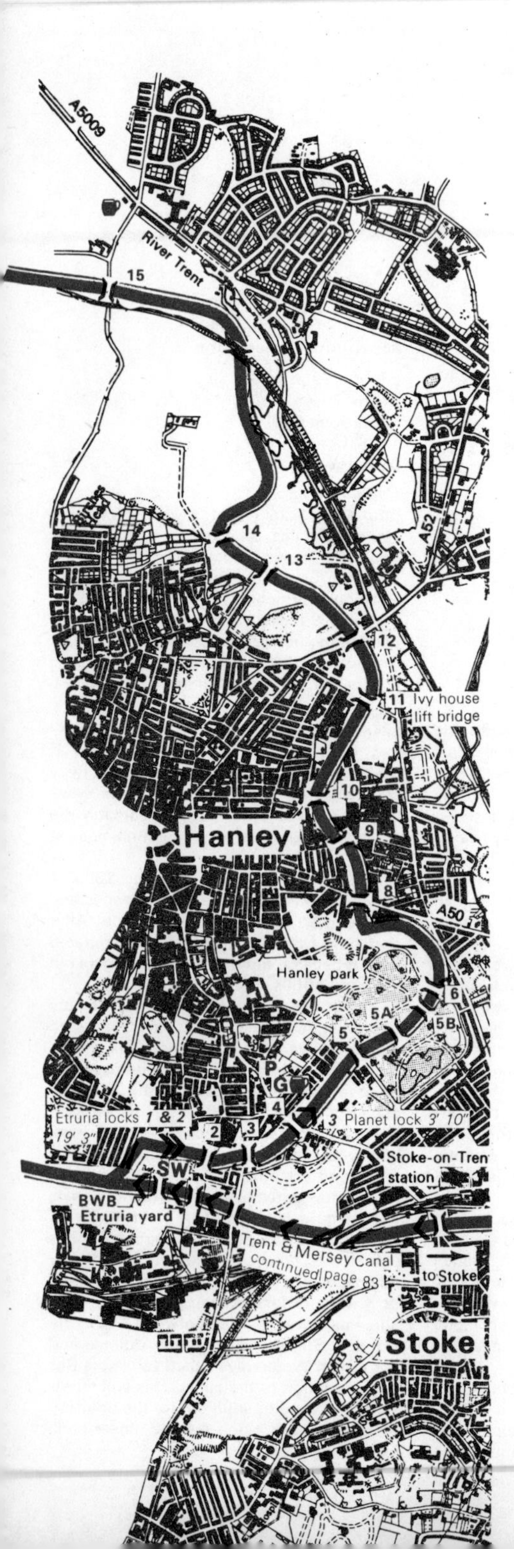

Hanley

4 miles

The Caldon branch of the Trent & Merse Canal leaves the main line at Etruria top lock, negotiating a series of amazing loop and turns that leave one wondering wher the canal will go to next. The first 2 locks up are 'staircase' locks—the only ones in north Staffordshire: they are set in an urba wasteland. All around, the little hills and valleys are crowded with terraced houses and factory chimneys. Planet Lock is soor reached; shops and pubs are close by. No one passes through Hanley Park with its meticulously kept flower beds, lawns and bowling greens; east of the park, the cana twists round the built-up hillside that is topped by Hanley. As industrial stretches go, this is an interesting one, for several 'bottle' kilns still stand near the navigatior and the 'Milton Maid' is usually moored along here. This eccentric-looking steel catamaran was specially built to carry pottery along the canal to Milton: the firm that operates it finds it substantially cheap and safer than shifting the fragile goods b road (and is therefore presently expandinc its fleet). It is ironic to reflect that Josiah Wedgwood used precisely the same argument when supporting the proposed construction of the Trent & Mersey Canal over 200 years ago.

Hanley
Staffs. All services. Hanley is one of the si towns that were amalgamated in 1910 to form the present Stoke-on-Trent. It has been modernised and redeveloped as the shopping and business centre of the distri There is a rather unusual circular building housing Lewis's store, with a striking statue 'Fire' by David Wynne. Arnold Bennett was born here in 1867. Stoke Cit Museum and Art Gallery is in Broad stree Hanley. (See page 83.)

BOATYARDS & BWB

BWB Etruria Yard at junction with Tren & Mersey Canal. (Stoke-on-Trent 25597). Water, sewage disposal, lavatory.

FISHING THE CALDON CANAL

Along the Caldon Canal, all the way from Stoke to Froghall basin, there are most of the usual coarse fish, including roach, bream, tench, gudgeon, pike—and some carp which have been recently introduced

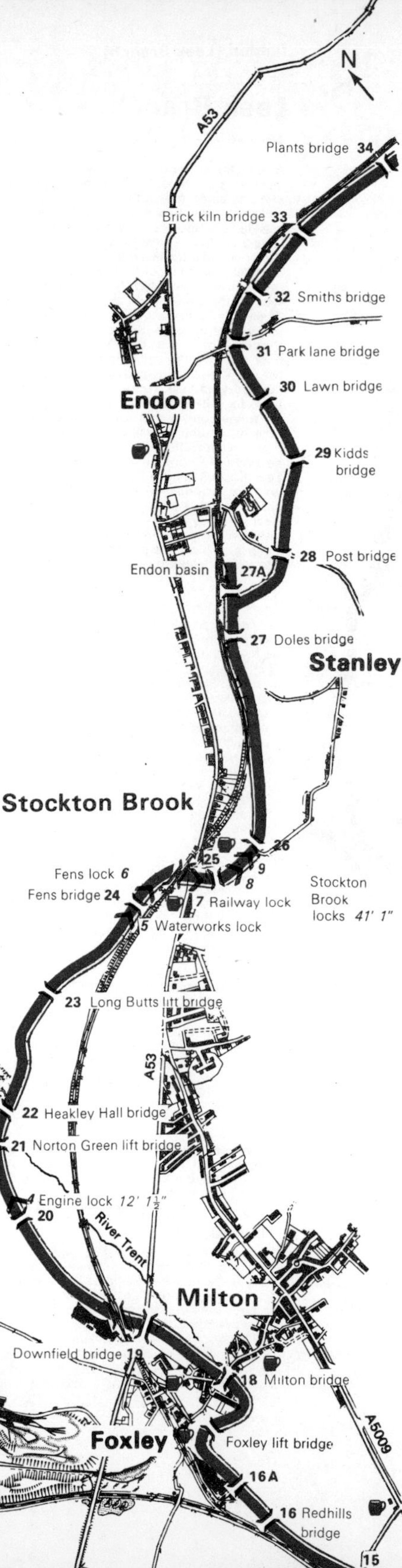

Stockton Brook

5½ miles

At Foxley the navigation turns sharp right under a little wooden lift bridge. There is a pub on the corner, which is where the ½ mile-long Foxley Arm used to branch off: it is now filled in and difficult to trace. Engine Lock is not far off; it is so called because a huge beam engine used to be housed just up the hill, employed to pump water from mine workings. At the next pretty lift bridge the (unnavigable) feeder from Knypersley reservoir joins the canal. By now the countryside is thoroughly attractive, and the Potteries are safely distant. 5 locks at Stockton Brook raise the canal up to the summit level 484ft above the sea. Soon the canal begins to hug once more the side of a hill.

Endon
Staffs. PO, tel, stores, garage, bank. The real village is up the hill just north of the main road and is attractive, especially during its traditional 'well-dressing' ceremony. Good views may be had from the Victorian church. Endon Basin is the local wharf, coming to life again now as the Stoke-on-Trent Boat Club's base after years of disuse. Near the basin are the remains of a former light railway swing bridge over the canal where it used to join the then busy main line.

Stanley
Staffs. PO, tel, stores. A stiff climb southwards from bridge 28 leads to a brown stone hill village, still looking much as it did when farming predominated. There is, happily, little new development. There are fine views across the valley to Endon.

Stockton Brook
Staffs. PO, tel, stores. From the canal, a pleasant and useful place. The 5 recently repaired locks are of course encouraging by their very navigability; but they also have a charming position, with views back down the headwaters of the river Trent. There is a splendid Victorian waterworks at the bottom of the flight, and pubs and shops near the middle.

Knypersley Reservoir
3½ miles north of Milton. This feeds water to the Trent & Mersey summit level via the Caldon Canal. The head of the river Trent is within its catchment area. Surrounded by woodland, the reservoir is a delightful setting for picnicking and rambling. The upper dam is covered with rhododendrons. Fishing rights are exercised by an angling club.

Milton
Staffs. PO, tel, stores. A little village on the side of a hill, forming an agreeable background to the canal.

PUBS

- **Plough** Endon. Food.
- **Travellers Rest** Stanley.
- **Sportsman** Stockton Brook, close to Railway lock.
- **Miners Arms** Milton.
- **Millrace** Milton.
- **Foxley** Canalside, at the junction with the former Foxley Arm.

FISHING

Stanley Pool is ½ mile south of bridge 28. This BWB reservoir is an excellent well-stocked fishing centre; fishing rights are leased to an angling association. Private sailing club. Access is at the northern end of the reservoir.

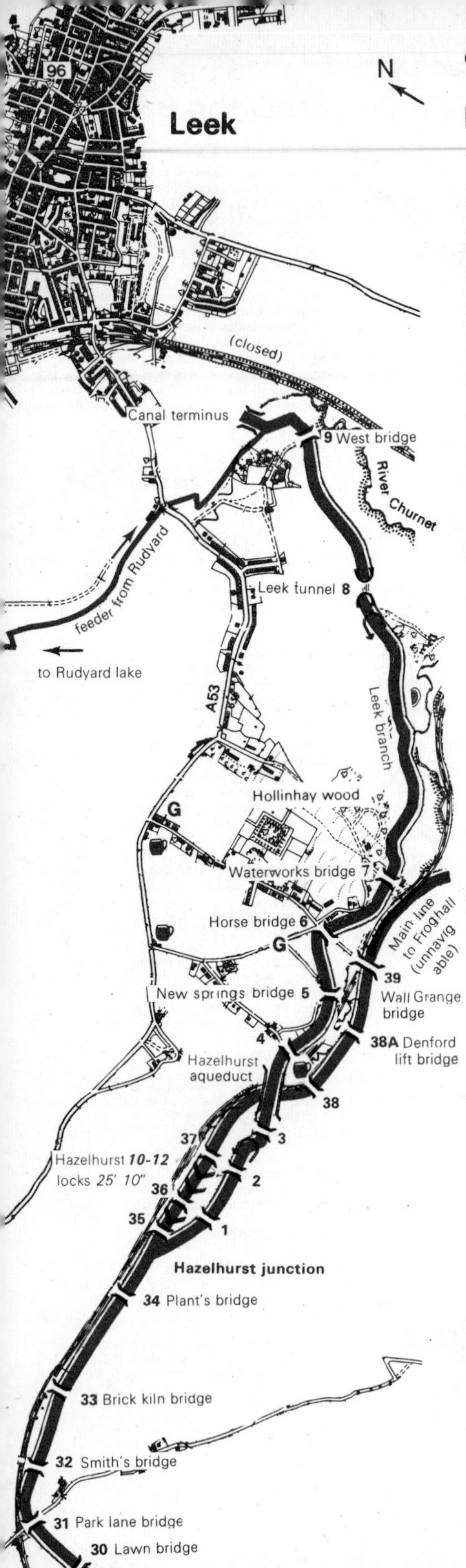

Leek Branch

4½ miles

At Hazelhurst the canal divides: the derelict main line falls through 3 locks before turning east and south to join the river Churnet, while the Leek branch bears right along the hillside, then crosses the main line on a large aqueduct. The railway and the Endon Brook are also traversed by aqueducts: thus the Leek branch reaches the north side of the narrow valley. After this very interesting section, the canal clings to the hillside, flanked by beautiful mature trees, as it follows the tortuous course of the river Churnet. The railway runs along the valley floor, but only the occasional goods train uses it. There is a large 'lagoon' just before the 130-yard Leek Tunnel: this is the last place for full-length boats to turn. Beyond the tunnel, only a short stretch of canal remains, ending on a fine stone aqueduct over the river Churnet. The last ½ mile beyond the Churnet and straight along to Leek Basin has been filled in and covered with a new industrial estate. However one can take a pleasant walk across the fields westwards by following the feeder that brings water down from Rudyard Lake into the navigation at its present terminus. An altogether delightful stretch of canal.

Leek
Staffs. Pop 19,100. EC Thur, MD Wed. All services. Essentially a textile town situated on the slope of a hill, and often referred to as the 'capital of the moors'. It was here that Thomas Parker, the first Earl of Macclesfield, was born in 1666, and his house can still be seen in the market place. James Brindley, the canal engineer, started in business as a millwright in Leek. The parish church of St Edward is 14thC, but was restored in 1856, and the chancel rebuilt in 1867.
Coombes Valley
3 miles SE of Leek. An attractive valley through which a trout stream runs. It is a reserve of the Royal Society for the Protection of Birds and it is possible to see kestrels, sparrowhawks, kingfishers, green and great spotted woodpeckers, dippers and redstarts. There are also a number of badger setts. *Open Apr-Aug Sat, Sun, Tue, Thur.* A nature trail has been laid out and guides may be obtained from the warden at Six Oaks Farm, Bradnop, nr Leek, Staffs.
Rudyard Lake
3 miles NW of the canal terminus near Leek. A very long, thin reservoir in a pleasant wooded setting used for feeding water into the Trent & Mersey Canal summit level via the Caldon Canal. Sailing of privately-owned dinghies is permitted. Licences are available from the address below (in the 'Fishing' section). The Rudyard Hotel adjoins the reservoir headbank.

PUBS

Wheel ½ mile N of Horse Bridge 6.
New Inn ½ mile NW of Horse Bridge 6.
Holly Bush Canalside, on main line of canal south of the crossover aqueduct. Telephone outside this little canal pub.

FISHING

Rudyard Lake, a well-stocked fishery, is very popular for both 'pleasure' and match fishing. Secretaries of angling clubs wishing to organise competitions here are advised to book well in advance. Several punts, each holding 3 anglers and their gear, are available for hire. Arrangements for all angling on this water are controlled by the resident reservoir attendant at Lake House, Rudyard, nr Leek, Staffs. (Rudyard 631).

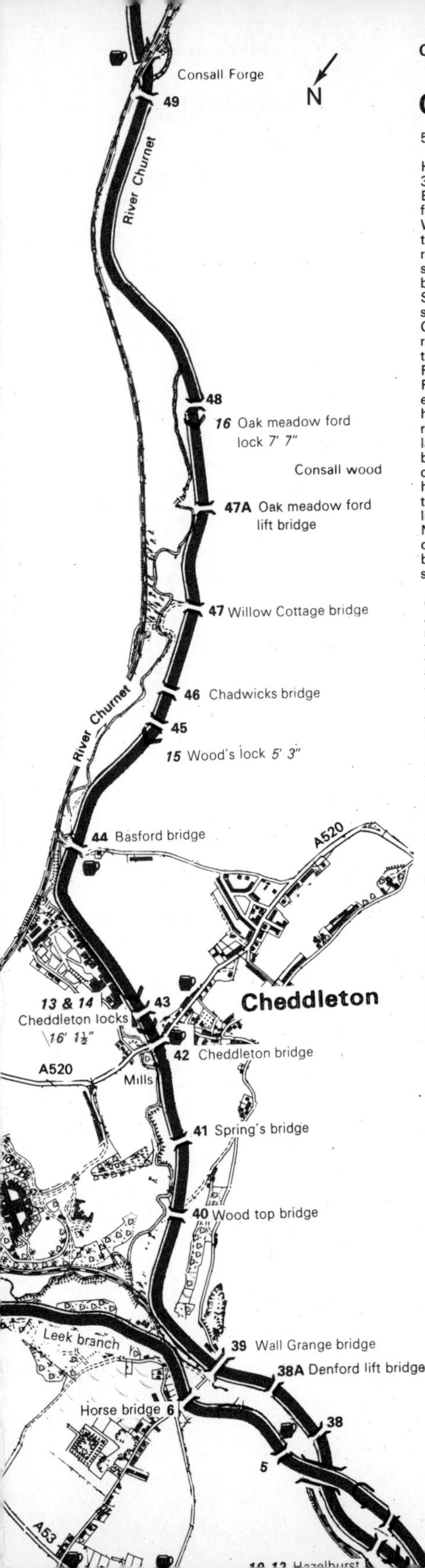

Cheddleton

5 miles

Here the main line to Froghall drops down 3 derelict locks and passes under the Leek Branch, soon taking up a position at the foot of the hills. At the former canalside Wall Grange station, the railway veers off towards Leek: it is soon replaced by the river Churnet, and the 2 waterways flow side by side for the next 7 miles. This must be one of the most beautiful valleys in Staffordshire, and the canal makes its own special contribution to the scenery. At Oakmeadow Ford lock the canal enters the river Churnet and the 2 waterways share the same course for 1 mile to Consall Forge.

For most of the way, the Churnet valley is enclosed by very steep and thickly wooded hills whose sides reach right down to the river and adjacent canal. It is a superlative landscape, almost untouched and unspoilt by man's incursions apart from the condition of the river water which is now, happily, improving. Yet it has been busy in the past, when boats and trains laden with limestone from Caldon competed for trade. Now the canal is derelict, and the railway only carries a few trains a day, so nothing breaks the peace of this splendidly secluded place.

Cheddleton
Staffs. PO, tel, stores, garage. A large main road rumbles through the village, but away from this are the 2 fine water mills, hard by the canal as it enters the village. These flint-grinding mills were restored to their former glory and opened to the public in 1969: the big wooden water wheels now turn at the touch of a lever. (Ground flint has always been a vital raw material for the pottery industry.) The mills may be visited on summer weekend afternoons. The village proper is up the steep hill, grouped about the ancient stone church of St Edward the Confessor. Little of the original building remains, but the 14thC work is worth examining.

PUBS

Boat Cheddleton. Canalside, at bridge 44. There is an old bridge across the Churnet nearby, also the remains of Cheddleton station.

Red Lion Cheddleton, on the main road.

Black Lion Cheddleton, near the church.

Holly Bush Canalside, near bridge 38. Tiny, popular canal pub. Telephone kiosk nearby.

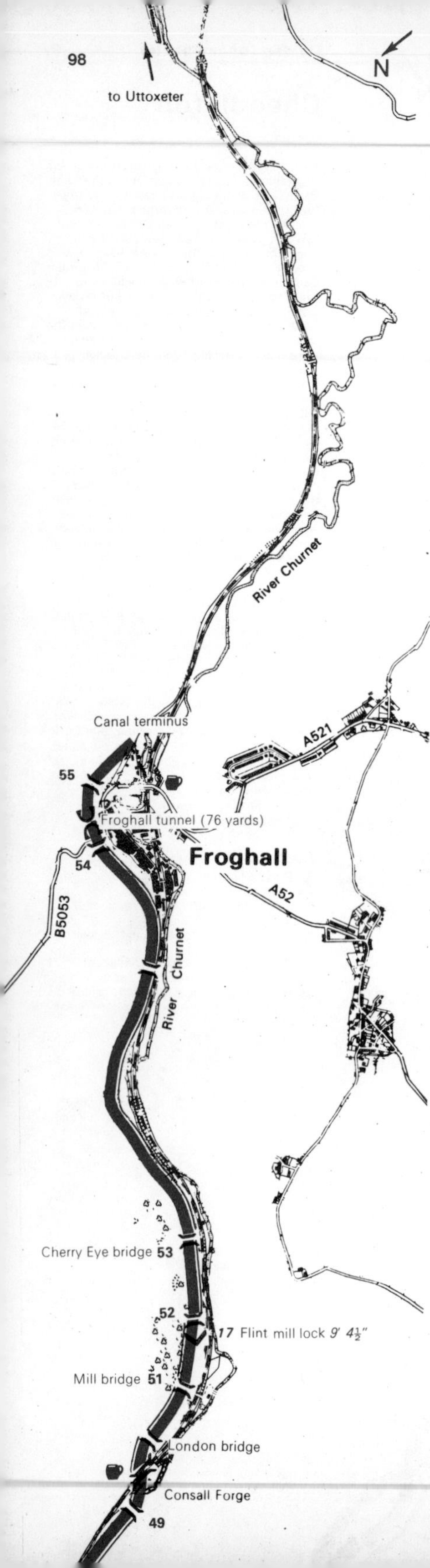

Froghall

2¾ miles

This is another very beautiful and secluded length of disused canal. Passing along the wooded valley that contains the river Churnet, one arrives at Consall Forge. This, once bustling with various mineral works, is now a quiet backwater, ruffled occasionally by passing goods trains. In this unlikely situation the visitor will find a pub with no apparent access save—once upon a time—the railway station (now closed) and the canal (now derelict). The canal and the river split at Consall Forge, the canal proceeding along the north east side of the steep valley to Flint Mill lock and the adjacent flint mill. This is, in a way, another piece of living industrial archaeology, where Australian sand is ground to dust for use in glazing pottery. The machinery is still run entirely by water power: water from the canal drops 15 feet to drive an underground turbine. The remains of the huge old water wheel can still be seen.
Beyond the mill, the navigation creeps along the side of a wooded hill as the valley floor drops away. Between the unique Cherryeye bridge and the tall chimneys of Froghall, a 100-yard stretch of the canal has been dammed off and emptied: the water is passed through in pipes. Beyond here, one finds the large scale industrial works that dominate Froghall. Froghall Tunnel (75 yards long) has subsided and is closed; Froghall Basin is also in a sorry state. All around, one can see the ruins of the lime kilns.

Froghall
Staffs. PO, tel. Tucked away in the heart of unspoilt Staffordshire, Froghall has been an outpost of industry ever since the advent of the canal fostered the growth of the Caldon lime quarries a few miles east. The limestone was carted down the hills by a plate tramway, being transhipped into waiting canal boats at Froghall Basin. Much of the trade was later lost to the railways. Just west of the final bridge by the basin, one can still see the junction with the old canal arm to Uttoxeter: this locked down to the Churnet valley. The branch was closed in 1847 and the present railway from Froghall to Uttoxeter now occupies most of the canal's course, although much of the canal bed can still be traced. Froghall nowadays comprises almost entirely the factories and dwellings associated with Thomas Bolton's big copper works.

PUBS

Railway Froghall, near the old station.
Black Lion Consall Forge. A canalside pub of outstanding isolation. Free house; sandwiches, teas, etc. usually available. (Wetley Rocks 294).

N
to Uttoxeter
River Churnet
Canal terminus
A521
55
Froghall tunnel (76 yards)
54
Froghall
A52
B5053
River Churnet
Cherry Eye bridge 53
52
17 Flint mill lock 9' 4½"
Mill bridge 51
London bridge
Consall Forge
49

Macclesfield

Maximum dimensions

Length: 70'
Beam: 7'
Headroom: 7'
(These dimensions apply also to the upper Peak Forest canal)

Mileage

Macclesfield Canal
Hardings Wood Junction (Trent & Mersey Canal) to
Congleton Wharf: 5¾ miles, 1 lock
Bosley top lock: 11½ miles, 13 locks
Macclesfield: 17 miles, 13 locks
Bollington: 20 miles, 13 locks
Marple Junction (Peak Forest Canal): 27¾ miles, 13 locks
Peak Forest Canal
Whaley Bridge to
Marple Junction: 6½ miles, no locks
Dukinfield Junction: 14½ miles, 16 locks
Ashton Canal
Duckinfield Junction to
Ducie Street Junction: 6 miles, 18 locks
Rochdale Canal
Ducie Street Junction to
Castlefield Junction (Bridgewater Canal): 1¼ miles, 9 locks

Ever since the Trent & Mersey canal had been completed in 1777, there had existed a demand for an alternative canal link between the Midlands and Manchester, and a more direct line through the manufacturing town of Macclesfield was an obvious choice of route.

However, it was not until 1825 that Thomas Telford was asked by promoters of the canal to survey a line linking the Peak Forest Canal and the Trent & Mersey Canal. The 28-mile line he suggested was the canal that was built, from Marple to just north of Kidsgrove, but Telford did not supervise the construction. (He left to go and build the Birmingham & Liverpool Junction Canal.) William Crosley was the canal's engineer. It is interesting to note that the Macclesfield Canal (which opened in 1831) was built so long after the peak period of canal construction that it was actually envisaged by some of its promoters as the route for a possible railway track.

The canal, which runs along the side of a tall ridge of hills west of the Pennines, bears the distinctive mark of Telford's engineering. Like his Birmingham & Liverpool Junction Canal (i.e. the Shropshire Union from Autherley to Nantwich), the Macclesfield is a 'cut and fill' canal, following as straight a course as possible, and featuring many tremendous cuttings and embankments. Apart from the stop lock at Hall Green whose 1-foot rise was insisted upon as a water preservation measure by the Trent & Mersey Canal Company—to whose Hall Green Branch the Macclesfield Canal connected at the stop lock—all the locks are grouped into the flight of 12 at Bosley. The canal is fed from nearby reservoirs, at Bosley and Sutton.

In spite of intense competition from neighbouring railways and the Trent & Mersey Canal, the Macclesfield carried a good trade for many years. Much of this was coal, and cotton from the big mills established along its northern reaches.

This was not greatly affected by the surrender in 1846 to what was to become the Great Central Railway Company. (The Peak Forest and Ashton Canals were also bought by that railway.) The railway company ran the 3 canals efficiently, but as narrow canals all 3 were bound to decline sooner rather than later.

The Macclesfield Canal today is relatively quiet, although towards Marple there are some well-established pleasure boating centres. When the lower Peak Forest and Ashton Canals are restored, it will once again become part of a through route. The quality of the scenery and the long pounds make this a canal deserving of more popularity.

Kent Green

$4\frac{1}{2}$ miles

The junction of the Macclesfield with the Trent & Mersey Canal is a curious one, for the former leaves the Trent & Mersey on the south side, then crosses it on Red Bull Aqueduct after the T & M has fallen through 3 locks. (In this respect the junction is identical to Hazelhurst Junction on the Caldon Canal (see page 96).
After passing through the stop lock in the cutting at Hall Green, one comes out into the open countryside at Kent Green. To the east, Mow Cop crowns the tall ridge of hills that stretches parallel to the navigation for miles to come. The canal wanders past the front lawn of the mansion that is Ramsdell Hall. Beyond this point, the canal loses itself in the countryside for several miles. A telephone box is near bridge 85.

Little Moreton Hall
NT property. $\frac{3}{4}$ mile west of canal. (Walk north west from bridge 86, along the footpath on the left side of the hedge.) This fabulous moated house is an outstanding example of black and white timbered architecture. It was built between 1559 and 1580, with carved gables and ornate windows and has scarcely changed since. It contains a fine collection of oak furniture and pewter. *Open Mar-Oct daily (except Tue) 14.00-18.00.*

Mow Cop
NT property. A hill nearly 1100ft above sea level, which gives a magnificent view across the Cheshire Plain, across Stoke and into Wales. (This looks particularly good at night.) On top of the hill is Mow Cop Castle, an imitation ruin built in 1750. It was on this spot that the Primitive Methodists held their first meeting in 1807 which lasted 14 hours.

Kent Green
PO, tel, stores. The main interest of this place is in its pubs, especially the little one on the canal by swing bridge 88.

BOATYARDS & BWB

David Piper Red Bull Basin, Church Lawton, Stoke-on-Trent, Staffs. (Kidsgrove 4754). By Red Bull aqueduct. Diesel, slipway up to 60 foot, moorings, winter storage. Boat & engine sales & servicing. Steel boats built & fitted out. Lavatory. *Open daily.*

PUBS

Bird in Hand Kent Green. A superbly old-fashioned canalside pub: the un-embarrassed landlord fetches beer up from the cellar in a jug.

Rising Sun Kent Green, near the canal.

Three Horseshoes Kent Green, near canal.

Bleeding Wolf Hall Green, near bridge 94. Food, except at weekends. *(PO, tel, stores nearby.)*

Canal Tavern Canalside, at Hardings Wood.

Blue Bell Canalside, at Hardings Wood Junction.

FISHING THE MACCLESFIELD CANAL

Along most of the Macclesfield Canal, the angler should find roach, carp, pike, perch, and some chub although much of the canal is rather shallow for the last-mentioned. There are big roach, particularly in the Bollington, Higher Poynton and Adlington reaches. Several 2-pounders have been caught from the canal with the best weighing over 3lb. The canal's record roach scaled 3lb 5oz.
Season tickets are issued to cover the Macclesfield and the adjoining Peak Forest canals. It is advisable to enquire locally.

Watery lane aqueduct
Oak farm bridge 81
Hockenhall bridge 82
Gravel pit bridge 83
Deakins bridge 84
Simpson bridge 85
Rowndes No. 2 86 bridge
Ramsdell hall
Little Moreton hall
Mow Cop
Kent green 87 bridge
A34
88 Lownde's swing bridge
Kent green
89 Morris bridge
90 Glovers swing bridge
91 Tramroad bridge
92 Hall green bridge
93 Hall green foot bridge
Hall green lock 1′ 0″
P
W
94
95
BWB yard
Hardings Wood junction
A50
Trent and Mersey canal
continued page 84
Red bull aqueduct
98
Kidsgrove bridge 97
Kidsgrove station
Kidsgrove

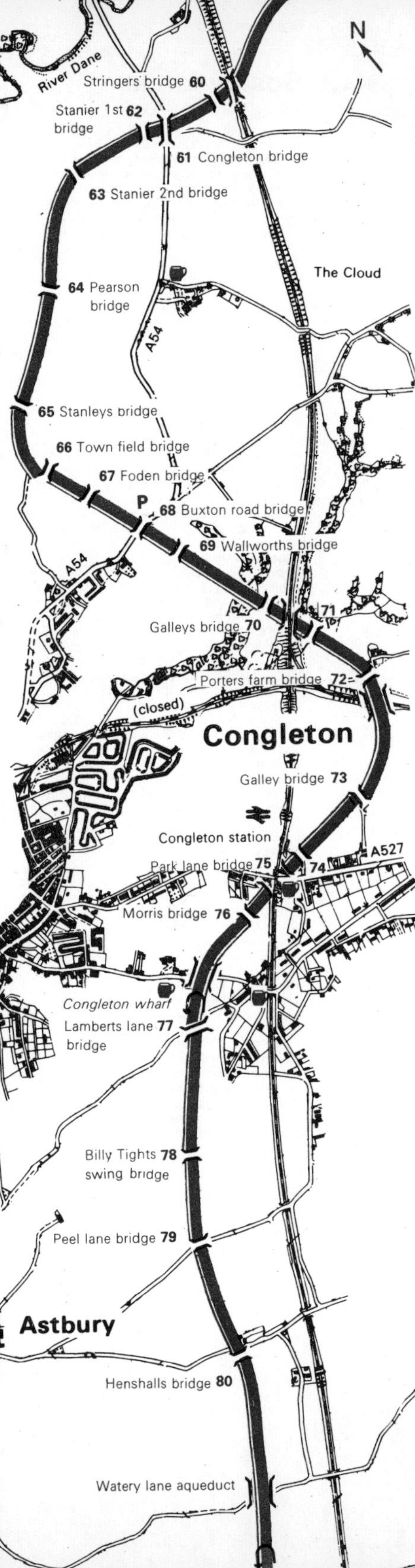

Congleton

$5\frac{1}{2}$ miles

The canal continues north east. On one side, the land falls away gradually; to the east, the ever-present range of substantial hills reminds one that the Pennine Chain lies just beyond. Passing a golf course, one arrives at the embanked wharf that overlooks Congleton: there is an aqueduct over the road that runs down into the town and then a beautifully symmetrical 'roving' bridge (76). Past Congleton railway station, the canal is carried by a high embankment – a common feature of the Macclesfield – across a narrow valley, affording a good view westward of the tall and elegant railway viaduct crossing the same valley. Meanwhile the looming fell known as The Cloud (over 1000ft high and with remains of ancient earthworks) is given a wide berth as the navigation continues on its lonely lockfree course through this very fine landscape. Fish and chips may be found near bridge 68.

Congleton
Ches. Pop 20,000. EC Wed, MD Tue, Sat. All services. A compact, busy market town hemmed in by hills. The Victorian Town Hall in the High street, looks like a cross between a 17thC Dutch guildhall and St Mark's, Venice.

Astbury
Ches. PO, tel, stores. A pretty village set back from the A34, about 1 mile north west of bridges 79 and 80. Tudor and 18thC houses are set around the green. The church is amazing; its roomy interior and wide aisles are complemented externally by generous battlements along the roof and a spired tower standing quite separate from the body of the church.

PUBS

Robin Hood $\frac{1}{4}$ mile SW of bridge 61. No dartboard here.
Railway near Congleton station.
Wharf near Congleton wharf.
Lion & Swan hotel Congleton. Restaurant.
Bull's Head hotel, Congleton (3388). Restaurant meals.
Egerton Arms Astbury.

FISHING

For fishing in river Dane, Goodwin's Pool and canal, contact Mr A. Turpin, Congleton Anglers Society, 'Everest', Canal rd, Congleton.

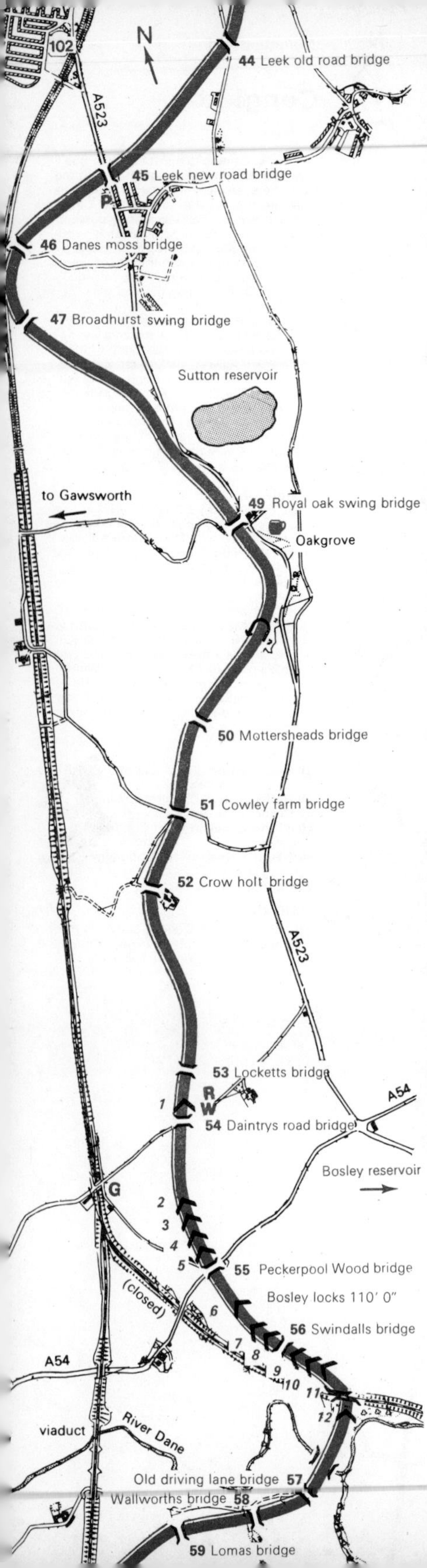

102
N
A523
44 Leek old road bridge
45 Leek new road bridge
P
46 Danes moss bridge
47 Broadhurst swing bridge
Sutton reservoir
to Gawsworth
49 Royal oak swing bridge
Oakgrove
50 Mottersheads bridge
51 Cowley farm bridge
52 Crow holt bridge
A523
53 Locketts bridge
R
W
1
54 Daintrys road bridge
A54
Bosley reservoir
G
2
3
4
5
55 Peckerpool Wood bridge
(closed)
Bosley locks 110′ 0″
6
56 Swindalls bridge
7
8
9
10
11
12
A54
viaduct
River Dane
Old driving lane bridge 57
Wallworths bridge 58
59 Lomas bridge

Bosley Locks

5¾ miles

Scenically, this is another impressive stretch. The massive hills to the right still dominate as the canal crosses the river Dane on an embankment and arrives at the foot of Bosley locks. These are in a really delightful setting which is semi-wooded and semi-pastoral, all the time overlooked by The Cloud from the south. Beyond the locks, the hills/mountains (some are over 1200ft high) spill right down to the canal near Oakgrove. The navigation follows the contour of the land as it begins to swing round the hills containing Macclesfield, which is now clearly visible to the north.

Sutton Reservoir
Close to the canal north of bridge 49, this reservoir holds up to 94 million gallons of water. There is a private sailing club; and the public are welcome to ramble and picnic here.

Oakgrove
A delightful spot incorporating a swing bridge over the canal, a nearby pub and a superb backcloth of tall, green hills which are ideal for energetic walks. The lane west of the bridge leads to Gawsworth. Sutton Reservoir is just north.

Gawsworth
Ches. 2 miles west of Oakgrove. A refreshingly unspoilt village with several small lakes and a lovely 13thC church, approached by a long avenue of elm trees. Facing the church is the old rectory, a half-timbered house built by Rector Baguley in 1470. Close to the church is Gawsworth Hall, a beautiful 16thC black and white manor house. The park encloses a mediaeval jousting ground. (*Open Mar-Oct Wed, Sat, Sun & G. Fri. 14.00-18.00.*)

Maggoty's Wood In this pleasant wood just outside the village is the grave of the eccentric fiddler and playwright, Maggoty Johnson. After being totally rejected by London critics he returned to Gawsworth where he died in 1773, having ordered that he should be buried far from the vulgar gentry who did not appreciate his genius . . .

Bosley Locks
Effectively the only locks on all the 27 miles of the Macclesfield Canal, these 12 splendid stone locks are relatively deep, raising the canal level by fully 118ft to well over 500ft above the sea. It is presumably for this reason that each lock has a pair of mitre top gates instead of only a single one– indeed Bosley locks are very rare among narrow locks in this respect. They are a good example of Telford's practice of grouping locks together in flights: here are 12 in 1 mile. *A PO, tel, stores is a few hundred yards west of the top lock.*

Bosley Reservoir
1 mile east of Bosley locks, along the A54. A canal reservoir with a wide variety of land and water birds, which holds 402 million gallons of water. An excellent rambling and picnic area. The fishing rights are exercised by an angling club.

PUBS

Fool's Nook Oakgrove. Horsebrasses and light meals.

FISHING

A large stock of chub has been introduced to the canal in the Bosley area. In addition there are some big pike (up to 20lb) around here and roach to 2¾lb have been reported.

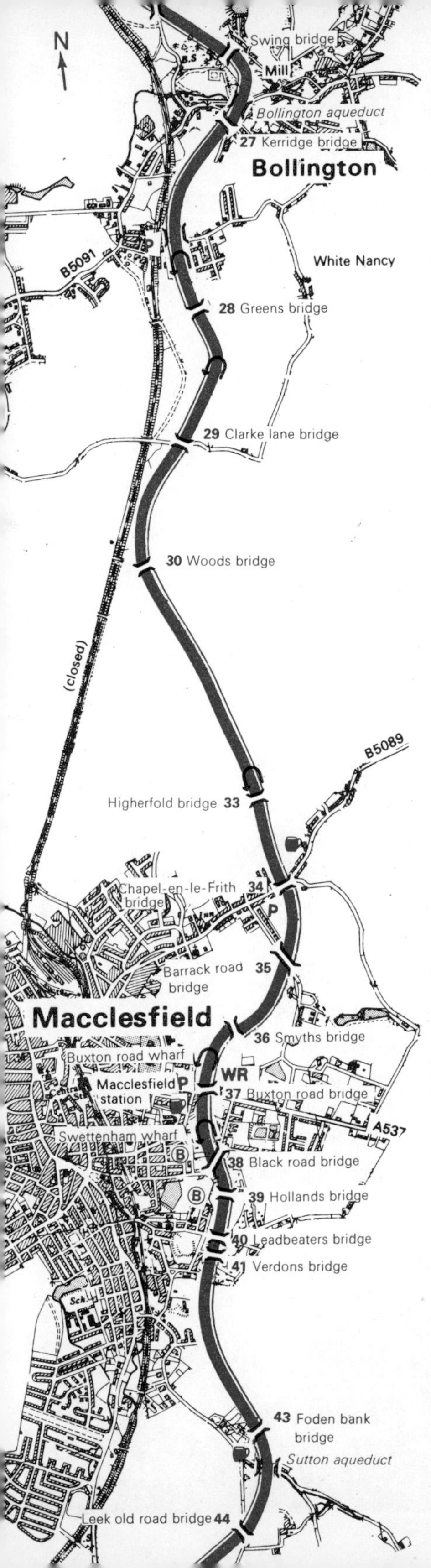

Macclesfield

5 miles

Leaving the green and hilly countryside, the navigation enters the outskirts of Macclesfield. A very wide stretch overshadowed by a vast, empty flour mill marks the site of the headquarters of the original Macclesfield Canal Company. The town centre itself is down the hill: the best place to moor is at the wharf north of bridge 37. Meanwhile the canal continues northwards near a closed railway to Bollington. A 60ft-high embankment and 2 aqueducts carry the navigation over the valley to the huge Clarence textile mill—one of several mills in the area which have closed in recent years owing to retrenchment and rationalisation in the major textile companies.

Bollington
Ches. Pop 6100. EC Wed. PO, tel, stores, garage, bank. One gets a good view of this stone-built town from the huge canal embankment that cuts across it. But the canal no longer serves the old cotton mills which close as Bollington gradually becomes a residential, non-manufacturing place. Hills crowd round the town, which is only a mile from the boundary of the Peak District National Park. The white tower on the ridge south of the town is called White Nancy. There are many speculative stories as to how this rather remarkable structure of white stone in the shape of a sugar loaf originated and how it gained its name. One popular story is that it was built to commemorate the battle of Waterloo by a member of the Gaskell family and took its name from one of the ladies of the family called Nancy.

Macclesfield
Ches. Pop 42,000. EC Wed, MD Tue, Fri, Sat. All services. An interesting combination of a thriving silk manufacturing town and an old market town with its cobbled streets and its picturesque mediaeval Market Place. There are several interesting classical buildings, making the most of the local stone. In the 18thC it was one of the leading silk producing centres and is still important for its textile and pharmaceutical industries. An interesting feature of the town is the Unitarian Chapel in King Edward street, approached through a narrow passage and guarded by a lovely wrought-iron gate: it is dated 1689 and is 'for William and Mary's subjects dissenting from the Church of England'.

St. Michael's Church Market Place. Very little remains of the original structure founded in 1278 by Queen Eleanor but it still contains many fine monuments, especially those in the private chapels of the Savage and Legh families, with their splendid altar-tombs and memorials.

Museum & Art Gallery West Park. It was built, equipped and presented to the town in 1898 by the Brocklehurst family, the largest silk manufacturers in Macclesfield. It contains exhibits of local interest, as well as sketches by Landseer, Egyptian craftswork and a stuffed giant panda. *Open Oct-Mar daily 9.30-16.30. Apr-Sep daily 9.30-17.30, Sun 14.00-17.00.* (Macclesfield 24067).

BOATYARDS & BWB

Deans Marina Swettenham Wharf, Brook st, Macclesfield, Ches. (20042). Dustbins, water, gas, chandlery, slipway up to 20 foot, winter storage. Boat & motor sales & repairs, agents for most major firms. Telephone, lavatory. *Open daily throughout year.*

Maclan Cruisers 146 Black rd, Macclesfield, Ches. (23358). At bridge 39 (Hollands bridge). Hire cruisers, narrowboat, canoes & dinghies. Dustbins, water, diesel, gas, moorings, winter storage. Antique shop, telephone, lavatory. *Open daily throughout year.*

Bridgewater Arms Macclesfield, near bridge 37.
Old King's Head beside aqueduct, 1 mile south of Macclesfield.

FISHING

The reed-fringed Bollington and Macclesfield length is particularly noted for big roach and hundreds of specimens have been caught. There are also bream, carp and pike here for the taking. Lobworm bait has accounted for many of the big roach.

Little Moreton Hall.

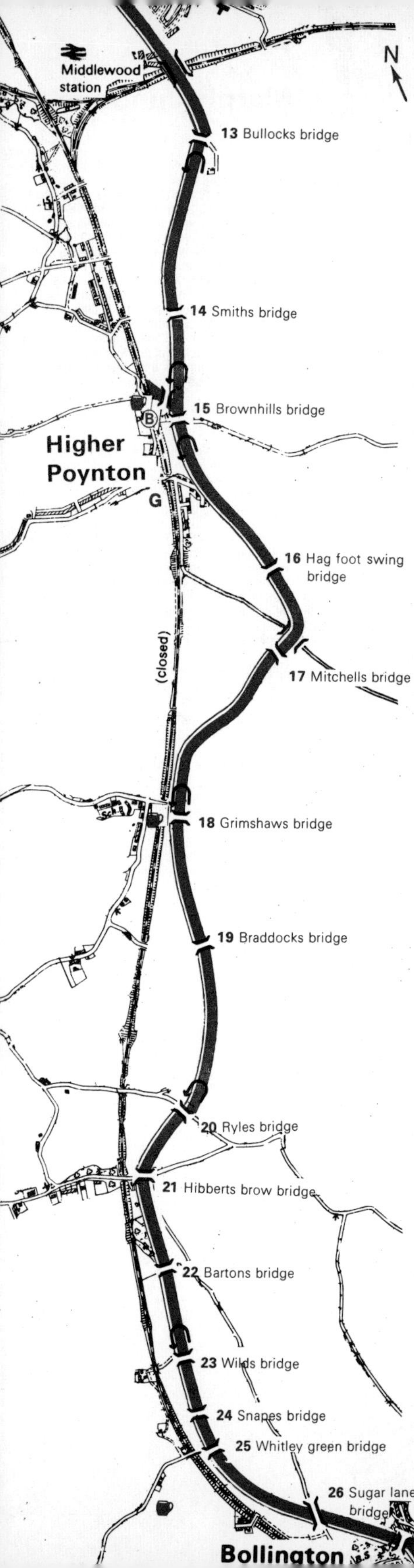

Higher Poynton

5 miles

This lonely stretch is typical of the Macclesfield Canal and in its beautifully quiet, rural isolation it is representative of much of the charm that most canals possess. Winding northwards along the summit level at over 500ft above the sea, the navigation generally follows the contours of this upland country, but crosses several valleys on embankments with fine aqueducts. There are few centres of population, only the odd pub here or there, and the countryside is entirely unspoilt. Around Higher Poynton (*PO, tel, stores, garage*) the canal becomes very deep, and in places wide: this is the result of ancient subsidence from a coalmine, which necessitated the continual raising of the canal banks and bridges (to hold the water in the sinking canal). An old branch near bridge 15 used to lead to the mine; now it is a mooring site. A mile north of here, one crosses yet another massive embankment and a tall aqueduct (over a railway) on the way into High Lane.

Lyme Park
NT property. 2 miles east of Higher Poynton. Pedestrian entrance at West Parkgate, $\frac{1}{4}$ mile SE of bridge 17. (Vehicular access from Disley, on the Peak Forest Canal.) In the centre of an extensive park containing deer, is a magnificent Elizabethan house that belonged to the Legh family from the 14thC until 1947 when it was handed over to the nation in payment of death duties. It has a fine interior containing many works of art and four Chippendale chairs claimed to be covered with material from a cloak worn by King Charles I at his execution. *House normally open: May-Aug 13.30-18.15. Sep, Oct, Mar, Apr 14.00-17.00. But closed in 1972 for restoration. Park & Gardens always open 8.00-dusk.* (Disley 2023).

Adlington Hall
2 miles west of bridge 21. An attractive manor house with a mixture of architectural styles: a Georgian south front and an Elizabethan black and white timbered wing. The banqueting hall contains a 17thC Bernard Smith organ. Pleasant gardens. *Open G. Fri-Sep: Suns & B. Hols 14.30-18.00. Also Sat in Jul & Aug.*

BOATYARDS & BWB

Constellation Cruises Mount Vernon, Higher Poynton, Stockport, Ches. (Poynton 3471). Near bridge 15. Diesel, gas, chandlery, slipway up to 25 foot, temporary & permanent moorings. Minor boat repairs, inboard & outboard engine repairs. *Open throughout the year.*

PUBS

Boar's Head Higher Poynton, down the hill from bridge 15.
Miner's Arms near bridge 18.
Windmill 250 yards W of bridge 25.

CARAVANS & CAMPING

Elm Beds Farm Elm Beds rd, Higher Poynton (Poynton 2370). Canalside. Overnight caravan & tent stops.

FISHING

Around Higher Poynton there is some excellent fishing. Local subsidence has made the canal very deep—up to 12ft in places, and these deep stretches harbour some big roach. Pike over 20lb have also been caught from this area, as well as carp over 10lb.

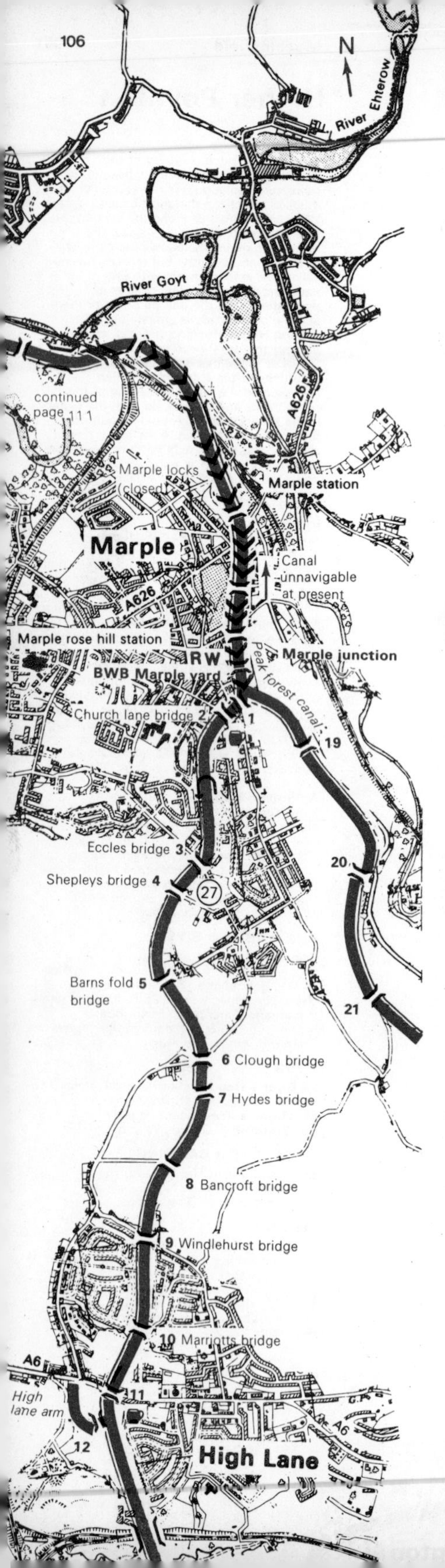

Marple Junction

4 miles

The canal proceeds northwards in a cutting through High Lane, passing the junction with the short High Lane arm—now used as a club mooring site. Beyond the town is a derelict mill, then open country intervenes, offering views westward of Stockport and the southern outskirts of Manchester. Yet another mill appears: it heralds Marple, a busy boating centre much enjoyed by the citizens of Manchester. The area of the junction with the Peak Forest Canal is delightful: an old turnover bridge, mellow wharf buildings and the nearby unnavigable flight of Marple locks are framed by the distant mountainous country across the Goyt valley. The canal here is 500ft above sea level—the highest usable pound on the English canal system.

Marple
Ches. Pop 24,000. All services. A typical residential town, serving as a dormitory base for Stockport and Manchester. Elements of the old village can still be seen, buried among the suburbia, but much the most attractive part is by the canal. It is a delightful tree-lined walk all the way down the locks, and half-way down there is a superb old canal warehouse. The rugged Ludworth Moor is not far away, where 'Robin Hood's Picking Rods' still stand, the supposed remains of a Celtic Druid's temple.

High Lane
Ches. PO, tel, stores, garage, station. More a spread than a village; useful for supplies. High Lane is effectively at the south-east corner of the Manchester conurbation, and is quite indistinguishable from its neighbours. The very long Disley railway tunnel passes deep underneath the place.

BOATYARDS & BWB

BWB Marple Yard Marple Junction (061-427-1079). Water, refuse disposal, lavatory.

PUBS

Ring O'Bells Marple, by bridge 2. Telephone kiosk outside.
Bull's Head High Lane, near bridge 11.

FISHING

Near Marple Junction there are some big pike: some specimens taken have weighed over 20lb.

Peak Forest & Ashton

THE ASHTON CANAL

This navigation was authorised in 1792 and opened shortly afterwards, as an isolated narrow canal from the centre of Manchester to Ashton-under-Lyne. It is short, at only 6½ miles, but several substantial branches were built, with a total length twice that of the main line.

From the beginning, the Ashton was a strong rival of the Rochdale canal—with which it connects in Manchester. The two canals were constructed simultaneously, partly to tap the big coal producing area around Oldham (north east of Manchester): in addition the Ashton opened a new trade route from Manchester to the textile mills of Ashton, while the Rochdale served as a broad canal link over the Pennines between the Mersey and the rivers of Yorkshire. Before long, the Ashton Canal was joined by the Peak Forest and Huddersfield Canals: both provided useful trade and the latter provided a secondary through route across the Pennines. And in 1831 completion of the narrow Macclesfield Canal gave the Ashton the added bonus of becoming part of a through route from Manchester to the Potteries.

The 1830s saw the peak of the Ashton Canal's prosperity. After this it was seriously threatened by railway competition, and the canal company sold out to the forerunner of the Great Central Railway Company in 1846. This company continued successfully to maintain and operate the canal for many years, but traffic declined in the present century and the branches began to decay.

The canal has been unnavigable for over 10 years now: all 18 locks are derelict and most of the branches have been filled in. For some years there has been a sustained campaign by the Peak Forest Canal Society, the Inland Waterways Association and others for the reopening of the canal as a navigable waterway for the benefit of all. This would reopen a circle of navigable wateways 100 miles long, encouraging pleasure craft through-traffic and turning an unsightly and unhealthy ditch into a lively and busy nagivation and a superb local amenity for boating, walking, fishing and idling. The campaign has, happily, been successful: agreement was reached in December 1971 between BWB and the councils along the canal. Full restoration is now scheduled: work started in March 1972, and should be completed within 2 or 3 years. The Peak Forest Canal Society will welcome volunteers (see page 174).

THE PEAK FOREST CANAL

This canal runs from the Ashton Canal at Ashton through Marple to Whaley Bridge and Bugsworth. Its name is misleading, for Peak Forest is only a small village 2½ miles east of Doveholes, and the canal never went to Peak Forest. Its history is similar to and tied up with its neighbour the Ashton Canal: authorised by Act of Parliament in 1794, it was aimed at providing an outlet for the great limestone deposits at Doveholes, a few miles south east of Whaley Bridge. However, since Doveholes is over 1000ft above sea level, the canal was terminated in a basin at Bugsworth, and the line was continued up to the quarries by a 6½-mile tramroad.

Construction of the canal and tramway and their 4 short tunnels was carried out by navvies directed by Benjamin Outram, a notable Derbyshire engineer and one of the founders of the famous Butterley Ironworks. The canal was completed in 1800, except for the flight of locks at Marple, which were not built until 4 years later. (A second, temporary, tramway bridged the gap in the meantime.)

Bugsworth soon became a bustling interchange point where the horse-drawn wagons bringing the stone down from Doveholes tipped their load either into canal boats or into limekilns, for burning into lime. This traffic, and the boats bringing coal *up* the canal for firing the kilns at Bugsworth, accounted for the greatest proportion of the canal company's revenue.

Like the Ashton Canal, the Peak Forest was greatly boosted by the opening of the Macclesfield Canal to Marple top lock in 1831. This made it (with the Ashton) part of a new through route from Manchester to the Potteries. In 1831 too, the Cromford & High Peak Railway was opened, joining up Whaley Bridge with the Cromford Canal on the far side of the Peak District.

By the early 1840s the Peak Forest Canal was suffering from keen competition on trade between Manchester, the Midlands and London. The competition came not only from the long-established Trent & Mersey Canal Company but also from 2 new railways. All the companies tried to undercut each other; the Peak Forest came off badly, so in 1846 the company leased the navigation in perpetuity to the Sheffield, Ashton-under-Lyne & Manchester Railway, which later became the Great Central. The canal declined slowly up to the present century. In 1922 the Bugsworth traffic finished, while (through) traffic on the 'lower' Peak Forest Canal—from Marple Junction northwards—gradually disappeared by the last war.

The situation now is that the upper section of the canal—south of Marple—is fully navigable to Whaley Bridge, and popular with pleasure boaters. Following a long and vociferous campaign, the northern section of the canal is now being restored, along with the Ashton.

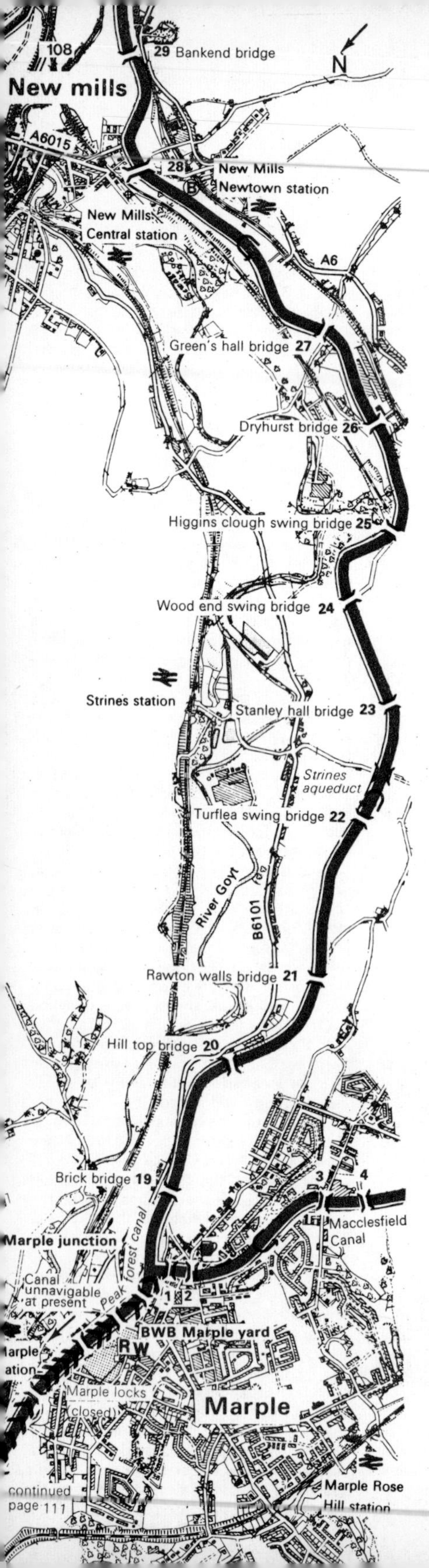

continued
page 111

New Mills

4¾ miles

As one passes through the old stop lock and bridge separating the Peak Forest Canal from the Macclesfield Canal, one enters at once dramatic, mountainous scenery. To the north and east, the land falls away sharply, with the Marple flight of locks emphasising the drop. The 'upper' section of the Peak Forest Canal leads off to the southeast; and it rapidly becomes apparent that this is a navigation set in a robust, handsome landscape. Clinging desperately to a wooded mountainside overlooking the steep, wide Goyt valley, it winds its precarious way to New Mills. The trains that traverse the opposite side of the valley look like tiny models on the distant, massive mountains. Near Disley, another railway pops out of the long Disley Tunnel, way below the canal; while yet another line appears above and beside the canal, from High Lane. Thus around New Mills the valley contains fully three operational and very picturesque railways. One of the pleasant features of this terrain is the easy co-existence of woods, fields and a canal on the one hand, and a certain amount of industrial urbanisation on the other. Usually, this mixture would tend to spoil the rural character of the area; but along this canal the steepness of the slope and the grandness of the landscape leaves the canal's charm unimpaired.

New Mills
PO, tel, stores, garage, stations. A mostly stone-built town on the Cheshire/Derbyshire border: its industries include textile printing, engineering and engraving. One can still see the ruins of the extensive canal stables just east of bridge 28.

Disley
Ches. Pop 2900. PO, tel, stores, garage, station. On the south bank of the canal. The centre of the village is quite pretty, slightly spoilt by the A6 traffic. The village is up the hill, SW of bridge 26. The attractive church stands among trees above the little village square. It was greatly renovated in the last century but the ancient tower with the griffin leering down at passers-by dates from the 16thC. Vehicular and pedestrian access to Lyme Park (see page 105) is from the A6 near Disley. 1½ miles SW of bridge 26.

BOATYARDS & BWB

Ladyline (New Mills) Hibbert st, New Mills, nr Stockport, Ches. At bridge 28. Diesel, chandlery, drydock, moorings, winter storage.

BWB Marple Yard at Marple Junction (061-427-1079). Water, refuse disposal, lavatory.

PUBS

Ram's Head hotel Disley (2019). Smart hotel with full restaurant. Baths available for boat crews who dine here.

Dandy Cock Disley. Bar lunches.

Romper Inn ½ mile uphill from bridge 21. Food.

Ring O'Bells Marple, near the junction. (On the Macclesfield Canal.

FISHING THE PEAK FOREST CANAL

The Peak Forest Canal contains most species of fish, but the best fishing is for roach. Hundreds of big ones have been reported caught, with several fish weighing well over 2lb. These big roach are partial to soft baits—bread flake is best—but the fish can remove it from the hook without the float showing a tremor. The angler needs to be skilful to catch a good specimen—especially as the clearness of the water makes these fish shy biters.
County Palatine AA holds much of the fishing rights on this canal and permits are obtainable. Local enquiries should be made.

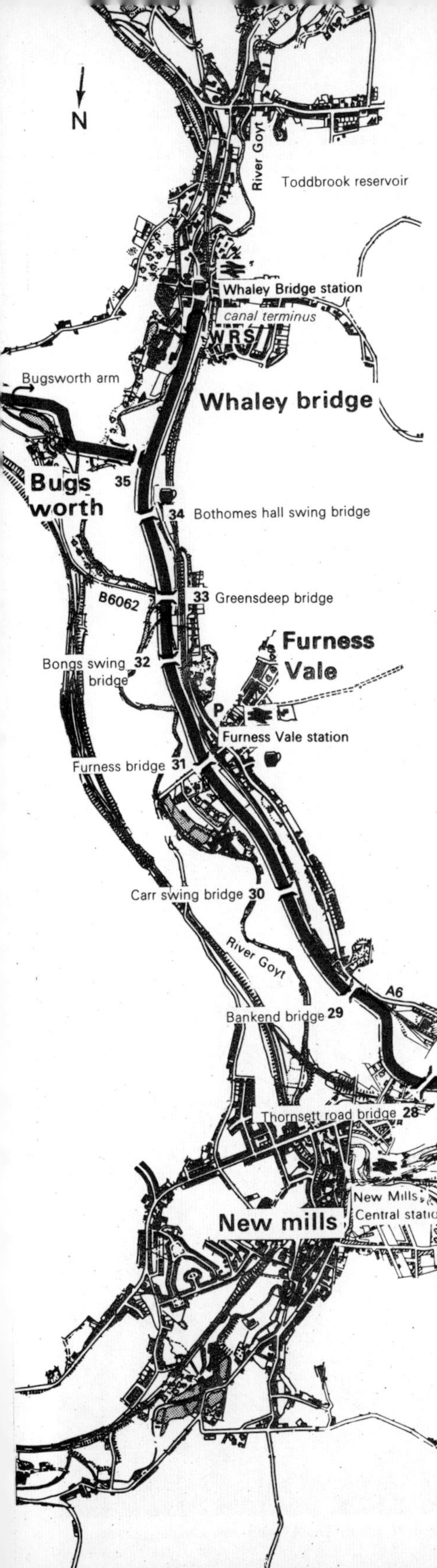

Whaley Bridge

2½ miles

The canal continues southeast along the mountainside towards Whaley Bridge. It is an enchanting stretch, passing plenty of woods, pastures and grazing horses. The A6 road and the railway are always close to the navigation, but they detract not at all from its isolation. There are charming stations at New Mills, Furness Vale and Whaley Bridge: from these one may take a magnificent railway trip past 2 canal-feeding reservoirs and over the hills to the summit, 1200ft above sea level, then down to the old Roman town of Buxton, now unfortunately the end of the line.

As the canal approaches Whaley Bridge, and the river Goyt comes closer, there are 3 more swing bridges to contend with—they can be hard work. South of swing bridge 34 the canal splits: the original main line, at present closed beyond the first couple of hundred yards, turns east across the Goyt on an aqueduct to Bugsworth (nowadays often politely called Buxworth) with its basin complex. The former Whaley Bridge branch continues for a short distance south to Whaley Bridge, where it terminates in a small basin at the north end of the town. There is a building at the basin of great interest to industrial archaeologists: it covers a dock and was built in 1832 at this, the junction of the Peak Forest Canal and the Cromford & High Peak Railway. Here, transhipment between canal, boat and railway wagon could take place under cover. The former railway's Whaley Bridge inclined plane rises to the south from this historic building. Whaley Bridge Council are proposing to demolish it in order to make way for a new swimming pool.

Coombs Reservoir
1½ miles south of Whaley Bridge. An 84-acre canal reservoir with public access from the three highways round it. It is used extensively as a sailing club centre and for angling.

Toddbrook Reservoir
Just south of Whaley Bridge. A very pleasant area for picnicking and walking. Private sailing club; fishing rights on this BWB reservoir are exercised by an angling club.

Whaley Bridge
Derbs. Pop 5400. EC Wed. PO, tel, stores, garage, station, banks. Built on a steep hill at the end of the canal, this village is now overwhelmed by the traffic on the A6 road. There are a lot of shops and pubs, and away from the main road it is a quiet and pleasant place, with good views across the Goyt valley. However the beautiful nearby hills are more noteworthy than the town.

The Cromford & High Peak Railway
In the early 1820s a physical connection was planned between the Peak Forest Canal at Whaley Bridge with the Cromford Canal, way over to the south east on the other side of the Peak District, using a junction canal. However a canal would have been impracticable through such mountainous terrain, and so a railway was constructed. Known as the Cromford & High Peak Railway, it was opened throughout in 1831, 33 miles long. With a summit level over 1200ft above the sea, this extraordinary standard gauge goods line was interesting chiefly for its numerous slopes and inclined planes, up which the wagons were hauled by either stationary or tenaciously locomotive steam engines. (The steepest gradient on the line was 1 in 7.) The C & HPR closed in 1967; much of the route is now being turned into a public footpath and bridleway. Around Whaley Bridge one may still see the remains of the short inclined plane which brought the goods down the hill, then through the town to the wharf at the terminus of the Peak Forest Canal.

Bugsworth
Derbs. PO, tel, stores. The main feature in Bugsworth (or 'Buxworth') is the old terminal basin system. This used to be a tremendously busy complex, and is of great

interest to industrial archaeologists. The canal line to Bugsworth was built to bring the canal as near as possible to the great limestone quarries at Doveholes, a plate tramway being constructed in 1799 via Chapel Milton to complete the connection. Known as the Peak Forest Tramway, this little line 6½ miles long brought the stone down the hills to Bugsworth, where it was transhipped into waiting canal boats. Throughout the history of the line, the wagons on the tramway were drawn exclusively by horse power—except for a 500yd inclined plane in Chapel-en-le-Frith, where the trucks were attached to a continuous rope so that the descending trucks pulled empty ones up the 1 in 7½ slope. The tramway was closed by 1926, and the sidings and basins at Bugsworth have been disused and overgrown since that time.
However the Inland Waterways Protection Society is working towards a complete restoration of the complex by voluntary labour and already part of the basin is cleared and reopened.

Furness Vale
Derbs. Pop 980. PO, tel, stores, garage, station. A main road (A6) village, useful for supplies.

PUBS

Jodrell Arms hotel Whaley Bridge. Lunches, dinners, etc (2164).
Station hotel Whaley Bridge. Lunches and dinners.
Navigation Whaley Bridge, near the canal terminus.
Navigation Bugsworth, by the canal terminus.
Dog & Partridge on A6, near swing bridge 34.
Soldier Dick Furness Vale.
Station hotel Furness Vale.

CARAVANS & CAMPING

Happy Vans Caravan Site Tunstead Milton, nr Whaley Bridge. (Stockport 6262). 1½ miles from canal, on A6. Overnight caravan stops. No tents permitted. Caravans for hire.
Ringstones Caravan Park Ringstones Farm, Whaley Bridge. (2152). 1 mile from canal, off A6. Overnight caravan and tent stops.

YOUTH HOSTEL

Windgather Cottage, Kettleshulme, Whaley Bridge. (Whaley Bridge 2153). 2½ miles south west of Whaley Bridge.

Marple Aqueduct, on the lower Peak Forest canal. The Marple–Manchester railway viaduct is in the background.

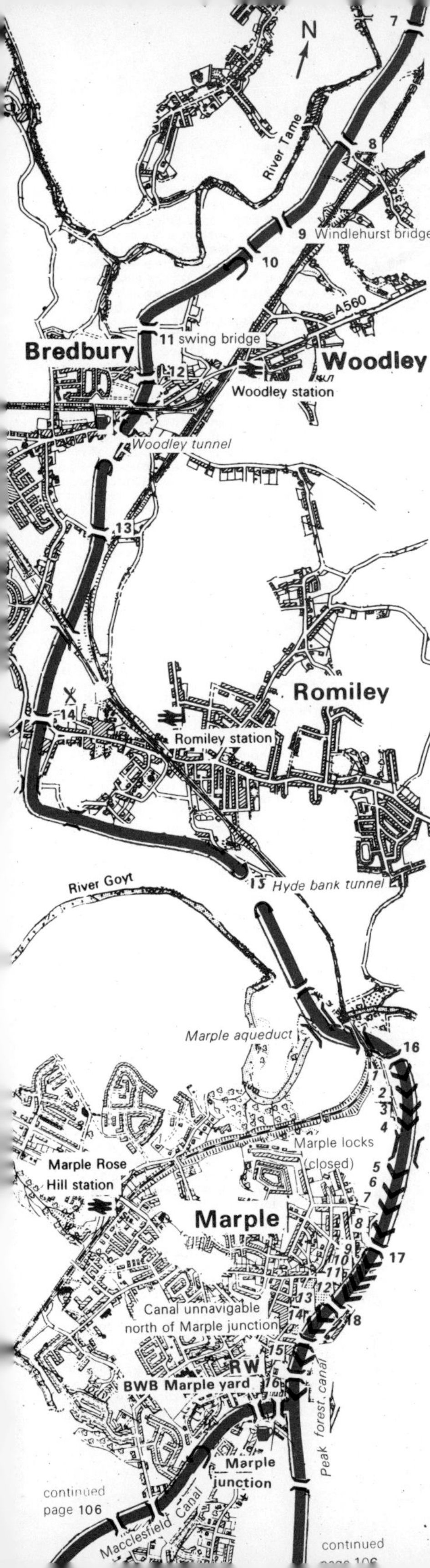

continued
page 106
continued
page 106

Marple Aqueduct

$5\frac{1}{2}$ miles

At Marple Junction the 16 narrow (standard 7ft beam) Marple locks carry the Peak Forest Canal down 210ft past the Macclesfield Canal towards Manchester. These locks, and the Peak Forest Canal beyond, are closed and unusable at the moment, as is the whole of the Ashton Canal. Soon these two derelict canals (with a combined length of over 14 miles) will be restored and reopened to cruising boats: this will complete a circle of navigable canals nearly 100 miles long. Meanwhile, the 2 canals are 'in water' and can be used by canoeists, anglers and walkers. The southernmost 5 miles of the 'lower' Peak Forest Canal (i.e. from Marple Junction northwards) are really very beautiful. The locks themselves, which are spaced out over 1 mile, have an unrivalled setting in an excellent combination of built-up area, parkland, tall trees and steep hillside; the river Goyt is hidden down in the wooded valley on the east. At the foot of the locks, where the river Goyt is crossed, one is treated to the double joys of a major canal aqueduct and an even bigger railway viaduct alongside. West of here, the canal traverses a wooded hillside before diving into the low, wide Hyde Bank Tunnel, 308 yards long. The towpath is diverted over the hill, past a farm. The other side, a couple of minor aqueducts lead the canal northwards, away from the Goyt valley and past Romiley, Bredbury and Woodley. Here is a narrow 176-yard long tunnel, this time with the towpath continued through it. Beyond these not unattractive outer suburbs of Manchester, the canal runs again along a hillside in unspoilt countryside, overlooking the tiny river Tame. There are plenty of trees and the occasional textile mill to add interest to the rural scenery. One should relish this length of the canal—it is the last one sees of the countryside before one enters the vast conurbation of Manchester.

Marple Aqueduct
Deservedly scheduled as an ancient monument, this 3-arched aqueduct over the river Goyt is a very fine structure, in an exquisite setting almost 100ft above the river. It was extensively repaired a few years ago after a partial collapse. Cheshire County Council paid a large part of the cost; BWB met the remainder.

Marple Locks
The 16 locks at Marple were not built until 1804, 4 years after the rest of the navigation was opened. The 1-mile gap thus left was bridged by a tramway, while the Canal Company sought the cash to pay for the construction of a flight of locks. This was obviously a most unsatisfactory state of affairs, since the limestone from Doveholes had to be shifted from wagon to boat at Bugsworth Basin, from boat to wagon at Marple Junction, and back into boat again at the bottom of the tramway. Not surprisingly, a container system was developed—using iron boxes with a 2-ton payload—to ease the triple transhipment. However this was no long-term solution, and when the necessary £27,000 was forthcoming the Company authorised construction of the flight of locks. The cost of restoring these locks today will probably represent the biggest single item in the scheme for the restoration of the Peak Forest Canal for pleasure craft.

BOATYARDS & BWB

BWB Marple Yard at Marple Junction, on the Macclesfield Canal. (061-427-1079). Water, refuse disposal and lavatory.

PUBS

Navigation Woodley, at north end of tunnel.

Waterside restaurant. Romiley, near bridge 14. *Closed Sun evening and Mon. PO, tel, stores, garage nearby.* (061-430-4302).

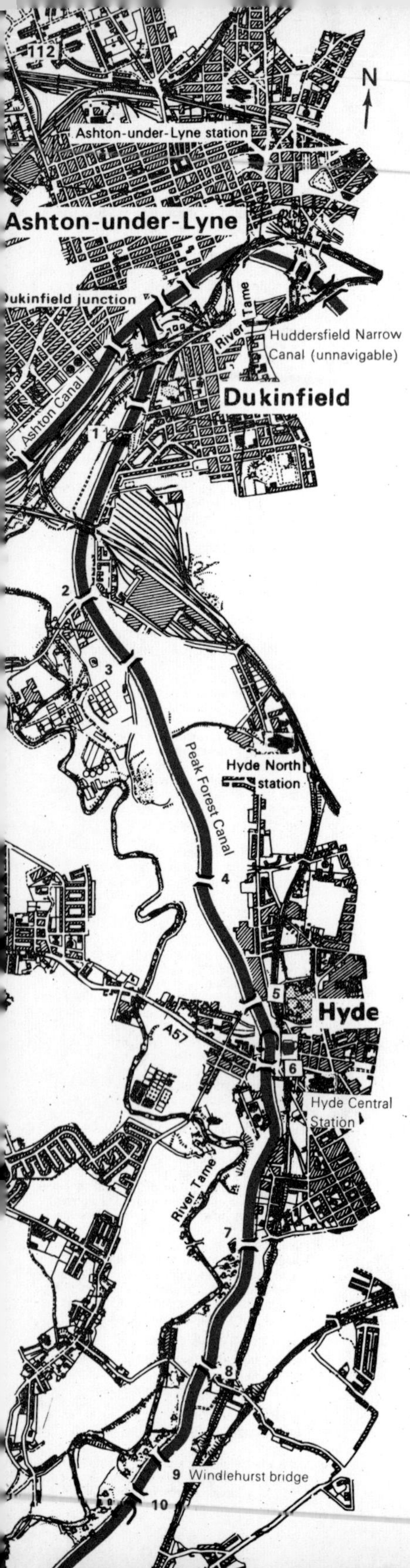

Hyde

4¾ miles

The canal continues northward through a landscape that becomes decreasingly rural or attractive. At bridge 7 the towpath changes sides; the building nearby is the Peak Forest Canal Society's headquarters. North of here the industrial tentacles of Hyde–outer Manchester–ensnare the canal traveller. Beyond Hyde, the canal traverses a great expanse of open wasteland, now used as a gigantic municipal rubbish tip. Seagulls enjoy the garbage. There used to be 2 short branches along here; they are untraceable now. As one approaches Dukinfield, a powerful sewage works lies to the left near an incongruously attractive farm (Plantation Farm). Further on, beyond several railway bridges, is a small aqueduct over the river Tame and the junction with the Ashton Canal.

The Ashton Canal continues for a short distance to the right–northeast–and then becomes the Huddersfield Narrow Canal. The latter has been infilled and piped for a short distance, beyond which many of the locks that used to lift boats on their way up and over the hills to Huddersfield have been filled in or weired. However the unnavigable Huddersfield Narrow Canal still fulfils the important function of carrying water down from its many reservoirs and streams high in the Pennines to feed the Ashton, Rochdale and Bridgewater Canals on the Lancashire side, and the Huddersfield Broad Canal and the Calder & Hebble on the Yorkshire side, as well as several factories along the way. It is with pleasant surprise that one finds the water in the upper part of the Ashton Canal crystal clear for many miles–a tribute to anti-pollution work done by BWB and the River Authority. However further towards the centre of Manchester, industrial pollution takes a heavy toll.

The Tame Valley Improvement Scheme
The river Tame flows close to the Huddersfield Narrow Canal from the Pennines down to Ashton Junction, where it is bridged by the Lower Peak Forest Canal. This canal then accompanies it as far south as Woodley, where the Tame turns west to join the river Goyt in Stockport. Here it joins the river Goyt, and from here onwards the 2 rivers form the headwaters of the Mersey. The Tame valley has for many years been an eyesore, little more than an ugly ribbon of neglected land between Lancashire and Cheshire. But now at last the valley is being brought back to life as a landscaped piece of parkland, under a scheme instituted by the Civic Trust and supported by the local authorities, Lancashire and Cheshire County Councils, the Mersey and Weaver River Authority and the British Waterways Board. Substantial improvements are now being undertaken, and when restoration of the derelict Ashton and Peak Forest canals (themselves an integral part of the valley improvement scheme) is complete, the whole area will form a valuable focus for recreation–in a district which badly needs it.

PUBS

Navigation a few yards E of bridge 6. *Shops and station are nearby.*

FISHING

From Whaley Bridge through the Marple, Hyde and Dukinfield lengths there are roach, tench, pike and some carp. The canal is popular with local anglers, and in places it gets heavily fished. The better chance of quality fish is had by the lone angler who approaches the water cautiously, so it is advisable to make up the landing net before starting to fish.

Droylsden

5¼ miles

From start to finish, the Ashton Canal passes through a densely built-up area in which the canal is conspicuous as an avenue of escape from the oppressive townscape that flanks it. Its clear water, its excellent towpath, its functional but dignified old bridges and the peace that surrounds it make it a natural haven for local schoolchildren, anglers, walkers and idlers, and for anyone else who enjoys an environment that is quite separate from and unrelated to his ordinary daily life. The canal has been decaying and unnavigable for several years, but happily it is at last being restored, assisted by volunteers from the Inland Waterways Association and the Waterway Recovery Group. In 1972 the BWB managed to persuade the 'riparian' councils that reopening the canal would not only produce a lively through navigation and the interest of visiting pleasure boats, but would simultaneously provide a unique local amenity. And so in future the citizens of Ashton-under-Lyne, Droylsden and Openshaw will be able to enjoy the rare pleasure, afforded only by an English canal, of stepping out of the noise and bustle of everyday life in a city suburb, into the peaceful and unpretentious atmosphere of the 18th century.

Leaving, then, Dukinfield Junction—where substantial old canal warehouses and docks face the Peak Forest Canal—one turns west towards Manchester. Electrified suburban railway lines jostle the canal, which enters a cutting and passes Guide Bridge. There are pubs, shops and a railway station nearby, but it can be difficult to scramble up the bank out of the cutting. Around Droylsden, 2 miles west, one finds the top of the 18 paired but derelict locks which fall gradually towards Manchester. At the top locks there was once a canal junction (Fairfield Junction): the 4½-mile branch from here to Hollinwood is now filled in. One can see the remains of several other old canal arms along the Ashton Canal: one of the more important ones was the 5-mile Stockport branch, leaving from Clayton Junction just below lock 11. Lock no. 9 is a sight to gladden the heart: it has been 'adopted' by an adjacent factory, the Anchor Chemical Company Ltd. Jointly with British Waterways, this enlightened firm, who own several factories along the canal, are undertaking a great scheme to improve the local canal environment by 'opening it out', tidying up their banks and planting trees. Already, lock 9 is resplendent with fresh paint and new paving. Below the lock a CIBA factory has landscaped its grounds beside the canal. These excellent projects are exactly the sort of development that the Ashton Canal needs so badly. If a few more firms along the canal were to contribute similarly to this form of 'social investment', then a precedent would be set for the long-overdue facelift of all our urban canals.

PUBS

Crabtree Canalside, at lock 13.
Yew Tree near the first lift bridge east of lock 16.

Manchester

4 miles

The canal now falls through the remaining seven locks into Manchester. The surroundings are generally drab and dreary, becoming more and more oppressively industrial until the canal becomes totally hemmed in by the back walls of tall factories—originally built there because of the canal's very presence—for half a mile above the bottom 3 locks. West of the bottom lock, the towpath is blocked off and one must take to the streets, leaving the canal to run its course over an aqueduct to the junction with the Rochdale Canal at Ducie Street. Even in an area like this there is great scope for developing an amenity feature, free from noisome road traffic.

The Rochdale Canal, which is still privately owned, used to stretch for 33 miles over the Pennines from Manchester to Sowerby bridge—where it joined the terminus of the Calder & Hebble Navigation. It has been closed to navigation, and in Manchester much of the canal has been reduced to a shallow, landscaped water channel. However the bottom mile of the canal is navigable, from the junction with the Ashton Canal at Ducie Street down to Castlefield and the junction with the Bridgewater Canal. This remaining mile of the Rochdale Canal is thus a vital link between the Bridgewater and Ashton canals in the 100-mile 'Cheshire Ring'. Persons wishing to navigate the 9 locks up from the Bridgewater Canal should apply in writing to the Head Office of the Rochdale Canal Company, 75 Dale street, Manchester 1 (061-236-2456). A charge is levied. The locks can accommodate vessels up to 74ft long and 14ft wide, drawing up to 4ft, with a height above water level of up to 9ft.

PUBS

City Barge 2 converted barges moored at the junction of the Ashton and Rochdale canals. One barge houses a bar, the other a restaurant. (*All meals bookable at 061-236-3720.*)

Navigation near lock 6, Ashton Canal.

TOURIST INFORMATION CENTRE

Manchester 119 The Piazza, Piccadilly Plaza. (061-236-0393).

Manchester Publicity Office, Town Hall Extension, Lloyd Street. (061-236-3377).

Weaver navigation

Mileage

River Weaver
Winsford Bridge to
Northwich: 5½ miles, 2 locks
Anderton Lift (Trent & Mersey canal): 7 miles, 2 locks
Acton Bridge: 11 miles, 3 locks
Sutton Bridge: 17 miles, 4 locks
WESTON POINT DOCKS (Manchester Ship Canal) 20 miles, 5 locks

Maximum dimensions

Winsford to Winnington
Length: 150′
Beam: 30′
Headroom: 29′
Winnington to Weston Point
Length: 176′
Beam: 30′
Headroom: 56′

Alone of all the waterways described in this book, the Weaver Navigation still carries a large amount of commercial traffic. In general terms, this must be due to its fortunate position in the centre of the salt and chemical industries, its endless supply of water, and the enterprising attitude of its past (and present) administrators.

The river itself, which rises in the Peckforton Hills and proceeds via Wrenbury, Audlem, Nantwich, Church Minshull and Winsford to Northwich and Frodsham, is just over 50 miles long. Originally a shallow and tidal stream, it was for long used for carrying salt away from the Cheshire salt area. The mineral was carried down by men and horses to meet the incoming tide. The sailing barges would load at high water, then depart with the ebbing tide. It was a somewhat unsatisfactory means of transport.

In the 17th century the expansion of the salt industry around Northwich, Middlewich and Winsford gave rise to an increasing demand for a navigation right up to Winsford. In 1721 3 gentlemen of Cheshire obtained an Act of Parliament to make and maintain the river as a navigation from Frodsham to Winsford, 20 miles upstream. Plans were drawn up, labourers were organised, and by 1732 the Weaver was fully navigable for 40-ton barges up to Winsford. It was naturally a great boost to the salt industry near Winsford, which now exported salt and imported coal via this splendid new navigation. And clay was also brought upstream to Winsford: it was then carted up to the Potteries by land.

When the Trent & Mersey was planned in 1765 to pass along the river Weaver the trustees of the Weaver were understandably alarmed; but in the event the new canal provided much traffic for the river, for although the 2 waterways did not join, they were so close at Anderton that in 1793 chutes were constructed on the Trent & Mersey directly above a specially built dock on the river Weaver, 50ft below. Thereafter salt was transhipped in ever increasing quantities by dropping it down the chutes from canal boats into 'Weaver flats' (barges) in the river. This system continued until 1871, when it was decided to construct the great iron boat lift beside the chutes at Anderton. This remarkable structure (which still operates) thus effected a proper junction between the two waterways. Trade improved accordingly.

The Weaver Navigation did well throughout the 19thC, mainly because continual and vigorous programmes of modernisation kept it thoroughly attractive to carriers, especially when compared to the rapidly dating narrow canals. The Weaver locks were constantly reduced in number and increased in size; the river was made deeper, and the channel wider; the docks at Weston Point (built in 1806 along with the canal from Frodsham cut to the docks) were duplicated and enlarged. Eventually coasters were able to navigate the river right up to Winsford. Much of this progress was due to the efforts of Edward Leader-Williams, who was the Engineer of the Weaver Navigation from 1856 to 1872, when he left to become Engineer of the new Manchester Ship Canal.

In spite of this constant improvement of the navigation, the Weaver's traditional salt trade was affected by 19thC competition from railways and the new pipelines. However the chemical industry began to sprout around the Northwich area at the same time, so the salt and clay traffic was gradually replaced by chemicals. Today, ICI's chemical works at Winnington supply all the traffic on the river: coasters up to 500 tons ship industrial chemicals out through the Manchester Ship Canal and to various ports in Europe. Meanwhile Weston Point Docks profit from being beside the Ship Canal (opened in the 1890s): well over 500,000 tons of merchandise are handled every year at this very flourishing port. A further boost to the river will be provided by the proposed new barge terminal at Winsford.

Winsford

6½ miles

Although Winsford Bridge (fixed at 10ft 8ins) is the upper limit of navigation for shipping and the limit of BWB's jurisdiction, canal boats can easily slip under the bridge and round the bend into the vast and wonderful Winsford Bottom Flash (controlled by Winsford U.D.C.). Navigation upstream of the Bottom Flash is unreliable, for the channel is shallow and winding, but can apparently be done by adventurous persons with small craft. The Top Flash is situated just beside and below the Middlewich branch of the Shropshire Union Canal; but there is no junction between them here.
Downstream of Winsford Bridge, there are some disused wharves—a good place to tie up. Further down is a winding stretch of little interest: each bank is piled high with the industrial leftovers of chemical industries. But soon the horizon clears as one arrives at Newbridge, beyond which is the superb stretch known as Vale Royal Cut.

Navigational Note
Boats with a headroom greater than 6ft 8ins will not clear the swing bridge known as Newbridge. Crews of such boats which are proceeding downstream should first telephone the BWB office at Northwich 74321 to arrange for the bridge to be opened.

Winsford
Ches. Pop 15,000. MD Sat. All services.
A busy salt-mining town astride the Weaver. The centre of town used to be very close to the river, but now a huge new shopping precinct has shifted the heart of the town well away from it. The riverside area is shortly to be redeveloped by the County Council. There has been no regular river traffic to or from Winsford for several years, and the wharves have decayed. However trade along the upper Weaver is now reviving: a company will begin shortly to operate a new barge terminal at Winsford, which will inject new life into the river. Winsford can be reached by barges of up to 400 tons and ships of up to 350 tons.
Winsford Bottom Flash This very large expanse of water (not owned by BWB) in an attractive setting among wooded slopes, was created by subsidence following salt extraction in the vicinity. It is a unique asset for the town, whose citizens obviously appreciate it to the full. 3 caravan sites and a sailing club are based along its banks, anglers crouch in the waterside bushes, and at the northern end (nearest to Winsford) one may hire dinghies and runabouts by the hour. To anyone on a canal boat, it is an unusual freedom from having to steer in straight lines all the time; and it must certainly be one of the few places accessible from BWB navigations where one is liable to encounter a full sailing regatta.

PUBS

Red Lion Winsford. Riverside, at Winsford Bridge.
Huntsman Restaurant Civic Centre, Winsford.

CARAVANS & CAMPING

Lido Caravan Park Newbridge, Winsford (2311). New riverside site for holiday caravans; overnight caravan and tent stops.
Cheshire Broads Caravan Site Stocks Hill, Winsford (2503). Beside Winsford Bottom Flash. Overnight caravan stops. No tents.
Ideal Caravan Park William st, Winsford (2198). Beside Winsford Bottom Flash. Overnight caravan stops. No tents.
Lakeside Caravan Park Stocks Hill, Winsford (4309). Beside Winsford Bottom Flash. Overnight caravan stops. No tents.

FISHING THE WEAVER NAVIGATION

The river Weaver, canalised in places, holds some exceptionally good fish. It is a popular venue for contests, particularly in the Hartford Bridge area, south of Northwich. Indeed, the fishing is not easy because it is so hard-fished by clubs.

The river has been extensively restocked, so it holds a tremendous head of roach and bream, which are the usual quarry. There are also good-sized tench and chub. Competitions are held by clubs and a catch of 40lb of roach in a 5hrs match stands as a local record. Good places are Hartford Bridge, Northwich and Winsford Bridge, where anglers are always to be seen, and where some fine fish are caught every season.

Navigating the Weaver Navigation

The Weaver Navigation is very much an 'odd man out' in this book. It is an old river navigation that carries a substantial traffic—transported not in canal boats or barges, but in small seagoing ships displacing up to 600 tons, which use the navigation at all times of day or night. The locks are correspondingly large and often paired. They are operated by keepers and may be used by pleasure craft only between the following times: Mon-Fri 8.00-17.00, Sat 8.00-11.00. They are also open on certain Sundays every year (dates obtainable from the BWB Area Office at Northwich 74321). The bridges are either very high, or are big swing bridges operated by BWB staff. With the exception of two very low ones, at Rock Savage and in Northwich, none of these bridges needs to be swung for any boat with a height above water of less than 8ft 10ins.

Although it is legally a 'Commercial Waterway' (and therefore there are very few facilities for pleasure craft), the Weaver Navigation is well worth a cruise up and down just to see the activity on it and the remarkably varied scenery. It is in fact best seen from a boat: walkers will find no towpath along much of its length, and motorists will find it extremely difficult to get at. But by boat one may easily enter the river, either from the Manchester Ship Canal or from the Trent & Mersey Canal, down Anderton Lift. Being largely canalised, the river presents no navigational problem to low-powered canal boats—except after heavy rain, when the sluices are opened and the current can flow reasonably fast and can be dangerous. Pleasure boats may be refused entry to the Navigation while such conditions prevail. One should always have a good anchor and a long warp, or chain cable, when using a pleasure boat on any river navigation—particularly one carrying commercial vessels. The giving of correct sound signals and compliance with the Byelaws and the 'Rule of the Road' is vital.

Winsford Bottom Flash, at the head of the Weaver Navigation.

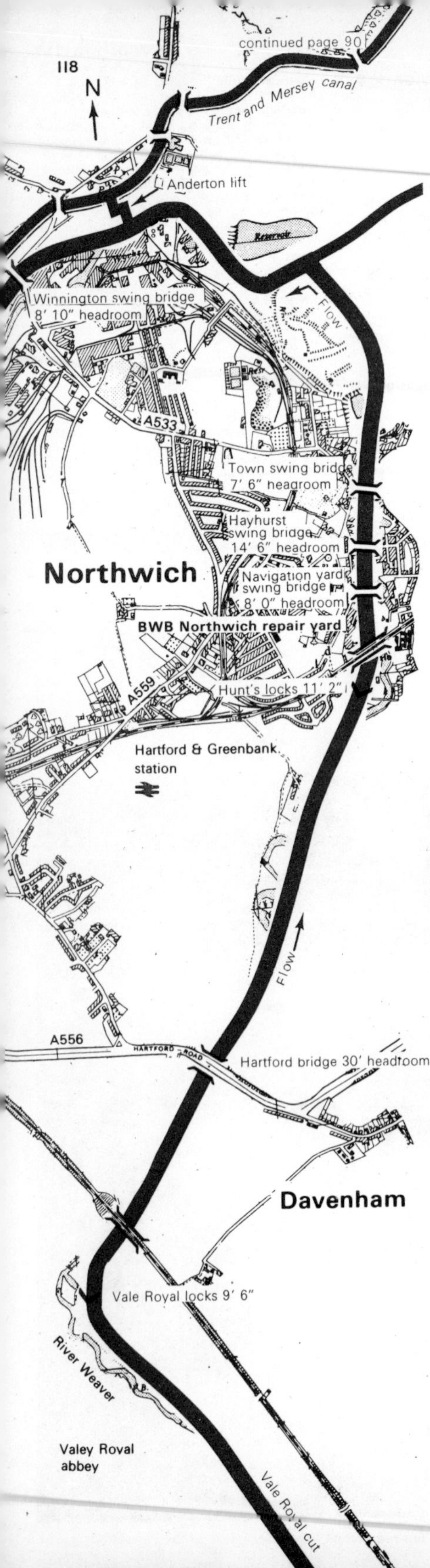

Northwich

5 miles

The Vale Royal Cut typifies the Weaver at its most attractive. The river flows along a closely-defined flat green valley floor, flanked by mature woods climbing the steep hillsides that enclose the valley. No buildings or roads intrude upon this very pleasant scene. Vale Royal locks are at the far end of the Cut; the remains of the old Vale Royal Abbey (believed to have been founded by Edward I and dissolved by Henry VIII) is just up the hill nearby. It is now much changed, and is a summer school for an electronics firm. Beyond is a tall stone railway viaduct, then Hartford Road bridge, a steel girder construction offering to ships a headroom of only 30ft– by far the lowest fixed bridge between Winsford and the Mersey.

Another stretch of pleasant water meadows leads to Hunts locks, another railway viaduct and the town of Northwich. The 3 swing bridges here are controlled by a keeper at Town Bridge (Northwich 74570); the very low one outside the BWB Repair Yard is normally left open at weekends. The trip through Northwich is pleasant enough, but north of the town the river twists and turns through a repetition of the industrial landscape that predominates outside Winsford. This stretch does not last long, and as the Anderton lift comes into view one rounds the bend to be confronted by the shipping tied up at the Winnington wharves.

Northwich

Ches. Pop 19,000. EC Wed, MD Fri, Sat. All services. A rather attractive town at the junction of the rivers Weaver and Dane. (The latter brings large quantities of sand down into the Weaver Navigation, necessitating a heavy expenditure on dredging.) As in every other town in this area, salt has for centuries been responsible for the continued prosperity of Northwich. (The Brine Baths in Victoria rd are still open throughout the year for the benefit of salt-water enthusiasts.) The Weaver Navigation has of course been another very prominent factor in the town's history, and the building and repairing of barges, narrow boats, and small seagoing ships has been carried on here for over 200 years. Nowadays this industry has been almost forced out of business by foreign competition, and the last private shipyard on the river closed down in 1971. (This yard–Isaac Pimblott's–used to be between Hunt's locks and Hartford bridge. Their last contract was a tug for Aden.) However the big BWB yard in the town continues to thrive; some very large maintenance craft are built and repaired here.

There is little regular river trade to the centre of Northwich at the moment, though it is hoped that this may be revived before long. In the meantime, the wharves by Town bridge are empty, and are an excellent temporary mooring site for anyone wishing to visit the place. The town centre is very close; much of it has been completely rebuilt very recently. There is now an extensive shopping precinct. Although the large number of pubs has been whittled down in the rebuilding process, there are still some pleasant old streets. The Weaver and the big swing bridges across it remain a dominant part of the background.

BOATYARDS & BWB

BWB Northwich Area Offices and Repair Yard (Northwich 74321). Alongside the extensive workshops is the Area Engineer's office–formerly the Weaver Navigation Trustee's offices. From here are controlled the Weaver Navigation, the Trent & Mersey Canal and a string of other BWB canals in the North West. Wet and dry docks for hire. As usual, this yard contains many mellow 18thC buildings. There is also an elegant clock tower on the office block.

PUBS

Northwich pubs include:
Beehive.
Crown hotel.
Sportsman.
Ko Wah in new shopping precinct. Chinese restaurant.

TOURIST INFORMATION CENTRE

Northwich Delamere Forest Centre, Linmere, Delamere. (Sandiway 2167).

CARAVANS & CAMPING

Daleford Manor Caravan Park Daleford lane, Sandiway (3391). 2½ miles west of Vale Royal locks, off A556. Overnight caravan stops; no tents permitted.

Anderton Lift from the Weaver Navigation. Both tanks are shown at the upper (Trent & Mersey canal) level.

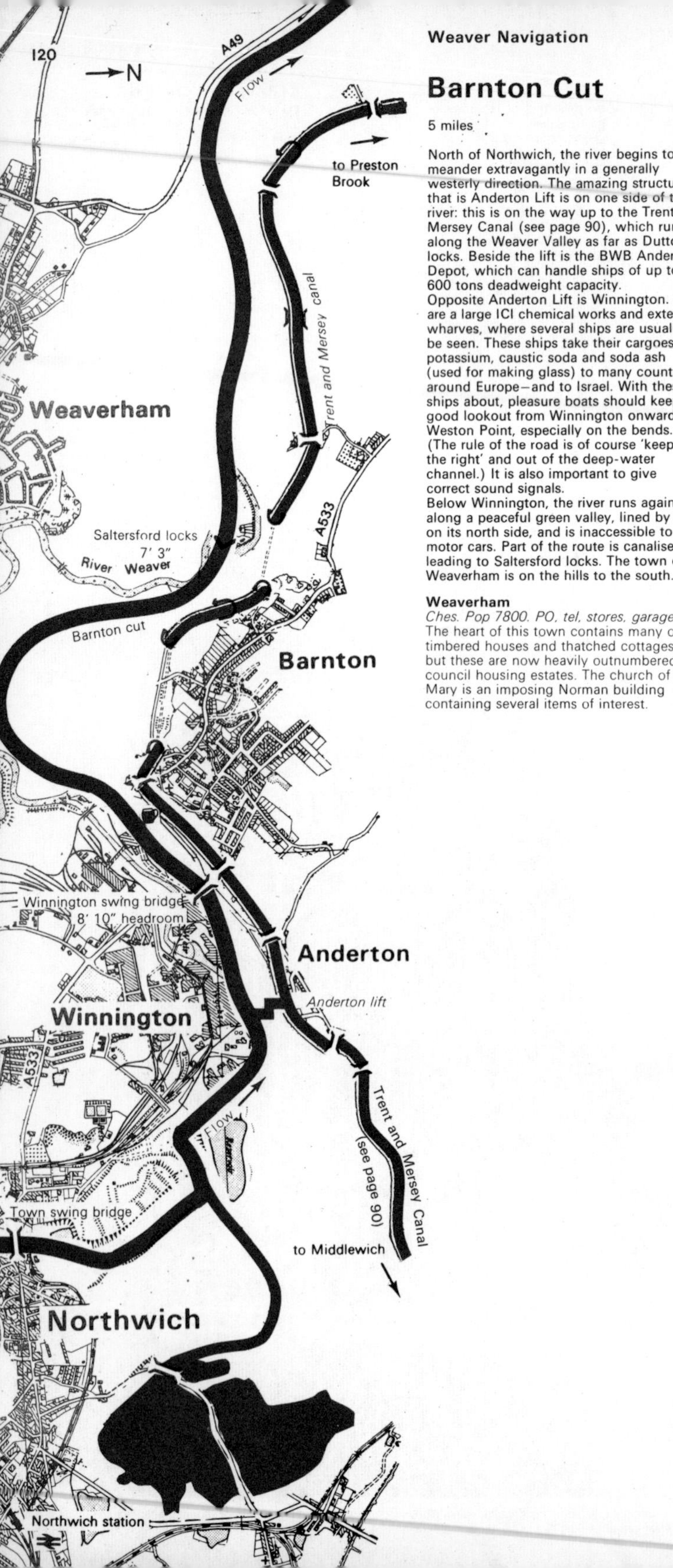

Barnton Cut

5 miles

North of Northwich, the river begins to meander extravagantly in a generally westerly direction. The amazing structure that is Anderton Lift is on one side of the river: this is on the way up to the Trent & Mersey Canal (see page 90), which runs along the Weaver Valley as far as Dutton locks. Beside the lift is the BWB Anderton Depot, which can handle ships of up to 600 tons deadweight capacity.
Opposite Anderton Lift is Winnington. Here are a large ICI chemical works and extensive wharves, where several ships are usually to be seen. These ships take their cargoes of potassium, caustic soda and soda ash (used for making glass) to many countries around Europe—and to Israel. With these ships about, pleasure boats should keep a good lookout from Winnington onwards to Weston Point, especially on the bends. (The rule of the road is of course 'keep to the right' and out of the deep-water channel.) It is also important to give correct sound signals.
Below Winnington, the river runs again along a peaceful green valley, lined by hills on its north side, and is inaccessible to motor cars. Part of the route is canalised, leading to Saltersford locks. The town of Weaverham is on the hills to the south.

Weaverham
Ches. Pop 7800. PO, tel, stores, garage.
The heart of this town contains many old timbered houses and thatched cottages—but these are now heavily outnumbered by council housing estates. The church of St Mary is an imposing Norman building containing several items of interest.

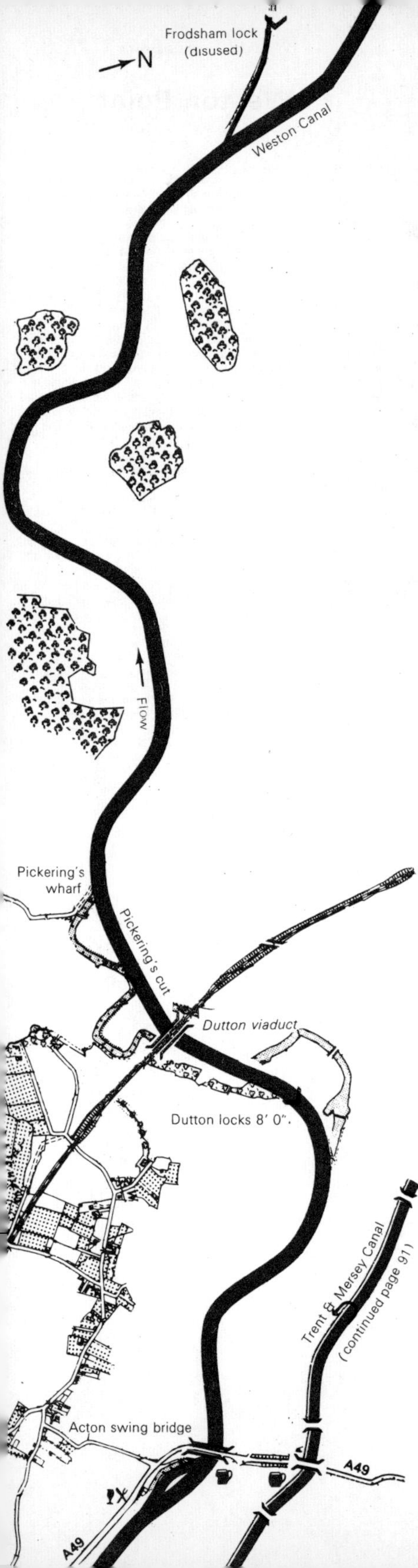

Pickerings Wharf

$5\frac{3}{4}$ miles

The A49 joins the river for a while, crossing at Acton bridge. A backwater here houses a boat club; pubs and a riverside restaurant are nearby. A mile further on, Dutton locks lead to the Dutton railway viaduct, whose elegant stone arches carry the main electrified West Coast line. Beyond the viaduct one comes to Pickering's Wharf, the site of a swing bridge long gone. From here down to Frodsham, the Weaver valley is a beautiful green, narrow cutting reminiscent of Vale Royal. Woods are ranged along the hills on either side. There are no roads, and no houses except one farm. It is a delightfully secluded rural setting.

As the valley gradually widens out to reveal the impending industrialism that stretches along the river from Sutton bridge, one may notice a branch off to the left. This is where a cut from the navigation leaves to fall through a shallow lock before rejoining the river course. This was the old line of navigation until 1827, when the Weston Canal was constructed to take the main line of the Weaver Navigation to Weston Point. One may still venture down the old cut to a swing bridge, now fixed, and the derelict lock. (The size of the lock reveals how much the navigation has been improved and enlarged in the past 100 years.)

PUBS

Horns Acton bridge, between the bridge and the Trent & Mersey Canal. Food at lunchtime and evenings. (Weaverham 2192).

Leigh Arms Acton bridge. Riverside, at the bridge.

Rheingold restaurant, Acton Bridge. Riverside, on south side of the river. Food served *except Sun evening and all Mon.* (Weaverham 2310).

CARAVANS & CAMPING

Woodbine Cottage Warrington rd, Acton Bridge (Weaverham 2319). Riverside. Overnight caravan & tent stops. Caravans & cabins for hire.

Nursery House Delamere rd, Norley. (Kingsley 777). $2\frac{1}{2}$ miles south of the river, on B5152. Overnight caravan & tent stops.

YOUTH HOSTEL

Delamere Forest Fox Howl, Ashton rd, Norley via Warrington. (Manley 393). $3\frac{1}{2}$ miles south of river.

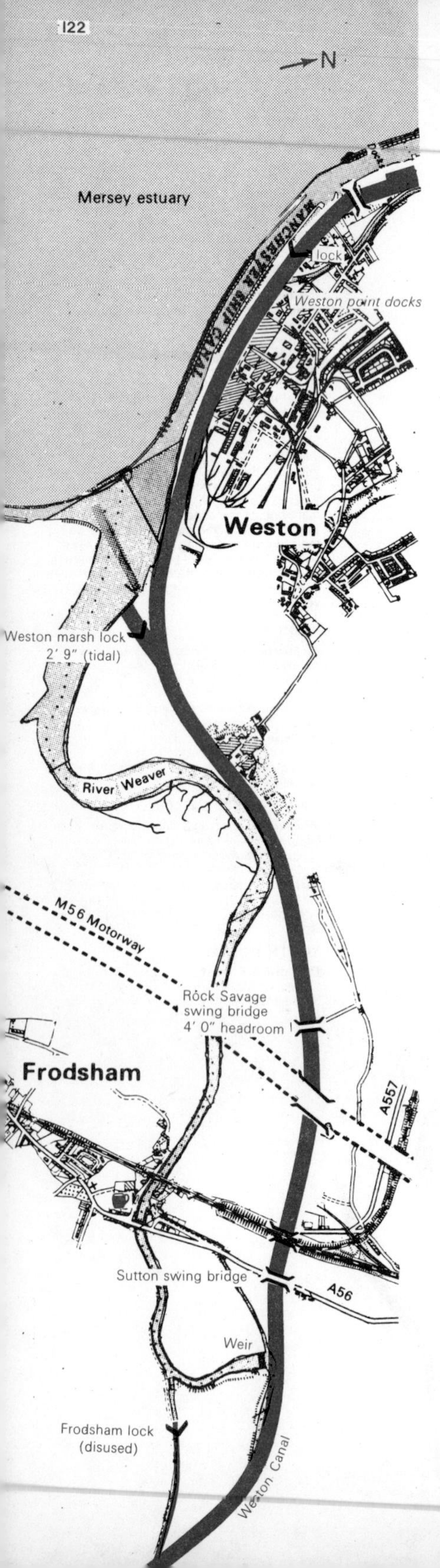

Weston Point

4¾ miles

Passing the former Sutton flood lock, now completely disused, the Weston Canal section of the Weaver Navigation now runs along the side of the valley, while the river follows its own twisting course down towards the Mersey. By Sutton (Frodsham) swing bridge one leaves for good the charming pastures that flank the Weaver; chemical works line one side of the canal all the way from here to Weston Point. The wooded hills and grassy fields of the Weaver suddenly seem very distant.
Rock Savage bridge is a little swing bridge with a maximum headroom of only 3ft 6in. The bridge-keeper is on duty during normal working hours. At Weston Marsh there is a lock down into the Manchester Ship Canal – this is the shortest way out of the Weaver Navigation (the lock is open during the ordinary working hours on the river). Beyond here the navigation goes right alongside the Ship Canal from which it is separated by a tall bank. Eventually, after passing the entrance lock up into the abandoned Runcorn & Weston Canal one arrives at a low (about 5 feet) swing bridge. Beyond it are the Weston Point docks and another lock into the Ship Canal. Pleasure boats may enter the dock only by arrangement with the Dock Manager's office (Runcorn 72218) and on payment of the appropriate fee.

Weston Point Docks
The BWB docks, at the junction of the Weaver Navigation's Weston Canal and the Manchester Ship Canal, are a bustling industrial centre. The docks are continually being modernised and their facilities expanded to handle ever-increasing tonnages (20% of which are now container traffic). In 1971, the docks handled a record 507,000 tons, earning for BWB a gross revenue of £591,000. Weston Point Docks are now one of the most important and profitable of BWB's Freight Services Division's undertakings.

Leeds & Liverpool

Maximum dimensions

Liverpool to Wigan, and Leigh Branch
Length: 72′
Beam: 14′ 3″
Headroom: 8′ 6″
Wigan to Leeds
Length: 60′
Beam: 14′ 3″
Headroom: 8′

Rufford Branch
Length: 62′
Beam: 14′
Headroom: 8′

Mileage

Liverpool to Leeds: 127 miles, 91 locks
Wigan to Leigh: 7¼ miles, 2 locks
Burscough to Tarleton: 7¼ miles, 8 locks

With a length of 127 miles excluding branches, the Leeds & Liverpool Canal is easily the longest single canal in Britain built by a single company. It is hardly surprising that its construction costs amounted to £1·2 millions, and that it took well over 40 years before the main line was completed.

The canal has its beginnings in the river Douglas, a little river made navigable by 1740—well before the canal age—all the way from Wigan to Parbold, Tarleton and the Ribble estuary. The navigation provided a useful outlet for coal from the Wigan area.

After a few years the idea of purely artificial canals as traffic routes became popular among businessmen, especially after the successful construction of the Duke of Bridgewater's canal from Worsley to Manchester. Several ambitious trans-Pennine schemes were mooted; one of these was for a canal from Liverpool to Leeds, where it would connect with the head of the Aire & Calder Navigation.

After much predictable argument between the promoters in Yorkshire and those in Lancashire about the actual route of the proposed canal, the Leeds & Liverpool Canal was authorised in 1770, and construction began at once, with John Longbotham as engineer. The first (lockfree) section from Bingley to Skipton was opened within 3 years; by 1777 2 long sections were open from the Aire & Calder at Leeds to Gargrave (incorporating many of the dramatic new staircase locks) and from Wigan to Liverpool. The river Douglas navigation had been embarrassingly close to the new canal's line, so the L & L had bought it out at an early stage to gain control of its valuable water supply. It was replaced by a proper canal branch to Rufford and Tarleton, where it joined the (tidal) river Douglas.

Construction was halted at this stage while trade flowed on to the separate lengths of navigation and the company summoned the resources to continue work on the canal. In 1790 a new money-raising Act of Parliament gave fresh impetus to the scheme for completing the difficult middle half of the canal. Work began again, with Robert Whitworth as the company's engineer; but after 1792 and the outbreak of war with France, the nation's purse strings grew steadily tighter while after the boom year of 1794 investment in canals declined steadily. With this unhealthy atmosphere prevailing, and in view of the difficulty of the terrain to be cut through, the canal company did not do badly to finish the whole of the main line from Leeds to Liverpool by 1816. (Under a convenient arrangement with the Lancaster Canal Company, the finished L & L line actually *shared* the channel of the Lancaster Canal for 10 miles.) This stretch is from Wigan top lock to Johnson's Hillock bottom lock. The Lancaster used then to branch off up what later became the Walton Summit Branch.

In 1820 a branch was opened to join the Bridgewater Canal at Leigh. A short branch (the Springs branch) was also made to rock quarries at Skipton and an important 3-mile long canal from Shipley to Bradford. (The cut down into the Liverpool Docks was not made until 1846.)

The prosperity of the company after 1820 was not, at first, greatly affected by the early advent of railways in that part of the country. The scale of the navigation (the locks were built—and remain—as barge locks 62ft by 14ft, allowing big payloads to be carried in each barge along the canal) no doubt contributed to the high dividends paid to shareholders for several years. Water supply was, however, a thorny problem from the very beginning, and in spite of the building of many reservoirs along the summit level, the canal had to be closed for months on end during many dry summers. Although through traffic has never been a very significant proportion of the trade on the canal, this lack of reliability tended, not surprisingly, to drive carriers' custom away to the railways. Use of the navigation for freight has declined throughout this century; the hard winter of 1962/63 finished off many traders. Today there is no Commercial traffic at all on the canal.

Liverpool

4 miles

The first ¼ mile of this canal has been filled in, so the navigation begins now at bridge 'A', near a Tate & Lyle factory. It runs north from the city centre for about 6 miles, parallel and close to Liverpool Docks, before turning east to Aintree, Wigan and the Pennines. The length of the canal from Liverpool to Old Roan Bridge at Aintree was classified by the 1968 Transport Act as a 'Remainder Waterway'. Discussions on its future are now taking place between BWB and the local authorities concerned. Liverpool is not an attractive place from the canal, which is completely shut off from the town by rows and rows of factories with their backs turned to the canal. For much of the way, substantial electricity pylons span the navigation. Access at the bridges to or from the canal is very difficult, because the towpath is officially closed to walkers, but naturally it is often alive with small boys fishing, playing and dropping or throwing things into the canal. The water, however, is surprisingly clear. This is because BWB have ceased to feed the canal with heavily polluted water from the river Douglas. Nowadays an alternative, cleaner source is used.

Navigational Note
Just north of the terminus is the Stanley Dock Branch. This useful connection from the canal down into Liverpool Docks and the river Mersey is nowadays the main raison d'etre of the west end of the Leeds & Liverpool Canal. There are 4 locks on the branch: they can be opened only by the resident BWB lock keeper in working hours between Monday morning and Saturday lunchtime. Any person wishing to use these locks would be advised to give prior notice to the lock keeper (tel 051-207-2449) or to the BWB Liverpool Section Inspector at Burscough 3160. Below the locks, one enters immediately the Stanley Dock: this belongs to the Mersey Docks & Harbour Company, whose permission should be sought before one enters the Dock. (Telephone the Waterloo Dockmaster at 051-236-1520.) The MD & HC are unlikely to refuse such a request, but do not like pleasure boats to tie up in the Dock. Navigators are encouraged to move straight on to the big lock down into the tidal river Mersey. (The lock is operated 24hrs a day.)

FISHING THE LEEDS & LIVERPOOL CANAL
In this canal there are roach, perch, bream, tench, carp, chub, gudgeon, eels and trout, but they are not all widely distributed throughout the canal—so they need finding. Despite being near some industrial areas the canal runs through some attractive country and offers enjoyable fishing.

TOURIST INFORMATION CENTRE
Liverpool Information Centre, 187 St John's Precinct, Elliot Street. (051-709 3631).

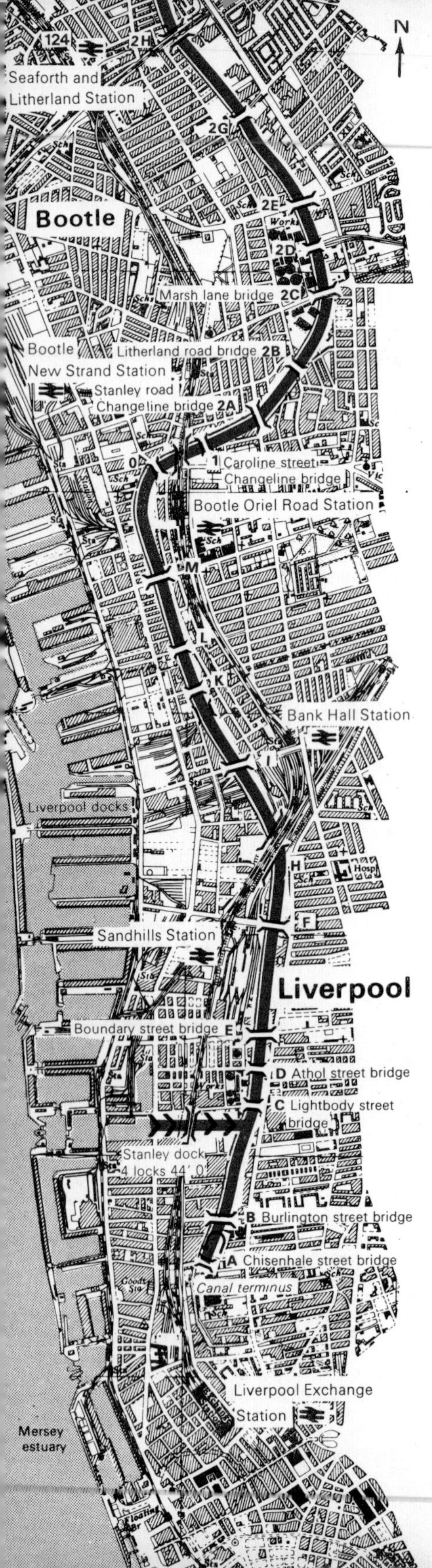

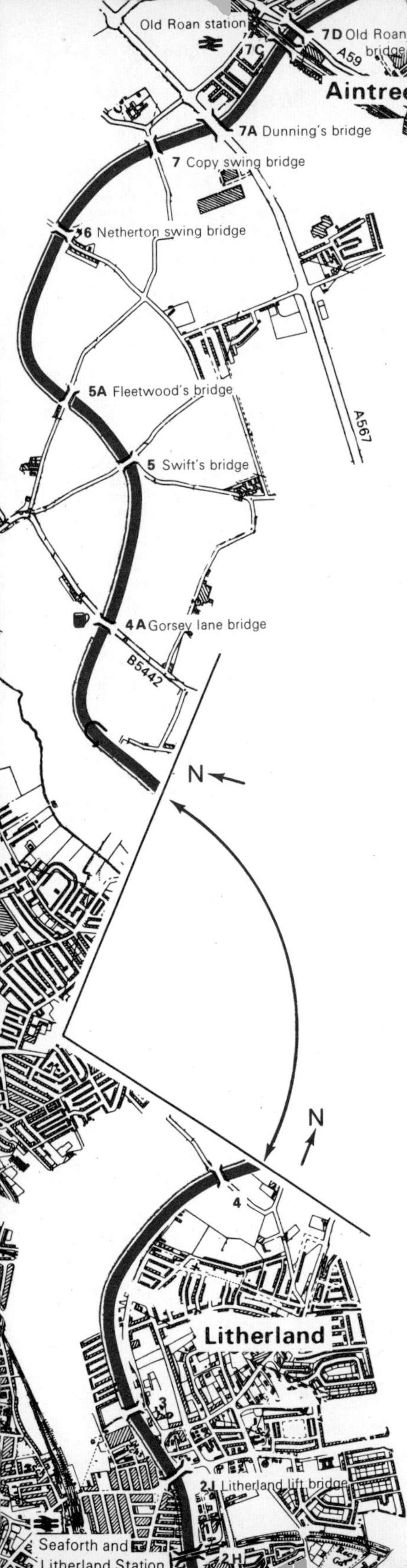

Litherland

$4\frac{1}{4}$ miles

Before one leaves the most heavily built-up area of Liverpool, one arrives at the Litherland lift bridge. This unusual structure is an electrically operated main road bridge complete with barriers, bells, lights and a resident bridge keeper—who should be given advance warning of any boat's approach (tel 051-928-3737 or Burscough 3160). After the operator has set in motion the barriers, bells and lights routine, the deck of the bridge rises vertically as 4 counterweights fall. It is very quick and efficient.

North of the lift bridge, the conurbation thins out and wastelands and suburbs appear, while the canal turns east to Aintree. Soon the first of many swing bridges is encountered; for the first few miles these bridges have to be intricately padlocked to combat vandalism, so progress through them is necessarily slow. All boatmen should ensure that they have the requisite key before reaching these bridges. (Keys obtainable from the lock keeper at Stanley Dock, or from the BWB Burscough Yard—see page 128.)

PUBS

Tailor's Arms Canalside, at bridge 4A.

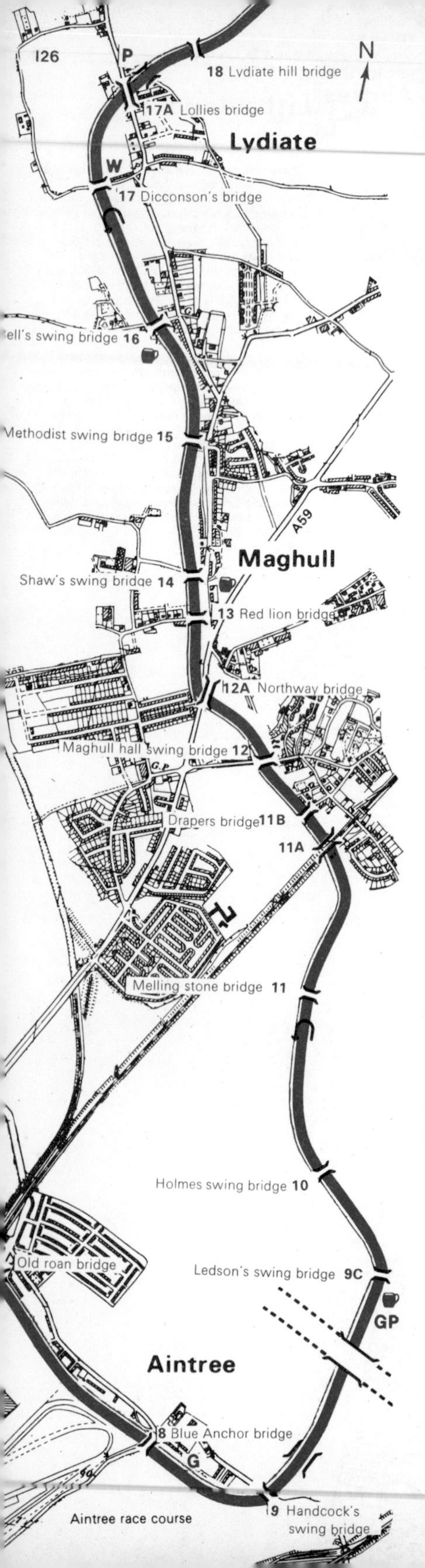

Maghull

$6\frac{1}{4}$ miles

Aintree marks the limit of the Livérpool outskirts. The great feature here is of course the Aintree race course: the famous Grand National steeplechase is run every year on a Spring Saturday. Much of the course lies right beside the canal, but would-be spectators from the canal will have to stand upon their boat's cabin top to see over the fence surrounding the course.
At the east end of the racecourse is another swing bridge; this carries a busy main road and traffic lights are installed, but boat crews operate the bridge themselves. Here the canal turns north again, and as the little church tower at Melling comes into view the navigation emerges at long last into open countryside, although Maghull soon looms up to interrupt this with a series of swing bridges.

Maghull
Lancs. Pop 16,000. EC Wed. All services
A small town astride the canal, convenient for supplies. Since the last war it has greatly expanded, but still maintains its former village atmosphere.
St. Andrew's Church Damfield lane (just north of bridge 12A). Though separated from the rest of the town by a well patronised dual carriageway, it is well worth a visit: it has a cosy setting among trees that seem to compete with the tower for height. It was built in the late 19thC but its style is in imitation of that of the 13thC to accord with the tiny 700-year-old chapel known as Old St Andrew's in its grounds. The chapel is a charming little building, said to be the oldest church in the Merseyside area.

Melling
Lancs. PO, tel. The sight of this little village is like a breath of fresh air to anyone coming along the canal from Liverpool, although southbound travellers probably find it unremarkable. The village stands on an isolated hillock at a safe distance from the big city. The church is a landmark in the area; it was built in the 15thC with rock from an adjacent quarry.

PUBS

Scotch Pipers Lydiate, north of bridge 17A.
Running Horses Maghull. Canalside, at bridge 16.
Hare & Hounds Maghull, near bridge 14.
Bootle Arms Melling.
Horse & Jockey near bridge 9C.
Old Roan Aintree, near Old Roan bridge 7D.

FISHING

The Aintree to Maghull length offers sport with roach, bream, tench, perch, pike and occasional chub. Match catches are steadily improving. Around Maghull itself, the fishing is good for most species. Bream, tench and roach over 1lb have been taken here. This stretch has been restocked extensively with different species. In the Lydiate area roach to $1\frac{1}{2}$lb are caught, and this is a popular fishing length with some big angling contests held. Restocking of most species has improved catches. The canal's match-weight record of 12lb of fish in 2hrs was made here.

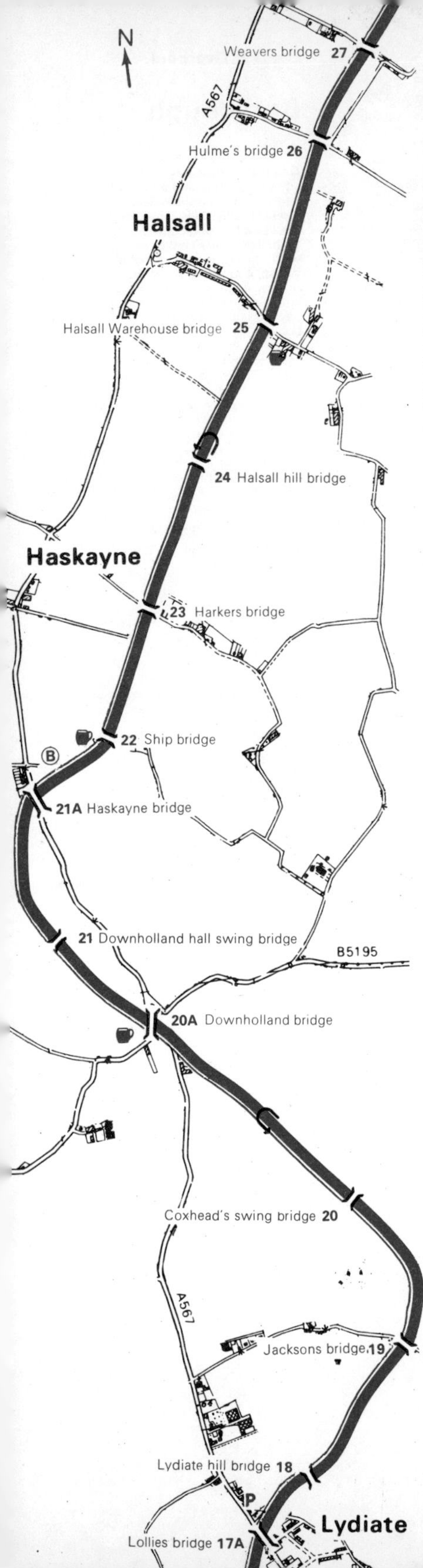

Halsall

5¼ miles

The canal now enters continuous open countryside, which soon establishes itself as extremely flat and intensively cultivated lowlands: indeed it is more akin to Cambridgeshire or Lincolnshire than to the rest of Lancashire. However it is pleasant enough and the canal forms one of its more important features—a view which is borne out by the large number of people usually to be seen walking and boating upon it, as well as the hundreds of anglers enjoying their sport in this well stocked length of canal. As if in compensation for the unexciting landscape, the traveller is offered a truly astonishing number of pubs on or near the canal all the way from Lydiate to Wigan.

Halsall
Lancs. PO, tel, garage. There is a handsome tall 14th-15thC church here (St Cuthbert's), with a fine spire. The choir vestry, erected in 1592, was formerly a grammar school. There is an interesting pair of pulpits/ lecterns. One of them is generously illuminated by a solitary overhead window; the other, more sheltered, one gives the occupant the unfortunate air of being behind bars . . .

Haskayne
Lancs. PO, tel, stores. There are just 2 pretty houses here: the post office and the old thatched cottage opposite. No sign of a church.

BOATYARDS & BWB

Canal Boats The Ship Inn, Rosemary lane, Haskayne, nr Ormskirk, Lancs. (Halsall 446). Hire cruisers. Water, diesel, gas, chandlery, dustbins. Moorings, winter storage. Boat sales, inboard engine sales. *Open daily throughout the year.*

BOAT TRIPS Traditional short boat 'Peace' operates from the Saracen's Head, Halsall. Available by charter for parties of up to 65 passengers. Enquires to: Flower of Gloster Moorings, Bridle Way, Bootle, Lancs. (051-525-93).

PUBS

Saracen's Head Halsall. Canalside, at Halsall Warehouse bridge.

Ship Haskayne. Canalside, at Ship bridge. A well-known canal pub.

King's Arms Haskayne. 100yds north of bridge 21A.

Scarisbrick Arms Canalside, at Downholland bridge.

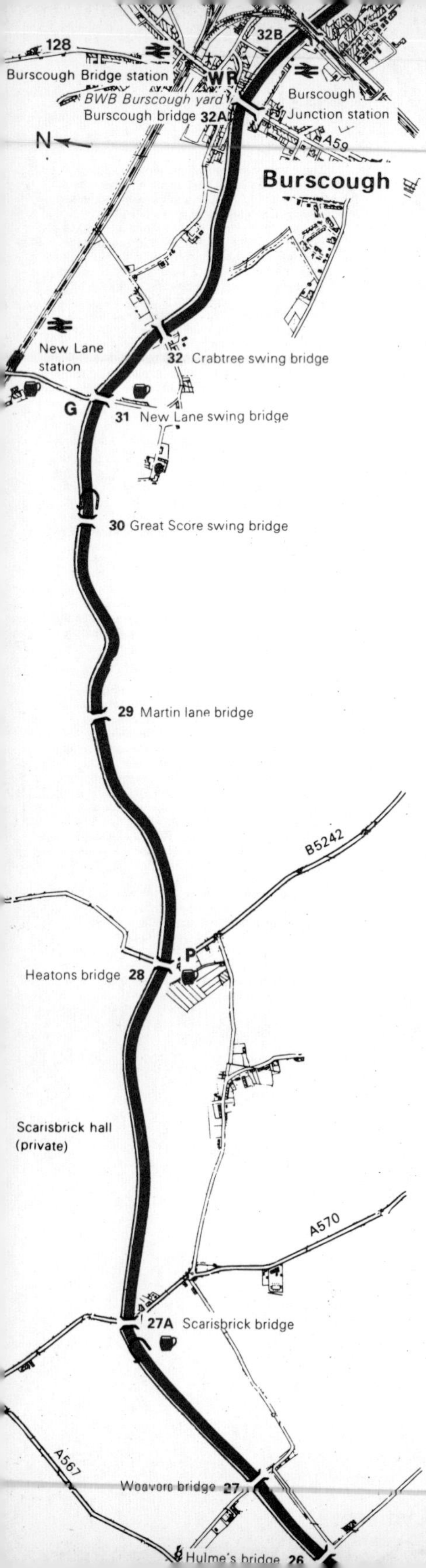

Burscough

5 miles

One moves now past a massive caravan site on one side and attractive woods containing the private Scarisbrick Hall on the other; then one moves out again into the open flat lands. The Southport–Manchester line converges from the north-west: it runs near the canal all the way into Wigan, and sports some wonderfully remote stations. A flurry of swing bridges brings the canal into Burscough: just beyond is the junction with the Rufford branch.

Burscough
Lancs. PO, tel, stores, garage, bank, station. Formerly a canal village and a staging post on the one-time Wigan–Liverpool packet boat run, this place attaches more significance nowadays to the benefits of road and rail transport. It still boasts 2 stations (one is on the Preston–Liverpool line) and suffers from heavy through traffic. A very convenient place for taking on victuals.

BOATYARDS & BWB

BWB Burscough Yard Water, refuse, dry-dock. (Burscough 3160).

PUBS

Royal Burscough.
Railway at New lane station.
Farmer's Arms Canalside, by swing bridge 31.
Heatons Bridge Inn Canalside: not a thousand miles from Heatons bridge.
Red Lion near Scarisbrick bridge. Food.

CARAVANS & CAMPING

Ormskirk Caravan Centre Scarisbrick Bridge, nr Ormskirk, Lancs. (Halsall 263). Canalside, at Scarisbrick bridge 27A. Overnight caravan and tent stops. Gas, chandlery. Big holiday caravan centre.

FISHING

In the Scarisbrick area re-stocking has been carried out and sport is pretty good from here to Wigan with roach, bream, perch, pike, etc.

128
Burscough Bridge station
BWB Burscough yard
Burscough bridge 32A
32B
WR
Burscough Junction station
A59
N
Burscough
New Lane station
32 Crabtree swing bridge
G
31 New Lane swing bridge
30 Great Score swing bridge
29 Martin lane bridge
B5242
P
Heatons bridge 28
Scarisbrick hall (private)
A570
27A Scarisbrick bridge
A567
Weavers bridge 27
Hulme's bridge 26

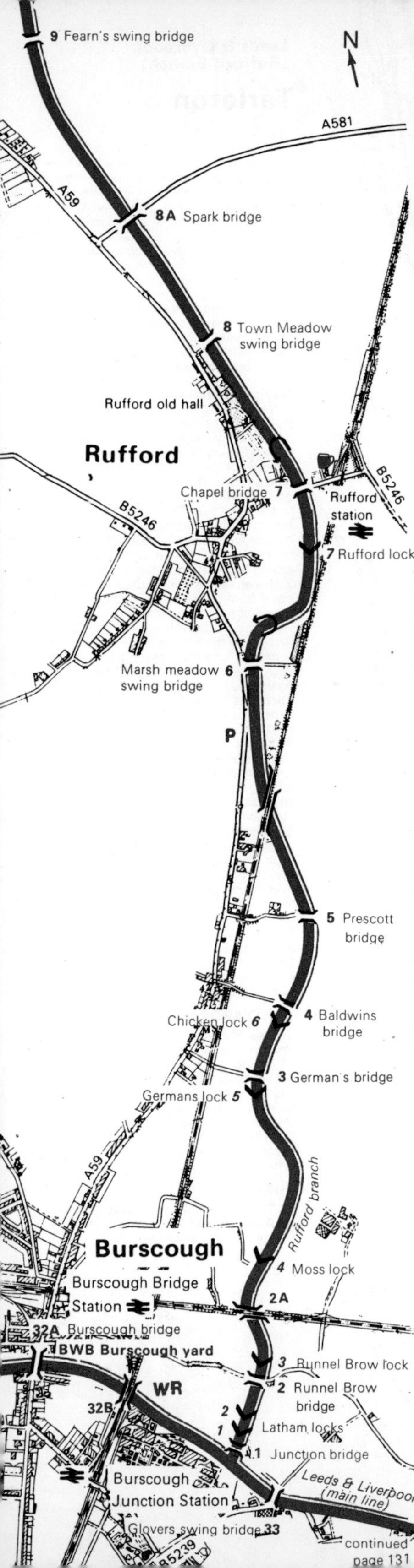

Rufford

5 miles

The Rufford branch leaves the Leeds & Liverpool main line just east of Burscough, through an imposing arched bridge dated 1816. A little canal settlement surrounds the top lock and the roomy drydock for barges here. The locks come thick and fast to begin with, as the canal falls through the very fertile and gently sloping farm lands towards the distant Ribble estuary. The country is generally quiet, flat and unspectacular but agreeable. A line of trees and the spire of Rufford church are followed by the beautiful Rufford Old Hall, on the west bank.

Rufford
Lancs. PO, tel, stores, garage, station. Main road village noted for its Hall. The church is a small Italianate Victorian building containing many monuments to the Hesketh family who owned Rufford Hall for many centuries; obviously a prolific family judging by one large sculpture depicting a brood of 11 children, dated c. 1458.

Rufford Old Hall *NT property.* On the west bank of the canal. A mediaeval timber-framed mansion with Jacobean extensions. The interior is magnificently decorated and furnished in period style, especially the great hall with its hammer-beam roof and 15thC intricately carved movable screen—one of the few still intact in England. The Hall also houses a folk museum. *Open weekdays 12.00-20.00 (or dusk if earlier), Sun 13.00-20.00 (or dusk). Closed Mon. Also closed Wed. from Oct-Mar and Thur in Dec and Jan.* (Rufford 254). Note: although the Hall is beside the canal, one may **not** enter the grounds direct from the canal. Boatmen should therefore tie up near bridge 7, then walk up to the village and turn right at the main road. The entrance is a few hundred yards along the wall on the right.

PUBS

Fermor Arms near Rufford station. A large old pub with an amazing tilt: it clearly won't stand for ever.

Hesketh Arms Rufford.

Ship Burscough, near 2nd lock down. An old canal pub formerly known as the Blood Tub. Old boatmen know why.

FISHING

The Rufford Branch is not so popular with club anglers as is the main line of the Leeds & Liverpool yet it once yielded a Lancashire record perch of 3lb 3oz. There are still a few big perch, but they need to be hunted.

continued page 131

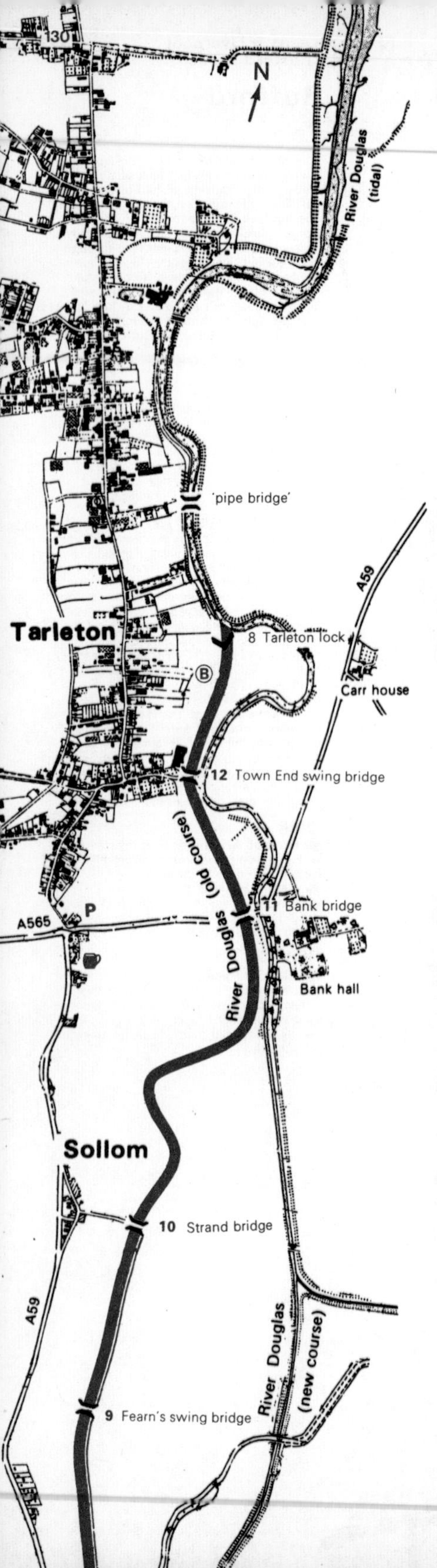

Tarleton

3 miles

At Sollom there used to be a lock until a few years ago, but now it is no more. This is where the canal turns into the old course of the river Douglas, and it twists and turns as though to prove it. The towpath has been ploughed up from here onwards. The 'new' course of the Douglas (which was once navigable from the sea right up to Wigan) comes along side the canal at the busy road bridge near Bank Hall, a derelict house hidden by trees. From here it is only a short distance to the final swing bridge and Tarleton lock, where the canal connects with the tidal river Douglas—which in turn flows into the river Ribble near Preston.

Navigational notes

1. Vessels wishing to enter or leave the Rufford Branch via Tarleton lock can only do so at high water. The Douglas is then a relatively easy navigation, and since the removal of the old railway swing bridge a mile downstream, there has remained only one limitation on headroom from Tarleton to the open sea. This is a pipe bridge not far north of Tarleton lock: the clearance at normal high water is about 20ft. The boatyard at the lock may help callers with advice regarding tide times, etc.
2. Navigators entering the Rufford Branch canal from the sea should remember that they will need a padlock key—as well as a windlass—to open the locks up the branch. Arrangements can be made with the BWB Burscough Yard (Burscough 3160) to have such a key left with James Mayor's boatyard.

Tarleton

Lancs. Pop 3400. PO, tel, stores, garage, bank. A large village luckily avoided by the A59 road. There are some useful shops.

Barry Elder Doll Museum Carr House, Bretherton (Croston 451). ¾ mile N of Bank bridge, on the A59. This remarkable collection numbers some 1200 dolls fashioned from all manner of materials, and gathered from all over Europe. The largest is 4ft high and the smallest less than ½ an inch. They date from the late 17thC up to the 1920s and almost seem to have taken over the whole house, as they fill every room. Carr House was built in 1613 and for a short time was the home of Jeremiah Horrocks (often called the father of English astronomy). The house was restored in 1965 and the museum, which was originally in Hammersmith, opened in it in 1966. *Open daily 10.00-19.00 Mar-Oct.*

BOATYARDS & BWB

James Mayor The Boatyard, Tarleton, Preston, Lancs. (Hesketh Bank 2250). At Tarleton lock. Caters mainly for sea-going boats. Dustbins, water, diesel, gas, chandlery, drydock, 6 slipways up to 90 foot, moorings, winter storage. Boat & motor sales & motor repairs. Steel & wood boats built & fitted out. Lavatories. Telephone. *Open daily throughout the year.*

PUBS

Tarleton hotel in Tarleton village.

Ram's Head Tarleton, ½ mile W of bridge 11. Bed and breakfast.

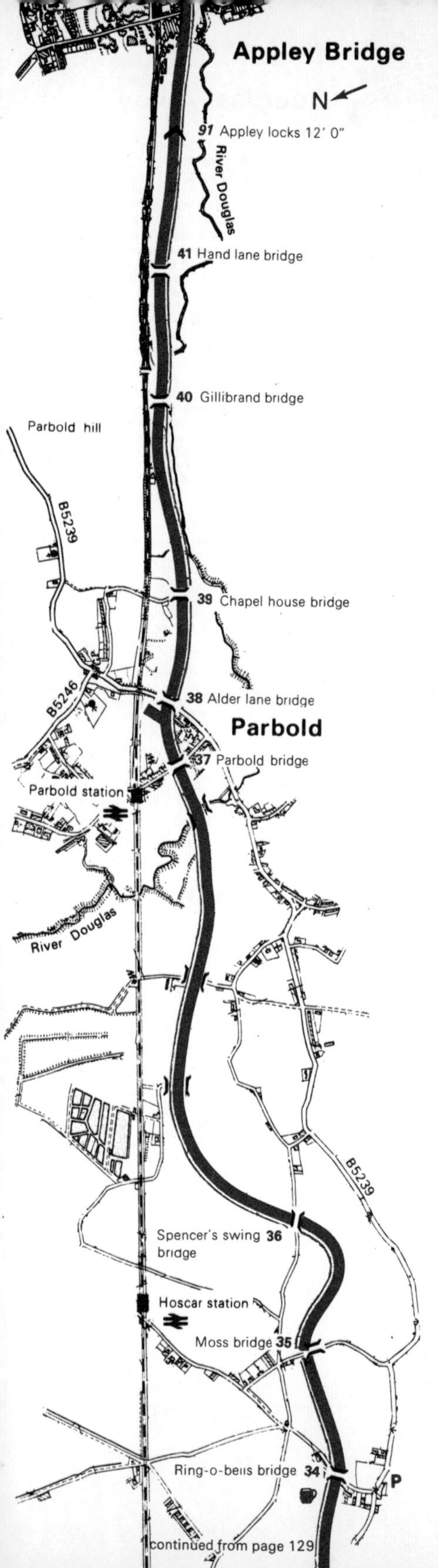

continued from page 129

Parbold

4¾ miles

East of the junction with the Rufford branch, the canal meanders through the flat countryside to the village of Parbold with its ancient sail-less windmill. Here the scenery changes completely as the canal crosses the river Douglas and then joins the Douglas valley. This is a very pretty, narrow wooded valley which the canal shares with the railway: there are several convenient stations along the line. Appley locks are reached: these were once duplicated to save water, one being used as a navigable sidepond to the other for boats passing in opposite directions. The present lock is extremely deep. **As with all subsequent locks, the gates should be closed and the paddles lowered and padlocked after use to combat vandalism and wastage of water.**

Parbold
Lancs. PO, tel, stores, garage, station.
A large village climbing up from the west end of the Douglas valley, Parbold is prettiest near the canal bridge, where the big brick tower of the old windmill is complemented by an equally attractive pub. Unfortunately the rest of the village is being engulfed by acres of new housing. Local landmarks are the tall spires of Parbold's two churches, and Ashurst's Beacon high on a hill to the south. The latter was built in 1798 by Sir William Ashurst in anticipation of an invasion by the French. (The beacon was intended as a local warning sign.)

The Douglas Navigation
The little river Douglas, or Asland, was made navigable in the first half of the 17thC, well before the great spate of canal construction. It provided the Wigan coal-field with a useful outlet to the tidal river Ribble, from which the cargoes could be shipped over to Preston or along the coast. When the Leeds & Liverpool Canal was built to share the Douglas valley, the old river navigation became superfluous. It was bought up by the new company, who constructed their own branch to the Ribble estuary (the Rufford branch). Between Parbold and Gathurst, the explorer may find many traces of the old navigation, including several locks.

PUBS

- **Windmill** Parbold, near bridge 37.
- **Ring O' Bells** Canalside, at bridge 34.

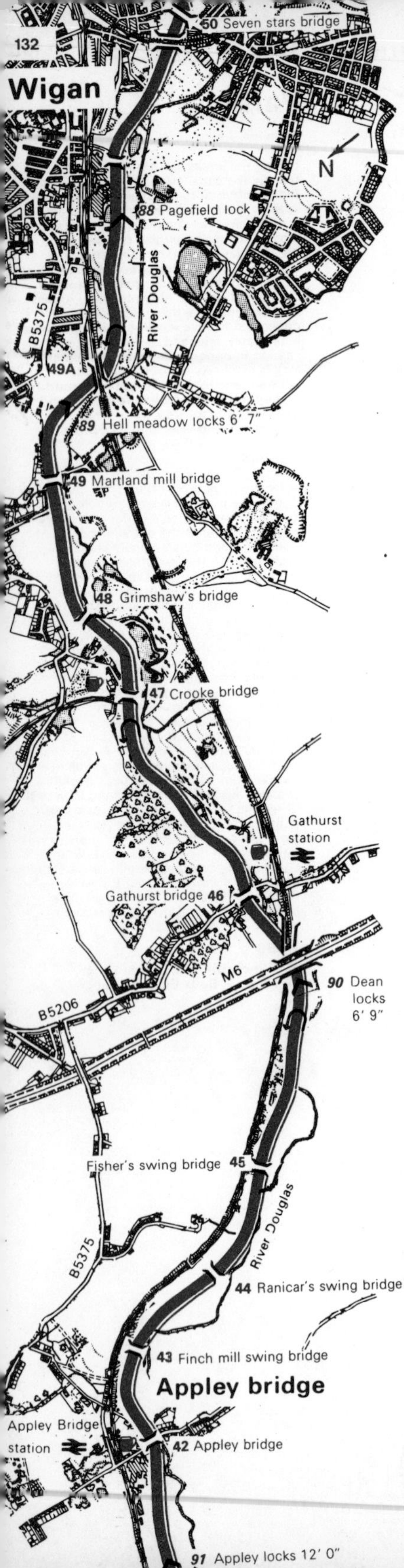

Douglas Valley

5 miles

The canal now goes through Appley Bridge and runs up the beautifully rural Douglas valley, with the river on one side and the Wigan–Southport railway on the other. Passing 3 consecutive swing bridges, one soon reaches Dean locks, a pleasant spot in spite of the high motorway viaduct nearby. This used to be a very busy place, for in addition to the duplicated canal locks (one of which is now derelict) there used to be a lock down into the river Douglas Navigation, when this was navigable before the Rufford branch was built. Just east of the locks is a pleasant canalside pub, then the valley widens out to reveal the chimneys and factories of Wigan. Hell Meadow (sometimes mistaken for 'Ell Meadow') and Pagefield locks lead the canal up through the now drab scenery towards the centre of Wigan. For those wishing to stop in the town, the best place to leave a boat is further on, at the BWB Repair Yard at Wigan bottom lock (no. 87). The BWB Wigan Area Engineer's office is here.

Appley Bridge

Lancs. PO, tel, stores, station. A canalside hamlet dominated by large mills and works, the place is nevertheless attractively situated in the wooded Douglas valley.

PUBS

Duncan Arms Crooke, near bridge 47.
Navigation Gathurst. Canalside, at bridge 46.
Railway Appley Bridge by the canal.

FISHING

Around the Wigan area roach over 2lb and perch over 3lb have been caught in recent seasons.

Abram

$5\frac{1}{4}$ miles

The Leigh branch leaves the main line of the Leeds & Liverpool Canal in Wigan, between the big power station and the 22nd lock. Descending through 2 locks, it enters the lock-free level that extends all the way along the Bridgewater Canal to Preston Brook and Runcorn, over 40 miles away. Unfortunately the branch passes through empty, flat wasteland that is devoid of any features, save a string of mostly closed railways. Most of the way, the canal is on an embankment, well above the level of the surrounding landscape: this is a relatively new situation and is due to severe mining subsidence in the area. (The canal has had to be built up—appropriately with pit waste—while the land on either side has sunk.)

BOATYARDS & BWB

BWB Wigan Yard at Wigan bottom lock. (Wigan 42239). Water, dustbins, lavatory. Drydock, slipway up to 60 foot. Sewage disposal at lock 86.

PUBS

Red Lion Canalside, at Dover bridge 4. There used to be 2 locks nearby: they were removed years ago, becoming unnecessary as the level of the land changed.

FISHING

The length from Wigan to Leigh is heavily fished at weekends by local club anglers who catch mainly roach and perch. There are big carp to double figures in this area. Fish of 20lb have been reported.

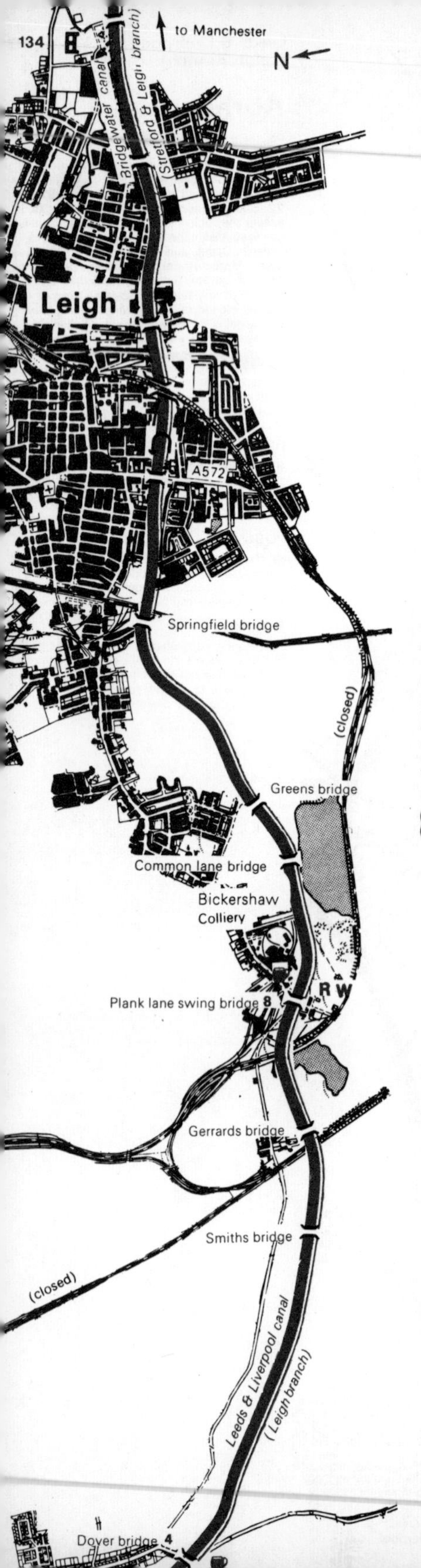

Leeds & Liverpool (Leigh Branch)

Leigh

4¾ miles

The Leigh branch continues eastwards through this desolate no man's land. There is just one working coalmine left along here now: this is Bickershaw Colliery, from which motor barges still carry coal to Wigan Power Station. Near this big colliery is Plank Lane swing bridge, which is mechanically operated. Navigators should knock at the adjacent house in daytime to ask the resident bridge-keeper to operate the bridge, which carries a busy road. Past the swing bridge, tall cotton mills mark the entrance into Leigh, where the canal suddenly becomes the Bridgewater Canal (without the customary stop lock), giving access to Manchester and—before the disastrous breach at the Bollin Aqueduct near Dunham in 1971—Preston Brook. This navigation is owned by the Manchester Ship Canal Company: boats licensed by BWB may use the Bridgewater without further charge for up to 7 days. (See page 171 for a map of canal connections from Leigh.)

Leigh

Lancs. Pop 46,000. EC Wed, MD Wed, Fri, Sat. All services. An industrial town centred around its old market place and parish church. Most of the town buildings are the result of a large redevelopment scheme, which provided housing estates and a new market; even the mediaeval church of St Mary was largely rebuilt between 1869 and 1873. Standing prominently in the Market Place, it is a forbidding, battlemented structure—an unlikely setting for the unusual ceremony taking place there every Maundy Thursday, when 40 poor people step over the grave of Henry Travice to qualify for his bequest of five shillings each. Mr Travice made out this bequest in 1626.

PUBS

- **Packet Inn** by Plank Lane swing bridge.
- **Britannia** Plank Lane, by the bridge.

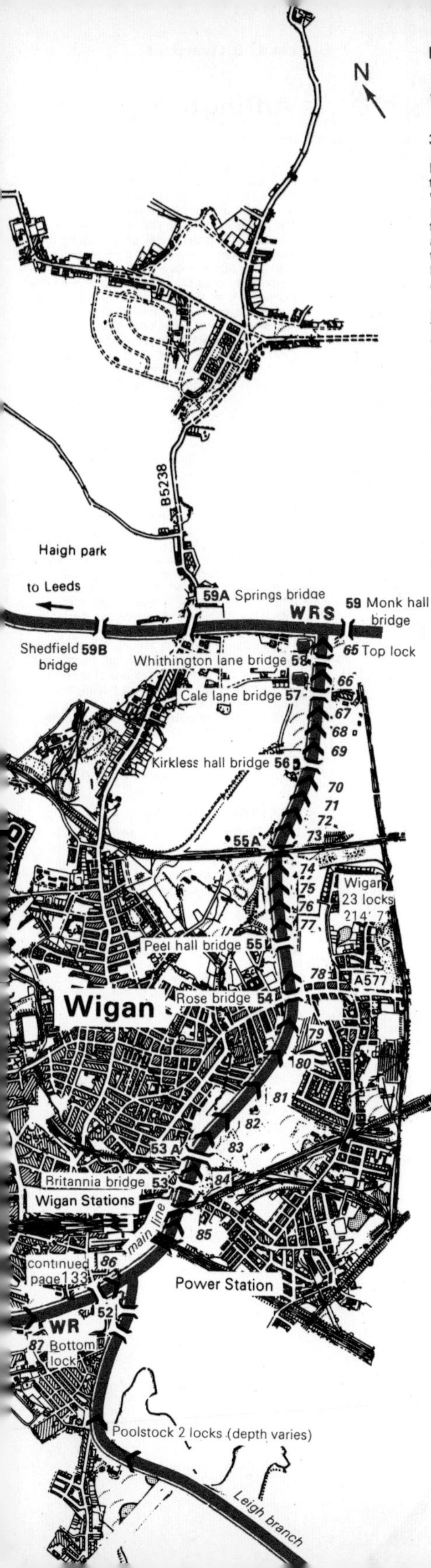

Wigan Locks

$3\frac{1}{4}$ miles

Leaving the junction with the Leigh branch, the main line of the canal passes the large Wigan Power Station—no longer served by the canal—and starts immediately on the Wigan flight of 21 locks. It is a long and arduous climb to the top by boat, for these wide, deep locks raise the canal level by over 200ft. For the faint-hearted, there are shops and pubs near bridges 53 and 54. Up at the top lock, however, are 3 canal pubs—a comforting sight. Here is a T-junction as the canal meets what used to be the southern end of the Lancaster Canal (see the history section) on its disjointed way to Johnson's Hillock, Walton Summit and Preston. Turning left, the traveller is soon aware of the great height he has climbed as the navigation winds along a hill. It soon enters the woods that precede Haigh Hall and Park.

Wigan
Lancs. Pop 80,000. EC Wed, MD Fri. All services. A large, heavily industrialised town whose skyline is now a mixture of industrial chimneys and towering concrete blocks of offices and flats. There is a good and extensive covered market. The old market place in the centre of the town has some attractive black and white timbered houses above the shops. The main railway station is presently being rebuilt, at a cost of £$\frac{1}{4}$ million, in connection with the current electrification of the West Coast railway line.
All Saints Church A very large and impressive parish church surrounded by beautiful rose gardens. Parts of the original mediaeval structure remain but it was largely rebuilt in 1845-50, still following the rather ornate design of the former church. There are several very fine stained glass windows and numerous monuments and effigies.
Wigan Art Gallery & Museum Station rd (Wigan 41387). Collections include geology, coins and local industrial development. *Open week-days 10.00-17.00.*

BOATYARDS & BWB

BWB Wigan Yard at Wigan bottom lock. (Wigan 42239). Water, dustbins, lavatory. Drydock, slipway up to 60 foot. Sewage disposal at lock 86.

PUBS

Top Lock Canalside, at guess where . . .
Kirkless Hall Canalside, near Wigan top lock.
Commercial Inn Canalside, at bridge 57.

FISHING

At Wigan the flight of 21 locks is popular among local anglers who find some big fish in the lock pounds. The constantly-moving water suits the big chub. There are also tench, carp and big eels.

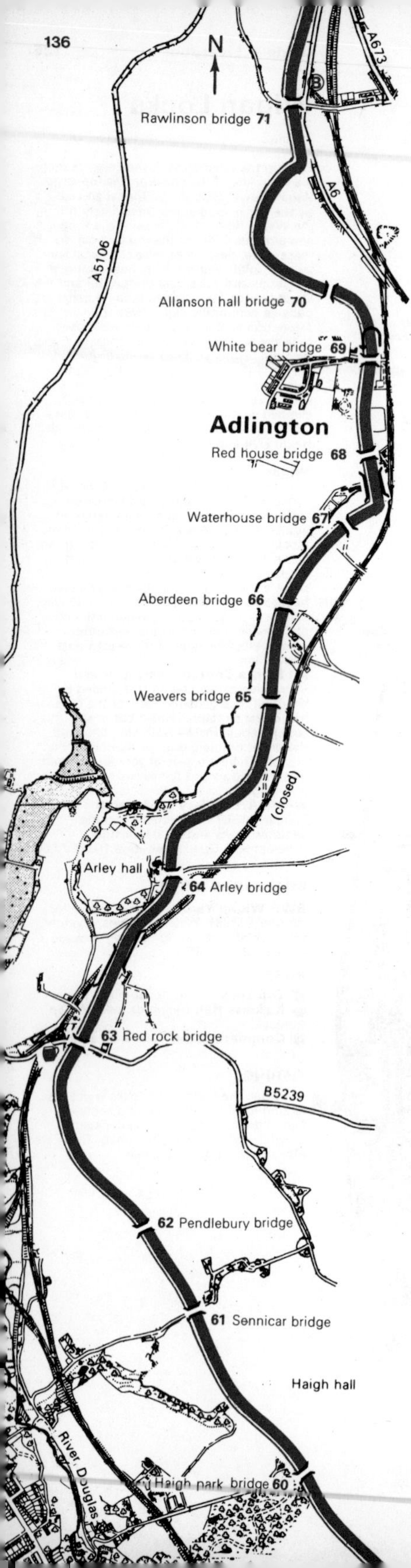

N
A673
A6
A5106
Rawlinson bridge 71
Allanson hall bridge 70
White bear bridge 69
Adlington
Red house bridge 68
Waterhouse bridge 67
Aberdeen bridge 66
Weavers bridge 65
(closed)
Arley hall
64 Arley bridge
63 Red rock bridge
B5239
62 Pendlebury bridge
61 Sennicar bridge
Haigh hall
River Douglas
Haigh park bridge 60

Adlington

5¼ miles

The canal continues to run as a 9-mile lock-free pound—known as the 'Lancaster Pool'—along the side of the valley from which the industries surrounding Wigan can be viewed in the distance. It enjoys a pleasant and quiet isolation in this lightly wooded area. Already the navigation is well over 300ft above the sea, and the bleak hills up to the east give a hint of the Pennines that are soon to be crossed. The conspicuous tower east of Adlington stands on a hill that is over 1500ft high. Points of interest on this stretch include Arley Hall, a large and elegant moated house that is now the club house of the local golf club, and the nearby skewed aqueduct over a closed railway track.

Adlington
Lancs. Pop 4610. PO, tel, stores, garage, station. A small industrialised town.

Haigh Hall
On east bank of the canal. The pre-Tudor mansion was rebuilt by its owner, the 23rd Earl of Crawford, between 1830 and 1849. The reconstruction was designed and directed by the Earl, and all the stone, timber and iron used on the job came from the estate. The Hall is now owned by Wigan Corporation, who allow the citizens to use it for private wedding receptions, etc. There is little to see in the house and it is not normally open to the public.
The park and grounds around the hall are *open daily all year*, and contain much that caters for the family: there are children's amusements, glasshouses, a nature trail and a big new golf course. There is also a tractor-trailer passenger service from the Wigan Lane entrance through the plantations to the Hall *every day from 14.00 to dusk.* Cafe in grounds. Further information from Wigan Council Parks Dept. (Wigan 46251).

BOATYARDS & BWB

J.M. Enser Stone Slack, Burnsall Ave, Whitefield, Manchester. (061-766-2769). At bridge 71 (Rawlinson bridge). Hire narrowboats, diesel, moorings, winter storage. *Open daily throughout year.*

PUBS

Clayton Arms Adlington. Light music.
Bridge Adlington. Canalside, at bridge 69.
Crawford Arms Canalside, at Red Rock bridge. Live music some evenings.

FISHING

Between Wigan and Johnson's Hillock there is a 9 mile length of lockless waters which is regularly fished by local anglers. Clubs frequently hold contests. Roach to 1½lb are to be caught from swims all through this length plus the occasional perch of 2lb.

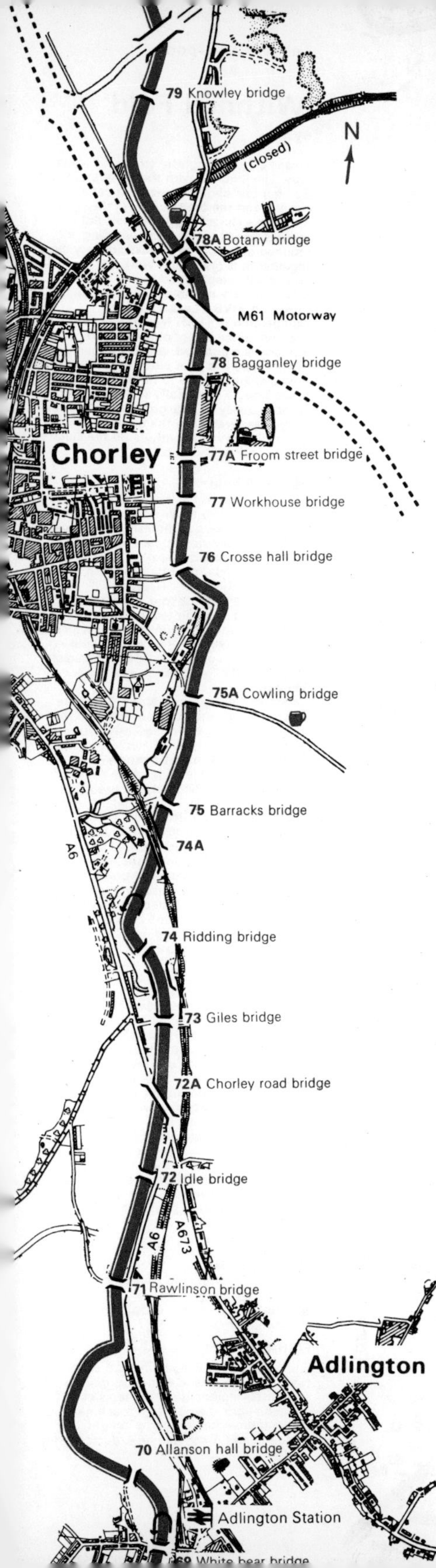

Chorley

4¾ miles

This is an initially attractive section as the canal wanders northwards from Adlington. Hemmed in for much of the way by woodlands, the canal is undisturbed by the railway and main roads that for a while follow it closely. Soon the greenery gives way to views of Chorley's rows of rooftops across the valley. The canal crosses this valley, but shuns the town: it passes instead some large and resplendent outlying textile mills. The new M61 motorway zooms up from Manchester around the mills and over the navigation before disappearing in the direction of Preston in a flurry of flyovers, feeder roads and roundabouts.

Chorley
Lancs. Pop 31,000. EC Wed, MD Tue, Fri, Sat. All services. On the west bank of the canal, a busy town based on the manufacture of textiles and spare parts for commercial and public service vehicles. (Leyland, where the vehicles are built, is just a few miles away, to the north west.) Chorley has avoided too much industrial grimness by maintaining its market-town traditions and by extensive new housing development. Sir Henry Tate, the founder of the Tate Gallery in London, was born in Chorley in 1819 and began his career here as a grocer's assistant.
St. Laurence's Church Church Brow. Surrounded by trees in the centre of the town, parts of the church date back to the 14thC. The bones that are enshrined in a recess in the chancel are believed to have belonged to St. Laurence.
Astley Hall At the north west end of the town just over a mile from Botany Bridge. Set in a large parkland beside a lake, the appearance of this Elizabethan mansion is very striking, for in the 17thC the existing timber-framing was replaced by a new facade that is lacking in symmetry. The interior is very fine with splendid ceilings, furnishings, tapestries and pottery. *Open daily May-Aug 14.00-20.00 Apr & Sep 14.00-18.00, Oct-Mar 14.00-16.00. Weekdays only.* (Chorley 2166).

PUBS

Railway Chorley. Canalside, at Botany bridge 78A.
Skinner's Arms Chorley. 150 yards uphill from bridge 75A.

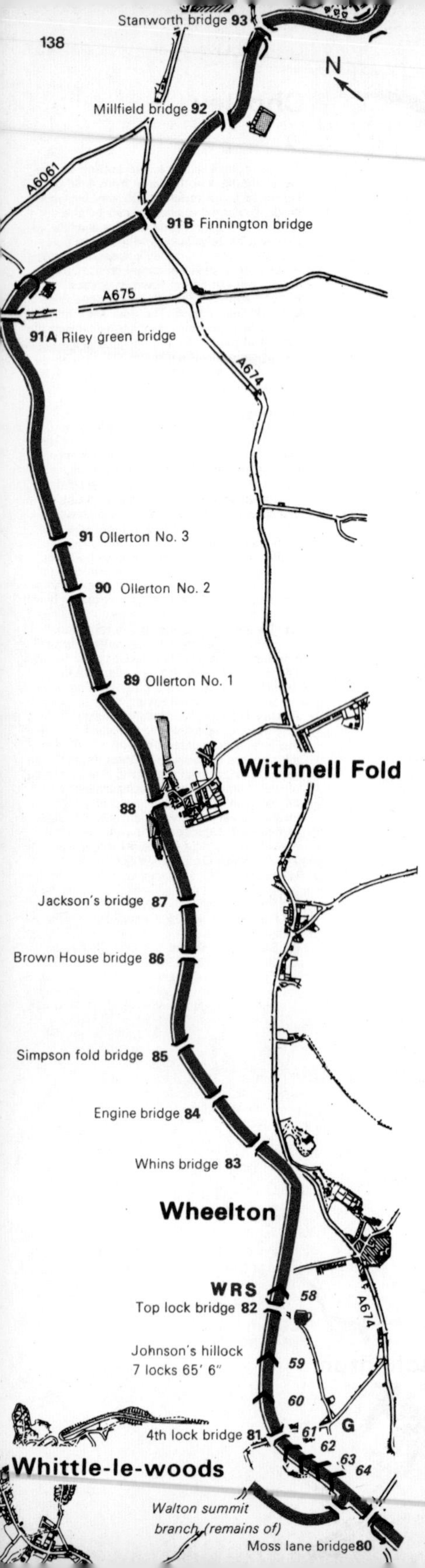

Withnell Fold

5¼ miles

This is a most delightful stretch of waterway. The junction with the old Walton Summit branch features an old canal cottage and the bottom lock in the Johnson's Hillock flight. A short but energetic spell of windlass-wielding is required here, for the 7 locks are very close together. It is rewarding work, for the steep countryside yields good views, and the locks are tidily maintained and painted: they won BWB's Lock Efficiency Competition in 1971. Near the middle lock is a post office, telephone and store; at the top lock is a pub and, usually, a medley of boats (there is a boat club here). The canal now changes course to northeast and flows along a beautifully secluded and often wooded valley at a height of over 350 feet above sea level. Even the old mills at Withnell Fold hardly intrude on the canal's private course.

Withnell Fold
Lancs. A remarkable village well worth a short visit. It is a small estate village, built to house workers at the canalside paper mills which are now closed and empty. They used to export banknote paper to all over the world until 'rationalisation' transferred their work elsewhere. Symmetrically grouped around 3 sides of a spacious square, the terraced cottages present an intimately united front which is almost unnerving to the casual visitor—especially as on the 4th side of the square is an old set of wooden stocks.

Wheelton
Lancs. PO, tel, stores, garage. There are steep terraces and cobbled streets in this village which has been recently bypassed and has thus rid itself of much road traffic.

The Walton Summit branch
The short branch leading off to the north from Johnson's Hillock locks used to be part of the Lancaster Canal, which was originally projected to run south from Preston past Wigan to the Bridgewater Canal. But the Lancaster Canal Company was very short of money, and, after arranging with the Leeds & Liverpool Company to share a common course between Johnson's Hillock and Wigan top lock, was daunted by the prospect of constructing a large and necessarily expensive aqueduct over the river Ribble in Preston. A 'temporary' tramroad was therefore built to connect the two lengths of canal between Preston and Walton Summit, about 3 miles north of Johnson's Hillock. The tramway, which opened in 1803, featured a short tunnel and a light trestle bridge over the Ribble. Through traffic now began to use the canal, and one may imagine the busy scenes at either end of the tramway as cargoes were transhipped from boats into wagons and back into boats at the far end.
The tramroad, although designed only as a short-term measure, was never replaced by a canal; indeed the whole line was closed by 1880. Most of the canal branch has recently been severed by the building of a motorway, although plenty of it still remains.

PUBS

Royal Oak Riley Green, ¼ mile NW of bridge 91A. Free house/roadhouse. Sandwiches daily.
Anchor Canalside, at Johnson's Hillock top lock.

FISHING

From Chorley to Blackburn most of the canal's species are in evidence, mainly small fish—including some shoals of gudgeon—but the odd 1½lb roach needs a skilful approach if it is to be caught. Gudgeon and roach can be expected along the Blackburn to Burnley length.

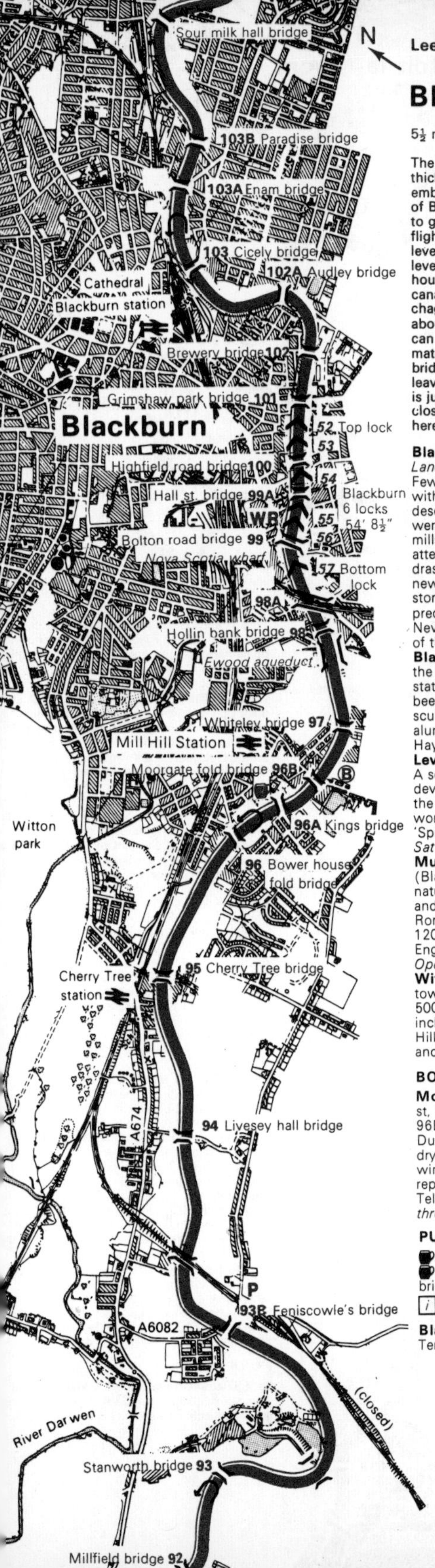

Blackburn

5½ miles

The canal now curls round a steep and thickly wooded valley, crossing it on a high embankment before entering the outskirts of Blackburn. It seems to take a long time to get through this large town, as there is a flight of 6 locks here, raising the canal's level to a height of over 400ft above sea level. Unfortunately the factories and houses have all turned their backs to the canal. Walkers will find to their possible chagrin that the towpath is fenced off for about half a mile in the town. However one can get an excellent view of local bowls matches from the embankment between bridges 97 and 98. The safest place to leave a boat for a short while in Blackburn is just above lock 56: shops and pubs are close at hand, and the lock-keeper lives here. He keeps a tidy flight.

Blackburn
Lancs. Pop 101,000. EC Thur. All services. Few of the Pennine towns which sprang up with the Industrial Revolution can be described as beautiful for aesthetic feelings were rarely consulted in the rush to raise mills and cram houses round them. In an attempt to rectify this, Blackburn has taken drastic steps in recent years to construct a new city centre, which includes multi-storey blocks of flats, a large shopping precinct and a vast covered market. Nevertheless the most impressive features of the town are still the old cotton mills.
Blackburn Cathedral Dating from 1820-6, the parish church was raised to cathedral status in 1926. Extensive renovations have been made inside. Very striking 13ft sculpture of 'Christ the Worker' in aluminium and black iron by John Hayward. Large churchyard.
Lewis Textile Museum Exchange st. A series of period rooms demonstrating the development of the textile industry from the 18thC onwards by means of full-size working models, including Hargreaves' 'Spinning Jenny'. *Open Mon, Tue, Thur, Sat 10.00-17.00; Wed, Fri 10.00-19.30.*
Museum & Art Gallery Library st. (Blackburn 59511). Exhibits include natural history, pottery, early manuscripts and a large collection of English, Greek and Roman coins. In the art gallery are over 1200 beautiful Japanese prints, as well as English water-colours of the 18thC-20thC. *Open Mon-Fri 9.30-20.00. Sat 9.30-18.00.*
Witton Park At the western end of the town, north of Cherry Tree station. Nearly 500 acres of magnificent parkland, including the beautiful landmark, Billinge Hill. Splendid abundance of rhododendrons and azaleas. *Open daily to the public.*

BOATYARDS & BWB

Moorgate Supplies Marina 67 Moorgate st, Blackburn, Lancs. (63350). At bridge 96B (Moorgate fold bridge). Hire cruisers. Dustbins, water, diesel, gas, chandlery, dry dock, slipway up to 24 foot, moorings, winter storage. Boat & motor sales & repairs. Fibreglass speed boats built. Telephone, lavatories. *Open daily throughout year.*

PUBS

Infirmary Blackburn. By lock 56.
Navigation Blackburn. Canalside, at bridge 96A.

TOURIST INFORMATION CENTRE

Blackburn Royal Chambers, Richmond Terrace. (53277).

Leeds & Liverpool

Rishton

8 miles

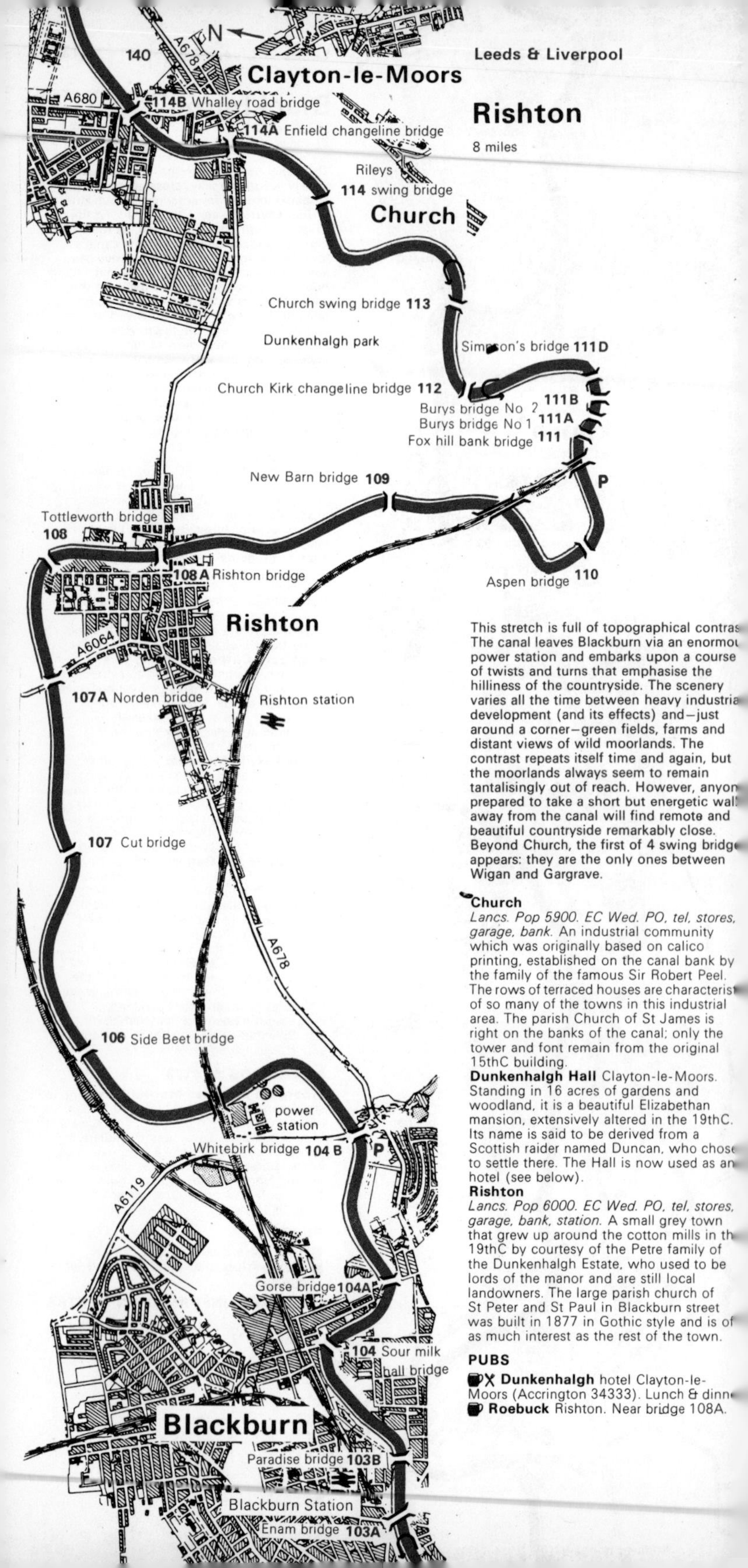

This stretch is full of topographical contras The canal leaves Blackburn via an enormou power station and embarks upon a course of twists and turns that emphasise the hilliness of the countryside. The scenery varies all the time between heavy industria development (and its effects) and—just around a corner—green fields, farms and distant views of wild moorlands. The contrast repeats itself time and again, but the moorlands always seem to remain tantalisingly out of reach. However, anyon prepared to take a short but energetic wal away from the canal will find remote and beautiful countryside remarkably close. Beyond Church, the first of 4 swing bridg appears: they are the only ones between Wigan and Gargrave.

Church
Lancs. Pop 5900. EC Wed. PO, tel, stores, garage, bank. An industrial community which was originally based on calico printing, established on the canal bank by the family of the famous Sir Robert Peel. The rows of terraced houses are characteris of so many of the towns in this industrial area. The parish Church of St James is right on the banks of the canal; only the tower and font remain from the original 15thC building.

Dunkenhalgh Hall Clayton-le-Moors. Standing in 16 acres of gardens and woodland, it is a beautiful Elizabethan mansion, extensively altered in the 19thC. Its name is said to be derived from a Scottish raider named Duncan, who chos to settle there. The Hall is now used as an hotel (see below).

Rishton
Lancs. Pop 6000. EC Wed. PO, tel, stores, garage, bank, station. A small grey town that grew up around the cotton mills in th 19thC by courtesy of the Petre family of the Dunkenhalgh Estate, who used to be lords of the manor and are still local landowners. The large parish church of St Peter and St Paul in Blackburn street was built in 1877 in Gothic style and is of as much interest as the rest of the town.

PUBS

Dunkenhalgh hotel Clayton-le-Moors (Accrington 34333). Lunch & dinn

Roebuck Rishton. Near bridge 108A.

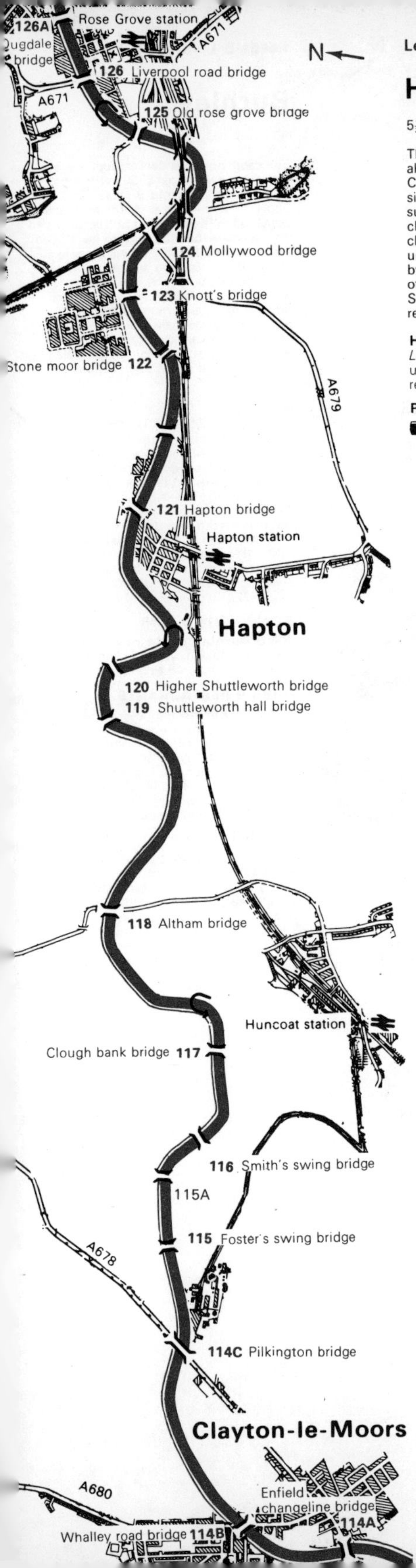

Hapton

5½ miles

The navigation continues to wind eastwards along the side of what turns out to be the Calder Valley. High ground rises on each side of the valley, and in the distance the summit of Pendle Hill (1831ft high) can be clearly seen when it is not obscured by cloud. This is an attractive length of canal, unspoilt by industry and greatly enhanced by the ever-changing views from the side of the hill along which the canal is cut. Soon the distant mass of dwellings is recognisable as the suburbs of Burnley.

Hapton

Lancs. PO, tel, stores, station. A small and unmistakably northern town, with its regular streets of terraced houses.

PUBS

Bridge House Hapton, by bridge 121.

126A Dugdale bridge
Rose Grove station
A671
N
126 Liverpool road bridge
A671
125 Old rose grove bridge
124 Mollywood bridge
123 Knott's bridge
Stone moor bridge 122
A679
121 Hapton bridge
Hapton station
Hapton
120 Higher Shuttleworth bridge
119 Shuttleworth hall bridge
118 Altham bridge
Huncoat station
Clough bank bridge 117
116 Smith's swing bridge
115A
115 Foster's swing bridge
A678
114C Pilkington bridge
Clayton-le-Moors
A680
Enfield changeline bridge
114A
Whalley road bridge 114B

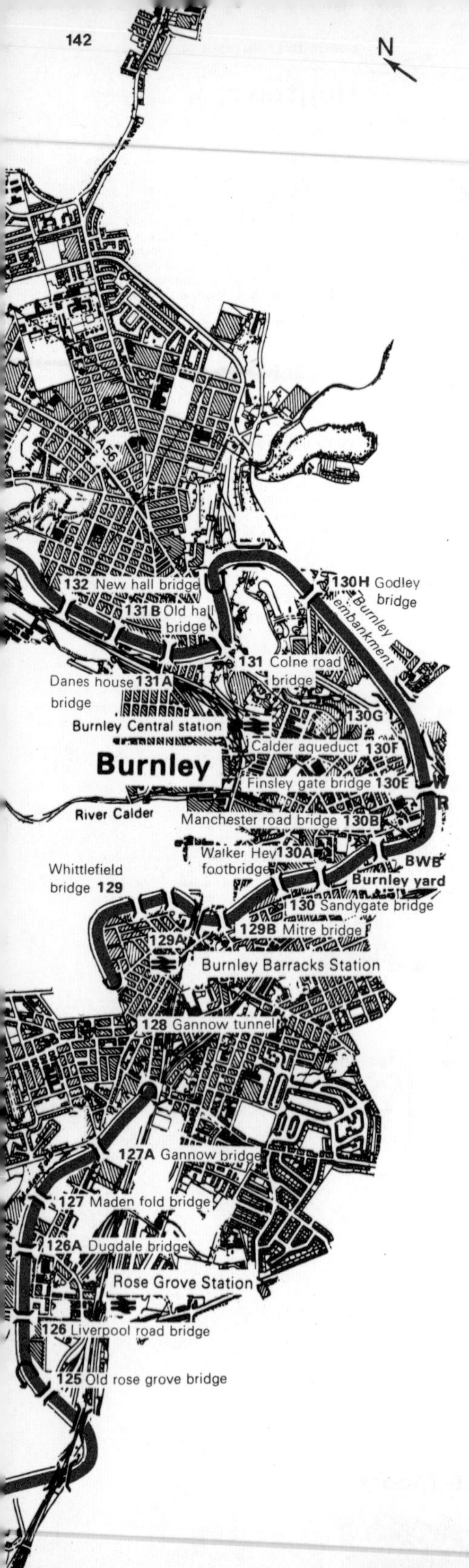

Burnley

$4\frac{3}{4}$ miles

The canal now wanders through the suburbs into Gannow Tunnel (559 yards long), then round the hillside into Burnley. This is an aggressively industrial stretch in which the canal, once the lifeblood of the town and its industries, now appears to have been forgotten or ignored. A huge embankment carries the navigation across part of the town: the bank, which is 60ft high, is $\frac{3}{4}$ mile long (although known as 'the straight mile') and incorporates an aqueduct over a main road. The BWB maintenance yard is at one end of the embankment: this is the only suitable place to leave a boat in the town. Shops are nearby.

Burnley
Lancs. Pop 77,000. All services. A large industrial northern town, which is now improving its appearance by means of a £5,000,000 rebuilding scheme.
Townley Hall On the southern outskirts of Burnley ($1\frac{1}{4}$ miles SE of the BWB yard). Set in extensive parklands, the grandiose, battlemented house dating from the 14thC was the home of the Townley family until 1902. It is now an art gallery and museum with the rooms lavishly furnished in period style. *Open weekdays 10.00-17.30. Sun 14.00-17.00.* (Burnley 24213.)

BOATYARDS & BWB

BWB Burnley Yard Finsley Gate. (Burnley 28680). Water, dustbins, diesel, moorings. Crane up to 3 tons.

PUBS & RESTAURANTS

Rosehill House hotel Rosehill ave, Burnley (27116). Once the baroque home of a cotton magnate, this hotel is run as a family concern by Mr and Mrs Hinchliffe. There is an extensive Tdh and interesting wine list. L 12.30-14.00, D 19.00-20.30 (closed Chr Day, Sun). Must book, no dogs. Good Food Guide since 1965.

FISHING

From Burnley to Nelson fish to be caught are roach, bream, tench, perch and pike. Some trout have also been reported. Further east towards Skipton there are also some large but elusive bream.

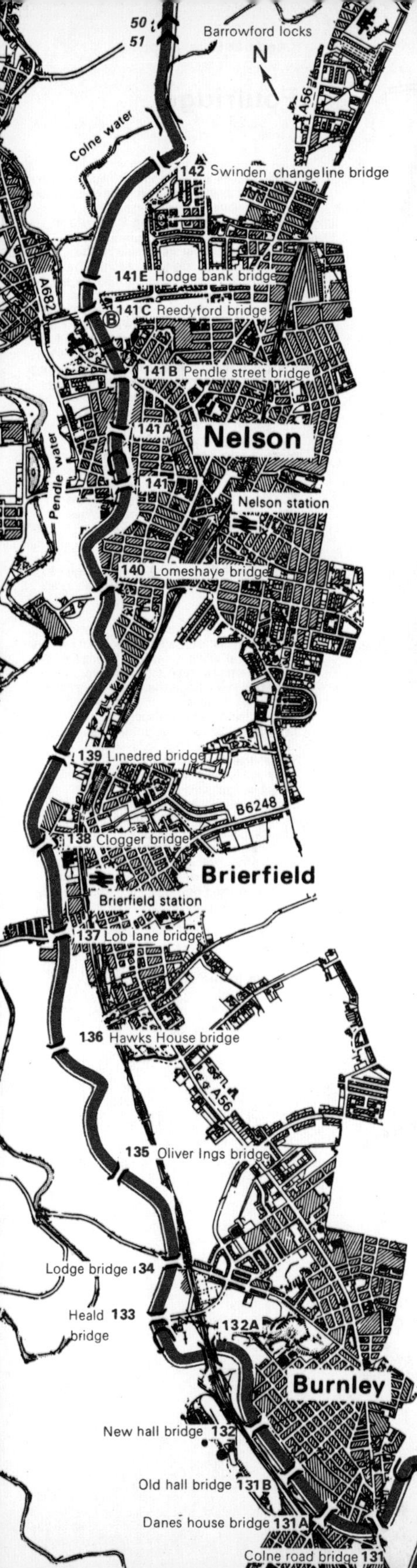

Brierfield

5½ miles

Here again the canal negotiates a landscape which alternates between open country, towns and semi-towns, with the massive distant bulk of Pendle Hill in the background. The navigation winds endlessly as it follows the hillside; but this ceases at Nelson, where it crosses the valley on a minor aqueduct and begins to climb the pretty Barrowford locks.

Nelson
Lancs. Pop 30,000. EC Tue, MD Wed, Fri, Sat. All services. Nelson is a conglomerate of a number of small villages that combined in the 19thC to form one industrial town. The centre has been redeveloped with a large covered shopping precinct. One of Nelson's more valuable assets is the easy access to the beautiful moors and Forest of Pendle, behind which looms Pendle Hill.

Brierfield
Lancs. Pop 7300. PO, tel, stores, garage, bank, station, cinema. A small industrial town merging into Burnley at one end and into Nelson at the other. The parish church of St Luke in Colne road is a Victorian building with an unusually designed clock tower culminating in a steep pyramid roof.

BOATYARDS & BWB

Nelson Marine Centre Fleet Street, Nelson, Lancs. (65273). At bridge 141C (Reedyford bridge). Moorings, winter storage, boat repairs. Fibreglass boats built & fitted out.

PUBS

Leeds & Liverpool Brierfield, up the hill from bridge 137.

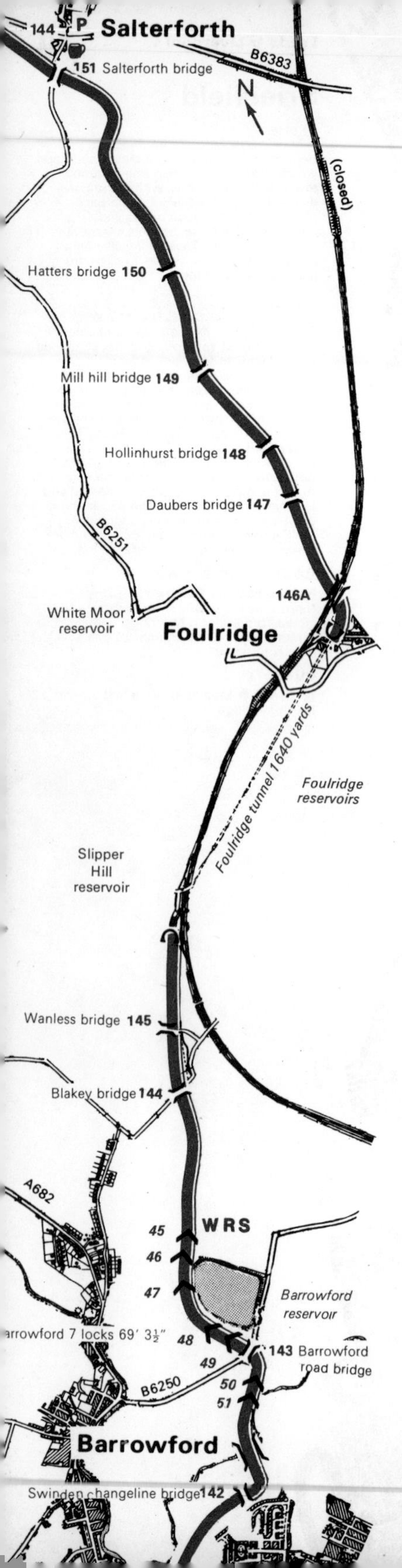

Foulridge

5 miles

This is a refreshing stretch, in which the canal shakes off for good the succession of industrial towns that dog it through much of Lancashire. It rises through the 7 Barrowford locks, passing Barrowford reservoir (in which the summit level's surplus water is stored), and at the beautifully kept top lock reaches the summit level of the whole canal. Soon one begins to notice the various feeder streams continuously pouring vital water supplies into the navigation. Meanwhile, distant mountainous country frames beautiful old stone farms nearer at hand. Soon everything is blotted out as one enters Foulridge Tunnel; at the other end, by the railway bridge, is an old wharf where one can tie up to visit the village. Meanwhile the navigation continues northward through this very fine countryside to Salterforth, passing into Yorkshire as it crosses over the little 'County Brook' between bridges 149 and 150. The railway crossing the canal at Foulridge used to be part of the Preston–Colne–Skipton line; now the Colne–Skipton section has been axed.

Salterforth
Yorks. PO, tel, stores. A small village of narrow streets and terraced houses in an upland setting.

Foulridge
Lancs. PO, tel, stores. An intimate village which with its unmade roads, pretty alleys and general air of quiet indifference to the world seems to have more in common with an Italian hill village than a place on the borders of Lancashire and Yorkshire. Around the village are scattered the reservoirs that feed the summit level of the canal.

Foulridge Tunnel
1640 yards long, with no towpath, this tunnel is, not surprisingly, barred to unapproved boats. The hole in the hill sprang to fame in 1912 when a cow fell into the canal near the tunnel mouth and for some reason decided to struggle through to the other end of the tunnel. The gallant but weary swimmer was revived with alcohol at the Foulridge end. Photographs in the nearby pub recall the incident.

PUBS

Anchor Salterforth. Canalside, at bridge 151.

Hole in the Wall Foulridge.

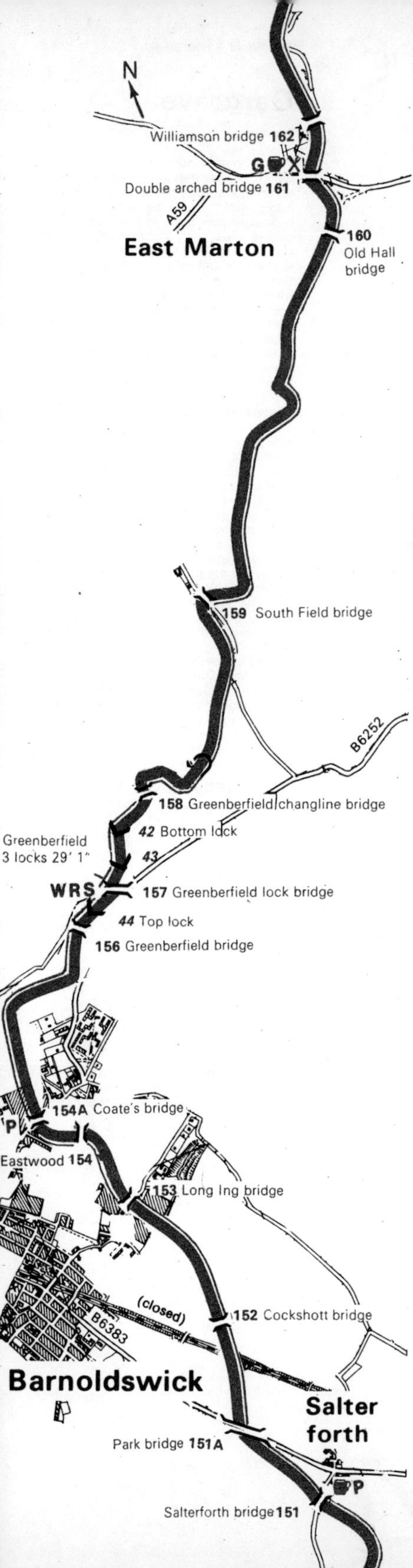

Barnoldswick

5 miles

This is one of the most remote sections of the whole canal. It is certainly the highest, and probably the most beautiful. Leaving Salterforth, one passes the old branch railway to Barnoldswick, up on the hill. Suddenly one rounds a corner and is confronted by Greenberfield top lock, which introduces the beginning of the long descent towards Leeds. (The feeder from the distant Winterburn reservoir enters the canal at the top lock.) The 3 locks here are set in wild, empty uplands; and for the next few miles the canal winds tortuously through this magnificently virile scenery that is composed of countless individual hillocks, some topped by clumps of brave, battered trees. This is Pennine scenery at its best.

Around East Marton, after skirting the isolated church, the surroundings change briefly: the navigation enters a cutting, passes under a curious (double-arched) main road bridge and enters a sheltered fold housing a farm, a pub and some moorings. But a steep wooded cutting leads the canal out of this pastoral interlude and back into the rugged moorlands.

Pennine Way

The Pennine Way is a walking route covering over 250 miles of Pennine highland from Edale in the south to Kirk Yetholm in the north. Because of the nature of the route much of the Way is rough, hard walking, but it gives a superb view from the mountains. At East Marton the Pennine Way shares the canal towpath for a short distance.

Barnoldswick

Yorks. Pop 10,200. EC Tue. PO, tel, stores, garage, bank. Set back from the canal, the mainstay of this town's existence is (still) the Rolls Royce factory, where experimental work is done on aero engines. The centre of the town is compact and dominated by the new Holy Trinity Church completed in 1960.

PUBS

Cross Keys East Marton. Large pub by bridge 161. Lunches (cold buffet) and dinners daily. (Earby 3485). *PO, tel, stores next door.*

Plenty of pubs in Barnoldswick.

YOUTH HOSTEL

Mill Brow, Earby, Lancs. 2 miles NE of Salterforth. (Earby 2349).

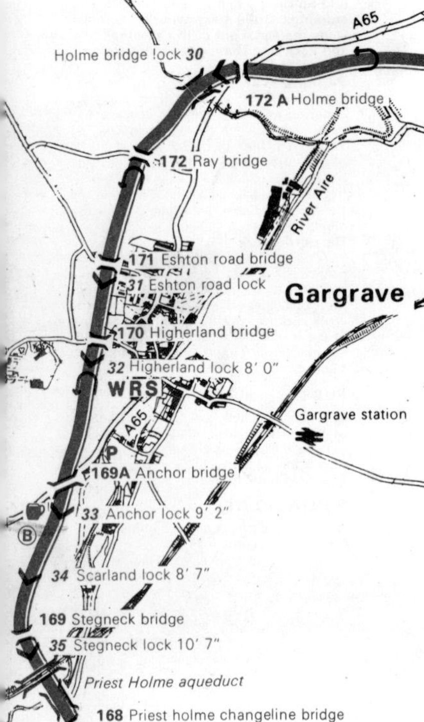

Gargrave

5 miles

This is another outstanding stretch, in which the navigation continues to snake amazingly around the splendid green and humpy hills that fill the landscape. The 6 Banknewton locks in their wooded setting lower the canal into upper Airedale, yielding excellent views across the valley to the hills and moors beyond. The river Aire flows in from the north, accompanied by the railway line to Skipton and Leeds from Morecambe, Settle and distant Carlisle. The canal crosses the river by a substantial stone aqueduct. Meanwhile, yet more locks take the canal round Gargrave, between the village and the hills; the beauty of the area may be judged by the fact that the Yorkshire Dales National Park borders the navigation along here.

Gargrave
Yorks. Pop 1400. PO, tel, stores, garage, bank, station. A very attractive and much-visited village. Holding an enviable position near the head of Airedale between the canal and the river, this place is the ideal centre for boat crews to explore the surrounding countryside. The river Aire cuts Gargrave in two, and the bridge over it forms the centre of the village. There is a charming station, and some pretty stone cottages along the green. The church is mostly Victorian, except for the tower, which was built in 1521. There is a BWB launching slipway at Higherland lock. Excellent home bakery.
Yorkshire Dales National Park
Some of England's finest walking country is contained in this area of fine views, deep valleys, open moorland and rugged hills. Designated as a National Park in 1954 the Dales, covering 680 sq. miles, are hardly scarred by habitation.

BOATYARDS & BWB

Rambler Boats Gargrave, Skipton Yorks. (Gisburn 372). Adjacent to Anchor lock. Hire cruisers only. BWB facilities next lock down.

PUBS

Grouse hotel Gargrave (242). Meals here.
Mason's Arms Gargrave, opposite the church. Attractive old pub.
Old Swan Gargrave.
Anchor by Anchor lock, Gargrave. Free house with canalside beer garden.

CARAVANS & CAMPING

Eshton Road Caravan Site Eshton rd, Gargrave (229). Canalside. Overnight caravan & tent stops.
New Brighton Caravan Site Marton rd, Gargrave. ¼ mile from Higherland lock. Overnight caravan & tent stops.

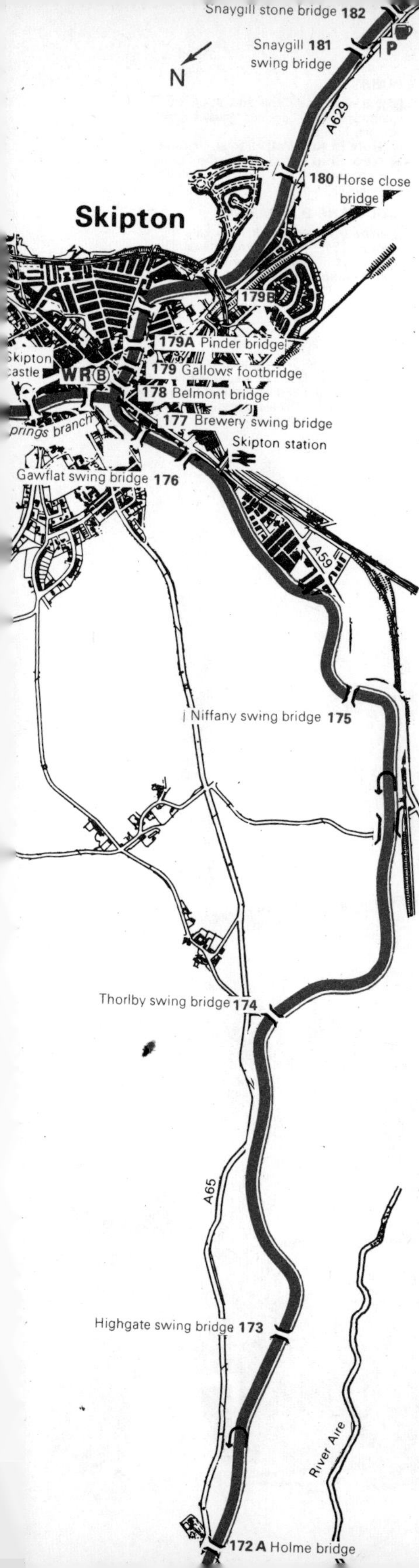

Skipton

5½ miles

The canal now turns south east and proceeds down Airedale, a valley which contains it from here right through to Leeds. Upper Airedale is a flat, wide valley defined by tall steep hills. The countryside is open, unploughed and very inviting to walkers, especially with the moorlands stretching away over the top of the hills. In this robust landscape the navigation hugs the hillsides just above the valley floor, enjoying a lock-free pound that is 17 miles long – although the boatman's relief at the absence of locks may be tempered by the abundance of low swing bridges across the canal.

Entering Skipton, which is usually bristling with pleasure boats, the navigator may find that the best overnight moorings are up the Springs Branch, a little arm that leads off past the town centre and soon finds itself in what is virtually a ravine, overlooked by the castle more than 100ft above. Boats longer than 35ft will find difficulty in turning round along the branch. At the junction is a boatyard: next door is a newly restored canal warehouse, now used as a sports shop.

Skipton
Yorks. Pop 13,000. EC Tue. MD Mon, Sat. All services (including cinemas). Skipton is probably the most handsome town along the whole Leeds & Liverpool Canal. It is an excellent place for visiting from the canal, for one can moor snugly and safely about 1 minute's walk away from the centre. It still maintains its importance as a market town which is referred to in its name: Saxon 'Scip-tun' means 'sheep-town'. The wide High street is very attractive, lined with mostly Georgian houses, and headed at the northern end by the splendid castle and the well-kept graveyard of the parish church. There is an interesting watermill beside the Springs Branch: this is often opened to visitors on summer Sunday afternoons.

Church of the Holy Trinity Standing opposite the castle, it is a long battlemented church, encircled by large lawns and flourishing gardens. It is in Perpendicular style dating from the 14thC, though it was greatly renovated after suffering serious damage during the Civil War. It has a fine oak roof and a beautifully carved Jacobean font cover.

Skipton Castle A magnificent Norman castle, with 17thC additions, that dominates Skipton High street. After a three-year siege during the Civil War, Cromwell's men allowed the restoration of the castle, but ensured that the building could never again be used as a stronghold. The six massive round towers have survived from the 14thC and other notable features are the 50ft long banqueting hall, a kitchen with roasting and baking hearths, a dungeon and the 'Shell Room', the walls of which are decorated with sea shells. *Open daily. Tours on the hour starting at 10.00 weekdays & at 14.00 Suns until sunset.*

The Springs Branch
A short (770yds) but very unusual canal that leaves the Leeds & Liverpool Canal, passes the centre of Skipton and soon finds itself in what is virtually a ravine, overlooked by the Castle that towers 100ft above. The branch is disused but navigable, and makes an interesting diversion by boat or foot. (The towpath continues past the arm, into Skipton Woods.) It was built by the Earl of Thanet, the owner of Skipton Castle, to carry limestone away from his nearby quarry. It was extended by 240yds in 1797 from the watermill bridge through the deep rock cutting, and chutes were constructed at the new terminus to drop the rock into the boats from the horse tramway that was laid from the quarry to the castle. This tramway was widened to standard gauge in 1899 and connected to the Midland Railway. The quarry still flourishes, but the canal and tramway have

not been used since 1946. Trains and motor lorries have replaced them.
The Springs Branch acted for many years as a feeder to the Leeds & Liverpool Canal, taking water from Eller Beck, which runs beside it. However the beck became so polluted in recent years that this intake has had to be sealed, with the unfortunate result that debris now tends to collect in the stagnant canal. However it is still a pleasant backwater.
Skipton Woods Fine woods leading up the little narrow valley from the Springs Branch. For access, just keep on walking up the towpath of the branch.

BOATYARDS & BWB

Pennine Cruisers The Boat Shop, 19 Coach st, Skipton, Yorks. (2061). At junction with the Springs branch. Hire cruisers, sewage & refuse disposal, water, diesel, gas, chandlery, winter storage. Boat sales & repairs, agents for all major firms. Steel boats built and fitted out. *Open daily throughout year.*

PUBS

Bay Horse Canalside, at bridge 182. (Skipton 2449). Lunches, snacks, grills, dinners, B & B.
Hole in the Wall High st, Skipton.
New Ship Canalside, up the Springs Branch; and 25 other pubs and hotels in the town.

CARAVANS & CAMPING

Overdale Trailer Park Harrogate rd, Skipton. (3480). ¾ mile from canal. Overnight caravan stops. No tents permitted.
Tarn House Caravan Park Stirton, nr Skipton. (Skipton 3136). 2 miles from canal, off B6265. Overnight caravan & tent stops.

FISHING

Throughout the Skipton length and through Bingley to Leeds, there are numerous small roach, plus pike and occasional bream and tench. There is also the occasional trout to be caught.

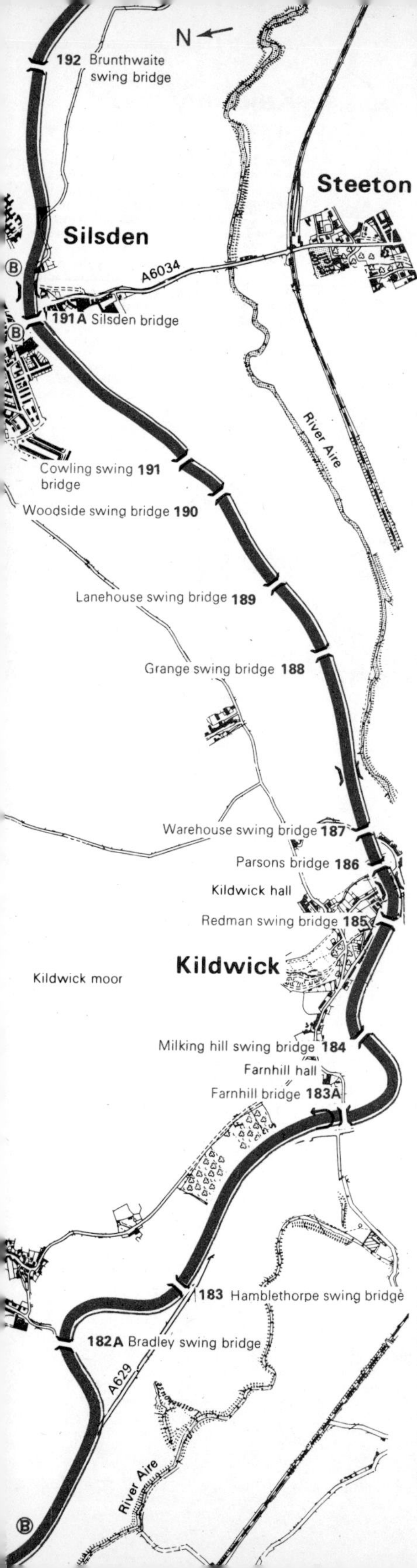

Kildwick

6 miles

The canal continues along the hillside down the valley of the river Aire, with the main road just beside and below the navigation. Excellent views are offered up and down this splendid valley and the surrounding countryside. There is a fine wooded stretch north of Kildwick; then one curves sharply round the outcrop on which crouches Farnhill Hall, a mellow stone building. The intriguing village of Kildwick brings quieter country: the main road and the railway cut the valley corner while the canal takes the longer route round to Silsden and beyond. This stretch of the navigation is liberally punctuated with swing bridges.

Silsden
Yorks. Pop 5200. EC Tue. PO, tel, stores, garage, bank. A well-contained, stone-built industrial town spreading uphill from the canal. In addition to its proximity to the Yorkshire Dales National Park, it offers plenty of shops near the canal. The canal-side warehouses are attractive; there is also an old corn mill dated 1677, but it is in a sad state of disrepair.

Kildwick
Yorks. PO, tel, stores. An interesting and unusual village spilling down the hillside. The streets are extremely steep; one of them goes under the canal through a narrow skewed aqueduct.

BOATYARDS & BWB

Pennine Boats 5 Manley Grove, Ilkley, Yorks. (Ilkley 3444). East of bridge 191A (Silsden bridge). Hire narrow boats. Dustbins, water, diesel, gas, chandlery, winter storage. Agents for all the major boat & motor firms. Boat & motor repairs. *Open daily throughout year, 24 hours a day.*
Langwith Boats Scarhead, West Bradford, Clitheroe, Lancs. Boatyard at Waterloo wharf, Silsden (at bridge 191A). Hire cruisers. Dinghies & chandlery for sale. Diesel. Crane (up to 3 tons). Fishing licences available.
Snaygill Boats Skipton rd, Bradley, nr nr Keighley, Yorks. (Skipton 5150). At bridge 182 (Snaygill stone bridge). Refuse disposal, water, petrol, gas, chandlery, slipway up to 30 cwt. Boat & motor sales, agents for all major firms. Lavatories & shower block.
Chalfont Cruisers Redman's bridge, Farnhill, nr Keighley, Yorks. (Crosshills 32972). Hire cruisers & narrow boats, day boats, moorings, winter storage, boat & motor sales & repairs. Boats fitted out.
Boat trips 16 passenger 'Long John' available for private hire only.

PUBS

Bridge Silsden. Canalside.
White Lion Kildwick.
Currergate Restaurant Skipton rd, Steeton (3204). This Italian restaurant has achieved a growing reputation for good food. Particularly recommended are the steaks and pizza. L 12.00-14.00, D 19.00-22.30 (closed Mon). Must book D, no dogs. Good Food Guide since 1971.
Kildwick Hall Kildwick. (Cross Hills 2244). This is a very fine 17thC stone manor in a rather superior position. However as a restaurant it depends for its reputation on good food, an exceptional wine list and solicitous service. The table d'hote menu is regularly changed and tends to be imaginative, offering such dishes as omelette Arnold Bennett and duckling Pretoria. Jacket and tie are obligatory at dinner. L 12.30-14.00, D 19.30-22.00. Book D; no dogs. Good Food Guide since 1971.

CARAVANS & CAMPING

Brown Bank Caravan Site Silsden. (Steeton 3241). 2 miles from canal, off A6034. Overnight caravan & tent stops.
Cringles Park Silsden. (Steeton 3109). 1½ miles north of canal, on A6034. Overnight caravan stops. No tents permitted.

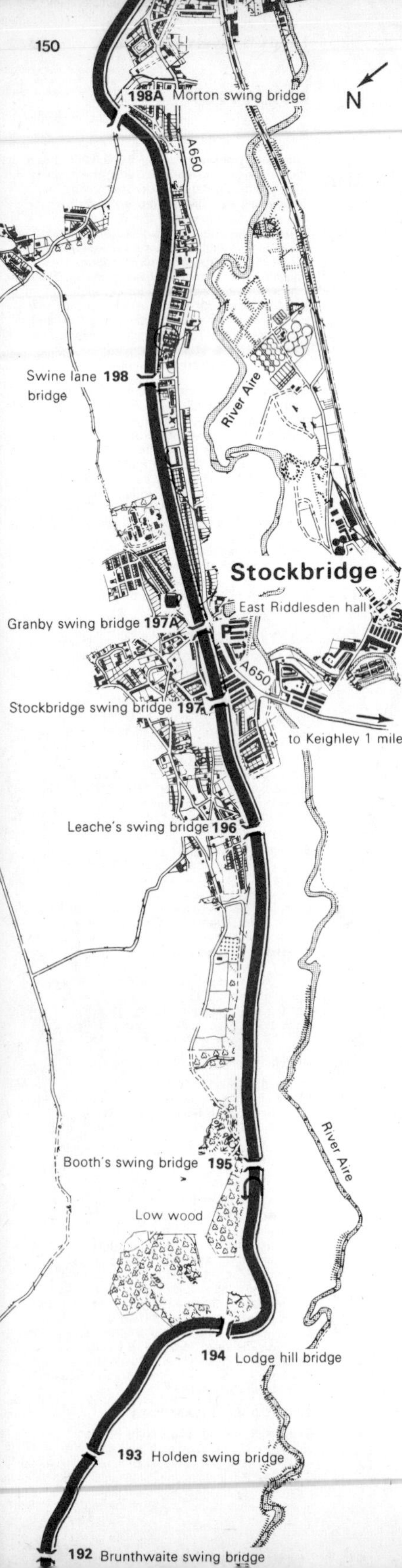

Keighley

4¾ miles

Here the canal continues south east along the side of the green hills that overlook Airedale. The hills are very steep and beautifully wooded in places. The distant rows of chimneys, factories and terraced houses across the valley comprise Keighley; most of its industrial and suburban tentacles are quickly passed by the canal, although the constant succession of little swing bridges intermittently impedes a boat's progress. Some of these bridges can be rather stiff to operate.

East Riddlesden Hall
NT property Just south of swing bridge 197A. A 17thC stone manor house complete with tithe barn. Fine collection of furniture, paintings and armour. Fishing is permitted in the ponds in the grounds. *Open daily except Mon 12.00-18.00. Closed Dec.*

Keighley
Yorks. Pop 56,000. EC Tue, MD Wed, Fri, Sat. All services. Compared with some other industrial centres in the area, Keighley is a clean and pleasant town. It boasts a large new shopping centre, much modern housing and some handsome older stone terraces. The oldest part is around the parish church of St Andrew, a large perpendicular building whose main attraction is its shady churchyard.

Cliffe Castle Spring Gardens lane. Once the home of the Butterfield family, it has been completely restored and now houses the Museum and Art Gallery. Local exhibits illustrate the archaeology, natural history and industrial history of the area. There are reconstructed craft workshops and a textile room. Picturesque grounds where band concerts are held. *Open all year: Weekdays 10.30-17.30, Sun 14.00-17.00. May-Aug open until 20.00 on Tue, Sat & Sun.*

Keighley & Worth Valley Railway
Privately preserved by volunteers of the Keighley & Worth Valley Railway Preservation Society, the line runs for 5 miles from the British Rail station at Keighley up to Haworth, the home of the Brontë family, and Oxenhope. British Railways closed the line in 1961, but with zeal and tenacity the Society eventually succeeded in reopening the line in 1968 with a regular service of steam trains. In the mornings, the service is operated by diesel railbuses but in the afternoons magnificent steam engines puff their way along the track. Train times may be obtained from Haworth 2595 (weekdays) and Haworth 3629 (weekends). In the goods yard at Haworth the Society has a splendid collection of 25 steam engines dating from 1874 and 22 carriages, mostly ancient. The line was made famous by the film 'The Railway Children'.

PUBS

Marquis of Granby at swing bridge 197A.

Bingley and Shipley

5¼ miles

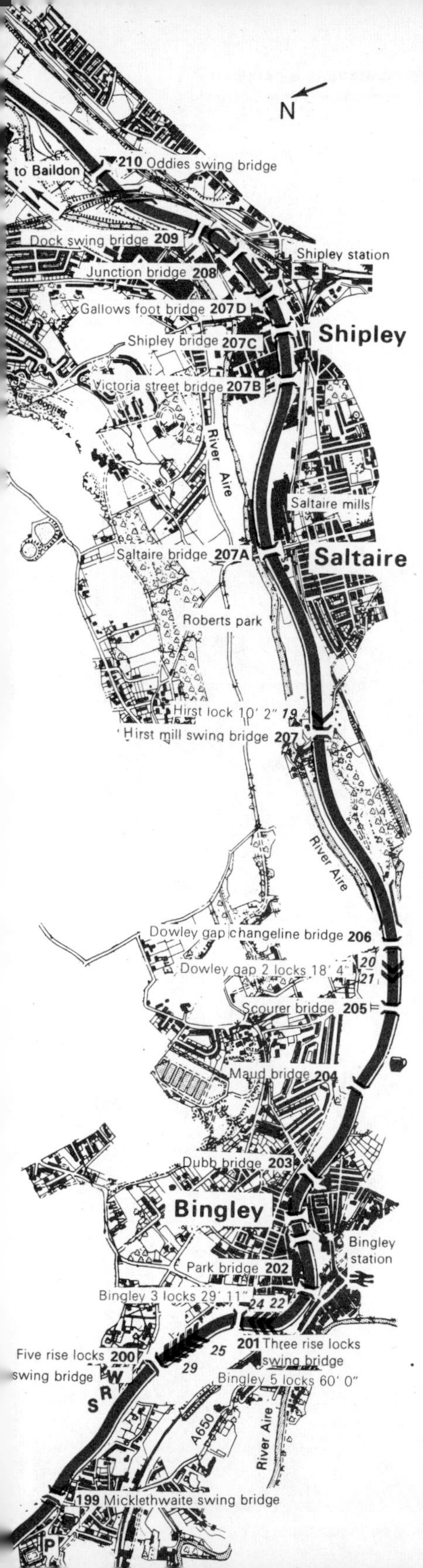

The awe-inspiring Bingley 5-rise staircase locks (see below) mark the end of the long level pound from Gargrave, and from here to Leeds there are no more views of a sweeping, uncluttered river valley. Just a few hundred yards south of the 5 locks are the 3-rise staircase locks; which bring one steeply down into Bingley. The canal bisects this town but one sees little of the place without getting off the canal. Leaving Bingley, trees lead to Dowley Gap and the 2 staircase locks. At the foot of the locks the towpath changes sides and the navigation crosses the river Aire via a stone aqueduct. Woods escort the canal along to the single Hirst lock; from here one moves past the big mills at Saltaire and right through Shipley.

Baildon
Yorks. Pop 14,000. EC Tue. All services. A very old industrial town, 1½ miles north of Shipley, huddled together on a hilltop on the edge of Baildon Moor. Stretching from Baildon to Bingley is The Glen, a wooded valley that curves below the heights of the moor. A splendid scenic tramway carrying two tramcars connects the coach road to the higher parts of Baildon Moor. (In summer a frequent service operates, but in winter it is arranged only to suit the needs of residents at the upper level.) .

Shipley
Yorks. Pop 30,000. EC Wed, MD Fri, Sat. All services. A dark stone town built on a generous scale and based on textile and engineering industries. There are powerful-looking mills to be seen, as well as the town hall and a suitably battlemented Salvation Army citadel. Shipley is lucky enough to be on the edge of Baildon Moor and Shipley Glen. The 3-mile long Bradford Canal used to join the Leeds & Liverpool in Shipley, by bridge 208, but this has all been filled in for years.

Saltaire
Yorks. A rather curious estate village that owes its existence to the Utopian dream of Sir Titus Salt, a wealthy Victorian mill owner. He was so appalled by the working and living conditions of his workers in Bradford that he decided to build the ideal industrial settlement. This he did in 1850 on the banks of the canal and the river Aire—hence the name Saltaire. He provided every amenity including high standard housing, but no pub—for he was a great opponent of strong drink. The village has changed little since those days; everything is carefully laid out and the terraced houses are attractive in an orderly sort of way. (And there is still no pub!) There is an Italianate church near the canal, and a large park beside the river. (Rowing boats can be hired here in the summer.)

Bingley
Yorks. Pop 25,000. EC Tue, MD Fri. All services. An industrial town. Standing at the south east end of it amidst several old cottages is the large parish church of Holy Trinity, with its massive spire conspicuous from the canal.

Bingley 5-rise locks
A very famous and impressive feature of the canal system, these locks are unusual for the beginner and can confuse even the experienced canal user. The reason for any apprehension felt is that the locks are in 'staircase' formation, i.e. they are all joined together rather than being separated by pounds of 'neutral' water. The top gates of the lowest lock are the bottom gates of the lock above, and so on. This means that one must think very carefully before proceeding through the locks. A lock-keeper lives at the top of the flight: there is an instruction board outside his house.

BOAT TRIPS

Apollo Canal Cruises 14 Ivy rd, Shipley, Yorks (52582). 'Apollo' is a traditionally decorated narrowboat shortened to 58 foot, licensed to carry 48 passengers. 'Achilles' is a recently built 62 foot narrow-boat licensed for 50 passengers. Both are available for charter to schools, parties, etc. Scheduled public service on August Bank Holiday from Leeds and Barrowford. Telephone for details.

PUBS

Fisherman Canalside, above Dowley Gap locks.
Plenty of pubs in Bingley and Shipley.
Royal 200yds down the hill from Micklethwaite swing bridge.

CARAVANS & CAMPING

Dobrudden Farm Baildon Moor, nr Shipley. (Shipley 51016). 2 miles from the canal through The Glen. Overnight caravan and tent stops.
Crook Farm Caravan Site West Lane, The Glen, Baildon. (Shipley 54339). 1 mile from canal. Overnight caravan and tent stops.
Harden & Bingley Caravans Goit Stock Estate, Bingley. (Cullingworth 3810). 2 miles from canal. Overnight caravan stops. No tents permitted. Caravans for hire.
Broadstones Caravan Park Sheriff lane, Gilstead, Bingley. (Bingley 2499). 1½ miles from the canal, off A650. Overnight caravan stops. No tents permitted.

Bingley 5-rise locks, with the mills of Bingley in the background.

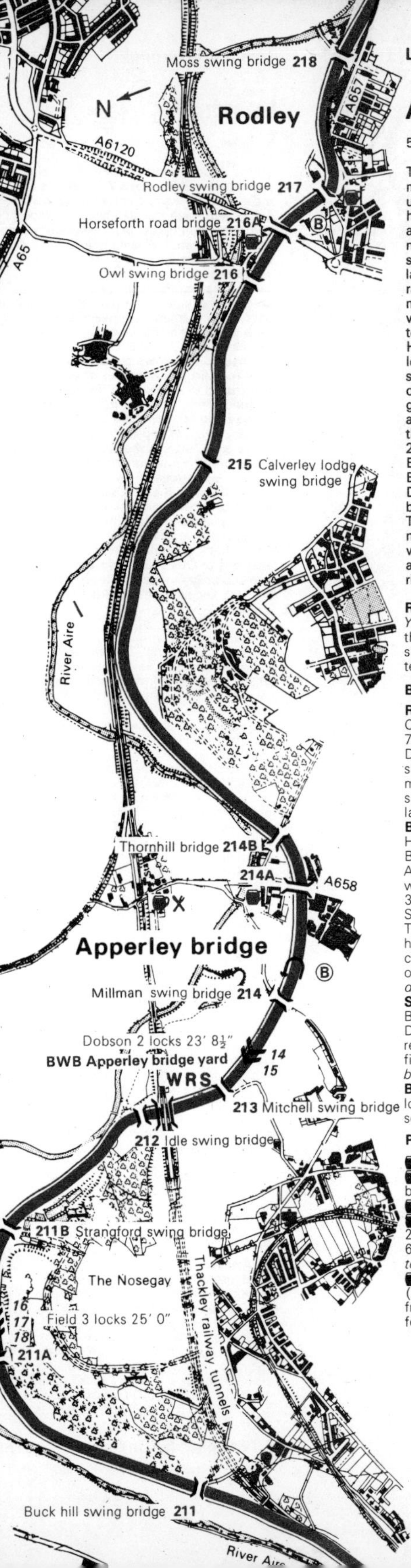

Apperley Bridge

5¾ miles

This section sees the end of the wide open moorlands that frame the scenery further upstream: from now on, industry and houses begin to feature more as one approaches the outskirts of Leeds. The navigation, however, is thankfully sequestered from these intrusions into the landscape. Leaving Shipley, the adjacent railway cuts through a 500ft high hill in 2 mile-long tunnels. The canal goes all the way round this delightfully wooded hill, tenaciously following the Aire valley. Halfway round the long curve are Field locks: there is an extensive but inconspicuous sewage works nearby, which boasts its own railway system. (An engaging little green tank engine called Elizabeth steams along the rickety track, which runs beside the towpath between bridges 211B and 212.)
Beyond the main railway bridge is a BWB maintenance yard at the head of Dobson's locks. The BWB facilities here for boats are housed in former canal stables. Temporarily traversing a built up area, the navigation emerges yet again onto a wooded hillside overlooking the still rural and charming valley that contains the river Aire.

Rodley
Yorks. PO, tel, stores. A useful village on the canal bank. There are 2 pubs, several shops and a laundrette, as well as good temporary moorings.

BOATYARDS & BWB

Rodley Boat Centre Canal Wharf, Canal rd, Rodley, Leeds, Yorks. (Pudsey 76132). At bridge 217. Hire cruisers. Dustbins, water, diesel, gas, chandlery, slipway up to 30 foot, 25 ton crane, moorings, winter storage. Boat & motor sales & repairs. Boats fitted out. Telephone, lavatories. *Open daily throughout year.*
Bradford Boat Services (Dales Craft Hire Cruisers), The Dockyard, Apperley Bridge, Bradford, Yorks. (Bradford 612827). At bridge 214. Hire cruisers, dustbins, water, diesel, petrol, gas, slipway up to 30 foot, 10 ton crane, winter storage. Steel GRP hulls built & fitted out. Telephone. Also, unique boats for weekly hire: caravan owners may put their caravan on a special boat, then sail off on a canalling caravan holiday. *Open daily throughout year, closed Sun am.*
Swiftcraft 27 Pellon Terrace, Idle, Bradford, Yorks. (Bradford 612681). At Dobson locks. Moorings, boat & motor repairs, wooden hulled boats built & fitted out. *Open daily throughout year, but hours erratic.*
BWB Apperley Bridge Yard at Dobson locks. (Bradford 611303). Water, refuse & sewage disposal.

PUBS

Owl Rodley.
Rodley Barge Canalside, near swing bridge 217.
Railway near canal, by bridge 216.
X **George & Dragon** Apperley Bridge, 200 yards NE of bridge 214A. (Bradford 612015). Restaurant *lunches Mon-Fri. PO, tel, stores, garage nearby.*
X **Stansfield Arms** Apperley Bridge. (Rawdon 2659). Just over the river Aire from the 'George & Dragon'. Well known for its lunches and dinners. *No food on Sun.*

Leeds

5¼ miles

This is a section full of contrasts, buildings and locks: and it probably represents the most pleasant way of entering the city of Leeds. Although the area becomes more and more built up as one travels eastward, yet still the canal remains unaffected by it, maintaining its privileged position on the wooded south side of the narrowing Aire valley. Leaving the ruined Kirkstall Abbey on the other side of the river, the navigation passes the Mackeson brewery and borders for a while the steeply sloping edges of an extensive park. Kirkstall power station is reached, with its own private canal 'lay-by': until the mid 1960s, scores of barges every week used to come up to fuel this establishment. Now the traffic has switched to road and rail transport, and the wharves are empty, silent and totally unused.
There are 6 locks in the last mile down to Leeds and the junction with the Aire and Calder navigations at River Lock. It is only in this last mile that the canal assumes the forgotten, unwanted look that characterises so many of our urban canals. A good place to moor a boat in Leeds is just above Office Lock or above River Lock. The environs of Office Lock are kept immaculately—in fact in December 1971 the lock keeper won a Leeds Civic Pride award.

Leeds
Yorks. Pop 506,100. EC Wed, MD Tue, Fri, Sat. All services. A vast industrial city whose mass of factory chimneys is the price it has paid for prosperity. Its major industry is the clothing and textile trade. There are many schemes for redeveloping the city and establishing industrial estates but it will take a lot of time and imagination.
City Art Gallery The Headrow. Large collection of Old Masters; French 19thC paintings, English watercolours and fine modern sculpture by Moore and Hepworth. *Open weekdays 10.30-18.30, Sun 14.30-17.00.* (Leeds 31301 Ext. 395).
City Museum Calveley st. Despite losing valuable exhibits when the museum was bombed in the last war, it still contains a very fine collection illustrating the natural history and archaeology of many parts of the world. *Open 10.00-17.00 weekdays; 14.30-17.00 Sun.*
Kirkstall Abbey
The large elegant ruins of a Cistercian abbey founded in the 12thC. The remaining walls narrowly escaped demolition in the late 19thC, but are now carefully preserved surrounded by a small, attractive park. (For opening times see below.)
Abbey House Museum Just near the abbey is the splendid folk museum illustrating the life and work of the people of Yorkshire during the last 300 years. As well as exhibiting toys, costumes and pottery, it houses three streets of fully furnished 19thC shops, cottages and workshops, including those of a saddler, chemist, tanner and blacksmith. *Open Apr-Sep weekdays 10.00-18.00, Sun 14.00-18.00. Oct-Mar weekdays 10.00-17.00, Sun 14.00-17.00.* (Leeds 55821).

PUBS

Ancestor just south of bridg 223.
Bridge 100yds E of bridge 222.
Abbey 50yds downhill from bridg 221.
Quebec Restaurant Quebec st, Leeds (26723). A converted wine cellar, the Quebec provides an alc menu and at lunchtime a cold buffet counter with one hot dish. House specialities are listed daily along with the standard carte. L 12.30-14.00, D 18.00-21.30 (closed Chr, public hols, Sat L and Sun). Must book D. Good Food Guide since 1967.

i TOURIST INFORMATION CENTRE

Leeds Central Information Bureau, Central Library. (31301).

Lancaster

Maximum dimensions

Preston to Tewitfield
Length: 75′
Beam: 14′
Headroom: 7′ 6″
Glasson Branch
Length: 70′
Beam: 14′
Headroom: 8′

Mileage

Preston to Kendal: 57 miles, 8 locks (disused)
Glasson Branch: 2¾ miles, 6 locks

The city of Lancaster has always been slightly unfortunate in being situated a little too far up the Lune estuary to allow easy navigation. By the late 18thC industrial developments in north west England created a great demand for better access from Lancaster to Preston, Manchester and the busy manufacturing areas near the river Mersey. A link such as a canal would enable much needed coal to be brought up from the pits around Wigan, while farm produce from the fertile plains of north Lancashire could be sent back to feed the teeming town workers to the south.

After various proposals had been bandied about, including suggestions for a ship canal up the Lune estuary and a canal along the coast, a smaller canal was promoted to run from Kendal to Westhoughton (a few miles east of Wigan). This was authorised as the Lancaster Canal by Parliament, and construction began in 1792, after a survey by John Rennie, the company's engineer. He designed the new navigation as a 'broad' canal, with locks 72ft long by 14ft wide, to take barges with a 50-ton carrying capacity. The water supply for the canal was—and still is—drawn from a reservoir at Killington (between Sedburgh and Kendal).

The route chosen included only 8 locks (at Tewitfield), but several aqueducts, the most important being across the river Lune at Lancaster. It was intended that the Ribble should be crossed at Preston by locking down to the river and up the other side, but this plan was constantly shelved because of lack of capital. By 1799 the canal was open from Tewitfield to Preston (including the great Lune aqueduct), and from Clayton to Chorley. There remained a 5-mile gap between the 2 sections, which became known as the North and South Ends respectively. The gap was closed in 1803 by a horse tramway from Walton Summit to Preston, which was carried over the river Ribble by a wooden trestle bridge. This tramway was intended only as a cheap, temporary solution to the gap, but it was never replaced by a proper canal line, so the North End was doomed to be separated for ever from the rest of the country's inland waterways. (The tramway was closed in 1857.)

On the South End, the Lancaster Canal Company agreed with the Leeds & Liverpool Canal Company to extend the former's line past Chorley to Wigan (they never continued it to Westhoughton). The L & L then shared the Lancaster Canal for 10 miles—for a substantial consideration. Meanwhile the North End was extended from Tewitfield to Kendal and opened in 1819. The branch down to Glasson Dock, near Lancaster, was opened in 1826 as the canal's only direct outlet to the sea. (Up to this time, tiresome transhipment had been engaged in at Hest Bank, where the canal is very close to the sea.)

There are several unusual aspects about the Lancaster Canal and its history. One is that the 75-mile long main line was constructed with only 8 locks, at Tewitfield. (There are of course also 6 locks on the Glasson branch.) This was naturally a great benefit to traders and helped to counteract the disadvantage imposed by the tramway at Preston. One may also notice that the towpath is on the same side all the way along the canal, except for a short stretch in Lancaster. This fostered the growth in the 1820s of an express passenger service along the canal. Using special 'fly-boats', a constant change of horses at special staging posts, and precedence over all other craft, this service lived up to its name, averaging up to 10mph along the run from Preston to Kendal.

Another interesting aspect of the Lancaster Canal was the extraordinary but canny interest the company took in the new railway companies, alternately leasing whole lines and then being leased by railways. Eventually, in 1885, the Canal Company sold out altogether to the London & North Western railway—except for the South End, which was already leased in perpetuity to the Leeds & Liverpool Canal Company.

Since the 1930s the canal has been progressively shortened from the Kendal end; and in 1968, after Tewitfield locks had been disused for several years, the canal north of Tewitfield was closed so that the M6 motorway could be driven across the canal in several places. In Preston the canal has been shortened by a mile; (most of the tramway has been closed for over 100 years, although the bridge across the Ribble still stands). The rest of the canal (from Preston to Tewitfield) and the Glasson branch has been designated a 'pleasure cruising waterway' by the 1968 Transport Act.

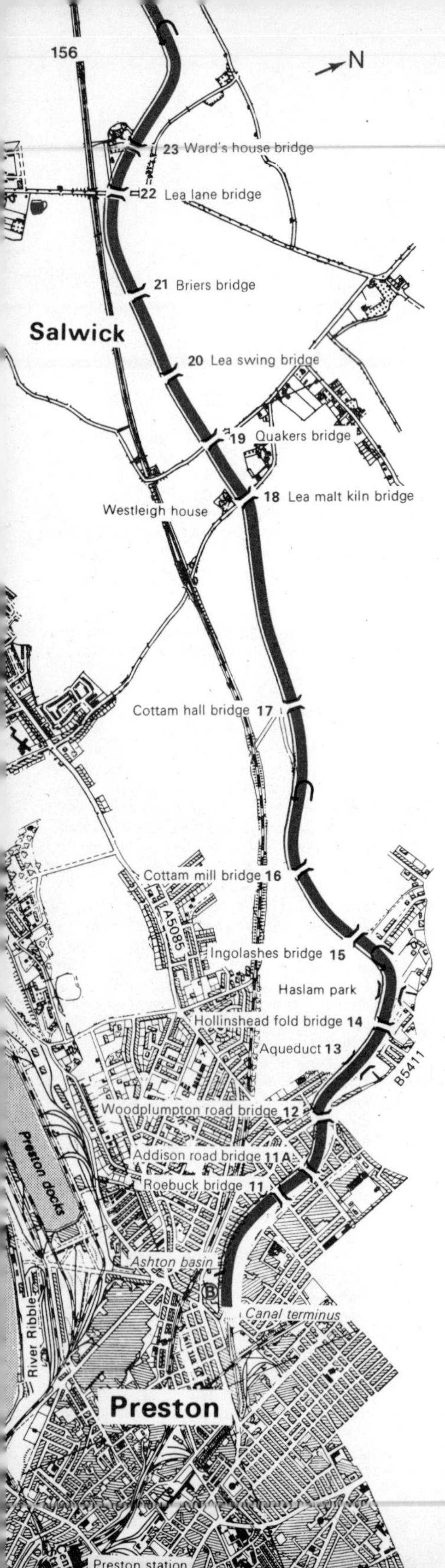

Preston

4 miles

The canal in Preston, shortened many years ago by over half a mile, now starts in the middle of nowhere, on an embankment by the old Ashton Basin, which has now been restored and turned into a thriving boatyard. (There is not much left of the original line, although pubs in Preston like the 'Lamb & Packet' recall the days when passenger 'fly boats' or 'packet boats' used to leave Preston to do the trip to Kendal in 8 hours—a remarkable speed.) From Ashton Basin, the canal runs through dull urban areas for a short while. There is nothing to see and no pubs or shops nearby except at bridge 11, where there is also a butcher. However, the attractive Haslam Park appears at bridge 12 and while housing estates line the offside bank for a mile, the towpath side of the canal is effectively already in the countryside. Soon Preston is left behind and the canal runs through flat and featureless but always green, open, agricultural countryside; the first of many sheep and cows are seen grazing along here. Passing Westleigh House and several farms, one begins to see the large industrial works at Salwick where fuel elements are made for atomic power stations. Farm eggs may be bought at bridge 18.

Salwick
Lancs. PO, tel, stores, station. A village scattered over a large area. The school, post office, telephone and pub are just ¼ mile south of bridge 22: the station is ¼ mile SW of bridge 25.

Preston
Lancs. Pop 107,000. MD Mon, Wed, Sat. All services. A large industrial town which prospered as a cotton manufacturing centre. The teetotal movement was founded in Preston in 1834, and Joseph Livesey's Temperance Hotel (the world's first) used to stand at the corner of Church street and North road. The Market Place is dominated by the huge classical building of the Harris Public Library and Museum, which is unfortunately spoilt by the grime of ages—as are several of the churches, whose tall spires are a distinctive feature of the town. Attempts to redevelop the centre of the town have resulted in a good new shopping precinct and a large modern bus station housed in a remarkably long multi-storey car park. Preston is an inland seaport on the Ribble and its docks enable it to serve as a distribution centre for the North of England. (Cargoes are mostly to and from Ireland.)

Harris Museum & Art Gallery Market Square. The museum has a specialised collection of the Devis family of painters in addition to exhibits illustrating 19thC art and industry, including porcelain, glass, toys, stamps and local history. *Open weekdays 10.00-17.00 all year. (Closed Sun and Bank Holidays.)*

BOATYARDS & BWB

Omissa Marine 52 Waterloo road, Ashton-on-Ribble, Preston, Lancs. (729210). At Ashton basin. Dustbins, water, gas, chandlery, slipway up to 9 foot, moorings, winter storage. Boat & motor sales & repairs, agents for all major firms. *Open daily throughout year.*

BOAT TRIPS

'Shelagh' is an old Leeds & Liverpool motor barge which runs charter trips in summer from bridge 12, in Preston. It is licensed to carry up to 100 passengers. Enquiries to D. Ashcroft, 12 Staveley Place, Savick Estate, Preston, Lancs. (Preston 728792).

PUBS

Smith's Arms Salwick, ¼ mile S of bridge 22.

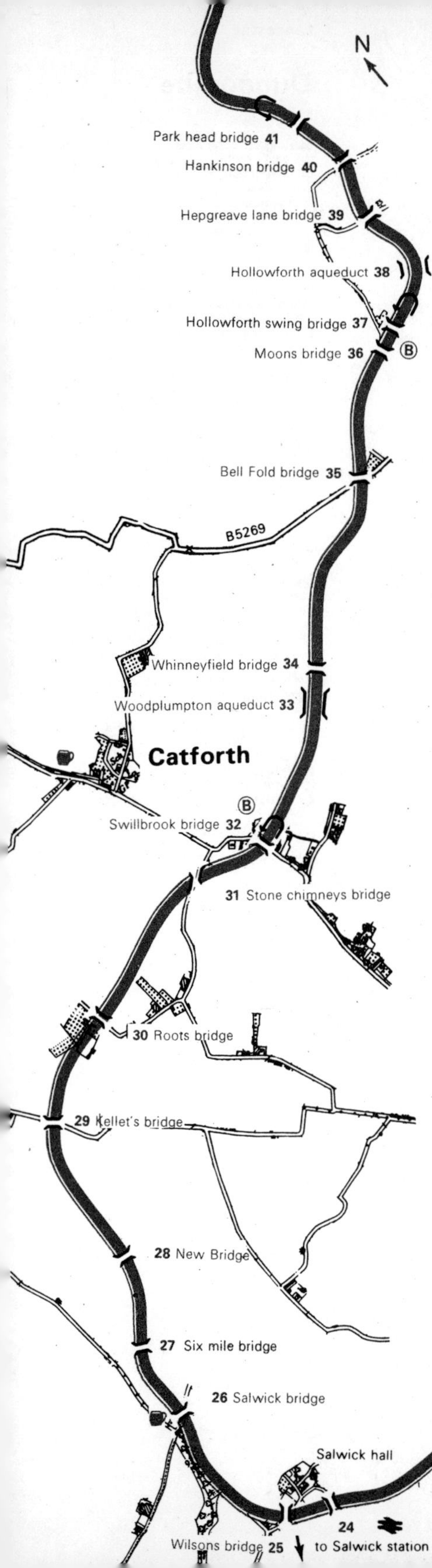

Catforth

5½ miles

The canal now reaches Salwick wharf, where the moorings are administered by the Duchy of Lancaster. On one side of the wharf is the moated Salwick Hall, screened by trees: on the other side is Salwick station, on the Preston–Blackpool line, and a disused windmill beyond. Here the canal turns north into a wooded cutting, passing a canalside pub–unfortunately a rare sight on this canal. At Kellet's bridge the navigation turns sharply east to Catforth (*PO, tel, stores*). All along this section the countryside is soft, open pastureland dotted with dairy farms, entirely peaceful and untouched by busy roads. At Swillbrook bridge there is one of the few boatyards on this canal: the proprietor's house was the old canal cottage with stables for the towing horses.

The Fylde
A large flat area of northwest Lancashire (west of the canal) which is the 'market garden' of the many industrial towns in Lancs. There used to be a wonderful array of windmills covering the land, but nearly all of these are gone now.

BOATYARDS & BWB

Preston Hire Cruisers At bridge 36. Enquiries to 4 Beech Avenue, Warton, nr Preston, Lancs. (Preston 632823). Hire cruisers. Dustbins, water, gas, chandlery, 5 ton crane, moorings, winter storage. Boat & motor sales & repairs, agents for Callum Craft. *Erratic opening hours, but usually open.*
Adventure Cruisers Jolly Roger Boating Haven, Preston, Lancs. (Catforth 690232). At bridge 32. Hire cruisers. Sewage & refuse disposal, water, gas, chandlery, slipway up to 30 foot, moorings, winter storage. Boat & motor sales & repairs, agents for most major firms. Groceries, telephone, lavatories. *Open daily throughout year.*

PUBS

Running Pump Catforth.
Bay Horse Catforth.
Clifton Arms Salwick. Canalside.

FISHING THE LANCASTER CANAL

This is a peaceful canal with fishing in picturesque surroundings. The canal holds a good head of roach, bream, tench, perch and pike; and there are eels to be caught throughout the waterway. Most of the fishing rights along the canal are leased to the Northern Anglers' Association, who also hold the rights along the Glasson branch. The Secretary is Mr S. Markland, 14 Humber Place, Norley Hall Estate, Pemberton, Wigan, Lancs. Membership of this Association is open, and local tackle shops will help enquirers with season permits.
At Preston the canal is well fished by anglers from the town, and regular competitions are held. Competitors go for the small fish but the top match weights usually run to 7 or 8lb. All species are to be caught, and fish of specimen size are there for those who seek them.

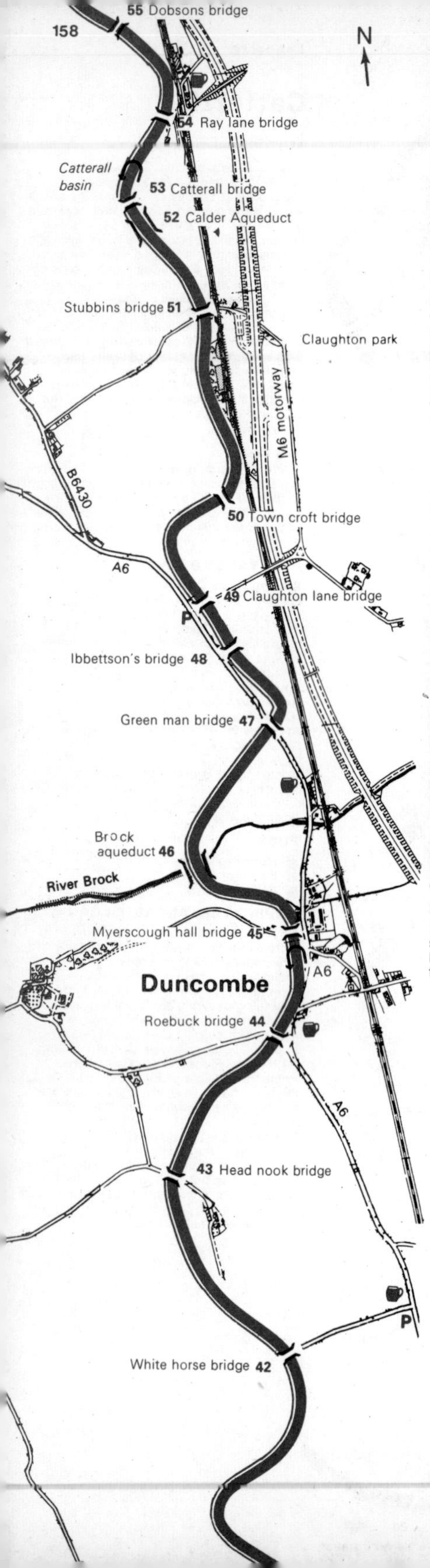

55 Dobsons bridge
N
54 Ray lane bridge
Catterall basin
53 Catterall bridge
52 Calder Aqueduct
Stubbins bridge 51
Claughton park
M6 motorway
B6430
50 Town croft bridge
A6
49 Claughton lane bridge
P
Ibbettson's bridge 48
Green man bridge 47
Brock aqueduct 46
River Brock
Myerscough hall bridge 45
A6
Duncombe
Roebuck bridge 44
A6
43 Head nook bridge
P
White horse bridge 42

Duncombe

5½ miles

Starting at White Horse bridge (¼ mile to the east of which is a pub, garage, post office and telephone kiosk), the canal sweeps round to enter the village of Duncombe on a minor embankment: the A6 joins the canal here and continues to dog it for many miles, as does the main railway line to Scotland, and the M6. When these rival transport routes keep their distance the canal is again delightfully quiet, still passing peaceful green farmland, while the foothills of the Pennines begin to converge from the east. Just south of Stubbins bridge can be seen the sadly derelict canal cottage and stable which was one of the places where towing horses were exchanged for fresh animals to pull the express passenger boats between Preston and Kendal. Near the former Garstang and Catterall station is Catterall Basin; both are now disused.

Claughton Hall
¼ mile east of the canal. This hall was originally an Elizabethan mansion built next to the village church for the Croft family, but in 1932-5 the whole house, except for one wing, was dismantled and reassembled on top of the moor north of the village. It was quite a remarkable undertaking and still stands there in defiant isolation.

Duncombe (or **Bilsborrow**)
Lancs. PO, tel, stores, garage. A village straggling along the A6, which must have been very noisy before the M6 was built. The church is set apart, up on a hill; there are two pubs very close to the canal.

PUBS

Kenlis Arms Garstang. 50yds east of bridge 54. Daily lunches and dinners bookable (Garstang 3307). B & B.
Green Man Duncombe. South of bridge 47.
White Bull Duncombe. Canalside.
Roebuck Duncombe. 30yds from canal.
White Horse ¼ mile east of bridge 42 on A6.

CARAVANS & CAMPING

Lodge Caravan Park Catterall Gate lane, Catterall. (Garstang 2246). 1½ miles from canal, on B6430. Overnight caravan stops.

FISHING

Between Preston and Garstang the good stock of varied fish includes small roach, bream to 3lbs and thousands of little fingerling carp.

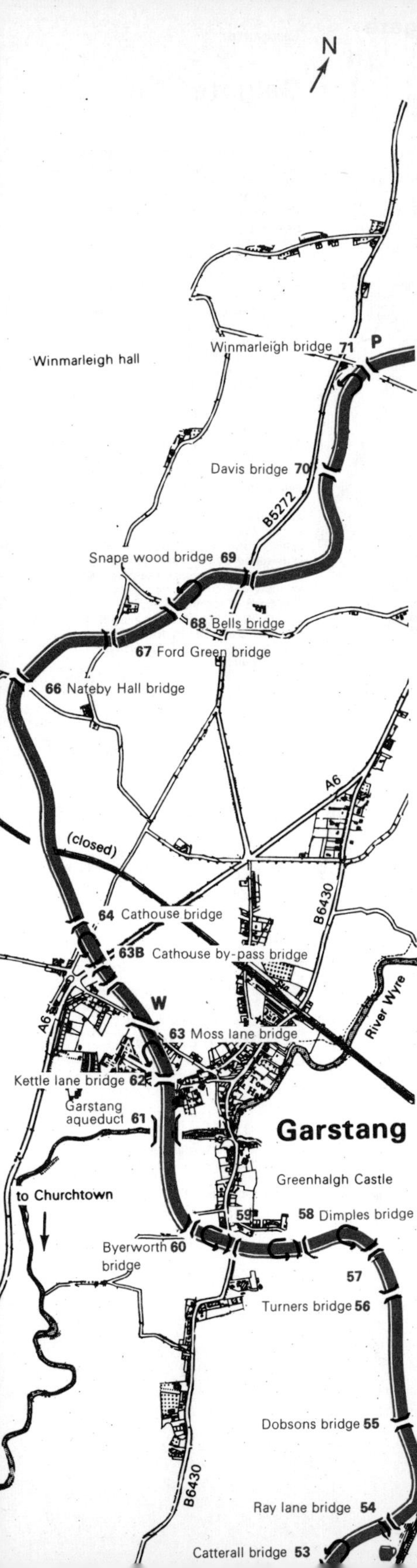

Garstang

5 miles

The canal moves away from the hills and the remains of Greenhalgh Castle, crossing the river Wyre on a fine stone aqueduct and passing the attractive town of Garstang; Garstang Basin is a popular mooring for pleasure boats now. It is hoped to restore the old wharf buildings and open a small restaurant in the barn here. The canal then winds through countryside that is as green and pleasant as ever but which is now overlooked by the steep slopes of the Pennines. Enthusiastic walkers up the hills will be rewarded with splendid views over Cockerham Sands and the Fylde.

Winmarleigh Hall
½ mile west of bridges 68 and 70. A red brick hall built in 1871 for Lord Winmarleigh. It was largely rebuilt after a fire in 1927. It is now an agricultural college.

Garstang
Lancs. PO, tel, stores, bank, garage.
A friendly town, touching the canal, which retains the feeling of a small market town. Just near the canal is the 18thC church of St Thomas surrounded by a tidy churchyard. Opposite the cobbled market place is the interesting little town hall with its diminutive bell-tower. The town hall, built in 1680 to acknowledge its promotion by the King to borough status, was rebuilt in 1939. There used to be a dozen ale houses in the town; but the present 6 seem quite enough.

Greenhalgh Castle
Just north of the canal on a grassy knoll are the modest ruins of Greenhalgh Castle. It was built in 1490 by the Earl of Derby, who placed Richard III's crown on Bolingbroke's head after the victory at Bosworth Field. In the 17thC it was destroyed by the Roundheads during the Civil War when the Royalists made a final stand there. Ask at the adjacent farm to visit the ruins.

St Helen's Church
1½ miles south west of the canal at Churchtown, west of the A6. A magnificent parish church known as the 'Cathedral of the Fylde', in an attractive setting of a shady churchyard near the river Wyre. Parts of the building date from c. 1300 and inside are 15thC arches on Norman pillars with the Creed written on them. The massive beams in the roof are from the four oaks that Henry IV granted to Churchtown when forests were the property of the monarch.

PUBS

Eagle & Child High st, Garstang.
Farmer's Arms Church st, Garstang.
King's Arms High st, Garstang.
X Royal Oak hotel Market Place, Garstang. (3318). Lunches and dinners. B & B.
Wheatsheaf Park Hall rd, Garstang.

CARAVANS & CAMPING

Smithy Café Caravan Site Winmarleigh, nr Garstang. (Garstang 2233). Canalside. Overnight caravan & tent stops.
Wharfe Cottage Caravan Park Winmarleigh, nr Garstang. (Great Eccleston 374). Canalside. Overnight caravan stops. No tents permitted.
Wyre Vale Park Garstang. (2776). ½ mile from canal, on A6. Overnight caravan stops. No tents permitted.

FISHING

The Garstang lengths are noted for big pike with fish over 20lb, plus roach to 1lb and bream to 3lb.

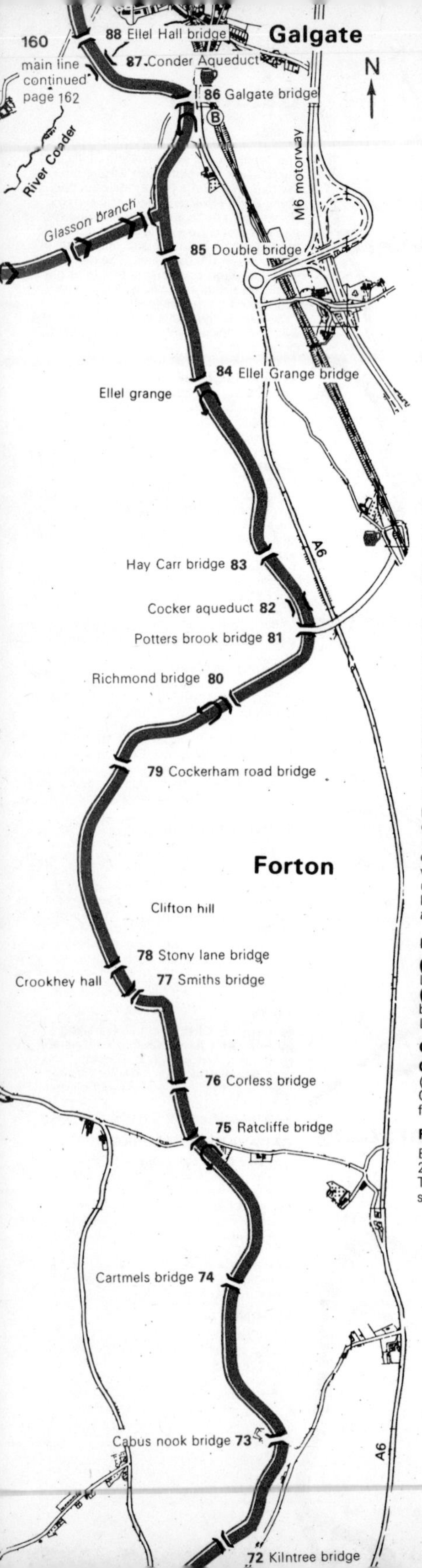

Lancaster

Galgate

$5\frac{1}{4}$ miles

Continuing northwards through quiet, modest and unspoilt pasture land, the canal passes countryside that is empty of villages but full of farms and houses dotted about the landscape. The absence of any locks certainly makes this an ideal waterway for restful cruising, while the wildlife and the generously-proportioned stone-arched bridges always supply interest along the way. Near Forton, a sharp S-bend carries the canal between Clifton Hill and Crookhey Hall, while from Potters Brook bridge a lane across the A6 leads to a post office, telephone and hotel beside what used to be Bay Horse station. Just north of Potters Brook is the Ellel Grange estate with its remarkable spired church, ornamental canal bridge and the Grange itself, shrouded by tall trees; unfortunately the estate is private. Double bridge is worth a closer look; beyond the rocky cutting that it spans is the junction with the Glasson branch, and round the corner is Galgate and a large boatyard and mooring site.

Galgate
Lancs. PO, tel, stores, garage. An unassuming village on the A6 but dominated by the main railway to Scotland, which strides through the place on a high embankment and an impressive viaduct. The back of the village up the hill is quiet; by the church of St John are the buildings of what is apparently the oldest surviving silk spinning mill in England (built in 1792).

Ellel Grange
On the banks of the canal. A very fine Italianate villa built for a merchant in 1857-9. It is a large mansion with two broad towers that compete in vain with the graceful spire of the charming little church of St Mary that stands in the grounds of the house. Both are private.

BOATYARDS & BWB

Ladyline (Nor' West Marina)
Canal Wharf, Galgate, nr Lancaster. (Lancaster 751368). At bridge 86. Hire cruisers. Sewage & refuse disposal, water, gas, chandlery, dustbins. Slipway up to 30 foot, moorings, winter storage. Boat & engine sales & repairs. *Open daily throughout year.*

PUBS

Plough Galgate, near bridge 86. Lunches.

Bay Horse hotel, $\frac{1}{4}$ mile NE of bridge 81, across the A6. (Forton 791204). Lunches, dinners and B & B.

CARAVANS & CAMPING

Claylands Farm Cabus, nr Garstang. (Forton 242). $1\frac{1}{2}$ miles from canal, off A6. Overnight caravan & tent stops. Caravans for hire.

FISHING

Between Garstang and Lancaster roach to $2\frac{1}{2}$lb and bream to $3\frac{1}{2}$lb have been caught. There are also perch, tench and ruffe, with some chub in places.

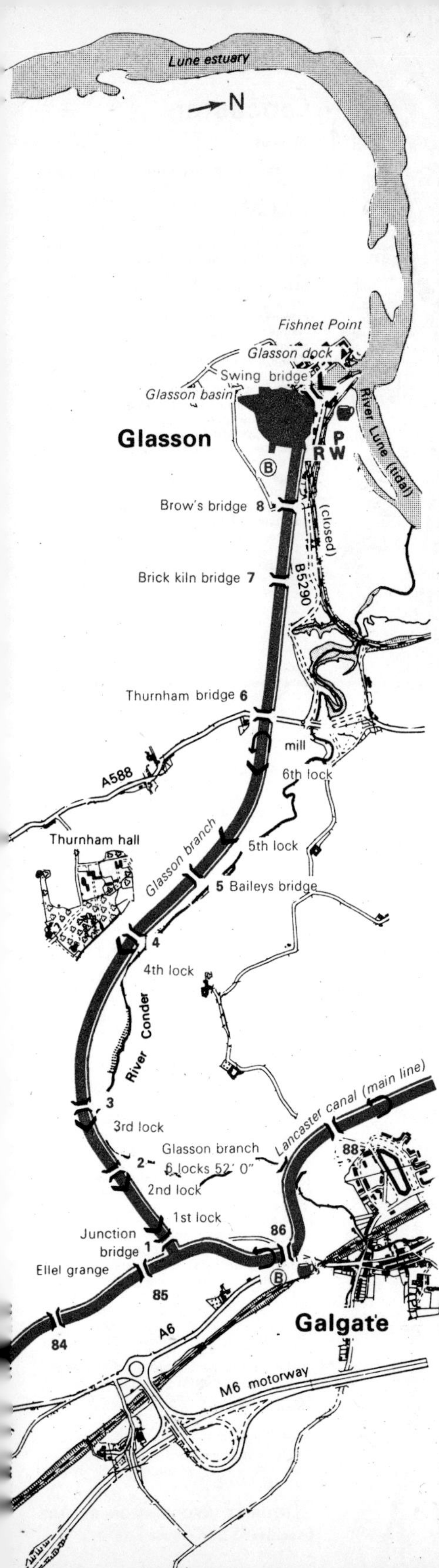

Glasson

3 miles

Between Ellel Grange and Galgate the Glasson branch leads off down to the west to connect the Lancaster Canal with the Lune Estuary via Glasson Dock. The branch was finished only in 1826, long after the main line of the canal was completed, and provided the canal with its only direct link with the sea. There are 6 wide locks whose bottom gates feature the same excellent type of sliding paddles as one sees on the Leeds and Liverpool Canal. The top gates are all kept padlocked for security reasons: boatmen should ensure that they have the requisite key on board (available from BWB staff) and are asked to lock the gates after use, and also to leave the locks **empty** after use, even when going up the locks. The Arm falls through the Conder valley, a pleasant, quiet stretch of countryside whose proximity to the sea is betrayed by the many seagulls cruising around. The spire in the trees on the south bank belongs to Thurnham church; Thurnham Mill is beside the bottom lock, and its mill race shows that it still takes water from the canal. After the bottom lock, the canal runs in a straight line through saltings and marshland to Glasson Basin, where there is a large boatyard, mainly for seagoing yachts, and BWB moorings.

Navigational notes

1. The entrance lock from the Glasson Dock up into Glasson Basin will take boats up to 95ft long, 26ft wide and 12ft draught. Anyone wishing to use the lock or to take up a mooring in the Basin should contact the BWB lock-keeper at Galgate 566.
2. The locks on the Glasson branch will take boats up to 72ft long, 14ft wide and 5ft draught.

Glasson

Lancs. PO, tel, stores, garage. A fascinating tiny port that is still busy with trade from coastal and continental vessels. The canal no longer contributes to this trade and the huge Basin is only occupied by an assortment of pleasure boats using its excellent sheltered mooring. In the tidal dock, however, there are usually plenty of coasters that discharge into lorries, since the old railway line from Lancaster has now been dismantled.

Thurnham Hall

On SW bank of canal. This ancient family home of the Daltons is a battlemented 16thC mansion that was given a new facade and beautiful chapel in the 19thC.

BOATYARDS & BWB

Glasson Basin Yacht Company
Glasson Dock, nr Lancaster. (Galgate 754491). Boatyard for sea-going vessels. Dustbins, water, diesel, petrol, gas, chandlery, slipway up to 70 foot, crane (up to 15 tons), moorings, winter storage. Boat & motor sales & repairs, agents for most major firms. Boats fitted out. Telephone. Lavatories.

Ladyline (Nor' West Marina) Canal Wharf, Galgate, nr Lancaster. (Galgate 368). At bridge 86. (See page 160 for details).

PUBS

- **Caribou** hotel Glasson Dock.
- **Dalton Arms** Glasson Dock.
- **Victoria** hotel Glasson Dock.
- X **Ba Ba Gee** Café mounted on an old Lancaster Canal barge, floating in Glasson Basin.

FISHING

Fishing in the Glasson branch has always been rewarding, with a few interesting catches at times. There are some enormous bream (up to 7½lb) about, also good tench and very big eels. Down in the area of Glasson Basin there is a good variety of fish—including brown trout, which were introduced in 1970.

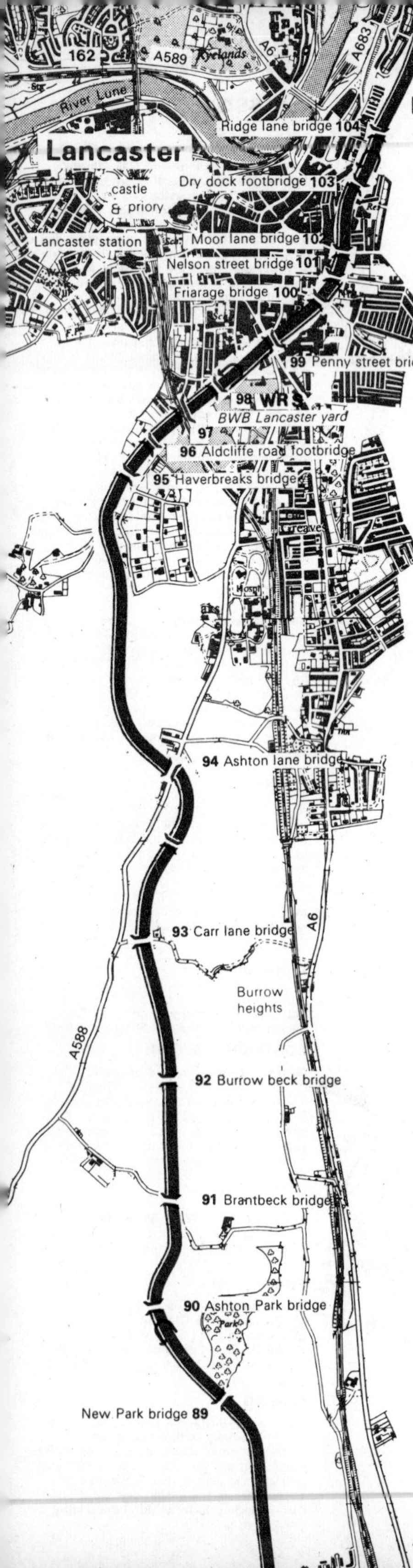

Lancaster

5¼ miles

The canal continues northwards through beautiful undulating green countryside, then passes through an unusually long wooded cutting which ends in the outskirts of Lancaster. Going underneath the main line railway, one can see the gaunt shell of the 2-storey building where the old packet boats used to be refitted, being hauled out of the water from pulleys on the beams of the upper floor. (This building now has a Preservation Order on it.) The BWB maintenance yard is nearby, at the bridge where the towpath changes sides. Past the bridge, the old Aldcliffe basins and wharves which were once the headquarters of the canal company are disused and forlorn, but are shortly to be developed as an amenity area by the City Council who now lease them. Opposite are some canal stables which have been tastefully converted into a place for punting, eating and drinking. At bridge 101 the towpath returns to the left side of the canal, where it stays for the rest of the journey northwards. The navigation now leaves Lancaster, on the side of the hill that overlooks the Lune estuary.

Lancaster
Lancs. Pop 48,000. EC Wed, MD Sat. All services. The name Lancaster is derived from a combination of Lune (after the river) and Latin 'castrum' meaning 'camp', which refers to the Roman fortress that once stood on this site. Today the quay, once a great shipping port, is only a quiet backwater, with a pleasant walk provided by the tree-lined quayside promenade. A large new university was opened at Bailrigg, south of the town, in 1964. The Boat Regatta takes place annually in May and the Agricultural show in August.

Lancaster Castle A handsome but forbidding building on the site of Roman fortifications; mainly 13thC and 14thC construction, except for the Norman keep, which is surmounted by a beacon tower known as John of Gaunt's Chair. The Shire Hall contains an impressive display of over 600 heraldic shields. Most of the castle has reverted to its earlier function as a prison. *Escorted tours mornings except Wed, Sat & Sun 11.00. Afternoons except Sun 14.30 & 15.30. Closed while Assizes, Quarter Sessions or County Courts are sitting.*

Priory Church of St Mary Vicarage lane, by the Castle. Attractive 15thC church in late Perpendicular style though the original Saxon western doorway still remains and the belfry was added in 1754. Elaborately carved choir stall c. 1340 and fine Jacobean pulpit.

Town Hall Dalton sq. A very impressive building of classical design, with a grand marble staircase and domed council chamber. It was the generous gift of Lord Ashton to Lancaster city in 1909. It is open to visitors, who are shown the magnificent entrance hall, the council chamber and concert hall, as well as the historic charters. To arrange a visit contact the Town Clerk.

Lancaster Museum Old Town Hall, Market sq. Prehistoric, Roman and mediaeval exhibits; pottery and porcelain, firearms and topographical paintings. *Open weekdays only, 10.00-17.30.*

Ashton Memorial Williamson Park, Quernmore rd. Yet another generous gift from Lord Ashton to the city as a memorial to his family. In the centre of a beautiful park, containing a palm-house and ornamental lake, the memorial is a vast structure consisting of two domed chambers, one on top of the other. It was designed in neo-classic style by J. Belcher and constructed of Portland stone in 1907-9.

BOATYARDS & BWB

BWB Lancaster Yard at bridge 98. (Lancaster 2712). Water, refuse & sewage disposal, lavatory.

TOURIST INFORMATION CENTRE

Lancaster 7 Dalton Square. (65272).

BOAT TRIPS

'Lady Fiona' is an old canal motor barge, converted and licensed to carry 100 passengers. Trips Easter-Sep: Sun, Tue, Wed, Thur, at 14.00. Trips last 3½hrs and leave from opposite the Infirmary just east of bridge 98. Licensed bar and snacks on board. Enquiries to D. C. Fox, 1 Woodland Ave, Thornton, Blackpool, Lancs. (Thornton 2568).

The Stables on the towpath east of bridge 98. Punts for hire; snacks and drinks served from the former canal stables.

PUBS

Large number of pubs, hotels, etc. in Lancaster: none on the canal bank.

X🍷 **Portofino** 23 Castle street, Lancaster (2388). An Italian restaurant owned and run by three brothers, specialities being the starters—of which there are over thirty. Praise has been given to most dishes, amongst them fried squid, cannelloni, and prawns on savoury rice. L 12.00-14.00, D 19.00-23.30 (closed public hols, Sun). Must book D, no dogs. Good Food Guide since 1961.

The Lune Aqueduct, near Lancaster.

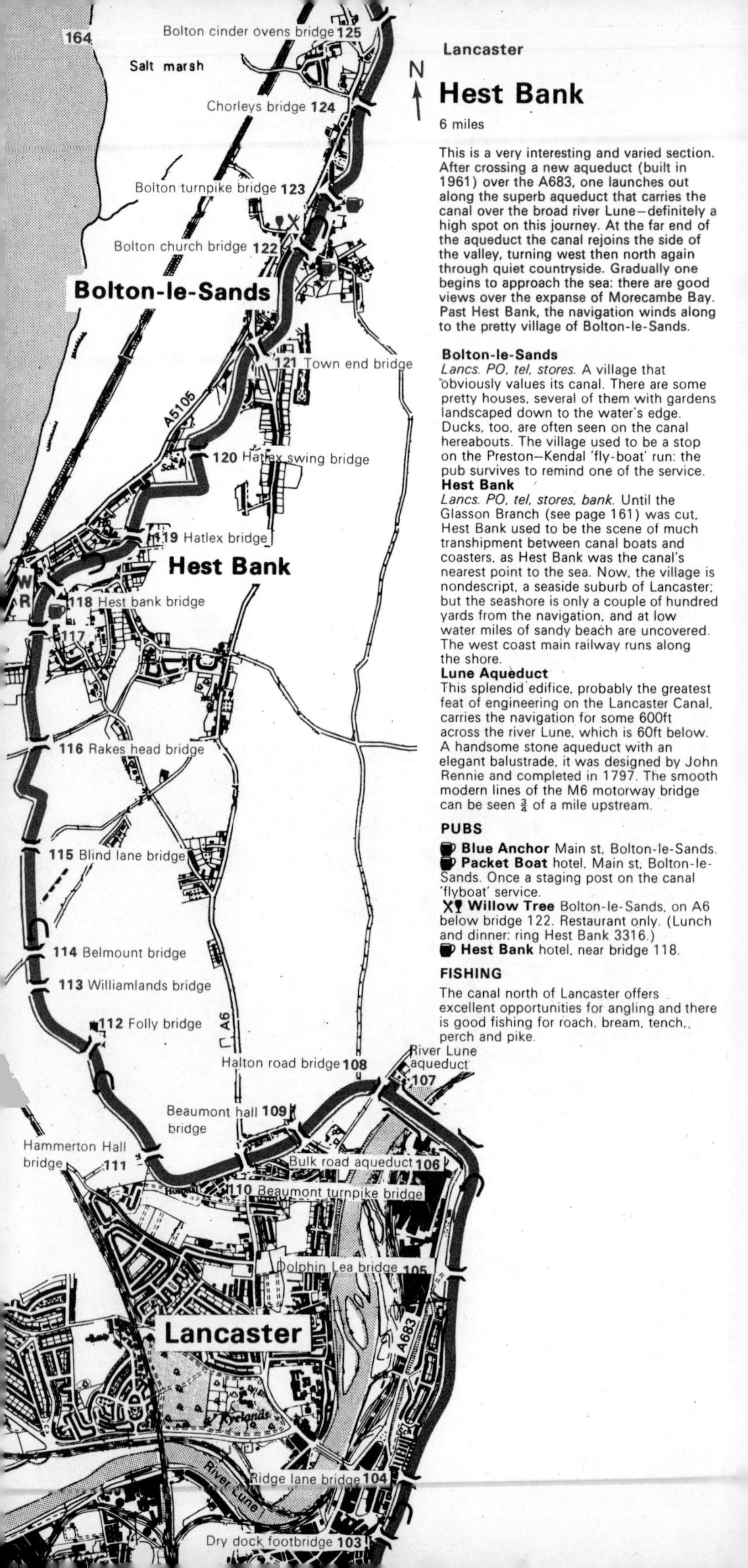

Hest Bank

6 miles

This is a very interesting and varied section. After crossing a new aqueduct (built in 1961) over the A683, one launches out along the superb aqueduct that carries the canal over the broad river Lune—definitely a high spot on this journey. At the far end of the aqueduct the canal rejoins the side of the valley, turning west then north again through quiet countryside. Gradually one begins to approach the sea: there are good views over the expanse of Morecambe Bay. Past Hest Bank, the navigation winds along to the pretty village of Bolton-le-Sands.

Bolton-le-Sands
Lancs. PO, tel, stores. A village that obviously values its canal. There are some pretty houses, several of them with gardens landscaped down to the water's edge. Ducks, too, are often seen on the canal hereabouts. The village used to be a stop on the Preston–Kendal 'fly-boat' run: the pub survives to remind one of the service.

Hest Bank
Lancs. PO, tel, stores, bank. Until the Glasson Branch (see page 161) was cut, Hest Bank used to be the scene of much transhipment between canal boats and coasters, as Hest Bank was the canal's nearest point to the sea. Now, the village is nondescript, a seaside suburb of Lancaster; but the seashore is only a couple of hundred yards from the navigation, and at low water miles of sandy beach are uncovered. The west coast main railway runs along the shore.

Lune Aqueduct
This splendid edifice, probably the greatest feat of engineering on the Lancaster Canal, carries the navigation for some 600ft across the river Lune, which is 60ft below. A handsome stone aqueduct with an elegant balustrade, it was designed by John Rennie and completed in 1797. The smooth modern lines of the M6 motorway bridge can be seen $\frac{3}{4}$ of a mile upstream.

PUBS

Blue Anchor Main st, Bolton-le-Sands.
Packet Boat hotel, Main st, Bolton-le-Sands. Once a staging post on the canal 'flyboat' service.
Willow Tree Bolton-le-Sands, on A6 below bridge 122. Restaurant only. (Lunch and dinner: ring Hest Bank 3316.)
Hest Bank hotel, near bridge 118.

FISHING

The canal north of Lancaster offers excellent opportunities for angling and there is good fishing for roach, bream, tench, perch and pike.

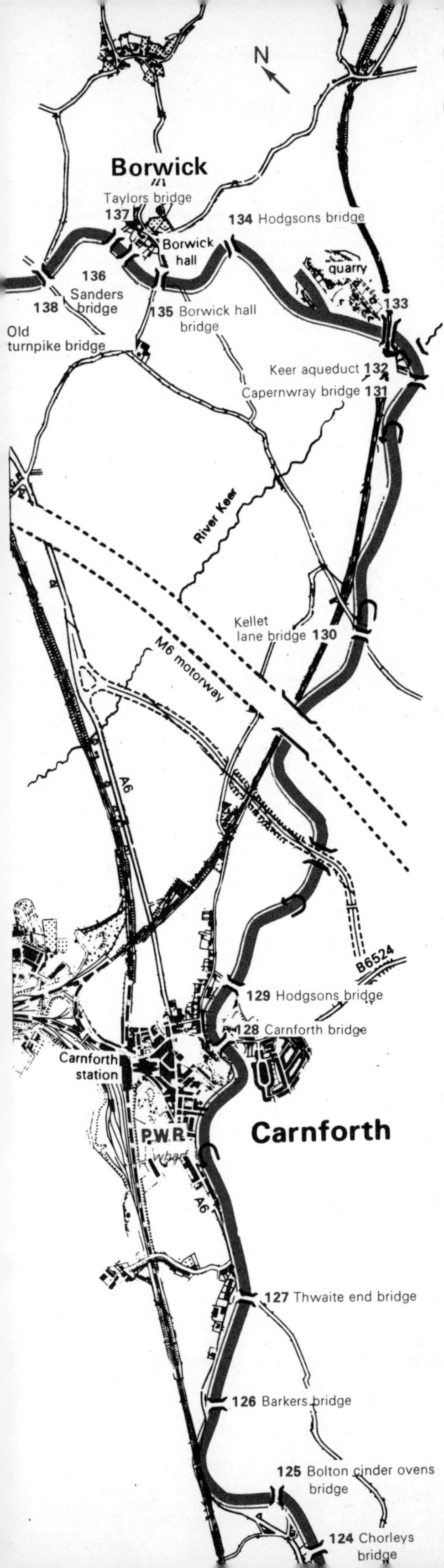

Carnforth

$5\frac{1}{2}$ miles

The A6 now runs beside and below the canal into Carnforth. One may catch occasional glimpses westward of the distant shores around Morecambe Bay, then the canal passes Carnforth, mostly in a cutting. A few small abandoned quarries are scattered between the canal and the M6. After passing under the motorway spur road, the canal finds itself diverted along a new channel for several hundred yards before going under the main line of the M6: this diversion was presumably cheaper to build than a long, finely angled skew bridge over the navigation. Beyond the motorway lies peaceful green countryside backed, unmistakably, by the foothills of the Lake District. At Capernwray the canal crosses the river Keer on a minor aqueduct: the nearby railway, which leads to Leeds, crosses the Keer on an impressive viaduct, framing a tiny old derelict watermill. Past the railway bridge is a short and rather shallow branch to a worked-out quarry, then the canal winds round the hillside to Borwick. Carnforth and the M6 can be easily seen from here, the latter getting ominously close.

Borwick
Lancs. Tel. A small, old and attractive village, spread around a green. Overlooking the canal is Borwick Hall, a large and sombre Elizabethan manor house, built around a high 15thC tower. Extensive gardens. It is now used as a residential training centre by the Lancashire Youth Club Association. *Open B. Hols and by appointment* (Carnforth 2508).

Warton
Lancs. PO, tel, stores. About two miles W of Borwick. Ancestors of George Washington lived in this village and their family crest containing the famed Stars and Stripes is to be seen on the 15thC tower of the church of St Oswald.

Carnforth
Lancs. Pop 4100. PO, tel, stores, garage, bank, station. Not particularly attractive to most people, Carnforth is of interest to some as an important railway junction. One may catch trains not only north–south but east over the beautiful green hills to Skipton and Leeds, west to Barrow and right round the coast to Carlisle. Carnforth was the last town in the country to lose its regular British Rail steam locomotive service in 1968. Since then a company of steam engine enthusiasts and volunteers have privately set up the 'Steamtown' museum—a depot with 5 miles of track along which preserved engines steam on certain weekends. The growing collection of motive power includes the French National Pacific locomotive that used to haul the famous Golden Arrow express. (For details contact Carnforth 2625.) At Carnforth wharf are some useful facilities: BWB moorings, slipway, dustbins and fresh water. A petrol station is nearby.

PUBS

Carnforth hotel, Market st, Carnforth (2902). Lunches, dinners.
County Lancaster rd, Carnforth. (2469). Lunches, dinners, bar food.

CARAVANS & CAMPING

Intack Caravans Nether Kellet, nr Carnforth. (Carnforth 2884). 2 miles from canal, off A6. Overnight caravan stops. No tents permitted.
Marsh House Farm Crag Bank, Carnforth. (Carnforth 2897). $\frac{3}{4}$ mile from canal, off A6. Overnight caravan & tent stops.
New England Caravan Park Capernwray, nr Carnforth. (Carnforth 2612). Canalside, near the old arm to the quarry. Long term caravan parking only. No tents permitted.

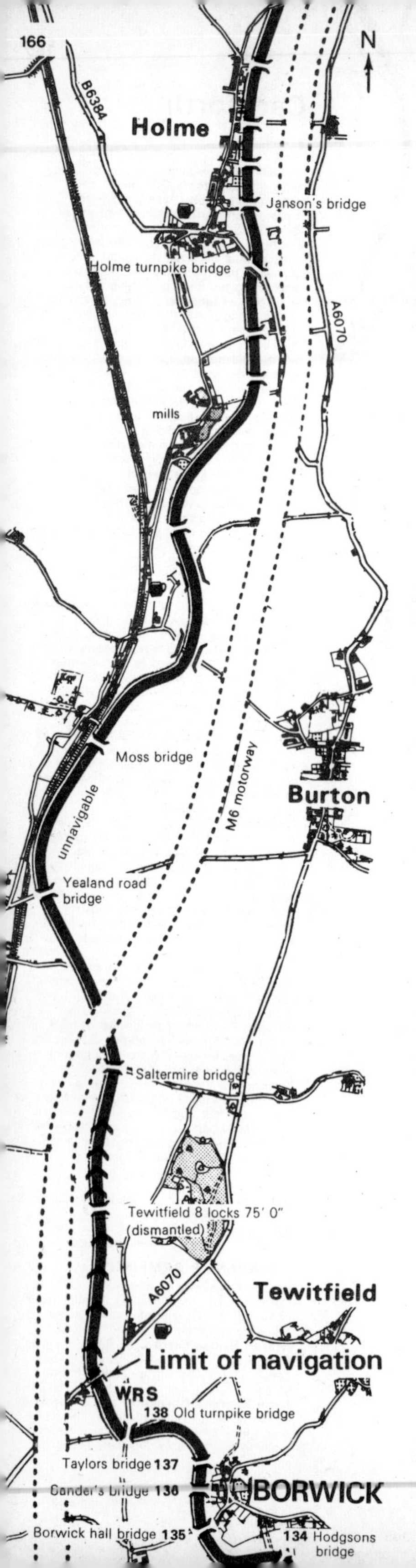

Holme

5 miles

As one turns the corner and passes bridge 138, one finds that the Lancaster Canal comes to an untimely end. When the M6 motorway was built alongside the former Tewitfield locks, a large bridge was constructed to carry the A6070 over the new motorway, but was not extended over the adjacent canal—so now the navigation is completely and permanently blocked by a massive embankment with the A6070 on top of it. Similar crossings exist at 5 more places further north.
Tewitfield therefore represents the northern limit of the Lancaster Canal for cruising boats. However the now unnavigable section of the canal still feeds water down to the south from the distant Killington reservoir, so there is still water in the canal for another 8½ miles, to Stainton. The water is normally at least 2' 6" deep, so canoeists should find this an attractive length. Apart from the 8 at Tewitfield there are no locks, but portaging is necessary to cross the motorway or its feeder roads at the 7 points along the route.
Anyone wishing to explore the unnavigable portion of the canal on foot will find it a worthwhile excursion. One can quite easily walk right through from Tewitfield to the original terminus in Kendal. There is an excellent towpath all the way, the countryside is very fine, and there is a bus service from Kendal right back to the Longlands hotel at Tewitfield. In addition to this, one can safely leave a boat tied up at the present terminus at Tewitfield, where there are BWB moorings and facilities and a winding hole. The only obstacle to such a walk is presented by the few road crossings along the way.
Walking away, then, from the canal terminus and under the road bridge, one strides up the hill past the late Tewitfield locks, with the M6 traffic roaring alongside. Above the top lock, the motorway goes straight through the canal at an oblique angle. The other side of the road, the canal re-enters peaceful, hilly land. One seems at first to be relatively high up (the railway line is well below) but in fact it is less than 150ft above sea level. The village of Holme is passed; then one arrives at a minor road driven across the canal bed. By now the motorway has reappeared to the east, and Westmorland is entered.

Tewitfield Locks
These 8 locks, which are evenly spaced over ¾ of a mile, are the only locks on the main line of the Lancaster Canal in the 57 miles between Kendal and Preston—which says a lot for John Rennie's choice of route for the canal. The locks are all dismantled and weired now. They are—or were—wide locks: in fact these locks took small seagoing vessels from Glasson Dock en route for Kendal. And when the express passenger boats from Preston arrived at the foot of the locks, the passengers had to disembark, walk up the locks and get into another 'packet boat' waiting at the top lock. This rather drastic procedure had to be followed for the horse-drawn packet boats to maintain their remarkable *average* speeds of up to 10mph.

Holme
Westmorland. PO, tel, stores. There are some old stone terraced cottages by the canal, but otherwise the houses in this village are uninteresting and mostly new. The Victorian stone church looks pretty from the outside, with a stream running past the graveyard. But inside it is gloomy and disappointing.

Leighton Hall
1½ miles west of Tewitfield locks, at Yealand Conyers. (Carnforth 2729). A Neo-Gothic facade was super-imposed in the early 1800s on this Georgian mansion, the interior of which contains some examples of furniture made by R. Gillow the Lancaster cabinet maker, who was for a time owner of the house. It stands in large attractive grounds near the coastline. *Open*

May-Sep Wed, Sun, B. Hols 14.00-18.00.
Leighton Moss
2 miles west of Tewitfield locks. This area is a nature reserve of the Royal Society for the Protection of Birds. A reed marsh surrounded by limestone hills, its large meres are famous for the breeding of bitterns and reed warblers. It is a fine site for observing the birds (which include shovellers, kestrels and redpolls) at close quarters from hides without disturbing them. *Open Apr-Sep (escorted by warden) Sat, Wed; (unescorted) Sun, Tue, Thur. Access permits, for which at least 7 days' notice must be given, are available from Reserves Dept, The Lodge, Sandy, Beds.*

PUBS

Commercial Holme, opposite the church. B & B, bar food. (Burton 302).
X Station hotel Burton, 150yds W of the 2 aqueducts. The station has been gone for nearly 20 years, but the London–Scotland trains still thunder past this pub. Lunches and dinners bookable. (Burton 225).
Longlands hotel Tewitfield, 100yds NE of canal terminus. Free house, bar food. (Burton 256).

CARAVANS & CAMPING

Beetham Caravan Park Beetham. (Kendal 23204). 2 miles west of canal, on A6. Overnight caravan & tent stops.
Fell End Caravan Park Slackhead rd, Hale. (Milnthorpe 2122). 1½ miles west of canal on A6. Overnight caravan & tent stops.

YOUTH HOSTEL

Broadlands, Church Hill, Arnside (about 5 miles west of Holme). (Arnside 701).

FISHING

Above Tewitfield locks, several miles of the canal are to be developed into a new mixed fishery by the Northern AA in conjunction with the Lancashire River Authority and BWB. All species of coarse fish will be stocked, plus trout.

A typical stone-arched bridge on the Lancaster canal.

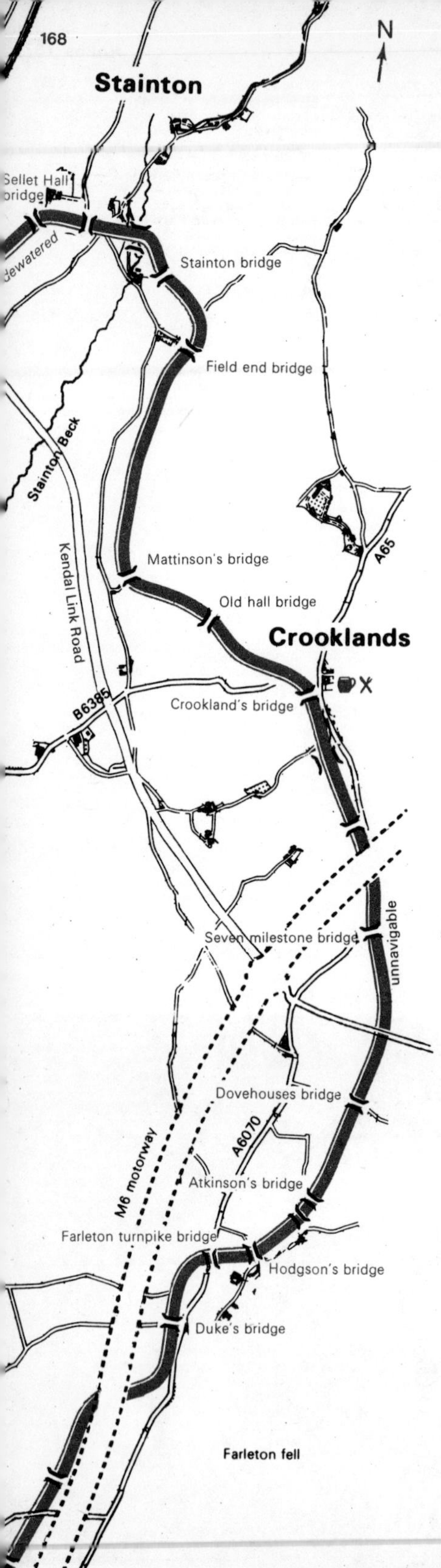

Crooklands

5 miles

Leaving Holme, the canal is run over by the motorway as it passes the steep and towering mass of Farleton Fell. The canal continues its lonely way past a forlorn wharf and stables, then leads straight to where a new road realignment has entailed the construction of a large embankment across the canal bed. Fortunately, a pedestrian tunnel in the bank allows an easy crossing of this highway. North of this the canal is contained in a narrow cutting, culminating in yet another motorway embankment across the former navigation. Again, this is an easy crossing, as the M6 bridges an adjacent road. Here at last the motorway heads off to the north east, but unfortunately our modern road network has not finished with the Lancaster canal yet, for the Kendal Link Road has recently been built, cutting the canal in two places and spoiling the formerly delightful character of the upper reaches of the canal. So the swans and ducks and other wildlife on the canal are rarer now, and the beautiful uplands that form the south end of the Lake District are permanently marred by yet another 20th century scar. But presumably the motorists enjoy it. At Crooklands the feed from Killington Reservoir flows into the canal; there are subsidiary feeders at Farleton and Stainton. At Stainton the canal is abruptly dammed off: from here to Kendal the canal bed is completely dry and empty, so canoeists and anglers will find no sport beyond this point. However walkers will doubtless enjoy the isolation of the canal beyond Hincaster, and also the fact that it is mostly embanked or cut along the side of a hill, yielding excellent views of the countryside.

PUBS

Crooklands hotel 50yds from canal. (Crooklands 374). Restaurant, grill room and bars. *Open daily.*

CARAVANS & CAMPING

Millness Hill Preston Patrick, Milnthorpe. (Crooklands 306). Canalside, at Seven Milestone bridge. Overnight caravan & tent stops.

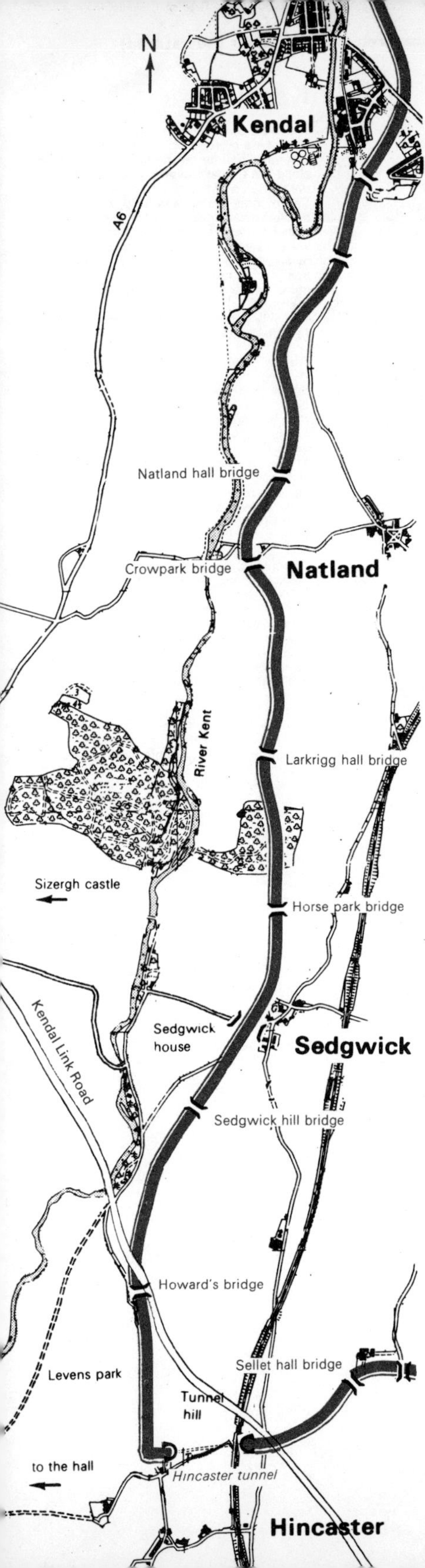

Kent Valley

5 miles

At Stainton the now dry canal bed turns west to pass under Hincaster Hill in a tunnel. The tunnel roof drips a lot, so the canal bed is usually boggy; and as there is no towpath, it is best to walk up past the railway and over the top of the hill, along the path that was made for the barge horses. At the west end of the tunnel the canal turns 90 degrees, and heads north for Kendal. This is splendid country, and the canal is carried along a steep hillside overlooking the woods of Levens Park and the hidden Kent valley. One walks over Sedgwick via an aqueduct: north of the village the canal bed in places merges almost unrecognisably into the pastures on either side. Only the stone arched bridges remain in defiant but bizarre isolation to remind one that this was once a water-filled channel carrying trading boats from Preston.

Crowpark bridge, near Natland (*PO, tel, stores*), marks one further stage in the progressive disappearance of this once-busy navigation: from this point northwards, the canal bed vanishes completely, as it has been filled in and incorporated into the adjoining fields. However the towpath remains, as a fenced footpath and a public right of way. And still the old bridges stand, bridging nothing. It is in a way an eerie sight.

Sizergh Castle
NT property. 1 mile north west of Sedgwick, on the A6. A large battlemented castle built around a 14thC tower. It has many fine ceilings, tapestries and furnishings. Attractive gardens. *Open Apr-Sep Wed 14.00-17.45. Gardens also open Tue & Thur afternoons.* Access along roads from Sedgwick or Natland, across the river Kent.

Sedgwick
Westmorland. PO, tel, stores. Hincaster Tunnel (380yds long) was originally opened in 1817 to divert the canal past a gunpowder works in Sedgwick. There is no sign of such an industry nowadays in this very pretty hamlet, which is dominated by the canal embankment with its aqueduct. The baronial-looking Victorian Sedgwick House is now a school.

Levens Hall
The hall is an Elizabethan mansion, privately occupied, that was converted c. 1586 from a mediaeval 'Pele' tower used as a refuge from marauding Scots. It contains richly carved panelling and plasterwork and possibly the finest collection of Charles II and William & Mary furniture in England; it also houses a splendid collection of working steam engines (all types except railway locomotives). The gardens around the hall are a fascinating demonstration of topiary skills, with trees and hedges rising in all sorts of weird and wonderful shapes. *House and Steam Museum open May-Sep Tue, Wed, Thur, Sun 14.00-17.00. Gardens open May-Sep daily 10.00-17.00. No dogs.* (Sedgwick 321). Access to the hall may be gained either by walking westward from Hincaster tunnel, or one may enter the park ¼ mile NW of Howard's bridge, then go back (south west) along the famous avenue of trees. The latter makes a superb walk.

CARAVANS & CAMPING

Gilpin House Café Levens, nr Kendal. (Witherslack 206). 2 miles west of canal, on A590. Overnight caravan & tent stops. Caravans for hire.

Sampool Caravan Site Levens, nr Kendal. (Witherslack 265). 2 miles west of canal, on A590. Overnight caravan & tent stops. Caravans for hire.

Kendal

The route of the canal's last 1½ miles into Kendal are pretty dismal. It can be traced without difficulty, as the public right of way along the former towpath extends right to the terminus of the canal, below Kendal Castle; most of the canal bridges and buildings have gone, but the ground one covers is mostly wasteland, and the gas works–which once had all its coal brought by canal–has now extended over the canal bed. It is all rather an anti-climax, and quite out of keeping with the character of Kendal itself.
One may catch a bus back from Kendal to Tewitfield locks and Carnforth.

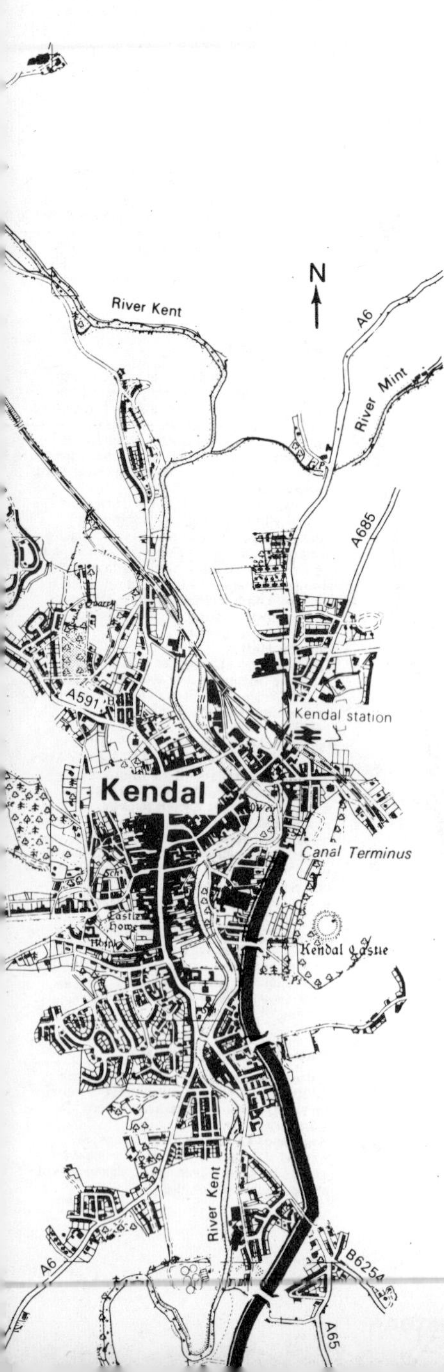

Kendal
Westmorland. Pop 20,000. EC Thur, MD Sat. All services. A very fine old stone market town astride the river Kent. The town contains much of interest and charm, and has not been spoiled by the few light industries that have sprung up round it. There is a mediaeval 'Shambles' as in York, and there are narrow cobbled streets leading down to the river Kent, which is fairly wide and shallow. A variety of bridges span the river: most of them are elegant 18thC stone structures. Beside the river, surrounded by a pleasant spacious churchyard, the Gothic parish church is a handsome and rather unusual building. It is one of the largest churches in England, a title that refers to its width rather than its height, for it has fully five aisles and spreads out broadly on each side of the tall central tower.
Town Hall Stricklandgate. A typically elaborate Victorian hall whose claim to fame is the selection of Welsh, Scottish, Irish and English folk tunes that issue forth six times a day from the bell tower. The repertoire includes such rousing songs as 'When the King enjoys his own again' and 'All through the Night'.
Kendal Museum Station rd. Special feature is the natural history section which exhibits a large collection of birds and wild animals from all over the world. *Open 10.00-16.30 weekdays.* (Kendal 21374).
Abbot Hall Art Gallery Adjoining the parish church in Kirkland. A Georgian mansion surrounded by lovely gardens, opened as a gallery in 1962. The ground floor has been completely restored and furnished in 18thC style. *Open weekdays 10.30-17.30. Sat & Sun 14.00-17.00.* (Kendal 22464).
Abbot Hall Museum of Lakeland Life and Industry Collections of local industries and culture. *Open weekdays: 10.30-12.30, 14.00-17.00. Sat, Sun 14.00-17.00.*
Kendal Castle On the east bank of the river. Only ruined fragments remain of the original Norman castle. Its most notable inhabitant was Katherine Parr, who became Henry VIII's last queen in 1543. Her father was lord of the castle and she lived there throughout her childhood.

PUBS
Plenty of pubs etc. in Kendal.

YOUTH HOSTEL
Stone Cross, 107 Milnthorpe rd, Kendal (24066).

[i] TOURIST INFORMATION CENTRE
Kendal Tourist Information Office, Town Hall. (23649).

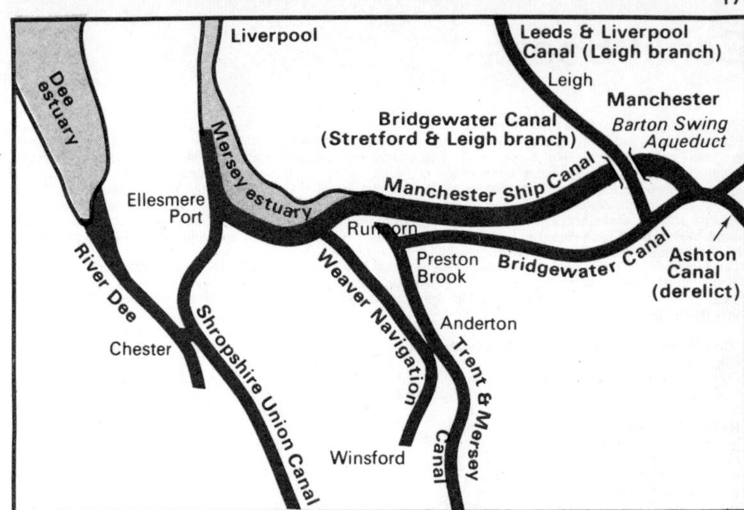

The Merseyside Canals

Five of the waterways covered in this book terminate in independently owned canals around the Manchester–Merseyside area. The map above shows how they link up.

The Manchester Ship Canal

The Shropshire Union Canal and the Weaver Navigation both flow into the Manchester Ship Canal, which is owned by the Manchester Ship Canal Company. This very big canal, opened on New Year's Day 1894 at a cost of £15½ million, carries ships displacing up to 15,000 tons. Navigation along the Ship Canal and through its locks cannot be undertaken freely by pleasure craft and is restricted to boats of proven seaworthiness in the charge of thoroughly competent skippers. All boats must carry adequate ropes, fire-extinguishers and lifebuoys, an anchor and cable, navigation lights, a tide table, the relevant Admiralty chart, a copy of the Company's bye-laws and insurance covering 3rd party liability up to £50,000. Owners of boats thus equipped should get an application form from the Harbour Master, Manchester Ship Canal Company, Dock Office, Manchester M5 2XB. (Tel: 061-872-2411.) This should be returned to the above address—with the insurance and seaworthiness certificates—not less than 48 hours before the entry onto the Canal.

The Bridgewater Canal

This canal is owned by the Manchester Ship Canal Company (who had to buy it before building the Ship Canal) and is controlled by the Company's Bridgewater Department. There is insufficient space in this book to be able to cover the Bridgewater Canal fully. However the canal is a most important link route and, as the first major navigation of the canal age, is of great interest historically. It was the first canal built by James Brindley and featured the famous aqueduct at Barton over the Mersey & Irwell Navigation. (This was later replaced by the unique Barton swing aqueduct over the Manchester Ship Canal.)

The Leigh branch of the Leeds & Liverpool Canal flows straight into the Bridgewater Canal, with no change in level. Indeed, since the canal that linked Runcorn with Weston Point was closed a few years ago, there has been only one lock on the whole of the Bridgewater Canal. (This is on the very short branch down into the Ship Canal in Manchester.) The Trent & Mersey Canal is joined to the Bridgewater by Dutton Stop Lock, where there is a drop of only a few inches.

At the Manchester end, the unnavigable Ashton Canal joins the Rochdale Canal, which locks down through the city centre to the eastern terminus of the Bridgewater Canal. (The Rochdale Canal is privately owned: the company's address is on page 114.)

Under a reciprocal arrangement, any boat holding a normal BWB craft licence may cruise freely on the Bridgewater Canal for up to 7 days; but periods longer than this require a proper Bridgewater licence. Application should be made to:

Manchester Ship Canal Company
Bridgewater Department
Chester Road
Manchester M15 4NU
(061-872-2411).

Prospective navigators along this canal should note that the Barton Swing Aqueduct over the Ship Canal is closed for one or two weeks a year for repairs. This usually takes place in the summer: the date can be ascertained by enquiring to M.S.C.Co.

In 1971, a serious breach of the Bridgewater Canal main line occurred at the Bollin Aqueduct, near Lymm, cutting off the Leeds & Liverpool Canal from the Trent & Mersey and the other navigations in the North West. However in February 1972 the Manchester Ship Canal Company announced that the canal would be restored, and it is now hoped that the Bridgewater Canal will be reopened to through navigation by autumn 1973. The Bridgewater Department of the M.S.C. Co. will inform enquirers of the current position.

Canal Books

Very few bookshops carry more than a handful of different books on canals. The best place to find the books listed below is probably St John Thomas Booksellers, 30 Woburn Place, London W.C.1 (01-580 9449), who will post books all over the country. The Inland Waterways Association at 114 Regent's Park Road, London N.W.1 also have a complete range of canal books, and this is the best place to get hold of all specialist publications. Both establishments will post a list of their stock to anyone interested. Apart from these, the British Waterways Board have a wide selection of canal books and pamphlets available to visitors at the Canal Shop at Farmer's Bridge, Birmingham (in Kingston Row) and of course at the Waterways Museum at Stoke Bruerne. Finally, many boatyards on the canals (especially those offering chandlery) have a selection of books for sale.
The publications listed below are either general canal books or those that deal specifically with waterways in the North West (including some non-BWB navigations). Publications that deal with canals in other parts of the country will be mentioned in the appropriate book list of one of the three remaining titles in this BWB series.

'Canals of the British Isles' history series:	**Author**	**Publisher**
British Canals	Charles Hadfield	David & Charles
The Canals of the West Midlands	Charles Hadfield	David & Charles
The Canals of North West England (in 2 volumes)	Charles Hadfield & Gordon Biddle	David & Charles
Reference Works:		
Inland Waterways of Great Britain and Northern Ireland	L. A. Edwards	Imray
A General History of Inland Navigation (reprint from 1805)	J. Phillips	David & Charles
Historical Account of Navigable Rivers & Canals of Great Britain (reprint from 1831)	J. Priestley	David & Charles
Bradshaw's Canals & Navigable Rivers of England and Wales (reprint from 1904)	Henry de Salis	David & Charles
Cruising books:		
Holiday Cruising on Inland Waterways	Charles Hadfield & Michael Streat	David & Charles
The Canals Book (annual)		Link House Publications
Canal Cruising	John Hankinson	Ward Lock
General books:		
James Brindley Engineer, 1716–1772	C. T. G. Boucher	Goose & Son
The Decorative arts of the mariner	G. F. Cook (ed.)	Cassell's
Slow Boat through England	Frederic Doerflinger	Allan Wingate
Slow Boat through the Pennines	Frederic Doerflinger	Allan Wingate
The amateur boatwomen	Eily Gayford	David & Charles
Canals in Camera	John Gagg	Ian Allan
English Canals (in 3 volumes)	D. D. Gladwin & J. M. White	Oakwood Press
The Canal Age	Charles Hadfield	David & Charles; and Pan Books
The Canal Enthusiast's Handbook	Charles Hadfield (ed.)	David & Charles
Canals and their Architecture	Robert Harris	Hugh Evelyn
A tour of the Grand Junction Canal in 1819 (reprinted 1968)	J. Hassell	Cranfield & Bonfiel
Journeys of the Swan	John Liley	Allen & Unwin
The Canal Duke	Hugh Malet	David & Charles
The Canals of England	Eric de Maré	The Architectural Press
Canal & River Craft in pictures	Hugh McKnight	David & Charles
Discovering Canals	Leon Metcalfe & John Vince	Shire Publications
Water Highways	David Owen	Phoenix House
Water Rallies	David Owen	Phoenix House
Narrow Boat	L. T. C. Rolt	Eyre & Spottiswoode
Navigable Waterways	L. T. C. Rolt	Longmans
The Inland Waterways of England	L. T. C. Rolt	Allen & Unwin
Thomas Telford	L. T. C. Rolt	Longmans
James Watt	L. T. C. Rolt	Batsford
Lost Canals of England and Wales	R. Russell	David & Charles
Canal Fishing	Kenneth Seaman	Barrie & Jackson
Voyage into England	John Seymour	David & Charles
Lives of the Engineers (in 3 volumes–reprint from 1862)	Samuel Smiles	David & Charles
Maidens Trip	Emma Smith	Penguin
Waterways Heritage	P. Smith	Luton Museum
The Flower of Gloster (reprint from 1911)	Temple Thurston	David & Charles
Hold on a Minute	T. Wilkinson	Allen & Unwin
River Navigation in England 1600–1750	T. S. Willan	F. Cass

Ordnance Survey Maps

The following 1in. ordnance survey maps refer to the canals covered by this book:

89	Lancaster & Kendal	Lancaster canal
94	Preston	Lancaster and Leeds & Liverpool canals
95	Blackburn & Burnley	Leeds & Liverpool canal
96	Leeds & Bradford	Leeds & Liverpool canal
100	Liverpool	Leeds & Liverpool and Trent & Mersey canals
101	Manchester	L & L, T & M, Peak Forest, Macclesfield and Ashton canals
109	Chester	T & M, Shropshire Union and Llangollen canals; also Weaver Navigation
110	Stoke-on-Trent	T & M, S.U., Macclesfield, Llangollen and Caldon canals
111	Buxton & Matlock	Peak Forest and Caldon canals
117	Bala & Welshpool	Llangollen and Montgomery canals
118	Shrewsbury	S.U., Llangollen and Montgomery canals
119	Stafford	T & M, S.U., and Staffs & Worcs canals
120	Burton upon Trent	Trent & Mersey canal
128	Montgomery & Llandrindod Wells	Montgomery canal

David & Charles have brought out a reprint of the First Edition of the Ordnance Survey, dating from 1860 to about 1870. 97 separate sheets cover England & Wales. Available from David & Charles.

Specialist publications:	**Author**	**Publisher**
The Staffordshire Moorlands & Caldon Canal	H. Bode	
It happened round Manchester	A. H. Body	University of London Press
The Facts about the Waterways	British Waterways Board	HMSO 1965
Leisure and the Waterways	British Waterways Board	HMSO 1967
British Waterways Board Annual Report	British Waterways Board	HMSO
Birmingham Canal Navigations	British Waterways Board	BWB 1971
The Caldon Canal		Caldon Canal Society
New Waterways	Inland Waterways Association	IWA 1965
The Bridgewater Canal		Manchester Ship Canal Company
The Cromford & High Peak Railway	A. Rimmer	Oakwood Press
The Peak Forest Tramway	D. Ripley	Oakwood Press
The Offa's Dyke Path	A. Roberts	Ramblers' Association
The Pennine Way	T. Stephenson	Ramblers' Association
Bridgewater Canal		Manchester Ship Canal Company
Cruising Guide		Manchester Ship Canal Company

Boat Clubs

The following is a list of boat clubs on waterways covered by this guide book, classified by the navigation on which each club has its main mooring site.

Lancaster Canal
Lancaster Canal Boat Club

Leeds & Liverpool Canal
Airedale Boat Club
Craven Cruising Club
Elwy Boat Club
Mersey Motor Boat Club
Wheelton Boat Club

Macclesfield Canal
North Cheshire Cruising Club

Shropshire Union Canal
Autherley Marina Boat Club
Nantwich & Border Counties Yacht Club
Wolverhampton Boat Club

Staffs & Worcs Canal
Stafford Boat Club

Trent & Mersey Canal
Armitage Boat Club
Ash Tree Boat Club
Fradley Junction Cruising Club
Lostock Gralam Cruising Club
Stoke-on-Trent Boat Club

Weaver Navigation
Acton Bridge Cruising Club
Weaver Motor Boat Club

An up to date list of all the clubs shown above may be obtained from the British Waterways Board at Melbury House, Melbury Terrace, London NW1 6JX. This list gives the name and address of each club's current Honorary Secretary.

Prospective canoeists, campers and walkers may find the following addresses useful:

British Canoe Union
26 Park Crescent
London W1

Canoe Camping Club
11 Grosvenor Place
London SW1

Ramblers' Association
1 Crawford Mews
York Street
London W1

Canal Societies

The Inland Waterways Association is 'the' national society of canal enthusiasts. It is the oldest, biggest and most influential of the canal societies and has permanent offices and staff. It now has 10,000 members and publishes a regular Waterways 'Bulletin'. There are at least 2 subsidiary branches of the IWA in north west England: their addresses can be obtained from the General Office at 114 Regent's Park rd, London NW1 8UQ.

Other, generally local, canal societies in the North-West—most of which are affiliated to the IWA—include those listed below.

Caldon Canal Society

Inland Waterways Protection Society

Lancaster Canal Trust

Peak Forest Canal Society

Railway & Canal Historical Society

Shropshire Union Canal Society

Staffordshire & Worcestershire Canal Society

An up to date list of all canal societies may be obtained from the British Waterways Board at Melbury House, Melbury Terrace, London NW1 6JX. This list gives the name and address of each society's current Honorary Secretary.

BWB Offices and Yards

Headquarters

Melbury House, Melbury Terrace, London NW1 6JX (01-262 6711). General and official enquiries and correspondence.

Willow Grange, Church road, Watford, Herts (Watford 26422). Pleasure craft licences and registration, mooring permits and angling arrangements.

Northwich Area Engineer

Navigation road, Northwich, Ches. (Northwich 74321). Responsible for maintaining the waterways listed below, via the named BWB maintenance yards on those canals. The numbers in brackets refer to the pages in this book on which the yards occur.

Caldon canal Etruria Junction (94)
Llangollen canal Ellesmere (54)
Macclesfield canal Marple Junction (106)
Montgomery canal
Peak Forest canal Marple Junction (108)
Shropshire Union canal Norbury (31)
Chester (43)
Staffs & Worcs canal
Trent & Mersey canal Fradley Junction (76)
Etruria Junction (83)
Weaver navigation Northwich (119)

Wigan Area Engineer

Swan Meadow road, Wigan, Lancs. (Wigan 42239). Responsible for maintaining the waterways listed below.

Ashton canal
Lancaster canal Lancaster (163)
Leeds & Liverpool canal Burscough (128)
Wigan (133)
Burnley (142)
Apperley Bridge (153)

Supervisor (Amenity Services)

Nantwich Basin, Chester road, Nantwich, Ches. (65122). Enquiries about BWB hire cruisers at Nantwich and Hillmorton, and general enquiries about amenity uses of the canals in the North West. Permits for match fishing and day fishing on the Shropshire Union and Llangollen canals, and all permits for fishing from boats. Craft licences and mooring permits can be obtained by calling at this office: postal applications should be made direct to the Craft Licensing Officer at Watford (see above).

Index